Mike,
with
best wishes

Hank & Graham

D1420476

FORTY YEARS
OF MURDER

Professor Keith Simpson CBE

FORTY YEARS OF MURDER

AN AUTOBIOGRAPHY

HARRAP LONDON

First published in Great Britain 1978
by GEORGE G. HARRAP & CO. LTD.
182 High Holborn, London WC1V 7AX

© *Keith Simpson* 1978

ISBN 0 245 53198 X

Designed by James Campus

Filmset by Woolaston Parker Ltd, Leicester
Printed in Great Britain by offset lithography
by Billing and Sons Ltd, Guildford, London
and Worcester

CONTENTS

ILLUSTRATIONS

CHAPTER 1

WHY CHOOSE PATHOLOGY?

You might well ask what could possibly persuade any young doctor, unmarried and without ties, to take up the study of the dead—the diseased, mutilated, sometimes even dismembered dead, whose bodies seem to come to light at such odd hours and in such queer places. Why not a nice clean laboratory job in a white coat with keen technical staff, or a challenging research project? Or surgery, with the glamour of the operating theatre, the appeal of brilliant results snatched from the jaws of disaster? Why not patient scholarly physicianship—or neurology, obstetrics, children's diseases? There they all were, and if you'd had a successful medical studentship, as mine had been at Guy's, the choice really was wide open. So why the dead body, the often smelly morgue, exhumation, lust and violence, the inconvenience of calls to derelict premises, dells in Epping Forest, ponds, prostitutes' bedrooms, at all hours; of sudden challenge, hard duels with lawyers, pompous old judges and obtuse juries? Why?

Well, few doctors can enjoy a more exciting life, such a challenge to be constantly on the qui vive, or should it be the qui meurt? There could be few jobs so full of new possibilities, so certain to bring new and colourful slices of vivid life, new acquaintances with other doctors of all kinds, with detectives, with policemen and prostitutes, barristers and barmen, distinguished lawyers and drug-addicted layabouts. It's so different from looking into ears or throats muttering 'Say Ah' or 'Now breathe in', handling distasteful skin diseases or trying to persuade hysterical women they haven't got cancer. The smell? No worse than the unwashed. Harrowing? There is, as H. E. Bates wrote, a 'beauty of the dead'. And wasn't it John Wesley who wrote:

Ah, lovely appearance of Death,
What sight upon earth is so fair?
Not all the gay pageants that breathe
Can with a dead body compare.

Isn't it more exciting than 'Doctor, little Willie's been sick again', to
hear an urgent 'Doctor Simpson? Oh, glad to find you in, sir' (as if
you spent the night on the Embankment or in Soho night clubs).
'Inspector Read here, sir. Got a man stabbed in the back in Lambeth
public toilets. Could you come and see him? Ten minutes? Splendid,
sir; meet you outside the Underground station.'

So there you are once again in overcoat and muffler, crouching on
the floor of a stale public lavatory in the glare of police spotlamps
trying to see everything, literally every clue that might later be vital to
yet another murder trial. A stray hair from the assailant clinging to
the jacket, an indistinct footprint, blood smeared over here, dripping
first there, then trickling over there. Buttons undone, trousers torn
and muddied. Black eye and bruised lip. Another homosexual
quarrel? The knife and the stab wound can have attention much
later—comparatively unimportant, just the last fatal stab, and of
course never to be touched or explored at the scene.

First, photographs and fingerprints, cellophane bags for the
hands; head, clothes, another search with the CID, then the
undertakers to carry the body to the nearest mortuary, and finally yet
another look around at the scene for clues. One stray button torn
away on the window sill of a pub in Portsmouth pointed at
Loughans: a Luton dyer's tag in a discarded piece of coat at Bertie
Manton; a shell case in Chelsea Square at Boyce. Each proved guilty
(although Loughans was wrongfully acquitted) on such tiny observations. Finally everyone round the body in the morgue—Yard men,
photographer, fingerprint, liaison and 'scenes-of-crime' scientific
detectives—and it will go on patiently until the job's done, all day and
all night if necessary.

No fun, you say? Nothing to laugh at in the ugliness of crime, the
grimness of poverty, the tragedy of death; not a smile's worth of fun in
the weeping wives and the sad and sometimes savage face of
humanity? No, it isn't funny; and that is why laughter has to break
through, probably more than in other jobs.

I have a vivid memory of standing in the Shoreditch Public
Mortuary one morning, sharpening my knife, about to examine the
body of an old man lying stiff on the slab, prepared for post-mortem

an hour or so previously by the attendant, a cheerful Cockney named Hart.

'Tell me something about him,' I asked Doughty, the Coroner's officer. 'What did he do, and how did he come to die?'

'Well, sir, this man was an actor, and . . .'

But before Doughty could say another word, the Cockney wit of the attendant was out:

'Gor blimey, if he's acting now, he's bloody good!'

We all laughed freely and easily. It was the joke of a compassionate, not a callous man. The dead actor could have appreciated it.

Fun, without disrespect for the dead, is where you look for it. I've had many a chuckle roving round the tombstones in churchyards whilst waiting for a body to 'come in'. Undertakers are always said to be 'out on the job' or 'on way' (never 'on the way here') if one arrives first, so often there's time to look around the graveyard. Epitaphs often have a diverting macabre humour of their own. How about this?

> Poor Martha Snell her's gone her way
> Her would if she could but
> Her couldn't stay.
> Her had two bad legs and a baddish cough,
> But her legs it was that carried her off.   (1797)

Some tombstones sound a Salvationist note: one in Hammersmith reads:

> The trumpets sounded, a voice said 'Come',
> The Pearly Gates opened—and in walked Mum.

Laughter can erupt in even less hilarious places than a cemetery, and a drab scene can at any time suddenly light up with some gem of humour or Gilbertian situation. There is nothing remotely amusing about the mutilated head of a dead girl, and I could not have been further from laughing when I took one away, in a cardboard box, from a murder in a ryefield near Saxmundham during the latter years of the war. I wanted to study the pattern of some knife wounds on the head. I returned to London by the milk train, which rattled into Liverpool Street station at 5 a.m. A Scotland Yard car met me, and deposited me at the street door of my block of flats in Weymouth Street, close to Broadcasting House, driving away as I mounted the few stairs to the front door. I was fiddling with the key in the Yale lock, quite alone in the bare light of dawn, when a constable strolled round the corner. He looked at me, half in and half out of the building, and with this cardboard box under my arm. One could almost see him thinking ''Ullo, 'ullo, now what's all this?' He came across to me.

'May I ask', he said very politely, 'what you have in that parcel under your arm?'

'Why—er, yes,' I said. 'It's a head.'

He looked at me hard. Then: 'A *what*, sir?'

'A specimen. I'm a doctor. I've been on a job. . . .'

'If you don't mind, sir, I think I must ask you to just step inside', I'd got the door open by now, 'and let me see.'

We both got inside the front door, and I untied the parcel, exposing first a rather bloody crown of brown hair, then eyebrows, then . . . but he'd had enough.

'Good God!' he muttered, clutching his face. 'Good God!'

I explained. He didn't know me, but it must have dawned on him that I wasn't a crank.

'You might perhaps like to ring the Yard for confirmation?'

'No, sir.' He was distinctly white in the face. 'No, thank you, sir. And it's the last time I'll ever ask anyone what they're carrying in a parcel!'

A charred body in a burnt-out house isn't intrinsically amusing either, and there was nothing to laugh about when, one Saturday night in Bedford, I searched with fire officers and the local CID chief for traces of a second burnt body. For a man and a woman who had been drinking and quarrelling at a local pub had been seen entering the house soon after 9 p.m. and by 10.30 a fierce fire had destroyed it. Only one body had been found. The possibility of murder must always lie at the back of a CID officer's head, so a full-scale search was started just before midnight.

Padding around in the soaked charred debris for some sign of human remains, we suddenly lit upon what looked like a human forearm, charred out of recognition. Carefully handled, it was laid in a cardboard box and carried off to the local mortuary under police car escort, together with other fragments destined for the forensic science laboratories. Ten minutes later, under the tense scrutiny of Scotland Yard and local CID chiefs, Chief Fire Officers and the Police Surgeon of Bedford, I made a half section of it so as to get down to the bone that I thought would prove it was human.

Suddenly, as the charred crust gave way under my knife, we all burst into laughter, for there, split open on the bench, was . . . a French loaf! The laugh was certainly on me, and to this day, when I visit Bedford on a crime, I am likely to be asked if I would care for a slice of French bread with my tea!

If he worked alone the pathologist's spirits would fade, but he is one of a team. Cheerful policemen, eager young doctors, alert lawyers, matter-of-fact magistrates, counsel, judges, all help to provide a balance that preserves one's reason and sense of humour in the most dismal surroundings.

Stories are still told and told again of the devastating wit of famous counsel of the past like F. E. Smith, later Lord Birkenhead.

'Mr Smith,' a judge once interrupted him, 'I have listened to you with great care for some forty minutes now and I am none the wiser.'

'No, my lord,' answered Smith drily, 'merely better informed.'

Encounters in court are seldom dull, for so few counsel are; most will either challenge or respond to a thrust with pleasure. A ghost of a smile, perhaps, then: 'Doctor, are you seriously saying that A plus B equals A^2 plus $2AB$ plus B^2?'

No one could possibly say the practice of medicine in court is a dull branch of professional life. It teems with personalities and abounds in challenge and surprise. I always enjoyed the drama of an Assize trial: a duel with the lawyers, the tensing of intellects in a cross-examination on the medical and scientific aspects of the case, with opposing counsel coached by one of one's colleagues like Donald Teare or F. E. Camps to probe the weakness and strength of one's case. Camps in particular seemed to relish throwing variously sized and weighted 'spanners in the works' of a good Crown Case. But it was good for me: it kept standards of work high, demanded careful attention to detail and accuracy.

Able lawyers are a constant spur to performance, a challenge that prohibits any pathologist from the easy-going indifference into which doctors may so easily drift in private practice.

'Doctor,' they say, in a slow emphatic challenge, 'are you seriously saying that the injuries you describe exclude the possibility of an accident?'

Well, you hadn't thought of the possibility, perhaps, but here is the challenge, and, unlike Members of Parliament or Judges, you are going to have to answer *now*, not later, after further thought. 'I don't think they could have been accidental,' you say, a little uncertain as to

the line he may adopt. What other information had he up his sleeve?
'Come, doctor, this is a serious charge, and you are the expert.'
Counsel is relentless. 'Do you or do you not exclude that possibility?
Yes or no, doctor?'

Lawyers all want a black or white 'Yes' or 'No'. There's no grey
anywhere, no 'It might be'. I once had a young barrister thunder at
me:

'Tell me, doctor, *in what order* were these injuries sustained?' And
before my mouth had opened . . .

'And I want "yes" or "no" for an answer, not a long lecture!'

All this testing is good for professional standards. No one is
allowed to go to seed, drop off, or muddle a way through. It is a life of
challenge, and no one is allowed to drift along. Any ordinary intellect
needs it: an alert mind thrives on it.

Of course there are difficulties and intense irritations. The
ponderous, slow-moving majesty of the processes of law, for one.
Every pathologist contends with inconveniently timed or unnecessary calls, extremes of cold and heat, bodies with scores of wounds
(when one would have sufficed), decomposed, fly-ridden, disintegrated remains, long waits for the undertakers or some expert to
arrive, dirty premises and sloppy morticians.

Add to all this the prospect of a prosecution at some unfixed future
date in an Assize Court often seventy or eighty miles distant.
Warnings to attend often come after 6 p.m. on the eve of the trial
through the DPP or a local police station. 'Doctor, you're wanted tomorrow morning at Nottingham Assizes; 10 a.m., please, case against
Pitts from Slough.' Never mind what you've got on next morning,
who's expecting you or what other court has already engaged your
services (the Assize and Civil High Court have precedence). Never
mind that after 6 p.m. it's impossible to find everyone on your list for
tomorrow to tell them what has now happened.

Never mind, either, that your holiday may be due to start tomorrow, and you're packed ready to travel. Or, worse, that you have
already travelled!

The day I married my secretary, Jean Scott-Dunn, in 1956, I left for
Paris with a 'Recognisance Notice' in my pocket warning me to be at
the Old Bailey next day at 10 a.m. I'd hardly arrived before I was back
again on the platform at Gare St Lazare, finding my way to the night
train for London. Some honeymoon!

Worse, but far more amusing, I was on holiday in the Atlas

mountains, right in the middle of Morocco, in April 1966, when, at the end of a long and very hot drive from Marrakech I was relaxing in a bath in the Palais Jamais at Fez. The telephone bell rang.

'Eet eez ze foyer, Monsieur Simpson. Ze Police are here. Pleez to come down. And Pleez also to bring ze passport.'

I dressed hurriedly. The police can be awkward in a foreign country. What had I done? Run over a dog with my hired Simca car? Perhaps. Or, worse, some exchange deal in Tangier?

Sure enough, there in the foyer stood two Moroccan police officers—pretty high-up stuff by their braid. Attention.

'Monsieur Simpson?'

'Mais oui, messieurs. Qu'est-ce que vous voulez?'

'Ici, monsieur, s'il vous plaît.' We withdrew into an office.

My passport was closely inspected, and my photo checked. An official black briefcase was produced, and from it the senior officer drew a thin telegram headed 'Interpol'.

'You are wanted,' the officer read menacingly, slowly, 'on a charge of murder. To be at the Gloucester Assizes at 10 a.m. to-morrow, Friday 19th.'

What excitement! The Fez Police had never in their lives had a telegram from Interpol. And they'd got their man! Wanted for murder—Keith Simpson!

Unfortunately, in the excitement of transmitting the Yard message from Tangier to Fez, three words that meant so much had been omitted. A telephone call to Scotland Yard elicited the information, as I suspected, that the original Interpol message had read, 'Wanted *to give evidence* on a charge of murder'. It made all the difference! A few drinks in the bar, and the tension settled. The officers left, not a little deflated. I felt almost sorry for them. It had looked so much like their big moment.

Anyone who thinks pathologists run well-planned days dealing with the dead at their own convenience, and taking holidays when the weather's fine, should spend a few days going round the morgues, dashing at short notice for court, often miles out of London, back to the lab, or to give lectures, trying to receive visitors and dictate letters, obeying summonses to be here, then there, 'As soon as possible, doctor. The body's in the open air, sir. We're rather worried about it, and a man's in the station. *As soon as possible?*' 'I'll come straightaway.' It was the sort of response every CID chief hopes for, and I always went out of my way to give it if I could. I knew how much it meant to both of us to get down to a murder job before the body had cooled off and the scent had gone stale.

How nice to have an ordered life! Or would it be too dull for words? *Chacun à son goût*, I suppose, for it isn't everyone who would choose to spend so much of his professional life with the dead. For me it is the spice of life; an ever-changing stage with an unending stream of characters: public, the police, the Bar, doctors, scientists, old lags, young students. Every day brings some new surprise, some sort of challenge, some humour, some pathos. There is an air of challenge and intellectual test so unlike 'just another day at the office'. Any moment the telephone can start anything, from a strangled Pimlico prostitute to an urgent call to Canada.

Why choose pathology? For Heaven's sake, how could one choose anything else?

CHAPTER 2

EARLY DAYS

I became a doctor because my father was one. A very good if rather old-fashioned G.P., he had a vast following of devoted patients to whom he was both general adviser and doctor, and he would have been intensely disappointed if one of his sons had not followed him into medicine. Denis, my elder brother, disliked all forms of study, so it was as well that no career other than medicine ever crossed my mind. My mother, a calm talented woman, who spoke and wrote well, wisely refrained from putting other ideas into my head.

My father came of Scots parentage but his family moved south while he was still a medical student, so that he qualified from Edinburgh and then University College Hospital in London. He bought a practice, as one did then, in Brighton and Hove, where I was born. It was a flagging practice, but he built it by his industry and deep concern for his patients' welfare into a 'four-man practice' of which, when I was at school and later at Guy's, he was senior partner. He was a splendid representative of the older G.P. He seldom indeed read the *British Medical Journal* or *Lancet*, but he knew when a patient was ill—there were few specific treatments then—and he also knew when a case was beyond his standards of care . . . when to call in a specialist like the great Lord Horder for an opinion and guidance. He was undoubtedly happiest out on his rounds driven in his favourite Buick by his deaf chauffeur Wood who, like most of his flock of patients, was devoted to him. Brisk, fresh, alert, and always keen, 'the Doctor' would nearly always be out of the car before it had drawn to a standstill and with a double knock on the door was in most homes with a 'May I come in?' whilst many would still be peering about for the number of the house. In the family he was a strong disciplinarian, and I never found a way of speaking at all intimately with him, even when, late at night, he at last relaxed with a book. His work was his passion and his pleasure, and being on holiday obviously bored him after the first forty-eight hours.

School never held any terror for me. My first teacher, a Madame Gengoult, Head of a preparatory school in Preston Park, had the twin gifts of enthusiasm for her art and the ability to impart knowledge as if it were an exciting cult. She spoke her native language, French, by interjections of 'du tout' and 'ma foi' between her deliveries in English, and always started any more difficult subject with an affectionate 'Now, mes enfants. . . .' This warm-hearted Frenchwoman inculcated in me a desire to learn which has given me the greatest pleasure ever since.

I was fortunate, too, when I went on to the old-established Brighton Grammar School. The Head was the portly 'T. Read, M.A.'(I can still forge his signature!), a delightful fatherly scholar of English and 'the Scriptures' who also taught applied maths. An occasional 'Good, my boy' was earned with difficulty, but well worth the effort. I learned with pleasure, even wore 'gig-lamp' brass-rimmed spectacles at one stage, and was despised as 'a swot' by my brother Denis, who was firmly determined to avoid all kinds of education. He left the school at sixteen, being quietly withdrawn after making no real progress for some years, falling behind all his fellows irretrievably, to go to farm in Sussex and later, unsuccessfully, in Rhodesia. A most amiable brother, just lacking in ambition.

The lasting impression that stayed with me through my school, medical school, and university life at Guy's, was the deep tie of regard and affection that develops between teacher and pupil; they are akin to those between master and apprentice when both are devoted to acquiring the same expertise. I enjoyed the power a teacher has to impart the one thing that matters in academic life, learning, and at the same time to acquire affection. Touring India, Thailand, Hong Kong, Australia, and New Zealand years later I found a long stream of charming past pupils, students and post-graduates keen to lavish the warmest hospitality on me for no better reason than 'warm regards to my teacher'.

Languages attracted me as a boy, and my first taste of travel came from a French travelling scholarship I was awarded at school. I lived for a short time undergoing 'tutorials' in a French country family home near Pithiviers (noted for its lark pâté) and I never found the language troublesome thereafter. Years later, on a lecture tour of

France for the British Council, I had the great honour of speaking at the Sorbonne University in Paris. I had prepared this lecture with great care, in French that was given a final Roget-like polish by a French teacher in London University (for a substantial fee). A sad anti-climax ensued: on the way from dinner near Etoile with my hosts, the Anglo-French Society, driving with Monsieur Corbin, a former French Ambassador, this distinguished white-haired old gentleman leaned over towards me in the car, placed a hand on my arm and said conversationally, 'By the way, Doctor, I quite forgot to mention to you. This particular audience would be much flattered if you would address them in your own English language.' Alas for my skills, and tutored veneer, in French! And my Roget polish expenses! All down the drain.

My father showed no discernment about my studies and regarded school, matriculation, and some kind of medical education and qualification as 'necessary' for my future. All good Scots have to be industrious and earn a living, an honest living, and any thoughts I had about going to one of the older universities—which was easy enough then for those with the means—failed altogether to appeal to him. Learning, for its own sake, was 'wasting time', and I had to accept the decision. When I went from school to medical school I was still a schoolboy of 17: the maturity that a couple of years at Oxford or Cambridge would have given me was almost painfully lacking.

In the years between the wars, medicine was still a rewarding professional career, and there was no difficulty then in finding a place in any of the university schools. London was the obvious choice, and Guy's was the nearest medical school, so, armed with a pretty good-looking matriculation certificate from my Brighton school, I presented myself one 1924 August morning, red hair brushed, and in a tidy blue suit, at Guy's.

'I wish to enrol at a medical school,' I said to the clerk, a delightful Edwardian character called Croucher, black coat, striped trousers.

Now these days it's only after a strict perusal of papers by the Advisory Board, letters of outrageously extravagant recommendation and a tough interview with the Dean and a School Selection Board that you may perhaps be offered one of the one-in-twelve (one-in-seventeen if you're female) places for next year.

Not so in 1924. The School Clerk had the entire authority.

'Do you have the money for the fees?' asked Croucher courteously.

I had—and Croucher himself enrolled me on the spot.

University and state backing for the medical schools did not then exist. Guy's was a 'voluntary hospital', living largely on the rich foundation with which the bookseller Thomas Guy had in 1720 endowed it, and the school depended largely on the students' fees. On the annual 'rag' day the students, attired in a variety of fancy dress—I had a tough bright-spotted orange and blue (Guy's colours) harlequin outfit—poured out on to the London streets, boarding taxis and buses, pestering the good old English businessman around London Bridge for contributions for the Hospital. 'Something for Guy's, guv'nor . . . ma'am. Go on, sir, you might find yourself in there tomorrow.' And several thousand pounds would come in to support the tottering structure of the Voluntary Hospital System.

Guy's then had several remarkable teachers, headed by T. B. Johnson, our Dean, a strict Scots disciplinarian Professor of Anatomy who at that time edited the famous *Gray's Anatomy*. And when we moved over to 'walk the wards' we found a new breed of man—the physician, the West End Consultant who, if he was worth his salt, came down twice weekly to Guy's in his Rolls to do a voluntary afternoon round. This was indeed an occasion. The Registrar, his House Physician and the 'firm' of students, perhaps eight or ten of us, would assemble in white coats at the Front Lodge where, punctually at 2 p.m., the great man would arrive. My idol at the time was Dr Herbert French; tall, handsome, successful, he was always immaculately dressed in grey Ascot tails and topper. He would bound up the front steps from his Rolls, leaving his grey liveried footman to collect his letters at the Lodge as 'Lofty', the top-hatted Head Porter, saluted him 'in', and was striding out down the famous Colonnade, where the great Bright and Addison and Hodgkin had trod before him, and into the Park before most of his 'firm' of students had got into gear to stream after him.

Another of my heroes was Dr E. R. Boland, then Clinical Tutor and later, as Sir Rowan, Dean of the Faculty in the university. He had been sadly knocked about in the First World War but was incisive, slim, clean, fresh-faced, wore a black monocle to conceal an eye wound and was always well dressed. He taught generations of Guy's men the courtesies of doctoring. It was 'Bo' who as Dean of the School backed my inclinations for pathology, and a Gold Medal in Bacteriology, a 'Gull Exhibition' in Pathology and a Demonstrator-ship which enabled me to start teaching in the subject helped me to justify his support.

. I had been increasingly drawn towards teaching when, soon after I qualified, a sudden vacuum on the staff of the Pathology Department gave me the opening I was looking for. One day I was a struggling young casualty officer, next day a white-coated Senior Staff teacher in the Pathology Department. The doors to a career had opened miraculously wide for me at the age of twenty-five. The few prizes or awards I had had the good fortune to collect in my 'finals' year had stood me in good stead when the vacancy had so suddenly arisen.

Long after, in the Old Bailey, at a murder trial, a passing success I had had at Guy's came to roost. I had been a pathologist for twenty years when one morning Counsel, seeking to cut to size a remark I had made in evidence about an 'evident need to relieve the internal bleeding by operation', remarked:

'Doctor, what can you, a pathologist, know about clinical surgery?'

It was a good question. Experts in court are always being warned not to exceed the strict limits of their own fields of specialization in giving opinions. Counsel must have felt he had me by the traditional short hairs. It suddenly came to me that I had an 'escape' hatch.

'I hold,' I said, 'a gold medal in clinical surgery.'

He was plainly shaken. Who could ever have anticipated such a disastrous answer from a pathologist? If only he had had known that it had been awarded twenty years previously for writing knowledge-able papers and an essay in the subject, and that I had never in my life held a surgical knife in my hand! But he didn't know, and after a moment's flush of chagrin at the reverse he moved away to another line of questioning.

In the year of my sudden promotion, 1932, I married a Guy's nurse, Mary Buchanan, and we were to have three children.

My fundamental interest when at Guy's as a young teacher was in pathology, and this was—it still is—the only sound foundation for a crime pathologist. Until he has become familiar with the ravages and strange variants of disease, he is not ready to branch off into a study of injury, far less of criminal injury. Forensic pathology is a specialized branch of pathology, not open to the young tyro.

As the Senior Demonstrator in the Pathology Department I was doing the majority of all the post-mortems at Guy's, including those reported to the Coroner, Douglas Cowburn, at Southwark. It was my good fortune that Cowburn happened to need a pathologist to handle his own cases. In the ordinary way he would have used Bernard

Spilsbury, who dominated medico-legal practice at that time, but
Cowburn disliked Spilsbury and only called on him when he was
forced to—in major crime work. He had once paid Spilsbury a *single*
post-mortem fee for examining conjoined twins! Spilsbury fumed.
There were two bodies and he'd examined both: But Cowburn was
adamant. Feeling never entirely died out, and though the incident
was trivial it resulted in a certain 'needle' between the men. So
Cowburn asked the Superintendent of Guy's, Sir Herbert Eason, to
permit me, whose services he found he was employing (presumably
satisfactorily), to handle some of his cases in the public mortuary.
Eason and the Professor of Pathology agreed, the latter created the
new post of 'Supervisor of Medico-legal Post-Mortems' for me, and I
was off. It was the autumn of 1934.

Of course I still saw only a handful of criminal cases each year.
Murder is not rife in England, as in some countries: it is
comparatively rare. The London area, which has more than its fair
share, gets only about 50 murders a year; and only about 150 to 160
cases—the figure has been remarkably constant since the beginning
of the century—occur annually in the whole of England and Wales.
This figure is insignificant when set against a total mortality of some
600,000, of which about 90,000 cases come to the attention of the
coroners. When, years later, I made an analysis for the Ministry of
Health of 20,000 coroners' autopsies that I had performed, 55 per
cent resolved into a mere identification of a natural (but until then
obscure) cause of death, and another 30 per cent were concerned with
the assessment of some kind of accident or injury in relation to death:
an accident at home, in hospital, in the street or at work resulting in
injury at some date. Some 4 to 5 per cent were suicides, and only 2 to 3
per cent involved injury that raised suspicion or gave frank evidence
of crime.

One morning towards the end of 1934 the telephone rang in my small
laboratory at Guy's.

'Dr Keith Simpson? Scotland Yard here, sir. Detective Superintendent Young speaking. We've just been called to a murder at the York
Hotel, opposite Waterloo Station, and we'd like your help.'

'Why-er, yes,' I said, trying to sound calm and collected, 'of course.
I'll come straightaway. Be there in ten minutes.' (Better be, I thought,
or they'll call someone else and bang will go my chances of getting a
foothold with the Yard.)

Still a very young pathologist, I was thrilled by this first call from Scotland Yard. In fact, I have never lost the thrill of the sudden call to crime, of dropping everything, leaving a dinner party, even getting up at dead of night, to drive to some new case. It might be another Heath, or Haigh or Hanratty, or 'nothing', but whatever it turned out to be I never sensed any kind of disappointment or boredom. The life of a crime pathologist is so packed with colour and interest he has no time to get bored—hardly even to feel tired.

Ten minutes later that first morning I drew up in my Rover 14 among the police and press cars outside the very modest little York Hotel, since demolished to make way for the Festival Hall, and walked up the steps to the front door, already guarded by a constable. The pressmen gathered around took not the slightest notice of me, for I was entirely new to the scene: any important murder always had 'Spilsbury called in'. I climbed upstairs to the first floor. I felt very much alone, but was young enough to be full of confidence.

'Ah, there you are, Doctor,' said the tall grey-haired man who stood on the landing. I can see this distinguished Scotland Yard detective, later to become Commander Hugh Young, eyeing me shrewdly, assessing this new recruit, as vividly today as I did that morning.

'A young couple booked in last night,' he said, 'and the man was seen just after 9 a.m. today running down the steps and over to the station. The manager thought he might be welshing his account, so he went up to the room. The girl was in bed, dead.' He led the way in.

I tried to appear calm. I was absolutely green, and I had a shrewd suspicion the Superintendent knew how I felt.

'Before you touch anything, Doctor, let me tell you we've had the photographs done, but Mr Cherrill, here, hasn't done the place for fingerprints. She was last seen alive at 11 p.m. when they went to bed.'

I put my professional bag on the floor. This earned me my first good mark, for it lay in contact with nothing but the tattered carpet where we stood.

I just stood there thinking what came next. My notebook, of course! I carefully noted the time, the place, the officers at the scene, then a rough sketch of the girl as she lay in bed, face up, head squarely in the middle of the single pillow of a small double bed, body straight out, arms and legs beneath the counterpane, the face suffused and the mouth very tightly stuffed, gagged, with a corner of the coverlet and with a handkerchief. In those days the pathologist had no 'instant' photographs by Polaroid to eliminate the need for a sketch.

This note-taking helped me to steady my nerves, and it also earned me my second good mark. Too many doctors start by pulling things about, disturbing the evidence.

'She's dead all right, Doctor,' said Mr Young with a smile. 'The Police Surgeon came in to certify about half an hour ago. You can move the body now, if you want. There doesn't seem to be any rigor mortis.'

Of course! He was giving me guidance. How long had she been dead? The body temperature, showing the heat loss since death, and stiffening of the muscles, coming on some five to seven hours after, would help. I had nearly forgotten that timing is almost more important to the police than how the murder was committed. It helps them check on a suspect's statements.

I pulled the counterpane gently aside and inserted a zero-reading thermometer deep into the rectum. It measured 102 degrees F.! Nearly four degrees *above* normal! *The body had warmed up, not cooled!* I could not detect any muscle stiffening—none. What did this mean?

'I suppose it's pretty obvious she died of asphyxia,' suggested Young.

Of course. The body temperature rises in deaths from asphyxia (how had I missed those tiny but pronounced asphyxial haemorrhages on her face and brow?) and it had not yet dropped back to normal.

'She can't have died long before that young man ran out at 9 a.m.,' I said. 'Early this morning.' My confidence grew, and I examined her neck. 'Those marks look like a strangling,' I added cautiously.

'We rather thought so,' said Young. (No score for me here.) 'Like a right hand, do you think?'

I accepted his guidance. This grey-haired detective had seen more than I had.

'Yes, it would do very well.'

And so I felt my way, gingerly, accepting all the helpful comment this grim-faced but kindly old man handed out. Years later he said I had impressed him by my calm and unhurried step-by-step examination. It really was precisely what it was—a practical examination *for me*. I'd passed.

As the years went by and counted off scores of similar situations I grew in confidence for I knew what I was looking at. I learned there was no hurry—the body wouldn't walk away far—I had time: time to get a proper stock of the situation, to do things in the right order, without disturbing a hair or a piece of clothing until it had been recorded and photographed; time to think and talk over the possibilities, there at the scene; not to rush off to the mortuary.

When I started to do medico-legal post-mortems in London in the middle thirties, the standards of work were deplorably low. Coroners had the power by a 1926 Coroners' Act to call 'any duly qualified medical practitioner' to perform an autopsy; and most coroners, qualified solicitors, knowing nothing of the technique of such post-mortem work, did just that. 'Any duly qualified practitioner.' Many without the slightest training in pathology or post-mortem work, without equipment or laboratory resources, some called Police Surgeons since they attended to drunks under arrest, examined assault cases, or looked after the medical welfare of the local police, and a very small handful who found coroners' work profitable financially, were doing the vast majority of post-mortem examinations.

Almost the only persons in England with any real idea what they were doing were the general pathologists in charge of the larger provincial hospitals—like Smith of Exeter, Faulds of Carlisle, Biddle of Ipswich and Grace of Chester—together with two men in London, Bernard Spilsbury and John Taylor, both real pathologists by training and instinct, both with real insight into the problems of obscure death or insurance, pensions, industrial, suicidal and homicidal cases.

Spilsbury in particular showed an aptitude for seeing criminal investigations with the eye of the police, meticulous for detail, a patient investigator with a logical mind for deduction and a gift for picking out the important factors in a case. Although not highly regarded by his academic colleagues, the professors in the medical schools or universities, he was undoubtedly the authority in his subject and an unchallenged expert of the greatest integrity, pretty well unchallengeable. Tall and good-looking, courteous, a lucid but firm witness using as few words as were necessary, he had for twenty years been head and shoulders above anyone in the country in this branch of pathology. His services were called for, and promptly given, in any important crime anywhere in England. 'Spilsbury called in' on the placards meant that a big crime job was in the offing. 'Spilsbury in the box' meant that the net was tightening. 'Fox Guilty' meant that once again this great figure had carried a judge and jury with him.

Well might J. D. Cassels, Q.C., complain, as he did at the trial of Sidney Fox: 'It will be a sorry day for the administration of criminal justice in this land if we are to be thrust into such a position that, because Sir Bernard Spilsbury expressed an opinion, it is of such weight that it is impossible to question it.' Spilsbury kept no statistics, but would recollect (with an assurance no one was in a position to challenge) that he had 'seen such a case on two occasions previously'. Counsel were far too frightened of him to challenge his word—indeed, in the Merrett case at Edinburgh, to which Spilsbury had gone for the defence, counsel at one stage addressed him as 'Saint Bernard' instead of 'Sir Bernard'! It was, as Cassels has remarked, 'an unhealthy state'.

Spilsbury's world was England. Only three times in his life did he give evidence abroad; twice in Scotland and once in Jersey over a stillborn. He never saw the Americas, never lectured or worked in any part of the British Empire, as it then was, never attended international congresses to meet and sharpen his wits with his famous contemporaries. He never troubled to speak to his fellows: Sydney Smith, Glaister, Webster at home, or Ponsold of Berlin, Gonzales of New York, Balthazard and Piedelievre in France, Mackintosh in South Africa. Not one of them would have asked his advice, for he did not appear to welcome such requests. He had no confidants among his colleagues with whom he cared to discuss his cases; he never took post-graduate visitors on his 'rounds' or in court. He stood like a monolith, alone, aloof, respected but unloved; and unmourned, too, when he finally committed suicide, in his tiny laboratory in University College, London.

Spilsbury has often been called the greatest pathologist of his day. His stature in the practice of criminal pathology was certainly unique, and the trust placed in his integrity was not misplaced. The trouble about such careers is that they die, as completely as the men who live them. It is in teaching, training pupils, writings, the media, and in lecture travelling that a lasting repute lies. Spilsbury did none of these things. He never wrote a guide to the subject—the textbooks in forensic medicine had all come for years from Glaister, Littlejohn, and Sydney Smith in the Scottish schools—and his name does not appear in academic literature of his day. He never took an assistant, though at times he was much overworked, and never trained anyone. It was not possible to sit at the great man's feet, far less his bench or table. I would have leaped upon any chance of seeing him at work: 'Yes, of course,' he would say without a smile. 'Some time.' But it never came off for any of those who, like myself, followed him in England.

So though I had then five years of laboratory training at Guy's as a pathologist, teaching at some hundreds of autopsies in the hospital post-mortem room, with a modest excursion into research behind me (I had been a Beaney Scholar in pathology and held a Gold Medal in bacteriology), Spilsbury took no notice of my entry into the field of forensic medicine. I was indeed very small fry, and I had no illusions about being 'fathered' into practice by him. It would have been entirely out of character. I had to go it alone.

So few pathologists were then in practice in London—the great Spilsbury, easy-going Taylor, Temple Grey and Arthur Davies, both of mediocre talent—that no difficulty arose in getting sufficient work to survive. Unlike the young barrister who had then to be content, whilst paying his master, to eat the crumbs that fell from the table in his first years at the Bar, I found the field of medico-legal and police post-mortem work literally cluttered with bodies: sudden death, suicide, street accidents, industrial compensation, assaults, and, if Sir Bernard was out on a case, the occasional crime. It wasn't a question of scratching sparse ground, but of picking up the plums that were falling every day from so many trees. Within a year I was ready to relinquish my teaching post in pathology, under way without help from the Great Man. I had a sneaking feeling he wasn't pleased to see me appear increasingly frequently at court to give evidence. It wasn't that he scowled at me or put obstacles in my way, but that he never actually spoke a word of welcome. Perhaps it was only in character. Cold and unemotional himself, he expected it everywhere and could not find it in himself to welcome any young man in his field. There was no question of challenging his status, for he was an astral figure in orbit, beyond all challenge.

I was not the only newcomer in London but one of a trio often referred to as 'the Three Musketeers' by the police, and privately among the Press also. The other two were Francis Camps and Donald Teare. We were all three much of an age. I had got into medico-legal practice a year or two earlier, while Camps tried his hand in general practice in Chelmsford, and Teare was getting his feet down in pathology at St George's, but soon we were sharing the work in and around London, pretty amicably on the whole, at least at first, since there was more than enough of it to keep us all very busy indeed.

At the time when Camps, Teare, and I were getting our foothold in medico-legal work in England, there stood a remarkable man in Scotland, Professor (later Sir) Sydney Smith. A New Zealander by birth and educated in Otago—where I myself lectured in his old school years later—he had everything the cold Spilsbury lacked. We three young pathologists found in him all the warm interest in young tyros that Spilsbury failed to show. He had flair and ability, an enthusiasm for police problems, tolerance of the human nature and pathos of crime and killing, and a real interest in his pupils. He was a brilliant and colourful teacher who knew how to thrill his classes at Edinburgh with the latest crime slides and he had an irrepressible wit.

Sydney Smith had graduated in Edinburgh, and after a brilliant career in Cairo he had returned to succeed Harvey Littlejohn in the Chair of Forensic Medicine, the oldest Chair in Great Britain. His sage advice was sought by young aspirants the world over, and freely and generously given. Twenty years older than I, he became an *alter pater* to me. I would have come even closer to him if he had accepted a very pressing invitation in 1934 from Lord Trenchard, the Commissioner of Metropolitan Police, to be the first director of Britain's first Police Laboratory in London. He refused, characteristically, out of loyalty to his Edinburgh students. Their gain was our loss.

Lord Trenchard, father already of the RAF and of the Police College at Hendon, had described himself to Sydney Smith as 'an old man in a hurry', and the need for a proper laboratory service was certainly urgent. At the time all scientific work was handled by independent experts like Churchill, the firearm dealer, who was a shrewd businessman, jealous of the only competitor in his field, Major Burrard; Roche Lynch, a fine chemist at St Mary's Hospital, persuaded disastrously to undertake glass, hair, fibres, dust and blood-grouping work of which he had no experience whatever; Mitchell, an ink and handwriting expert (the latter has always been mistrusted); and dear old John Ryffel, 'Junior Home Office Analyst' (at sixty), my own teacher at Guy's. It was a quaint and most unsatisfactory 'team' to cover laboratory service for the Home Office in crime investigation in England, but it committed no major blunders for nearly twenty years. It just creaked ominously under skilled cross-examination in court.

Without a Director of the calibre of Sydney Smith, the Metropolitan Police Laboratory was not an immediate success. It was ten years before Dr H. S. Holden took charge and put the laboratory on its feet.

CHAPTER 3

WAR AND CRIME

Emergency regulations, uniforms, drafting, service orders and a life of discipline cramp the freedom of many young men, and during the long periods of wartime training and waiting not a few of them got bored—'browned off' was the common term. Some missed their wives or girl friends and got into trouble with local girls and camp followers, or Waafs or Wrens or ATS girls, urged on by long periods of sex starvation. So during the 'phony' and training periods of 1939–43 there was a steady flow of rapes (some with strangling or other violence), of assaults (some fatal), of abortions and infanticides, of breaking into 'deserted' houses (sometimes with violence), all arising from the changes in life that were thrust by service conditions on ordinary people.

My professional routine deviated from ordinary peacetime work less than that of most specialists. It was just that bit more hectic and disturbed: there was more of it, and it was conducted under both day and night alerts and alarms and bombing; and later flying bomb and V2 attacks pretty well every day and night. Vast craters and outpourings of mains water or gas, or 'unexploded bomb' notices, caused frustrating changes of route, and occasionally a raid disintegrated a mortuary or a court. But everyone got used to living with the noise and uncertainty; we sheltered from blast, sometimes ducking to avoid flying glass, and once I took cover with 'Miss Molly', my attractive first secretary, on the marble floor of a mortuary at Leyton underneath a heavy-calibre slab on which the dead body lay, whilst a V1 flying bomb which had just shut off swooped down with its characteristic 'whoosh' on to an adjacent laundry, exploding with a shattering bang.

One morning, after Hammersmith Coroner's Court had been

shattered by an overnight bomb, the Coroner, Neville Stafford, who was always a stickler for 'form', entered a spare-room 'court' to the customary three knocks on the door and 'Oyez Oyez Oyez' by emerging with great dignity from his own tiny toilet into which he had retired a few minutes earlier! The Southwark Coroner, Hervey Wyatt, used occasionally to invite his court to 'come below' during day raids, to a store cellar, approached by a trap door through which witnesses, police, relations and doctors used to climb down into gloom and a dank, cadaverous atmosphere that really did seem to accord with the work of a morgue.

Most London courts did their best to minimize the constant interruptions of air-raid alarms by taking no notice of them, and in the end this was how Londoners carried on. Gas-mask drill and bolting for shelter like frightened rabbits several times a day quickly wore thin. The only anxiety I ever felt was being blown, lying in my bath on the first floor of my Hampstead home, out into the street with nothing on! It was mainly the 'East End' that returned in the morning from Underground tube platforms and night shelters to the comfort, or rubble, of their own homes. I spent many noisy nights in my 'fortified' basement living room at Haverstock Hill in pyjamas and dressing gown and slippers, dozing, writing my first textbook for students, *Forensic Medicine*, thinking how crazy war was, wondering what tomorrow would bring.

It brought every kind of case. People were 'found dead', committed suicide, fell under trains or were knocked down in the black-out that so crippled night work in London. Once, making my way home through this deep pall of black during an air raid, I myself walked into a lamp-post, and appeared in court next morning to give evidence— in a beat-up case, of all things—with a telltale plaster across my own split eyebrow. Poor street lighting has always helped the criminal, and it is surprising there were not many more assaults, robberies, and burglaries in those years of mandatory darkness: so many were, I suppose, occupied away fighting.

In 1937 I was appointed Medico-Legal Adviser to the Surrey Constabulary, and this led to my involvement in a number of typical wartime country crimes. Several of these concerned Canadian soldiers, because most of those who had come to England were stationed in Surrey.

In September 1941 I was called down to Weybridge, where an old lady named Miss Salmon had been found dead in her bedroom. She had lived as a recluse in a large Edwardian house near the Brooklands race circuit. Her body had been discovered at 7.45 a.m. by the postman, who, getting no reply to his knock, had put up a ladder against the back of the house and climbed up. Through the window he saw the old lady lying on the floor of her very disorderly bedroom.

The police, led by Detective Superintendent T. A. Roberts, head of the Surrey CID, found the bedroom door locked with the key on the floor inside, and also barricaded from the inside by a chair. The old lady, dressed only in an old flannel nightie, was clutching a glass tumbler containing brandy, as if she had just staggered about after drinking too much and injured herself fatally through collapsing on the floor. That did not, however, explain her two open and empty jewel-cases, and a more sinister explanation was apparently offered to the police even before they entered her room. On their arrival at the house they had found a drunken young seaman staggering about in the front garden, his pockets stuffed with jewellery, and a drunken Canadian soldier lying asleep on the kitchen floor, his battledress bulging with similar loot.

Dr Eric Gardner, the Coroner's pathologist, was on the scene at 9.30 a.m. He took her temperature (it was 91 degrees F.) and then waited until I arrived at the large mansion, inappropriately called 'The Nook', at 2.30 p.m. Gardner and I agreed that death had probably occurred between one and 2 a.m. There was a little blood around the dead woman's nose and mouth, some of which appeared to have been wiped away. The police had already noted a piece of bloodstained cotton wool and also a cigarette end and a broken comb on the floor. Miss Salmon had bruised lips, a black eye, and other serious head injuries that were plainly due to an assault. The puzzle was the locked and barricaded door, for I did not think she could possibly have put up these defences after the injuries to her head. I told Roberts, who suggested the key could have been pushed under the door from outside; and after some experiments he found also that the chair barricade could have been contrived from outside the bedroom door. The ruse rebounded, for it made it clear that at least one of her assailants was *not* incapable from drink at the time, and therefore capable of forming malice and an intent to kill. The glass of brandy had not been put in her hand after death for it was held by cadaveric spasm, which meant she had grasped it at the moment death took place. She could not have taken more than a few sips, for at the autopsy there was no smell of brandy in her stomach.

Besides the head injuries Gardner and I saw marks of a very rough gripping of the neck, which had failed to strangle only because her neck had been gripped too high up. It was not difficult to deduce the probable order of events. First, I thought, was a slapping blow on the mouth; next, and perhaps as a consequence, a heavy fall backward, with her head striking the floor; she was then pinned by her shoulders and arms and the rough and clumsy attempt was made to silence or strangle her; finally her head was punched heavily at least five times, probably in rapid succession. She had not died immediately. The bleeding inside her head showed that the circulation had continued for another hour or two. Perhaps an attempt had been made to revive her with brandy.

Who had inflicted all these injuries? I examined the two drunks who had pocketed her jewellery, and I thought they had probably both played a part in the murder. The young seaman, Patrick Cusack, was slightly built, and I did not think he had the brute strength for heavy face blows or the strangulation bruising, which was the roughest I had seen in a human neck. However, Cusack had fresh injuries on the back of his hand which he could very well have got in dealing the first blow, backhanded, at Miss Salmon's mouth. If I was right, this blow had made her fall and hit her head on the floor, and the man who had inflicted it could be charged with murder.

The Canadian soldier, Peter McDonald, bore only very slight fresh grazes on his right hand. There were no bruises; but in a man of his physique bruising would not easily develop. He was very powerfully built and formed a fist of great toughness.

Cusack made a statement admitting the first blow. 'I pushed at her with my hand, hitting her in the face. She fell down on the floor and stayed there.' McDonald said nothing. Later Cusack made a second statement, putting all the blame on the Canadian.

'She opened the door,' his statement ran, 'and McDonald caught hold of her, I believe round the throat. She did not have time to say anything. She struggled with him and tried to scream but she could not make much noise because he kept hold of her. He then laid her on the floor . . . and pulled a silk eiderdown off the bed and laid it over her. She was still struggling and was knocking her heels on the floor. He said, "Hold that over her." I held it over her. The old lady then got her head out from under the quilt and said, "What is all this?" (No crime novelist could have invented dialogue of this standard.) I then struggled with her and I put the quilt over her head again. I then went down the dressing-table drawers and I got out some jewellery. The old lady then started to struggle again and McDonald said, "I will attend to her. I think I will have to tap her." I said, "If you are going to, do not hit too hard because she is old."'

But McDonald had hit her hard, said Cusack, and after moaning a little she had become quiet. 'He then left her alone and we both went to the chest of drawers and took out some stuff. He said to me, "I think she is kicked out or dead."' Both men were charged with murder, but the outcome was unexpected.

Within a few months the frail Cusack was dead, but not from judicial hanging. He had been in an advanced stage of pulmonary tuberculosis at the time of the crime, and he died in Brixton Prison Hospital a few days before McDonald was put on trial. At once the Canadian became articulate, putting all the blame on Cusack.

When I gave evidence at McDonald's trial I repeated my opinion that death had occurred between 1 a.m. and 2 a.m. I had no reason to expect the defence to challenge this estimate, but the expert witness has to be ready for an attack on any part of his evidence.

'Do you agree,' I was asked in cross-examination, 'that such a conclusion is necessarily highly speculative?'

'No,' I replied. 'I admit it to be approximate but not highly speculative.' Early temperature measurement gives a pretty accurate basis. 'I think it might be reasonable to say it might vary half or three-quarters of an hour in either direction.'

'Then in reason she may have come to her death at a quarter after two?' counsel suggested.

'It is possible.'

'Perhaps two-thirty?' It sounded as if he was 'nursing' an alibi.

'I think that would be the maximum.'

Counsel then suggested Miss Salmon's temperature might have been sub-normal because she was old. 'Did your calculation take that into account?'

I had, in fact, allowed for this. 'It would make very little difference,' I said.

'Is it a fact,' counsel asked, 'that the body cools at a rate of something like 3·5 degrees F. in the first three hours?'

That was easy to answer. 'No, the conditions vary according to various factors. It varies considerably.'

Counsel went on to quote a passage from a rather out-of-date

Webster's *Medical Jurisprudence*, with which I said I strongly disagreed. That ended the cross-examination. We expected the defence to produce an alibi for a later time—perhaps an Army pal, prepared to say he had got back to camp with McDonald in the early hours. Perhaps my answers spoiled the alibi in advance, for no such witness was called. However, like many soldiers in wartime, McDonald was given the benefit of any slender doubt that existed, and acquitted of the charge. Posted back to Canada, he was killed in a road accident soon afterwards.

I had for some time been interesting myself in the measurement of loss of heat in the body as a means of estimating the lapse of time since death, and a few months later a case highly relevant to this was brought to my doorstep, or at least to Southwark mortuary, where I happened to be about to perform two other autopsies. The new body was of a woman who had been picked out of the muddy Thames foreshore by Waterloo Bridge. A local police surgeon had examined—well, he'd no more than looked at—the body at 9.30 a.m., noted a broken leg, inferred she had jumped off the bridge, 'another suicide, I suppose', and told the police he thought she had been dead four to seven days.

It was clear to me that this girl was pretty freshly dead when I saw the body at 2.30 p.m. There was still warmth in the body organs. I took the temperature: it was 47 degrees F., compared with 38 in the mortuary and 31 in the river. From this and the state of rigor mortis I estimated she had been dead only some fourteen hours, give or take half an hour, putting the time of death at about 12.30 a.m.

There were no signs of drowning, and it was clear from the injuries that she had not fallen into water but on to a hard, unyielding surface like a bastion or just the river bed. She had heavy impact injuries to both knees, both legs were fractured, her chest was crushed, and the internal damage was extensive and severe. Haemorrhage was so limited that she had evidently not survived her fall by more than a few minutes.

Suicide or accident? Neither, for when the mud was wiped away I found 'fingertip' bruises on the neck characteristic of manual strangling, and, beneath these, a fracture of the hyoid bone of the voice box and bruising of the soft tissues behind. Counter-pinning bruises on the back suggested her body had been held against some hard surface like a wall or parapet while the strangling attempt was made. There were no asphyxial changes so the attempt had failed. Both the bruises of the neck and of the back had spread rather more than her other injuries, so it seemed she had fallen, or been pushed, to her death a few minutes after the attempted strangling.

I sent a message to the Coroner's officer asking him to inform the CID, and I later went to Waterloo Bridge with Detective Superintendent Reece, who pointed out the spot where the body had been found, in the mud and debris of the foreshore fifty feet below. Evidently the shallow tide had come and gone without disturbing the dead body. The new bridge was then still under construction and closed to traffic, but it was easy to walk out on it and some parapet walls were completed. I thought these could very well account for the back injuries if she had been pinned face up on the parapet, perhaps for sex.

Reece was still trying to find out who she was. I could not tell him much, except that she had been about thirty-five or forty, was sexually very experienced and had had venereal infection, but there was no evidence of recent intercourse. No handbag had been found with or near the body. However, a watchman reported that he had heard a man and woman quarrelling on the bridge *at around midnight*, and when he went to investigate he saw only a man, a Canadian soldier, standing by the parapet; and a woman's scarf near by. My 'timing' appeared to have been correct.

Quite soon the police discovered her identity. She was a Deptford prostitute named Peggy Richards. Hardly a memorable name, but an alert constable remembered it from an identity card that he had inspected on the night of the murder. On duty at Waterloo Station, he had seen a soldier—a Canadian soldier—carrying a woman's handbag between 12.30 and 1 a.m. He had stopped the man, looked in the handbag and seen the identity card, and asked for an explanation. 'I had been with a girl, drinking. She hit me with the handbag when we came out of the pub. I got hold of it. She ran off. I got left with it.' He said he was on leave and was going to stay the night at the YMCA.

Peggy Richards had indeed spent part of the evening drinking in the near-by 'Wellington', which had been crowded as usual with Canadian soldiers having a last drink before taking the train back to their billets in Surrey. Peggy had been seen leaving the pub at closing time, with a Canadian soldier, walking towards Waterloo Bridge. The police questioned many Canadian soldiers who had slept out of

camp that night before they came to the scholarly-looking
McKinstrey, bespectacled and bald. He admitted drinking with
Peggy Richards and leaving the 'Wellington' with her at closing time.
He had paid her a fiver for her services, having bought some
contraceptives from a man in Waterloo Station, and 'had her' in a
dark doorway. They had quarrelled a bit, but then walked out on to the
deserted bridge, where he'd 'had her' again. Once more, he said, she
had raised her voice over something, and he'd told her 'Shut up, you
goddam bitch!' She had struck him with her handbag 'and had run
off'.

He told the same story at the Old Bailey, where I was rigorously
cross-examined. I had expected to be, for mine was the only real
evidence that it was a case of murder and not suicide or accident.

'Is not what you have told the jury—about the lapse of time
between the strangling and crushing injuries—mere conjecture on
your part?' counsel asked with a fine show of scorn.

'It is my opinion, but not a conjecture. It is an opinion based upon
my findings.'

'You formed that opinion *after* you heard of the charge, I suggest.'

'No, my opinions were expressed at the time I made the post-
mortem examination.' (They were, after all, before the court in black
and white, in my signed and dated p.m. report.)

'Might not post-mortem discolouration have affected the bruising
after four hours?'

That was an easy one. 'No. Post-mortem discolouration is a filling
of the vessels after death. The bruising is an escape of blood *from* the
vessels. These conditions can be distinguished with ease.'

'You have seen the picture?' Counsel pointed to the exhibited
photograph of the river bed.

'I have been to the place where the body was found.' (Louder.)

'When you were looking at the foreshore did you see a good deal of
heavy logs and lumps of wood?'

'Yes.' (What on earth was coming next?)

'And iron?'

'I did not see any iron but I could imagine it.'

'The flow of the tide comes very heavily at this point.'

'I have no knowledge of that.' (It is vital not to step outside one's
field of expertise.)

'Supposing the tide does come in there with a heavy force and some
wood were lying there, might not the bruises upon this woman's neck

be the result of blows from this wood?'

'I should then expect to find signs of drowning, as the body would have to have been alive to show bruising.'

'Supposing the woman's head was out of the water . . . ?'

'I should regard that,' I said politely, 'as very hypothetical.'

Counsel then challenged my estimate of the time she had survived after her fall. 'How are you able to say she did not live for half an hour, an hour, two hours, three hours . . . ?'

'The amount of bleeding from the crushed liver satisfied me that ten or fifteen minutes would have been the most she could have survived.'

'I suggest you cannot say how long she survived?' (Bluster, I thought.)

'The amount of blood from her injuries was so small that she had lived for only a few minutes.'

'Supposing the woman fell upon her face, would that cause bruising upon the part of the jaw you found marks around?'

'No, the marks were *under* the jaw, not over the jaw.'

'Supposing she struck the foreshore, do you suggest she could not sustain bruising to that part of the face?'

'I would not expect bruising on both sides of the jaw, only one one side of the jaw.'

Counsel again turned to the high tide and the blocks of wood.

'I think it a very remote hypothetical possibility,' I said. 'The marks I found were a classical example of a grip from the right hand.'

'I consider your conclusion rather a remote hypothetical possibility, to use your own words.'

'It is an opinion based upon facts.'

There was, of course, another possibility, which this shrewd defence counsel did not neglect. Peggy Richards had been out 'on business' that night. She could have picked up another customer soon *after* McKinstry, and he could have murdered her within the limits of my timing. Unlikely, but wartime juries were reluctant to convict a soldier on a capital offence. McKinstry, like McDonald, was given the benefit of the doubt and walked out of court to freedom. He too was posted back to Canada; and he too was cut down by fate, for he died soon after, by accident, in his case in a fire.

A few weeks after the McKinstry trial I performed an autopsy on the body of 'Old Moules' (Leonard Moules) seventy-one years of age, pawnbroker, of Hackney Road, Shoreditch, who had spent the last nine days of his life in Bethnal Green Hospital with a relay of police officers sitting at his bedside in the hope that he would open his eyes and give them a description of the person or persons who had so mercilessly clobbered him as he was closing up his shop at 1 p.m. But Old Moules did not regain consciousness.

His scalp had been split by five successive blows with a blunt instrument of moderate weight. Four of the injuries were set close together and parallel to one another: this suggested to me that these blows had been struck when the old man was already incapable of resisting or moving, or perhaps when his head was being held steady for the purpose; and deep bruising of the neck muscles did, in fact, indicate that the neck had at some point been gripped strongly by a left hand. The fifth injury lay apart, being set in a different place and at a different angle. It was distinctly heavier than the others and I thought it would have been sufficient to disable the victim although not, perhaps, to knock him out completely. It could well have been delivered as Moules approached with his head slightly bent forward, and I thought it quite likely that this disabling injury had been the first. If I was right, Old Moules had been knocked out and then deliberately and cold-bloodedly battered to death.

Divisional Detective Inspector Keen, who watched me perform the autopsy, produced a wrench that had been found at the shop. 'Could this have done it?' The wrench weighed 1½ pounds. 'It would do,' I said, and Mr Keen knew he had to keep on looking. So many blunt tools 'would do', but there were neither hairs nor blood on the wrench and I wanted both.

The only clue the police had found in the shop was a single palm print inside the safe. Unfortunately Scotland Yard did not at that time have any record of palm prints, though as long before as 1931 a conviction for housebreaking had been obtained on one against a man called Egan.

Keen, who knew the area and its crooks like the back of his hand, started a big comb-out. The pile of statements grew daily, but after two weeks of inquiries no progress had been made. Then a soldier was heard to remark in a Bethnal Green café that he had seen two men—'George' and 'Sam', he called them—examining a revolver in another café near-by. Inspector Keen heard this and decided to follow it up for though no shots had been fired, revolvers can also be blunt instruments. A little more 'information', and Keen was interviewing a 23-year-old machinist named George Silverosa in Pitsea, Essex. Without the blustering denial that is so common at first interview, Silverosa launched into a statement incriminating himself and his friend Sam Dashwood.

'Two weeks ago last Thursday, 30th April 1942'—the date of the attack on Old Moules—'I went with Sam to a café where we had dinner.' Midday dinner. 'He told me he had a gun and showed me a revolver. He told me he was going to do a job. I asked him "Where?" and he said, "Anywhere, I don't care as long as it is something." We went along the Hackney Road and he said the gun was only for putting the frightening power in. We were going past a pawn-broker's. He said, "We might as well go and do this if you are coming." I said, "All right, only no violence." He said, "All right." '

It was early-closing day, and they waited till Old Moules had come out and put up the shutters. They followed him back in, Dashwood leading.

'I closed the door,' Silverosa continued, 'and when I turned round I saw the old man falling down. I didn't see Sam strike him but I surmised what he had done. I said, "You silly sod, what did you do that for?" He said, 'I had to. He was going to blow a whistle." I wiped some blood off the old man's head with my overcoat. I said to Sammy, "Well, we've done the damage, we had better do what we came here to do.". We took some rings from the safe and off the table. . . .'

Keen lost no time in picking up Dashwood. 'Silverosa has admitted being concerned in the murder and has involved you.'

Dashwood, like his crony, was a former Borstal boy, with a long record for a man of twenty-two. He gave a different version of events. 'The dog started barking. I hit the dog between the eyes. George and the old man were scuffling and the old man went down. The old man then got up again and we both jumped on him to hold him down and he started shouting. I said, "For Christ's sake quiet down, or you will get hurt." The old boy went on shouting. George said, "Look out!" I bent over the old boy to shut him up and he put his arms round my neck. I bent over him and hit him on the top of the head with the revolver. . . .'

The revolver, a ·45, weighed 2½ pounds and the back of the long barrel was much like the spine of the wrench. Again there was no contact trace of hair or blood. 'It would do,' I told Keen again. In court this became 'I have been shown the pistol, Exhibit 4. The injuries I found on the head could have been caused by blows from this weapon.' I also filled in one vital omission in Dashwood's statement: he had not mentioned how many times he had struck Old Moules on the head.

Superintendent Fred Cherrill, Head of Scotland Yard's Fingerprint Department, gave evidence to show that the palm print in the safe, had been left there by Silverosa. He later told me he had given fingerprint evidence, as young Inspector Cherrill, to convict Egan of housebreaking eleven years before. Silverosa's counsel, the famous Sergeant Sullivan, said his client admitted the robbery but argued that there was no common design to kill. 'Only one man used violence, and that man was not Silverosa.' The judge explained the law to the jury, leaving them no option but to find both men guilty of murder.

'Hard luck, George,' called a woman's voice as they left the dock.

'Don't worry,' Silverosa replied, waving a hand. His own worries were soon over, for there was no royal clemency, in spite of their youth.

After this old man, a very young boy: David, aged three months, the son of a Lieutenant-Commander, R.N., and the grandson of a Vice-Admiral. His well bred mother took him out in his pram one June morning in the country, and stopped to pick rhododendrons. Shortly after, she ran screaming towards a gardener on the estate: 'Come and help, a man has thrown David into the lake!' She fell in a faint, and the gardener ran to save the baby. He snatched it out of shallow reedy water and applied artificial respiration, but David was already dead. The police began a manhunt, based on the mother's story.

I found not a single bruise on the little body, although a child's tissues bruise easily. No violence, then; not even rough handling such as one would expect, almost inevitably, in a case of baby-snatching. Not a sign of injury on any part of the body; just the usual features of drowning and asphyxia. Was it conceivable that the baby could have been so gently handled by some crazy murderer almost with loving care? I added one further observation to my p.m. report: 'Psychiatrists and criminal mental specialists do not recognize a disease of the mind *in men* of which stealing or snatching babies to drown or kill them is a feature. This fact alone might arouse doubts as to the veracity of the statements made by the deceased child's mother.' The

police, growing more suspicious, saw her again, and she confessed
that the man they were looking for did not exist.

'This is a pathetic story,' began Christmas Humphreys, K.C.,
prosecuting at the Old Bailey. She had heard the news that her
husband's ship had been sunk, and had assumed—as it turned out,
wrongly—that he had gone down with it. Already depressed, she had
decided, she told her psychiatrist, to do away with her child and then
herself. She pleaded guilty to 'Infanticide' and was bound over for two
years. This offence is always regarded by the law with great sympathy
for the mother: a binding over (i.e. not to repeat the offence or
commit any other within a prescribed period) is usual, and this
lenience is rarely misplaced.

CHAPTER 4

STRANGLING AND SUICIDE

Spilsbury, typically solitary, never had a secretary, and of course a pathologist who dabbles in crime is hardly the kind of employer every fond mother would think of for her darling daughter. Noel Coward might well have coupled it with the stage in his advice to 'Mrs Worthington'. Deaths, dismemberment, dirty hovels, ditches, dried-up infants in lockers or suitcases, drunks, the sort of clinging smells that cause your boy-friend to go off you, late hours, constant pressure: it needs an unusual type of girl to 'go the rounds' with this sort of doctor. Molly Lefebure, my first secretary, came to me from journalism, and when she left me five years later, to get married, she wrote up her experiences in a fascinating book, *Evidence for the Crown*. Young, blonde, lively, and amusing, she was with me for most of the war, and never seemed to have time for reflection on the disadvantages of working for a man who always seemed to have got his hands on some malodorous body in a mortuary, who never seemed to notice the time, who was mad at secretaries who got colds, and who didn't on the whole agree with 'time off'.

One of my favourite relaxations when living alone in London in wartime was wining and dining in Soho with close colleagues and talking shop. I used to meet my two London contemporaries, Francis Camps and Donald Teare, regularly at the French restaurant L'Etoile, in Charlotte Street, where good food and wine were still available in spite of shortages and rationing. Nino, the proprietor, had devised a substitute for the dry Martinis and Pernods of peacetime, a powerful aperitif which he called 'ARP' (wartime short for Air Raid Precautions) which consisted of absinthe, rum, and paregoric—or so Nino said. A shot or two of this certainly helped to restore our flagging spirits!

We had little contact with our elders—Spilsbury, John Taylor, or the Home Office analysts of the day, Roche Lynch and Ryffel. They were much older, and seemed to have little or no interest in living outside their official jobs, unless it was to browse in their London clubs. But Eric Gardner, the Surrey pathologist, would sometimes join us, chauffeur-driven in his sleek blue Railton, to pull out of his capacious greatcoat the last ''orrible specimen' or a few skeletal remains, rather as L'Etoile might produce the *plat du jour*. Occasionally, also, I might have a call from Dr Grace, the Home Office pathologist to the Chester and Liverpool area, to talk over some problem; but he preferred the spacious Euston Hotel, now alas pulled down, since he could walk straight out on to the Stygian gloom of the adjacent station platform to catch his night train home with the hundreds of service men and women who were daily being 'posted' somewhere.

Our complaint of the Euston Hotel was that too much notice was taken of air-raid alarms, and also that there was no place of privacy in which to produce a piece of bloodstained clothing or a mangled larynx, or even the latest 'filthy' pictures of some new crime we wished to show each other.

One evening Gardner and I had an argument in the Euston Hotel that led to an experiment which I recalled years later, when taking part in a radio programme on the pros and cons of capital punishment. Someone on the panel had said hanging was painless, and added that the victims of murders did not usually die so easily. I retorted that strangling was not very painful. Ears were pricked up. The BBC interviewer said, 'How do you know, Doctor? Have you ever been strangled?'

'Well, yes, almost. . . .' I was thinking of that evening with Gardner in the summer of 1941, in the Euston Hotel.

Our disagreement was over the death of a woman named Marjorie Fellowes, who had died of asphyxia due to strangling. Gardner, who had performed the autopsy, said she could not have done it herself, and the Coroner's jury had returned a verdict of murder by some person or persons unknown. The only person who had had an opportunity to kill her was her husband, with whom she had been on bad terms. The police had found no other evidence against him, and the Chief Constable had asked me if I would review the medical evidence as to whether it justified a charge of murder. Or was it possible that she had committed suicide?

Most strangling is done with the bare hand or hands, and that, of course, is always murder. It is physically impossible for a person to strangle himself manually because as he begins to lose consciousness he will inevitably relax his grip and so recover. But in the case of Marjorie Fellowes a ligature, a silk stocking, had been used. It had been wound *twice* round her neck and *knotted twice*. At his p.m. Gardner had found clear signs of asphyxiation, and he did not think she could possibly have had the time before losing consciousness to tighten the ligature herself.

'You may be right about that,' I said, 'but I believe she could still have managed to strangle herself.' It was a question of time, really.

Her husband had said he heard her coughing at 2 a.m., very close to the estimated time of death. Gardner had found quite a lot of undissolved veronal in her stomach; not perhaps a lethal dose for a healthy person, but she had been riddled with tuberculosis and was already showing signs of heart failure. Nobody doubted that she had herself taken this obvious overdose either by accident or, more probably, with suicidal intent, and it seemed quite likely that she had taken the drug shortly before she tied the ligature. The drug would have caused venous congestion and swelling of the neck, which could have increased the strangling tension of the ligature.

Gardner then objected that she still could not have tied the double knot (a reef). The stocking was too short for her to have remained conscious long enough after looping twice and tying one knot to be able to tie a second. He had brought the stocking with him, and we measured it. It could be stretched to 46 or 48 inches. The circumference of her neck was 13 inches. Twice round would be 26 inches. That left 10 to 11 inches for each end, and I thought this quite enough. 'No one with a neck measurement of 13 inches could do it,' Gardner insisted. I asked him to measure my neck. At the level in question it was exactly 13 inches. I looked for some privacy in the lounge of the Euston Hotel: hopeless. I could think of only one place that offered the necessary seclusion. . . .

We went to the men's toilets, both got inside one and, locking the door, turned to our experiment. I wound the stocking twice round my neck, tightly, and set about the tying of a double knot before (I hoped) losing consciousness. Blue in the face and already seeing things a little mistily, I succeeded, *and* got the tie loosened before getting enough breath to gasp 'How's that?'

How very foolish we both were neither of us had for a moment contemplated: quick tightening of a hand or a ligature round the neck can kill like a karate chop—suddenly, of reflex vagal nerve stoppage of the heart action. Next morning's papers might well have carried the headlines:

KEITH SIMPSON FOUND STRANGLED IN HOTEL TOILETS: NOTED PATHOLO-GIST HELD ON SUSPICION

or

MYSTERY OF HOME OFFICE PATHOLOGIST'S SUDDEN DEATH: TWO IN LOCKED MEN'S TOILET AT LONDON HOTEL

It was only when we both crossed the corridor to the hotel bar that the real stupidity of our act began to dawn on us. We had to laugh, but my point was made, and no charge of murder was brought.

I never tried that again; but a colleague in the Midlands attempted to repeat my experiment, collapsed, and was saved by prompt police action.

The case of Marjorie Fellowes was unusual but not unique. Other cases had been recorded of self-strangling with a ligature. Yet in my first twenty-five years of medico-legal practice I saw only three such cases, including Marjorie Fellowes; and as I had by then seen some 40,000 cases of all kinds I thought it must be rare indeed. Statistics can be misleading; for in the next year, in another 2,000 post-mortem examinations, I saw three more. This encouraged me to write a paper on all six cases for the *International Criminal Police Review*, the organ of Interpol, in the hope that it might help world police officers to avoid error and injustice.

Three of my six cases plainly admitted no other interpretation but suicide. In one, a woman of seventy-two had wound a thin rope round her neck, tightly enough to constrict the veins, *eighteen times*. There was no knot, both ends lying loose in front. Her husband was gravely ill in hospital, and she had threatened suicide.

Another woman, aged fifty-seven, had made a cord noose with a slip knot which she set under her left ear; then she pulled the loose end tight round the back of her neck by holding the cord wound round her right hand. This was a remarkable case, for her husband was trying to stop her. She had woken him in the night, moaning and crying, and had swallowed a carton of sleeping tablets, about thirty-two of them. Then she had left the room and returned with the noose round her neck. Her husband had managed to loosen it, but she was stronger and, standing by the bed, set it again and strangled herself, collapsing on the floor. He had then tried to loosen the ligature again before she died, but without success. Finally he had gone into another room and attempted to gas himself, but was discovered in time. His account of the incident was verified by the way the ligature was held and by the finding at autopsy of a substantial overdose of sleeping tablets in the stomach.

The third plainly suicidal case was of yet another woman, a recluse of sixty-five, who was found dead sitting in a chair. A cord ligature was set round her neck in a single loop, and a half-hitch held it on the left side under the ear. She had placed a pencil between this half knot and a second hitch so as to make a tourniquet, twisting the pencil several times and finally holding it in position with one end under the jaw and the other stuck into the neck above the collar bone. In a similar case that occurred some years later, a man had tightened a noose of ordinary string by passing an umbrella handle through the loop and twisting it around at the back of his head. It is probably unfamiliarity with this method that has led historians to suspect Napoleon I of the murder of General Pichegru. The general was found strangled in prison by a ligature that had been tightened by means of a stick, which had been twisted and then fixed behind one ear; there was no lividity of the face. The evidence for homicide was very weak, and the suggestion that the ligature had been added as window-dressing after he had been strangled or suffocated seems very far-fetched.

The other three cases I described for Interpol were more intriguing because they were hardly distinguishable from murder. One was Marjorie Fellowes. In another a woman of eighty-two was discovered lying peacefully in bed in her night attire with her head on a pillow, face upward, and a stocking round her throat, looped twice, tightly, and held tight by a single half-hitch in front. Only minor asphyxial changes were present, and at the autopsy many capsules of amytal, partly dissolved, were found in her stomach. Evidently she had swallowed poison and, not dying at once, had set the noose round her neck. It was tight enough to constrict but had added only a little to the course of events leading to her death. There was no disturbance in the room, and the door was locked on the inside with the key still in the hole.

The most sinister-looking of my six cases was of a Berkshire woman of seventy-three, known to be suicidal, who was found by her son lying dead on her bedroom floor. A piece of string encircled her neck tightly twice, and was tied by a double knot under the right ear. A minor injury to her right index finger had bled slightly, soiling the carpet. The consequences for her son would have been less unpleasant if he had acted like a good detective and not touched the body until the pathologist arrived. Instead he had acted like a son, loosening the knot and releasing the ligature, and trying to bring his mother back to life. Neither the local police nor their pathologist had had such a case, and they were uncertain whether such a self-strangling could ever be suicidal. Fortunately I was able to clear him of suspicion. The woman's dentures lay on the floor close to her face, and I thought probably she had strangled herself whilst sitting on the bed and had toppled off, injuring her finger in her fall.

In cases of homicidal strangling a pathologist is often asked how much time might have elapsed between the assault and loss of consciousness, and between the onset of this and death. These can be difficult questions, and the answers are sometimes surprising.

One terrible evening in March 1943, no fewer than 173 men, women, and children died in what became known as the tube shelter disaster. An air-raid alert had sounded in Central London, and people were walking down to Bethnal Green Underground Station shelter in a perfectly orderly manner when a woman with a little girl slipped and fell at the bottom of a flight of stairs. The people behind her could not stop, and there was a horrifying human pile-up. When the pressure was relieved 161 bodies were extricated, and a further 12 died after admission to local hospitals. The Coroner instructed me to carry out autopsies on the bodies of four selected age groups of the victims.

In each case I attributed death to asphyxia due to suffocation by compression (pinning of chests in the pile of bodies). Three of the four bodies showed changes quite out of keeping with prolonged asphyxia, and in my evidence at the inquest I said death 'could have occurred very quickly, perhaps within thirty seconds of being crushed'. A great deal of sceptical interest was shown in this opinion, which was so obviously at variance with everyday experience in holding one's breath. But the Greek word from which 'asphyxia' is derived means 'pulseless', not 'prevented from breathing'; and the Greeks may have been closer to the truth than we are, for their word is pregnant with a meaning which our own adopted interpretation has lost. Many different factors may be involved in asphyxia, and some—a vagal reflex from neck compression, for example—are capable of precipitating death within a few seconds. Such a case could be due to momentary restraint without malice or intent while several minutes of tight constriction of the neck could only reflect a deliberate intent to cause grievous harm. In law, this is the difference between manslaughter and murder.

CHAPTER 5

HARRY DOBKIN AND
THE SKELETON IN THE CELLAR

I was only thirty-five when I had the sort of case every young pathologist dreams of, 'the case of a lifetime', Molly Lefebure called it. It certainly had all the ingredients, and, but for the heavy shadow of a war that still hung desperately in the balance, it would have hit the news headlines as Crippen did in Spilsbury's younger days.

On 17th July 1942, a workman helping to demolish a bombed Baptist church premises in Vauxhall Road, South London, drove his pick under a heavy stone slab set on the floor of a cellar under the vestry and prised it up. Underneath lay a skeleton with a few tags of flesh clinging to it, which he assumed to be the remains of another victim of the Blitz. He put his shovel under the skeleton and lifted it out. The head stayed on the ground.

Detective Inspectors Hatton and Keeling, who were called in to investigate, wrapped the bones in a brown paper parcel and took them to the public mortuary at Southwark, where I inspected them the next morning. The sight of a dried-up womb tucked down in the remains of the trunk established the sex. There was a yellowish deposit on the head and neck. Fire had blackened parts of the skull, the hip, and the knees.

Could she have been the victim of a bomb explosion? Hardly likely, considering she had been lying neatly buried under a slab of stone, neatly set in the floor of a cellar; this was no bomb crater. The detectives told me there had been an ancient cemetery on the site: could the body have been there fifty years? I shook my head. Soft tissues do not last so long. I thought the body was only about twelve to eighteen months dead. The church had been blitzed in August 1940, almost two years before.

Who was it? How had it got there? Was it murder? These questions

were obviously going to take a lot of answering, and neither the cellar
nor an old-fashioned mortuary was a suitable place for a scientific
reconstruction. I asked the Coroner, Hervey Wyatt, for permission to
take it to my laboratory at Guy's to sort it out in the only way
possible—a slow step-by-step laboratory reconstruction.

The head had not broken off when the workman had shovelled up
the skeleton, as he had thought. It had been cut off. Further, both
arms had been cut off at the elbow, and both legs at the knee. Bomb
blast could do strange things, I knew from experience, but not as
strange as that. Someone had dismembered the body.

Pieces of the limbs were missing, and the first job was to try to find
them. I spent two afternoons with the police sifting nearly three tons
of earth from under the floor of the cellar. We found animal bones
but nothing human. However, I noted two interesting things in the
cellar: a yellowish powder on the earth where the body had been
buried, and a wooden chest slightly less than five feet long.

John Ryffel, the Home Office analyst and Head of the Department
of Clinical Chemistry at Guy's, analysed both the powder from the
cellar and the yellowish deposit on the body, and reported that she
had been buried in slaked lime.

I reassembled the body and measured it. After making due
allowance for missing bones and soft tissues, I calculated the height as
5 feet ½ inch. I checked this by reference to the well-known 'Pearson's
formulae' and also the less reliable Rollet's tables, both of which give
estimates of height based on one of the long bones of the limbs. I had
one long bone, the left humerus. Pearson and Rollet differed slightly,
but the mean was 5 feet ½ inch.

The woman's neck was bent at a fairly sharp angle upon the trunk,
and if she had been like that in life she would have been a conspicuous
figure. I had X-ray photographs taken to see if there had been any
disease to cause curvature of the spine. Nothing was found, and I
concluded the neck had been bent after death. Why? Perhaps, at some
stage, to cram the body into a space that was a little too small for it.
As it was, it would have just fitted into the wooden chest. I examined
this for bloodstains, but all the tests were negative.

How old was she? I had X-ray photographs taken of the skull
plates, which join together at pretty constant periods between the
'teens and old age. Her brow plates were completely fused, fusion was
in progress between the top plates, and there was no fusion between
the two groups. That put her age between forty and fifty.

The person who had dismembered the body had evidently tried to make her utterly unidentifiable. The scalp and hair, face, eyes, hands and feet had all gone. No, not quite all: I found a fragment of hair sticking to the back of her skull. It was dark brown, going grey.

The uterus was enlarged. Another X-ray photograph, in case there was a pregnancy. No foetal bones. Instead, the swelling proved to be a fibroid tumour, three to four inches in diameter, for which she might well have sought medical attention.

Teeth? Her lower jaw had gone completely, but in the upper jaw I found as much dental information as a portrait, if her dentist could ever be found. Three molars on the right, two of them filled; the first molar on the left also filled. Marks from the metal claws of a dental plate. A high palate, and considerable thickening of the bone in the region of the back teeth. It was a mine of information. 'If you trace her dentist, and he has kept proper records, you'll identify her beyond doubt,' I told the police.

Inspector Keeling thought he might have found her. Working through the lists of missing persons, he discovered that Rachel Dobkin, the wife of the fire-watcher to the bombed Baptist Church premises, had disappeared after setting out to visit him to collect arrears of maintenance fifteen months previously. Her sister, Polly Dubinski, had reported her disappearance to the police.

Rachel was forty-seven,, Polly said. Height about 5 feet to 5 feet 1 inch, 'the same height as me'. Dark hair going grey. She had been going to hospital about 'something internal'. Her dentist was Mr Kopkin—a strangely close spelling!—of Stoke Newington. Polly gave the police a photograph of Rachel.

Yes, said Dr Marie Watson, of the Mildmay Mission Hospital, Bethnal Green, she had examined Mrs Rachel Dobkin in October 1939, and found fibroid growths of the uterus. Yes, confirmed another doctor, at the London Hospital, fibroid growths of the uterus: an operation had been advised, but Mrs Dobkin had refused.

Yes, said Barnett Kopkin, the dental surgeon, recognizing Rachel Dobkin from the photograph—yes, she had been his patient for six years. From April 1934 to March 1940, to be precise; and Kopkin could be very precise, for his record cards were the most comprehensive that Inspector Keeling had ever seen.

'From these cards', he asked, 'could you draw a picture of her upper jaw as it was when you saw her last?'

Kopkin sat down in his consulting room and drew the diagram. At

Keeling's request he signed and dated it: 3rd August 1942, at 11 a.m. Then Keeling brought him to my laboratory at Guy's, where the skull of Rachel Dobkin lay upside down on the bench.

'That's my patient!' he burst out excitedly, before I had time to greet him. 'That's Mrs Dobkin! Those are my fillings!'

It was as dramatic a moment as I can remember. Molly Lefebure nearly fell off her lab stool.

Inspector Keeling produced the diagram the dental surgeon had made. It was an exact replica of the upper jaw from the cellar—teeth in the right positions, fillings just so, gap for the denture, claw marks—but also a couple of possible extra: tiny fragments of the roots of the first and second pre-molars on the left side that Kopkin thought he might have left in the jaw when extracting those teeth in April 1934. These did not appear on our X-ray photographs.

We had the jaw X-rayed again, this time by Guy's own senior dental surgeon, the famous Sir William Kelsey Fry. He found the fragments.

Meanwhile I had been feeling my way in photography myself, with the help of Mary Newman, who was in charge of the Photographic Department of Guy's. Now that we had a photograph of the missing woman, a full-face portrait, I wanted to try to superimpose it on a similar photograph of the skull. This identification technique had been used first in 1936, by Professors Glaister and Brash, in the famous case of Buck Ruxton, the Indian doctor who had murdered his wife and her maid and thrown their dismembered bodies into a ravine. Having the jumbled remains of two bodies, Glaister and Brash had been concerned with sorting out the pieces. I had only one head and one photograph, and I wanted to see how far they matched.

Miss Newman photographed the skull and photographed the portrait, and enlarged the latter to the same size. Then she made fresh photographs on X-ray film, a negative of the skull and a positive of the portrait, and placed them together superimposed. We found no dissimilarities whatever. The portrait fitted the skull like a mask.

Keeling was so pleased you would think he had caught the murderer. And in a sense he had; at least, he had him half in the bag.

Murderer? It is all very well to say you do not find yourself in several pieces under a slab of stone in the floor of a Baptist Church cellar unless something sinister has been going on, but that is not enough for a charge of murder. What evidence was there that she had been killed?

Probably there would have been none, but for a very important contribution by the murderer himself. In sprinkling slaked lime over the body he had no doubt intended to keep down the smell of decomposition and perhaps to destroy the soft tissues. Lime has a reputation for burning human flesh. But slaked lime has little or no destructive action; on the contrary, by killing maggots and beetles it acts as a preservative. Thanks to the lime, certain injuries to the throat, in part to the voice box, had been preserved in this way.

It was another dramatic moment, late in the evening, when I was alone in my laboratory and dissected out the voice box and saw that the upper horn of the thyroid cartilage on the right side was fractured. There was a little blood clot round it, so the workmen had not done the damage with their picks and shovels. It had occurred in life.

Now this little bone never gets broken, alone, except when the neck is gripped tight by a strangling hand. It is the pressure of a finger tip or thumb that does it.

'Are you quite sure, doctor?' Could I really say it was strangling without the classic signs, the imprint of fingers, the asphyxia? Both Hatton and Keeling were very tense.

'I'm certain. This means strangling. This little bone gets broken in no other way. I am quite prepared to say so in court. And if any other pathologist wants to confirm the injury for himself, well, there it is. We'll keep it and I'll have microscopic sections made to confirm the bruising.'

I found another possible bruise on the back of the head. It could have followed upon the throat being gripped and the head bashed against the ground, but it might equally have followed upon a fall. This was a much less significant injury, and as there were no tissues left for microscopical examination I could not be so sure it had occurred before death.

My work was done. I had, I thought, enough evidence to convince a jury that the skeleton was Rachel Dobkin, and that she had been murdered by strangling some fifteen months previously. It was for the police to show who had killed her.

Rachel Dubinski had married the future fire-watcher in September 1920. The union had been arranged, according to Jewish custom, by a marriage-broker, and it was an immediate failure. The couple separated after three days; but nine months later a child was born, a boy. In 1923 Mrs Dobkin obtained a maintenance order. Dobkin was most irregular with payments, from 1923 to 1940 or so, and several times he served a term of imprisonment in default. Rachel had been reduced to waylaying him in the street to obtain some payment, and he had come to regard her as a pestering nuisance. On four separate occasions she summoned him for assault, but each time the magistrate dismissed the charge.

On 11th April 1941, Good Friday, the couple had tea together in a café in Dalston. They left at about 6.30 p.m., and Rachel was never seen again. Next day at 3 p.m. her sister Polly reported her disappearance to the police, saying she suspected Harry of foul play. But London was at war, the police were undermanned and overworked, and Harry was not interviewed until 16th April. Meanwhile, on the night of 14th–15th April, a mysterious fire had occurred on the Baptist Church premises.

It was mysterious because there had been no enemy action that night, and no inflammable material was kept in the cellar behind the church where the fire apparently began. Another mystery was that Harry Dobkin, the fire-watcher, did not give the alarm. The fire was first noticed by a patrolling constable, at 3.20 a.m. He summoned the Fire Brigade and went into the premises, where he met Dobkin. 'I'm glad you've come, gentlemen,' the fire-watcher greeted him. 'It's a terrible blaze, isn't it?'

The fire was put out, and the minister, the Rev. Herbert Burgess, went round taking stock of the damage. In the cellar he saw the charred remains of a straw mattress; it appeared to have been ripped open, and straw from it had been scattered in heaps over the floor. Mr Burgess sought out Dobkin and asked him what he knew about it. The fire-watcher said he had tried to put out the fire and then called the Fire Brigade. Mr Burgess felt very strongly that the fire had been deliberately caused and he made an entry to that effect in his diary.

The next day, 16th April, there was what was officially called an 'incident' at Kennington Oval, less that 250 yards from the church, killing 23 persons and injuring more than twice as many. Enemy planes had dropped a land mine. When such disasters were considered only incidental, it is not surprising that a small fire in an unoccupied cellar was just put out and forgotten. The police did not mention it when they asked Harry Dobkin that day about the disappearance of his wife. He told them he had not seen her since they had tea together on 11th April.

The police circulated a description of Rachel and inquired at hospitals and the other usual places, including the Central Air Raid Casualty Bureau. The police found out nothing more, but evidently had suspicions, for on 28th April, and again on 1st and 2nd May, they searched the Church premises, dug up the floor of the crypt, and discovered a freshly dug hole some 6 feet long by 2 feet wide. It was empty. The police finally published Rachel's photograph in the *Police Gazette* and then filed the case away.

All of which made very interesting reading for Hatton and Keeling more than a year later.

Dobkin had left his job as fire-watcher in May 1942 and was living in Dalston when his wife's remains were unearthed. Three weeks later a constable who knew him by sight saw him enter the Baptist Church premises at about 6 a.m. The constable, who was on a bicycle, stopped and watched, and presently saw Dobkin look out of an upstairs window.

Not a word about the skeleton had yet leaked into the press, Hatton waited until 26th August before asking Dobkin himself to 'assist the police in their inquiries'. Hatton took Dobkin to the cellar and showed him where his wife's strangled body had been found.

'I wouldn't strangle a woman,' he said. 'I wouldn't hit a woman. Some men might, but I wouldn't. I didn't know the cellar was here, and I've certainly never been down here in my life.' He also said he had not been back to the premises since leaving his job in May.

'I have information,' Hatton told him, 'that a policeman saw you going into the house on 4th August.'

'Show him to me, the liar!' demanded Dobkin excitedly. 'Show him to me!'

The officer, P.C. Wakeley, magically appeared. 'That's the man,' he said. 'I've spoken to him several times at Kennington Lane about lights he has shown. I know him well.'

'That's a lie!' shouted Dobkin. 'I've never seen him before and I wasn't there. He's lying, he's lying!'

Inspector Hatton then formally charged him with the murder of his wife.

The trial of Harry Dobkin opened at the Old Bailey on 17th November 1942. F. H. Lawton, not yet a K.C. but later to become Mr Justice Lawton, appeared for the defence, which consulted my friend Eric Gardner on the medico-legal aspects of the case. Gardner told me later that he had advised them not to challenge the identification evidence, but Lawton chose to fight identity step by step.

'Anybody with a neck with that curvature would be a very obvious sight in life, would they not?' he asked me.

'If it was present in life.'

'It would be obvious?'

'Very obvious indeed.'

'If it was present in life, it could not be Mrs Dobkin, could it?'

'It was not present in life.'

'That is not quite the question which I asked you: if it was present in life it could not be Mrs Dobkin?'

'But I am not prepared to consider the question whether it was present in life, because I found evidence to show it was not.'

With forensic skill and remarkable medical knowledge he challenged my opinion about the dead woman's age and teeth (and gave Kopkin, who followed me, an even harder time). He also questioned me, but with an ominous lack of scepticism, about the dead woman's height.

'Taking a combination of all three methods of calculating stature, what do you say are the outside limits of stature, both up and down?'

'Working from the average height I expressed of 5 feet ½ inch, I think the possible limits are really an inch in either direction.'

'So the maximum height would be what?'

'Five feet one and a half inches.'

'So if Mrs Dobkin in life was 5 feet 3 inches, then this body cannot be that of Mrs Dobkin?'

'Yes.' It was the only possible answer. But what was the point of the question? Counsel had something up his sleeve; he had asked Polly Dubinksi at the beginning of the trial if her sister could have been 5 feet 3 inches. Why that figure? And why did counsel seem so pleased with my reply?

He left it at that for the time being, and went on to challenge the evidence of the superimposed photographs, quoting from Glaister and Brash's book on the Buck Ruxton case.

'And you are saying in this case that the photograph and the photograph of the skull together help you to make a decision as to identity?' he asked lightly, casually, as if he was not going to bother me much longer on the subject.

'Yes,' I said.

'And a positive decision?'

'Yes.'

The trap had closed. 'Now may I turn,' counsel using his heaviest voice, 'to a passage on page 161 of Professor Glaister's book and see what you say about it.' I waited uneasily. ' "Owing to the novelty of the method and the uncertainty of some parts of the technique, a positive identification of the skulls, no matter how close a correspondence of skulls and portraits was obtained, would have been open to very grave objection." ' I had expected worse; I was relieved. 'Do you agree with that?' counsel asked earnestly.

'I think it has an element of truth: it is open to objection,' I said at once. 'It is being used to give assistance in indentification, not to prove identification.'

'It is just part of the circumstantial evidence?'

'It is not circumstantial.'

'You say it is direct?'

'It is scientific evidence.'

'You do not agree with the words at the end of the sentence which I read to you, that this method is "open to very grave objection"?'

'I think it is open to objection.'

'But not very grave objection?'

'I should not have used those words myself.'

'Now let us see why it is open to objection', and again this young barrister showed a disconcerting grasp of scientific data and technique. But I had disarmed him by conceding the limited value of the evidence.

As I had expected, counsel saved his heaviest guns for the evidence of strangling.

He asked me to imagine somebody standing in the road, or on a piece of waste land with a lot of rubble about, parts of bricks and so on, when a bomb exploded and the blast throws him violently forward so that in falling he catches his voice box on a kerb or a piece of brick or masonry or something like that. 'Is it not possible—I do not put it any higher than that—that a fall under those circumstances might break the horn of the right thyroid?'

'I have seen injuries under those circumstances on many occasions,' I said, 'and the injuries have never been confined to a fracture of the horn, as present here.'

I said I had seen the whole thyroid crushed, with fractures of both horns and both wings; I had seen only one wing and one horn broken together. But never only the horn. 'In fifteen years I have personally examined over 11,000 cases, and I have never seen this injury except in manual strangulation.'

'Do you say it is impossible?'

'I say that I have never seen it; and I have seen many falls and many strangulations.'

Counsel asked me how many of my 11,000 cases showed any fracture of the thyroid.

'I can obtain such figure from my records, if necessary. I cannot say off-hand.'

'Of course you cannot. I was wondering if I might suggest to you, then we can have a round figure'—counsel clearly hadn't consulted Eric Gardner about this—'that the number was well under fifty.'

'No.'

'More than that?'

'It would run into several hundreds.'

It was Lawton's only slip, and at the end of the trial he gave us a bad few minutes. Harry Dobkin had spent more than a day in the witness box, largely to his own detriment, and now Counsel for the Defence was asking for one of the Crown witnesses to be recalled. 'My lord, about twenty minutes ago a document came into my possession, and I wish to ask Miss Polly Dubinski a question on it. It is a matter of very great importance,' he urged, looking young and guileless, 'and, as I say, until twenty minutes ago I had no knowledge of it.'

The document was a copy of the *News of the World* of 4th May 1941. The 'Missing from Home' column included a description and photograph of Rachel Dobkin, both of which had been supplied to the newspaper by her sister Polly. Counsel began to read it out: 'Height, about 5 feet 3 inches.'

And he had got me to say that if Mrs Dobkin had been 5 feet 3 inches, the body from the cellar was not Mrs Dobkin!

But Polly denied she had told the newspaper 5 feet 3 inches. 'I gave my evidence of 5 feet 1 inch. She was almost my own height.'

Everybody was looking her up and down, literally, trying to guess her height. Dobkin would certainly be acquitted if Polly was 5 feet 3 inches. But neither the Crown nor the Defence suggested she should be measured then and there. Every pair of eyes followed her as she left the witness box and walked out of court.

Three more witnesses were called for the defence. Then Lawton: 'My lord, that is the case for the defence.'

L. A. Byrne, the Crown counsel, was on his feet. 'Your Lordship will recall that Miss Dubinski. . . . Since she was recalled I have had her measured. . . .'

The judge gave permission for Byrne to call the police officer who had measured her. No witness was listened to more attentively.

What is your name . . . What are you? . . . Did you take the height measurement . . . (On and on went the preliminaries.) Is *that* the woman? . . . Was that at Snow Hill Police Station? . . . .

And then, at last:

'What did you find her height to be?'

'Height without shoes, 4 feet 11¾ inches; height with shoes, 5 feet 1 inch.'

And that was that. The jury took only twenty minutes to find Dobkin guilty of murder. He was executed at Wandsworth, where I had the lugubrious duty of performing the routine post-mortem that the law demanded, if only to show that the sentence had been 'expeditiously carried out'. It had.

CHAPTER 6

AUGUST SANGRET AND THE WIGWAM MURDER

On 7th October 1942 a party of Marines was exercising in the sand dunes high up on Hankley Common, near Godalming, when one of them caught sight of a dried brown hand sticking out from a mound of earth. He looked more closely and saw, also shrivelled and discoloured, part of a leg.

The Surrey police were called in by field telephone, and when Superintendent Webb saw the hand and leg he decided it was a case for experts and simply posted a guard and covered the mound with a mackintosh sheet. By noon next day we were all there: Major Nicholson, the Chief Constable, and Detective Superintendent Roberts, head of the Surrey CID; sundry other police officers, including the photographer; my old friend Dr Eric Gardner, instructed by the Coroner, and I as medico-legal adviser to the Surrey Police. The famous Dectective Inspector Ted Greeno was on his way from Scotland Yard.

Roberts saw the area cordoned off and the photographer started taking pictures. I collected samples of the soil and examined the remains of the hand. The thumb and first two fingers had been bitten away close to their roots, as by rats. Both the hand and the leg were becoming mummified, so death had occurred at least a few weeks before.

I said Gardner and I had better do the digging, as the body was fragile, and we pulled away the turves and soil with gloved hands. 'Buried five or six weeks ago,' Gardner said confidently after turning over a sod of earth that had been lying upside down; the heather growing on it was still green and had already flowered, and Gardner knew his Surrey heaths. 'Heather finishes flowering about the beginning of September in these parts,' he explained. This obser-

The author (right) at the age of seven, with his mother, brother, and sister

1934: On holiday with Ian, his only son, who is now a Suffolk country doctor

The author leaving Caxton Hall, in March 1956, after having married his secretary, Miss Jean Scott-Dunn

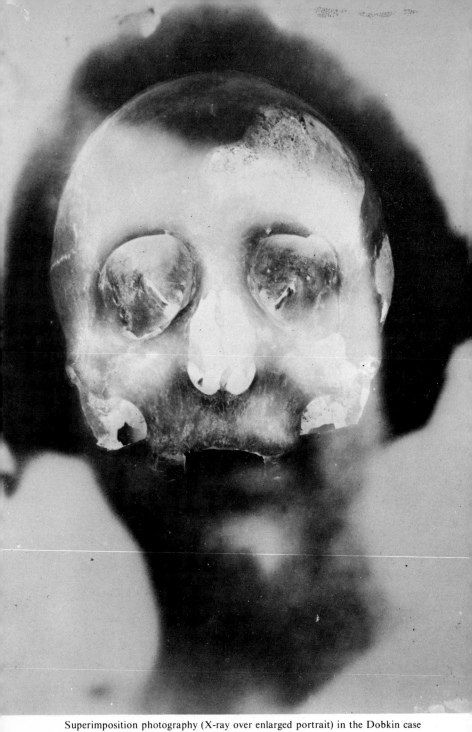

Superimposition photography (X-ray over enlarged portrait) in the Dobkin case

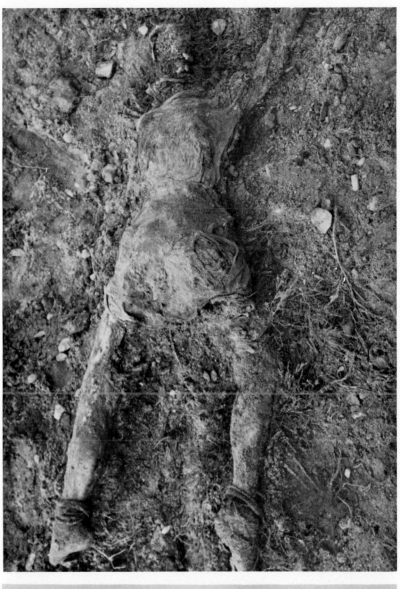

Body of Joan Pearl Wolfe; and knife with 'beak' end, recovered from drain in the wigwam murder

Loughans making his confession to *The People* in the John Barleycorn murder

Loughans' deformed hand which foxed Spilsbury

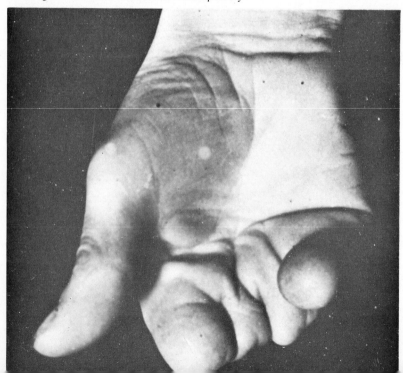

The author dictating to his first secretary, Miss Molly Lefebure

The author's assistant at Guy's, S. F. Ireland, giving instructions to 'an assistant'

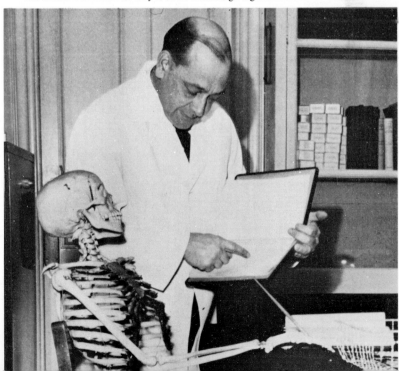

MURDER

POLICE ARE STILL ANXIOUS TO ESTABLISH IDENTITY OF THIS UNFORTUNATE WOMAN

HERE IS HER PICTURE ◄

If any person can help please communicate with

POLICE IMMEDIATELY

Her description is, age 30 to 35, height 5'·3", hair very dark brown, bobbed, eyes brown, heavy dark eyebrows, no teeth, appendix operation scar, 5½ months advanced in pregnancy.

Police poster shown at cinemas in the Luton sack murder

Fingerprint on pickle jar discovered on search of premises by Detective Chief Superintendent Fred Cherill of the Yard

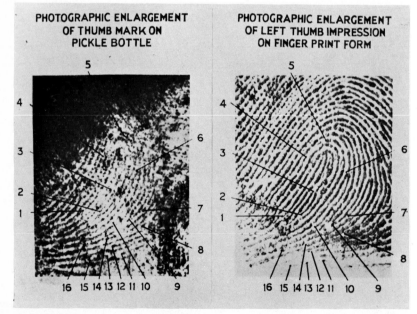

PHOTOGRAPHIC ENLARGEMENT OF THUMB MARK ON PICKLE BOTTLE

PHOTOGRAPHIC ENLARGEMENT OF LEFT THUMB IMPRESSION ON FINGER PRINT FORM

Body in the chalkpit case – as found on the hillside

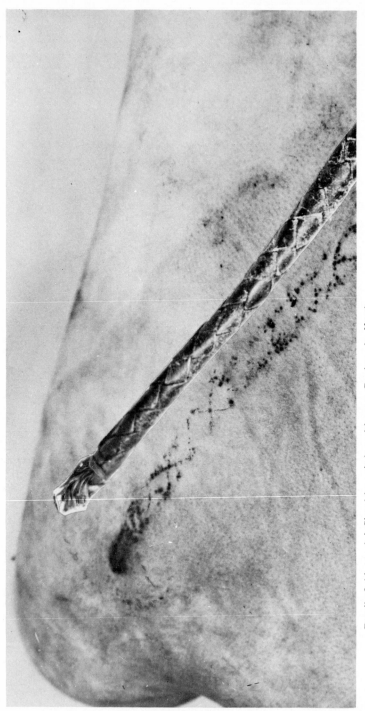

Detail of skin mark inflicted by switch on Margery Gardner, by Heath

vation initially 'timed' the murder for the police.

It was a very shallow burial and the body was disintegrating so we scooped more than we dug as we wondered what was going to emerge. A ritual burial on a hilltop? A sex assault and strangling? Concealment after a stabbing in London, or an abortion death in some near-by city? It could well be any of these.

The clothing was female: a soiled and rather tatty green and white summer frock with a lace collar, held round the waist by a string; a slip, a vest, a brassiere and french panties. All the underclothes were shabby but not disarranged, and her legs were only slightly apart. A head scarf was tied loosely round her neck, knotted in front, but the loop was much too slack for strangling. She lay face downward with her right arm outstretched. The back of her skull was smashed in, and as a result of vermin action her head was falling to pieces. 'A heavy blunt instrument,' I told the police. 'Perhaps an iron bar, or a wooden pole or stake.' She wore socks but no shoes. I saw one sock was torn, and found lacerations above and below the ankle with soil ground deeply into both. A short graze led down into each wound, and a third graze ran out of the lower wound towards the toes. 'I think she was dragged here, head first, probably by her right arm. I suppose her shoes fell off on the way.'

My secretary, Molly Lefebure, later recalled shivering in a cold wind on that unsheltered moor, but I only remember taking off my jacket because of the heat. The stench of putrefaction was strong, the air was buzzing with flies, and the remains of the body were crawling with maggots. It must have been exposed to the air before burial long enough for the blowflies to settle and propogate. 'Possibly even for one or two days.' I told the police. I thought there might have been two, less probably three, successive egg layings. 'The body could have been incompletely covered, perhaps by loose leaves or a cloth or blanket.'

Chief Inspector Greeno arrived and organized a search for the murder weapon and shoes, coat and handbag. The masses of blowfly larvae made it difficult for us to find out much more at the time. I could see there was some kind of wound in the right forearm, but the maggots obscured it. It would need a day or two in a Lysol bath to kill them off, and we probably had a week's work in the lab ahead of us, piecing the shattered skull together. I proposed to Gardner that we should ask the Coroner, Dr Wills Taylor, to let us take the body to Guy's to finish the job.

The Coroner agreed, and we carefully rolled the disintegrating body into the waterproof sheet. Maggots seethed out of the chest and the abdominal cavity when the body was moved, and by tea-time thousands more were struggling for life in a carbolic bath in the Guy's Hospital mortuary.

The police continued searching more widely over Hankley Common. One officer, Sergeant Smith, found a clasp-knife, open and rusty, and a canvas ration bag containing a piece of soap and a rosary. As he had not been told to look for them he threw both away!

When the maggots had died off Superintendent Webb came to Guy's and watched me remove the clothes. He thought he might have seen the frock before. The woman's features were unrecognizable, but I could build up some kind of description of her. Her teeth and bone X-rays put her age between nineteen and twenty. She was 5 feet 4 inches in height, with small hands and feet. Her hair was sandy brown, fine, bobbed, and had been bleached some weeks before death. Her two upper central teeth had been knocked out but I could see they had been very prominent, with sufficient overlap to be remarked on.

Not a great description, but good enough, with the clothing, for Superintendent Richard Webb. He remembered seeing her in his office six or seven weeks before her body was found. Her name was Joan Pearl Wolfe, and she had been living in the woods in a little hut improvised out of branches, leaves, and twigs: a kind of wigwam. It had been made for her by one of her soldier friends, a Canadian Indian named August Sangret, who was stationed at the near-by Witley Camp. She had told Webb she was pregnant, and he had sent her to a hospital from which she had recently discharged herself. The next day Sangret had called on Webb, asking for Joan and saying he wanted to marry her.

When had she died?

At first I thought she had been dead five, six, or seven weeks. Parts of her breasts and thighs had been converted to the white substance, foul-smelling and unctuous to the touch, called adipocere. This stiffening and swelling of the body fats usually takes at least five or six weeks in a temperate climate; but maggots generate heat. The heavy infestation could have raised the temperature of the tissues sufficiently for the formation of adipocere within a month.

How had she died?

Her skull had been shattered by a single blow, very violent and certainly lethal. There were thirty-eight major pieces, and Gardner worked all one Sunday and two evenings in my laboratory, sorting, drilling, wiring, and riveting them together until we had the cranium intact except for a gap at the back which had evidently been occupied by the smaller fragments we had left over. The blow must have caused immediate unconsciousness and death very shortly, perhaps within a few minutes.

But there were other serious injuries to explain, including three stabbing wounds on the front of the head. Without soft tissues I could not tell whether these had occurred before or after death. However, a section of tissue from another stabbing wound, below the right elbow, gave microscopic evidence of vital reaction to wounding. As the three head wounds were of the same character as this injury I could infer that they too were inflicted during life. I could go further. The head injuries were close together on the left side and on top, and had therefore been made by a right-handed person striking downward from in front. The natural defence against such an attack would be to raise the right arm to ward off the blows; hence the wound in the forearm. There were also several more similar stabbing injuries on the right hand. Evidently she had been alive and able to resist.

Two of the stabbing wounds in the head had penetrated the skull but to a very shallow depth. They would have caused great pain, some dizziness and later perhaps collapse, but not disablement. She would have been capable of further resistance, or of running away.

Her front teeth could have been knocked out either by a fall on the face (when running away?) or by a blow from a fist. A crush fracture of the right cheekbone appeared to me to have a different cause. Six long fissures radiated away from the gap at the back of the skull, and their paths indicated that the blow had been downward; the fractured cheek showed it had been struck when she was lying on her face. She had been struck after falling on to her face: it was no chance blow but a final bludgeoning—murder.

What weapons had been used?

All I could add to what I had said about the heavy blunt instrument was that it was a pole or bough with a diameter of 1¾ inches, the width of the gap at the back of the skull. The weapon that had made the stabbing injuries was more distinctive. A fragment of muscle had been drawn out of the wound in the right forearm, and a tendon had been similarly hooked out from a wound on the palm of the hand. The point of the weapon must have been something like a parrot's beak. The three holes in the skull vault were rimed or bevelled, like tiny dewponds with a small puncture in the middle of a crater hole; it looked as if the beak-like point of the weapon had been driven into the head and turned or twisted before withdrawal.

When the police were told to look for a stabbing instrument, Sergeant Smith reported the knife he had found and thrown away. In an intensive search the canvas bag was found but not the knife. Smith remembered it as an ordinary service knife without special features.

Inspector Greeno brought me a variety of stabbing weapons, including the bone-handled jack-knife issued to the Canadian Army, but none of them fitted the injuries . . . none had that important 'beak-shaped' point on the blade.

The police searchers worked down from the moor into the woods. They had nearly reached a rivulet at the bottom when they found the left shoe, 350 yards from the burial mound. About 30 yards away they found its partner. In the same area a constable found a heavy stake of birch wood with hairs crushed into the bark at the thicker end; it *had a diameter of exactly $1\frac{3}{4}$ inches*. It was not just a fallen branch or a piece of a dead tree, but had been cut as for use in a palisade, or as a strut in a wigwam. The wood was too rough to show fingerprints, and I did not expect to find blood as it would have been out of contact before bleeding began. The surface near the end was crushed, and the hairs had been held impacted in the shattered bark as might happen as a result of a crushing blow on the scalp. I found eight hairs with a lens, and compared them microscopically with hairs from the dead girl's scalp. They corresponded in all their natural characteristics and also in artificial bleaching. It was undoubtedly the murder weapon.

Meanwhile Greeno had decided to interview Sangret, the dead girl's soldier friend. He phoned Witley Camp beforehand, and Sangret was shut in the guardroom alone until Greeno arrived. He took Sangret to Godalming Police Station and showed him the dead girl's clothes. His face grim, he asked Sangret if he recognized any of them. Sangret, a Canadian-Indian, identified them impassively as Joan's. He said he had last seen her on 14th September and did not know where she had gone. He did not ask, and was not told, if anything had happened to her. 'I want you to tell me everything you can about your association with her,' said Greeno.

Sangret could not read or write but he could certainly talk, and with Greeno's encouragement he talked about Joan and himself for the next five days. A relay of sergeants wrote down every word he said, while other police officers brought his clothing and blankets to my laboratory. I found no hairs, but three interesting stains soiled one blanket. If the body of the girl had been wrapped in it before burial on the heath, the stained areas would correspond precisely with her head, her right hand, and her right foot—the injured parts. The stains all gave a positive reaction to the benzidine test, which is highly sensitive but not exclusively specific for blood. Dr Roche Lynch, the Home Office analyst, carried out more specific tests, but these proved negative because the blanket had recently been washed: it could also have meant that the stains were not blood. Sangret's battledress trousers, which had also been washed, gave the same dubious evidence. Grounds for suspicion, but not proof: washing had spoiled the tests.

No knife or other stabbing weapon was found among Sangret's belongings. When Greeno asked about his Canadian Army issue knife he said he had left it with Joan, who had used it to cut bread and open tins in the wigwam.

While Sangret was making his long, long statement, search parties found more of Joan's belongings on the other side of the rivulet. Her identity card (age 19½), a religious tract, a green purse containing religious tokens, a little white elephant mascot, a crucifix, a New Testament, and a letter dated 24th August written by her from hospital and evidently addressed to Sangret ('my darling'), discussing her pregnancy and their forthcoming marriage. Without comment Greeno showed all these articles to Sangret. Impassively he identified them as Joan's.

At last he finished and signed his statement. Then he said:

'I guess you found her. *I guess I shall get the blame.*'

'Yes, she is dead,' Greeno answered. He formally cautioned Sangret.

'She might have killed herself.' That was his only comment.

His statement ran to 17,000 words and it was quite a feat. Far from being in any way self-incriminating, it gave Greeno no option but to let Sangret walk out. Greeno was certain he had his man, but there was insufficient evidence to justify a charge—yet.

Two days later I went back to Hankley Common, with Greeno,

Webb, and Dr Gardner, to discuss our reconstruction of the crime.

I thought it had begun in the dell where Joan's papers were found, probably with the stabbing attack on her head. She must have ran downhill, screaming with pain and fear, inviting pursuit to silence her. Her crucifix ornament must have been torn or pulled away, and the contents of her handbag spilled out as she ran. Dizzy and faint because of her head wounds, and with blood running from her head wounds into her eyes, she was already stumbling at the rivulet, where a trip-wire had been laid down by exercising troops. She fell heavily, knocking out her vulnerable front teeth and further dazing herself, but was almost certainly still able to cry out for help, still inviting a silencing injury. She might have got to her feet, staggered, then fallen again, and was still lying prone, with her right cheek on the ground, when she was struck the final blow with the beech stake. She must have died almost immediately. Her killer flung the stake away and then dragged the body into the undergrowth, covering it with a blanket or leaves or both and leaving it for some hours of daylight, possibly a day or so (giving time for flies to lay eggs).

There is nearly always a loose end, some unanswerable question, an unsolved mystery. Why did the murderer go back, no doubt in the night, and drag the body up a fairly steep hill for nearly a quarter of a mile, from the relative seclusion of the woods to that open spot, and then cover it with a few inches of earth? Even a strong man could hardly have accomplished the climb and the burial in much less than an hour. It would have made so much more sense to spend the time and effort on burying the body more deeply among the undergrowth below. Was this a Red Indian burial rite?

Greeno was still looking for the knife. He had scores of Canadian soldiers up for questioning before he got a clue. Private Crowle, out blackberrying on the common in August, had found a knife stuck in a tree just above a shack where, the day before, he had heard people talking inside. 'It looked like a service knife but it wasn't Canadian Army issue. It had a black handle, and a hook on the tip of the blade.' Greeno checked the place. The shack was Sangret's wigwam.

Crowle said he had taken the knife to the provosts. Corporal Harding said he had given it to Sangret. 'It was British Army issue, not Canadian,' he remembered. '*The blade had a hooked point.*'

Greeno ordered another search of the woods round the scene of the crime.

A month passed, during which the British Eighth Army fought and won the Battle of El Alamein and the Russians trapped the German Sixth Army at Stalingrad. It was not the time for troops anywhere to be greatly interested in a trifle such as a blocked drain. One in the washhouse attached to the guardroom at Witley Camp remained obstinately blocked until Private Brown, performing a routine cleaning fatigue, took the trouble to reach down and pull out a soggy mass of paper and cigarette ends. As the water still would not flow away he thrust his arm in again, extracting more paper and cigarette stubs, *and a knife.*

It was an Army knife, but not Canadian—black-bone handled, and *with a blade that ended in a hook.* Crowle and Harding both identified it. Greeno took it to Scotland Yard for fingerprinting: no luck; then to Roche Lynch, and again positive to benzidine but negative to the confirmatory tests for blood; finally to me at Guy's, where Greeno watched intently as I put it into each of the three stabbing wounds on the front of the skull. It fitted each perfectly, and twisting the blade would cause the 'riming'.

Greeno did not produce the knife when he interviewed Sangret again, nor even mention it at first. Only after a number of harmless questions about various matters in Sangret's statement did he say, very casually, that the regimental police at Witley Camp had told him that when they had found a black-handled knife stuck in a tree near the wigwam Sangret had then identified it as his.

Sangret fell right into the trap. It was not his, he said; it was Joan's. 'I forgot to tell you about this knife before, I never thought about it. Joan used to carry it in her handbag. She told me she got it from the soldier she went out with before she met me.' Sangret said he and Joan had used it everyday at the wigwam, and he had left it stuck in the tree. 'I was shown the knife by one of the military policemen, and I told him it was Joan's.' It had a black handle, he said. Greeno asked if the military policeman had given it to Sangret. 'No, that knife was never given back to me, and it was never given back to Joan. I did not see it again.'

'Would you recognize it?' Greeno asked. Sangret faltered. 'I'm not sure.' He signed the second statement, and Greeno immediately asked Webb to arrest him and charge him with the murder of Joan Pearl Wolfe. This privilege is always left to the local police force.

Sangret was tried at the Kingston Assize five months after the

murder. I took the skull along with me to court. Arriving just before
the tea adjournment, Miss Lefebure and I were invited to take a cup
in the gaoler's room under the dock. It was a forbidding atmosphere
for a tea party, made gloomier by the presence near-by of Sangret,
who appeared to drink with his warders with more relish. Less than
half an hour later I was giving the evidence that he knew might hang
him.

There was little other evidence against him. Though known to
have been shut in the guard-room, nobody had seen him go to the
washhouse; there was some doubt when the drain had become
blocked. But for the trap set by Greeno's clever questioning, Sangret
could have denied all knowledge of a black-handled knife. As it was
he could only deny, rather unconvincingly, that the knife from the
washhouse drain was the one he had stuck in the tree.

There was a stir in court, as reporters call it, when I opened my
cardboard box. It was one of the few times that a victim's skull had
been produced at a murder trial. Knife in one hand and skull in the
other, I showed the jury how perfectly the weapon fitted each injury.

'It is an exact fit, is it not?' Eric Neve, K.C., asked me confidently.
Linton Thorpe, counsel for the defence, put it differently. 'It does not
really fit anywhere, does it?' he said scornfully after I repeated the
demonstration. 'It fits perfectly,' I answered. This was vital, and I
must not give way on the matter.

Thorpe changed direction. 'Any other knife would fit into that
wound in the same way?'

'Not *any* other knife.' (The hooked point was decisive.)

Later Thorpe tried to demonstrate that the knife could not have
made a triangular wound. I countered this with another demonstration.

'Then perhaps I have put the knife in the wrong way round,' he
said. 'Let me have the skull again and the knife.' I passed them over,
and he tried again. 'It fits into the left side, but not into the right one.'

'It cannot fit into both at the same time.'

'You think there must have been a second movement to cause it to
go into the other one?'

'Yes.'

'Or a knife with a rather peculiar-shaped back? An indentation in
the back of the knife would make these two marks with one stab?' I
explained why it could not have done and repeated my opinion that
the knife fitted the injuries with remarkable accuracy, and that any

other knife would have had to be ground to the same curious 'beak' point shape.

Surprisingly, my demonstration did not quite convince Mr Justice Macnaghten. 'Whether this knife does fit into the holes in the skull or not,' he said later to the jury, 'you may come to the conclusion that really the cuts on the skull are so surprising that you cannot tell what sort of a knife they were made with.' The judge attached much more importance to the arm and hand wounds—'what you may think is a more convincing piece of evidence'—he said, referring to the muscle drawn out of the forearm and the tendon from the palm.

The jury took the knife and the skull with them when they retired to consider their verdict, and they stayed out for two hours. They found Sangret guilty but with a strong recommendation for mercy, which was a surprise. He was hanged at Wandsworth Jail, and I performed the routine autopsy. Tattooed on his bronze arm was the name Pearl.

Sangret really hanged himself when he hid the knife in the washhouse drain. He could only have known then of Joan's stabbing injuries if he had inflicted them himself. Why otherwise hide the knife? If he had kept the knife in his pocket, and allowed Greeno to take it off him, the Crown would have had to rely solely on the medical evidence, and I doubt if the jury would have convicted him.

CHAPTER 7

HAROLD LOUGHANS AND OTHER STRANGLERS

'It's murder!' was a phrase commonly applied to the black-out, and sometimes it was literally true. Certainly the black-out helped to kill Caroline Traylor after she had been picked up in a Kent public house. She spent the evening of Whitsunday 1943 in the 'Mechanics' Arms' and left with a soldier at closing time, never to be seen alive again.

Just like Peggy Richards in the 'Wellington', except that Caroline was an auburn-haired girl of eighteen and a bride of six months, and worked as a cinema usherette. Her husband was serving in North Africa, and she had tired of spending Sunday evenings at home with Mum. It was her mother who reported her disappearance to the police, and they began a search of the many blitzed buildings in Folkestone. Four days after the crime they found her body in a bombed-out shop: I was called in the same evening, together with a 'Yard' team.

She had been strangled, and there had been rough sexual intercourse shortly before. Bruising of the vagina and thighs signified intercourse of some violence, though it had not necessarily been opposed when it began. Indeed, it seemed more probable that she had at first consented, for the outer sides of her calves were dirtied by contact with the floor, as if she had been lying with her legs flat on the floor and wide apart. From her injuries I deduced that she had resisted an attempt to grasp her neck from in front, and then had turned or been turned on her face and strangled from behind. It had been very quick, only about twenty to thirty seconds, perhaps because her face was buried in her left arm. I found six dark hairs, in striking contrast to her own auburn body hairs, stuck to her thighs. One of her fingernails was torn, probably through clawing at her assailant. I took scrapings from under the nail and found one short rust-brown wool fibre freshly torn away from the material to which it had belonged.

The trail led to gunner Dennis Leckey, who had gone absent the day after the body was found. Ten days later he was apprehended walking in London, and P.C. Briggs, who arrested him, recognized him as the man wanted by the Folkestone police. After being formally cautioned he exercised his right to decline to make a statement until he had obtained the advice of a solicitor; and, of course, the solicitor advised him to say nothing.

The police brought me samples of Leckey's body hairs, which I compared with the six hairs found stuck to Caroline's thighs. I found them identical in character, colour, and form. Meanwhile Dr Davidson, then Director of the Metropolitan Police Laboratory, had found an auburn hair identical with Caroline's clinging to Leckey's uniform trouser leg. The word 'identical' did not mean the hairs had necessarily come from the same person, only that they could have. That is the most one can ever say about hairs. Identical hairs are not compelling evidence like identical fingerprints for they carry so much less detail.

The police also brought me Leckey's clothing, and I found that the fibre from under Caroline's fingernail was 'identical' with one of the component fibres from which his khaki shirt had been made. Again, that was far from saying the fibre must have come from Leckey's shirt, for this was standard army issue. Identical fibres could have been found in thousands of other soldiers' shirts. But the evidence of the hairs and the fibres together would of course strongly corroborate any circumstantial evidence that might be brought to connect Leckey with the crime: this kind of evidence always has a strong influence on a jury.

In the event the jury returned a verdict of guilty after an absence of little more than half an hour. Mr Justice Singleton donned the black cap and in his impeccable Scots-English accent pronounced the death sentence. It was never carried out.

What went wrong? Sir John Singleton, an able and meticulously carefully spoken judge, had made one grave error, an almost elementary mistake. In his summing-up he had commented adversely on Leckey's failure to make a statement to the police. 'Of course, members of the jury, he is not bound to say anything, but what would you expect?' Three times in his summing-up he had suggested that Leckey's silence implied guilt. The Court of Criminal Appeal decided that these remarks amounted to a misdirection of the jury, the conviction was quashed, and Leckey walked out a free man.

A few months later another girl, a twenty-one-year-old probation nurse named Muriel Emery, was murdered in a copse outside the Three Counties Hospital at Arlesey, Bedfordshire, and again a soldier was suspected. The murder was 'timed' precisely by the girl's screams, which were heard by two army officers in the hospital shortly before midnight. Her body was found next morning, the Chief Constable phoned Scotland Yard, and within an hour Detective Chief Inspector Arthur Thorp, later to head the 'Fraud Squad', and I had set out for Bedford.

The local police had already discovered that Muriel had gone off duty at 8.35 p.m. to meet her boy-friend in the copse where her body was found. She had often done so, but this time she had walked out to die. It looked black for the boy-friend, a soldier from a near-by searchlight unit.

'We met at around 8.30 by the gate near my searchlight post. We chatted for about twenty minutes, and then sat down on the grass. We kissed and cuddled. She was a very decent girl, and there was no nonsense. Then she looked at her watch and said, "Good Lord, it's twenty past ten, I'd better be going".' They kissed again, and he saw her walking along the private road towards her hospital. 'It was a nice night; she was not in the least nervous. I went back to camp, to the sleeping hut, and to bed.'

She was indeed a decent girl, virgo intacta, and I found no injury to suggest any sexual assault. She had been half-strangled and then beaten several times on the head with a heavy blunt instrument, causing fractures of the skull and contusion of the brain. She had not been robbed, and there appeared to be no motive for the crime.

There were eleven other men in that searchlight post, and Thorp got nothing out of them. But he did find out that an NCO who ought to have been on duty was missing from around 10.30 p.m. until about 11.30 p.m.

Where had he been? 'Oh, out watching the sun go down, sitting on a grass bank.' It didn't seem likely at that late hour, and no one else had seen him during this time. Thorp took his clothing away for laboratory examination. The found a hair identical with the dead girl's, stuck to one of his shoes, and just a trace of blood—not enough to say whether it was human or animal. Unfortunately the hair was also identical with a sample from the NCO himself! It also emerged that he had been treating a dog with an injured leg a day or two before.

Thorp was far from satisfied. This wasn't the first girl to be assaulted in that wood since the arrival of the NCO. 'He had a peaked cap,' said the victim of one of the assaults another nurse. Only three men in the searchlight post had peaked caps, and this NCO was one. But that was flimsy evidence.

The Three Counties was a mental hospital. Indeed, as we all drove in we'd noticed an elderly man at the front gate sitting on a travelling bag heavily labelled with hotel stickers from Europe. He'd spent every day there 'waiting for transport, you know' for over ten years. He seemed harmless enough, but we wondered if one of the patients might be responsible for this motiveless murder. But every line of inquiry drew a blank—every patient 'off', sitting at the entrance, back late, absconding, it all came to nothing. Thorp went back to Scotland Yard with the case unsolved.

Nearly six months later an elderly woman, Miss Trotter, was assaulted in her general stores barely a mile from the hospital. Her attacker had suddenly gone berserk. 'He must have gone mad,' she said when she came round. She knew him, all right. He was a man named Rowley, aged twenty-four, who lived near the hospital and worked on a farm. He had been discharged from the army in 1940 as a case of major epilepsy. *He often wore an old railway cap with a peak.*

As soon as Thorp heard of the matter he tore down to Arlesey and asked Rowley where he had been the night Muriel Emery was killed. At first Rowley denied ever having met her. Then he confessed.

He said he had waylaid her as she walked back to the hospital in the moonlight, felling her with a piece of wood. He would show them where he had thrown it away in a dell afterwards—and there it lay still, to prove his guilt.

'I killed her,' he said. 'I hit her with a lump of wood, a thick bit . . . I don't know what made me do it . . . I knew what I was doing but I couldn't help myself.'

He was found guilty but insane at Bedford Assizes three months later. What a near thing for an NCO who'd only been 'watching the sun go down!' Or had he? What was *he* doing that night?

Rose Ada Robinson, who was strangled in her bedroom in Portsmouth in the night of 28th/29th November 1943, was not a young woman but a widow of sixty-three. She was also the licensee of the pub over which she lived, the 'John Barleycorn', and that was why she was murdered. It was her custom, unfortunately a well-known custom, to clear the till each night and put the takings in two large handbags: and it was well known, too, that since the bombings of the city had begun she had never let the handbags out of her sight. On the night of her death the bags contained about £450. When the police entered her bedroom in the morning they found the handbags empty and Mrs Robinson dead on the floor. When I saw her, just before 10 a.m., I estimated she had been dead seven or eight hours; and this was supported by the evidence of a neighbour who had been disturbed between 2 and 3 a.m.

On the ground floor the police found a broken window with a forced catch, and an unbolted and unlocked back door; from which they deduced, correctly, that the intruder had entered by the window and left by the door. He had left no fingerprints, but on the window sill they found a small black button with broken thread.

In the bedroom the black-out curtain had been pulled away, probably by Mrs Robinson in trying to open the window and scream for help. She had evidently struck her head against the window sill before being pulled back and down. From her injuries I thought she had probably been strangled as she lay on the floor, with her murderer either kneeling or sitting astride her. The fingermarks told a clear story: a deep bruise on the right of the voice box, presumably made by the thumb, and three lighter bruises in a line on the other side. Right-handed, four inches across. There were no curved fingernail impressions immediately related to these marks, but there were several scratches on the neck that could have been made by Mrs Robinson as she struggled to prise away her attacker's hands. She had certainly struggled, in spite of her age and an unduly senile heart.

That was about all I could tell the police, and although they searched the premises back and forth they found not a trace of the intruder except for that rather ordinary jacket button. All known local criminals were questioned and cleared, and the case was abandoned as insoluble.

Nearly a month after the murder, two plain-clothes constables picked up an old lag who was trying to sell a pair of stolen shoes in a café in Waterloo Road, London. 'I'm wanted for things far more serious than this,' the man told them. 'The Yard wants me. It's the trapdoor for me now.' They let him talk. 'I'm glad you picked me up;

it'll do you good.' In the police van he gave one of them a silver cigarette-box. 'There's a Christmas box for you; I know this will be my last Christmas.' They arrived at Kennington Road Police Station. 'Eh, I'm glad I'm in. I've been through hell for the past three weeks. I've been a bastard all my life, and I'll finish as I lived. I was sorry for it the moment I done it. I haven't slept since. It preyed on my mind. She must have had a weak heart, poor old girl.'

Someone asked him his name. 'Harold Loughans.' He gave an address, and began to cry. 'I've done a dozen jobs,' he went on. 'I tied a woman to a bed last week at St Albans, hit her on the head with a torch and robbed her. Got a cigarette-case and other things from there. I've done jobs at Mill Hill, Edgware, and other places I can't remember. I know this is the end of the road for me.' He paused; then, suddenly: 'I want to say I done a murder job in Hampshire about fourteen days ago.'

They waited for him to go on.

'It's a relief to get it off my mind. I had to stop her screaming, but I didn't mean to kill the old girl, but you know what it is when a woman screams. All the jobs I have been doing have been worrying me, and since I did the big job at Portsmouth, where I got the money when I strangled the old woman at the beerhouse, to get it off my mind I have been doing jobs every day.'

They asked him if he would like to make a written statement, and he dictated one. It contained some errors. 'I was looking through a room when the woman came in . . . I just put my hands round her throat . . . I think I got the money out of a little desk. . . .' But when Loughans was taken away by the Portsmouth police he made a more accurate statement; 'In the back room I saw a woman . . . I grabbed her by the throat with my right hand . . . There were two large handbags full of money. . . .'

There were no buttons on his coat that could be matched with the one found on the window sill, but his clothing was sent to the Metropolitan Police Laboratory, where they found a few items that he could have taken away from the scene of the crime: a hemp fibre on one boot, that could have come from one of Mrs Robinson's mats; a fibre of green wool, matching fibres from another mat; and a feather similar to those in the eiderdown. There was also a faint bloodstain, some weeks old, inside a cuff of his jacket.

One thing worried the police. 'He hasn't got any fingers on his right hand,' they told me.

It was not quite as bad as that. He still had four half-fingers, or stumps. In medical terms, he had lost the greater part of the distal two phalanges of each finger. His thumb was intact.

'That explains why there were no fingernail impressions,' I said. 'The hand could still have reached four inches, and the stumps would have had even greater leverage than fingers of full length. But, of course, if the old lady was lying on the floor he only needed to put the weight of his body behind that hand to strangle her.'

The defence did not challenge me about this at the trial, which was held at Winchester in March 1944. Instead, John Maude, Loughans' counsel, tried to trap me. Full of confidence and with his most theatrical delivery, he started on me with 'Now, doctor, I am going to quote, if I may'—as if he might not!—'from *Gray's Anatomy*. You are, of course, familiar with Gray?'

I replied, warily, that I was familiar with certain parts of it, but that no-one could be expected to know the whole of this great Bible of anatomy.

'Very well,' said Maude, only faintly checked. 'I am going to quote a certain section on the origin and attachment of the lumbrical—is that how you say it, doctor?—the lumbrical muscles to the fingers, on page . . .'

I thought I was down the ditch there, because he could ask me the small print in Gray and I could not possibly be familiar with all of it, and he would be able to expose my lack of knowledge of these unimportant little trivia. But I suddenly realized I had an escape door I could leap through. Only the day before, a copy of the new edition of Gray had come through the post, sent by the editor because I had, when a student, done several dissections for illustration in this famous textbook, and a complimentary copy was still sent to me when each new edition was published. It was an advance copy, and the edition was not yet on sale in the bookshops.

'May I know the edition from which you are quoting?' I asked.

'Of course, doctor,' said Maude, full of confidence as he thumbed over the title pages. 'It's the twenty-eighth edition.'

'Oh, I'm sorry,' I said, trying to look as if I was, 'but that is an out-of-date edition.'

'Oh,' said the judge, 'I can't have counsel quoting out-of-date textbooks in this court.' I was saved—by just one day!

When Loughans gave evidence he simply disowned his confessions, saying they had been invented by the police. Maude made the point that the statement to the Portsmouth officers corrected all the inaccuracies in the statement to the Metropolitan officers, who had not had the same knowledge of the details of the crime. But Maude's trump card, sprung as a complete surprise, consisted of four witnesses, rounded up by a private-detective agency, who swore Loughans had spent the night of the murder on the platform of Warren Street Underground station, in London, which was used as an air-raid shelter. They all identified him by his deformed hand.

J. D. Caswell, K.C., who prosecuted, was unable to shake any of these witnesses, and of course the police had not had any time to investigate Loughans's alibi. In the end the jury failed to agree, and the judge ordered a retrial.

It took place two weeks later at the Old Bailey. By then the police had collected some evidence to rebut Loughans's alibi, but the judge would not allow it, holding that it should have been presented at the first trial. Otherwise the trial followed the same pattern, except that Maude challenged my statement that Loughans could have strangled Mrs Robinson with his deformed hand.

Maude had another trump card up his sleeve when opening his new defence. 'Call Sir Bernard Spilsbury'; he declaimed this most dramatically, sounding like a toastmaster announcing the great man's entry.

Good Heavens! What was Spilsbury doing in this case? He had not seen the dead body, not made his usual authoritative autopsy, not even asked to come to my laboratory to inspect the scientific and medical evidence. What could he say?

He said he had been to Brixton Prison and he'd asked Loughans to grip his hand, as in a 'shaking hands'—and to hold 'with all the strength he had'. One could imagine how Loughans had performed. Faced with a murder charge by strangling he had been asked to show this great medico-legal expert how strong a grip he could set on a victim. One could hardly believe Sir Bernard's description of the limp, flabby handshake he had received, but this was the great man speaking:

'I do not believe', said Sir Bernard, 'he could strangle anyone with that hand.'

Casswell tried in vain to get him to admit the possibility of error in his judgment, suggesting that the accused might have made out the power of his hand to be rather less than it was. Had the great man been hoodwinked?

'No, I don't think so,' Spilsbury said disdainfully.

He was nearing the end of his great career, and of his life, and he was a sick man; and both lawyers and police officers knew his great powers were beginning to fail. But as a witness he was still as convincing as ever, and the magic of his reputation was too much for the jury. Loughans was acquitted.

Behind the scenes at the Loughans trial I had a characteristic brush with Spilsbury that was revealing. I met him passing to and fro meditatively in the corridor leading to the DPP's room.

'I find it difficult to separate fact and opinion in your report,' he said. 'You should keep the two apart.'

I sensed he was nettled at being on the 'wrong side': Spilsbury seldom indeed helped the defence.

'But, Sir Bernard,' I started.

'No, don't bother me now. I'm involved,' he cut in with a deprecatory wave of the hand.

I was dismissed: the 'Headmaster' had finished with me.

Had the old lag really deceived the great pathologist? I was left wondering whether Spilsbury, to whose star appearances mine were then a mere tyro's, might have been actuated by some other more personal motive. He had never given any indication of resenting my appearances in court in the sort of crime cases in which he had held unchallenged supremacy for so long, but—well, I wondered if a tinge of resentment had made him intervene. It was a 'spoiling' action that was unlike him; he should have realized he stood above us all, far beyond challenge by any young pathologist of his day. He spoke so little to me or any of his colleagues that the reason for his dramatic appearance in the case never emerged.

The case had two remarkable sequels.

When Loughans walked out of the court a free man he ran straight into the arms of the waiting police, who arrested him for the job he'd confessed to at St Albans, in which he had tied an old lady to a chair (using that helpless hand) with wire, nearly killing her. He was convicted and gaoled, and his fellow prisoners nicknamed him 'Handy' because of his skill with this poor lame right hand that Spilsbury had 'tested'.

In due course Loughans came out of prison, only to be sent in yet again, with a sentence of fifteen years' preventive detention. That should have kept him quiet, but in 1963 (nearly twenty years after the murder of Mrs Robinson) he brought a civil action for libel against the Sunday newspaper *The People* which published extracts from the autobiography of the barrister who prosecuted at both trials, J. D. Casswell K.C.; and Loughans claimed that Casswell's account of the 'John Barleycorn' case said quite clearly that he had been lucky to be acquitted.

This time it was for Loughans to prove his case, and this time he wasn't so lucky. Spilsbury had died, and one of the alibi witnesses confessed her memory for the events of twenty years ago was 'not very good'. The records had gone up in flames in a fire. Another alibi witness could not be traced.

I, as a professional witness, was the only one able to produce my faded original post-mortem report, together with photographs of Loughans' hand to scale, for they still lay in my files. My evidence stood word for word as it had been so many years before. I thought Loughans had had both enough stretch and plenty of strength in that deformed right hand, though Loughans had this time persuaded Francis Camps and an orthopaedic surgeon colleague to say, as Spilsbury had, that he had little strength in it. He in fact showed under test a grip of *14 pounds* on the machine! And this after it emerged that he had been much weakened in the previous six months by a stomach cancer. He was now sixty-seven, pale, haggard and worn out. How much stronger he had been twenty years before emerged from records (which were admissible in the civil action now being brought by him) of two crimes, including the one at St Albans only a fortnight after the murder at the 'John Barleycorn', at which he's tied an old lady to a bed and waved a crutch at her with that very hand! She had 'felt his hands' on her throat and thought he was going to choke her.

Joseph Molony, Q.C., for the defendants, was able, of course, to cross-examine Loughans, as the plaintiff in a civil action, on his long criminal record, his persistent lying, and his willingness to settle the case before trial. It was a novel case of 'unprecedented interest', the *Solicitors' Journal* wrote: to be thrice tried for murder and finally, as the High Court jury adjudged, be found guilty of the crime of which he'd been *autrefois acquit*—and in a civil action brought by him at that!

The second sequel came a few months later. The old lag walked into the offices of *The People*—the very newspaper he had unsuccessfully sued for libel—to make amends. 'They tell me I have cancer and haven't long to live,' he said. 'Before I die I want to make a confession.' They photographed him writing it, with his right hand, and for me it was a handsome apology and tribute:

'I want to say I done that job. I did kill the woman in the public house in Portsmouth.'

CHAPTER 8

BERTIE MANTON AND THE LUTON SACK MURDER

'I don't think her own mother would recognize her, if she had one,' said Chief Inspector Chapman when we saw the damage done to the dead woman's face by a single blow from the inevitable blunt instrument, actually a wooden stool. Chapman was right. Her mother would not have identified her anyway, being almost blind; but the dead woman's seventeen-year-old daughter failed to recognize her when a photograph was flashed on the cinema screen. It took the police three months' hard work to identify her and then only another forty-eight hours to locate her murderer and press the charge against him. It was an almost perfect murder, for the police had nearly had to write off the body as unidentified and give up; and yet, ironically, the murderer had done little to make his victim unrecognizable, as Dobkin had. All the damage to her features was done by the blow that killed her: only her dentures had been removed.

Chief Inspector Chapman, so deceptively angelic-looking that he was nicknamed 'the Cherub', was one of the then 'Big Five' at Scotland Yard when, one foggy afternoon in November 1942, he picked me up at my flat in Weymouth Street on his way to Luton, where the naked body of a woman, ankles tied together and knees trussed up to the chest, had been dragged out of the reeds of the little river Lea on the outskirts of the town. The trussed body had been tied in four potato sacks, and had been seen but ignored by several workers on their way to the near-by Vauxhall factory early the same morning.

The shallow river bed, which was grey with mist, had always contained a lot of refuse. But at 2.15 p.m., when Corporation sewer men clambered down the bank to test water levels, one of them tugged at the sacking and exposed a battered woman's face. A glimpse was enough for him, and the police surgeon could not have brought himself to look much more closely, for he saw only the split on her cheek—missing another ghastly wound across her eyebrow and a third that had nearly detached her ear—and declared she had been shot dead, so that the teletape message sent to me from Scotland Yard reported 'death undoubtedly due to a gunshot wound of the head'.

It is interesting that even some doctors don't like looking at the dead body. The well-known London surgeon E. G. Slesinger could hardly bear to come into my Guy's morturary, and if he did he would stand well off, handkerchief over nose and mouth, muttering incomprehensibly, seldom indeed seeing what he had come to see, which was how well his surgery had fared.

The wartime police surgeon at Luton had miscalculated badly, for I found the left side of the face had been shattered by a heavy blunt instrument, and any schoolboy could have seen the marks of strangling fingers on the throat. This was a strangling and bashing murder.

The attempt to strangle had come first. She had been gripped twice across the neck by a right hand in front, and bruises on her back and shoulders suggested she had also been pinned against a wall or the floor. She had struggled to free herself: there were bruises on both elbows and on the backs of her hands, including her finger knuckle. The grip round her neck had evidently been of considerable strength, for there was bruising behind the voice box; but there were no voice box fractures, no material asphyxial changes, and the grip on her neck had not contributed to the cause of death. This, clearly, was the single very violent blow that had crushed the left side of her face, fractured her jaws, loosened her skullbones and bruised her brain. Much less serious injuries on the right side of her face suggested either another blow or, more probably, a fall to the ground. A split in the scalp above the right ear could be explained by her head striking a piece of furniture.

She must clearly have lost consciousness at once after the fatal blow, and her attacker may well have thought she was dead when he began to truss her up. But she wasn't. There was unmistakable bruising on her legs where the ties had been made, showing that at the time she was being tied up the heart was still pumping blood round the body. From the extent of bleeding from the head injuries I estimated that she had died thirty to forty minutes, perhaps rather more, after the crushing blow. The absence of vital reaction to the ties round her trunk showed she had died during the trussing: the legs bore vital marks, but not the body.

The temperature of the body had fallen to that of the surroundings, and rigor mortis was fully established but had not yet begun to pass away. Immersion (in four to six inches of water) had been for a very short period, as there were only gooseskin changes and no sodden wrinkling. I thought death had occurred some twelve to twenty-four hours before the body was found. The sewer men were quite sure it had not been there when they had tested water levels in the same place at 4 p.m. the day before, so presumably the woman had been killed in the afternoon or evening and dumped in the reeds after dark.

The police had found tyre tracks by the wall of a bridge twenty yards away, but these were quickly traced to a milk van that passed that way every morning. However, there was no reason to think she had necessarily been brought by a motor vehicle. The only purpose for trussing the knees would have been to make the body more easily portable, and it could have been brought in a trolley, wheelbarrow, handcart, or bicycle. The sacks didn't help. One had contained soda, one sugar, and two potatoes. Only the potato sacks were marked— one 'MFD', the other with the name of a local dealer who had distributed hundreds without individual records. The string was equally common.

That left only the naked body of the unknown victim of the crime. She had certainly been stripped clean: no necklace, no ring or other ornament, and no teeth. Chafing of the gums showed she had worn dentures. When I had her jaws X-rayed we found three stumps or roots that had been left behind on extraction, a reminder of the Dobkin case. She was about thirty to thirty-five, dark bob haired, brown eyed, 5 feet 3 inches. She had borne at least one child, was again five and a half months pregnant, and bore the scar of an appendix operation. No deformities or distinguishing marks. Even her blood group was the commonest of all, O. Nothing informative found in her nail scrapings. No foreign hairs were found on her body or the sack. Her fingerprints were not on record at Scotland Yard.

The body had been found soon enough for photographs to be taken before the features could be disturbed by decomposition, but the bruising of the left eye and the resulting swelling of the face and lips were disastrous from the point of view of identification. They gave her features a thickened, coarse appearance that they had surely not had in life. Even the best of the police photographs, a right profile, had to be touched up before being released for the public gaze.

Chapman had the photograph published in the newspapers and displayed at police stations and in shops, and an enlargement was flashed on the screen at the local cinema, where it was seen but not recognized by the dead woman's teen-age daughter. Her sons, aged fourteen and fifteen, saw it some days later, exhibited in a shop window. They thought it might be their mother, but when they told their father he said she had called at the house since the murder to collect clothes. He had already told them she was staying with her brother at Grantham.

Under Chapman's command the police went through the lists of missing persons, and no fewer than 404 missing women were either traced or excluded. The police checked 681 addresses of women obtained through postes restantes or letters undelivered. The positive response to all this activity was no more helpful than the negative: thirty-nine identity visits were paid to the body, and nine persons identified it, in genuine error, as that of four other women.

Cleaners' records were searched for unclaimed or bloodstained clothing. Some two hundred and fifty Vauxhall lorry drivers who had called at the works about the time of the murder were traced and interviewed. Statements were taken from the many persons who had heard screams or seen suspicious persons or happenings. Street refuse collections and council dumps were searched for clothing. Casts were made of the dead woman's jaws, and X-ray photographs were published in the *British Dental Journal*. The police showed these and their own full-face and profile photographs to all the local dental surgeons, including the one who had fitted the woman with dentures and who had last examined them six months before her death, but he too only shook his head.

Chapman, tireless and determined, organized house-to-house inquiries throughout the area. Several times he came near to success. One officer called at the dead woman's house and showed the photograph to her sons, who did not mention they had thought it looked like their mother when they saw it in a shop window, or that she had left home about the time of the murder. A neighbour who wanted to go and tell the police the woman was missing was stopped— 'Don't be a damned fool'—by his wife. Other neighbours, who had last seen the woman on the day of her death, completely failed to recognize her from the police photograph. Her husband told inquirers she had first gone to her mother's in Luton and then to her brother's in Grantham. He gave the same reply to a Luton Food Office inquiry and to a midwife who made a routine call to check about the pregnancy.

Thousands of statements were taken, but after three months the police were no nearer than when they had begun. The deceased woman had long since been buried in a pauper's grave. The war was raging, manpower was short, and even Chapman began to lose heart. But instead of letting the investigation fizzle out as some do, he ordered a fresh examination to be made of all the bits of clothing and rags that had been garnered from dustbins and rubbish dumps. He had the whole filthy collection re-examined inch by inch, inside and out, for any clue that might have been overlooked.

Well, they found one possibility: a dyer's tag in the loose packing of a piece of a black coat. Just a few numbers on an inch of tape. It was weather worn, but the numbers were in indelible ink. It was easy to trace the dry-cleaner's, a local branch of Sketchley's, and their books gave the customer's name and address: Manton, Rene Manton, of Regent Street, Luton.

There was still nothing to connect it with the body from the River Lea, but Chief Inspector Chapman either had a hunch or was hoping desperately for he went to the house himself. The moment the door opened he knew he was near the end of the hunt, for the little girl of eight standing there was, in his eyes, the living image of the dead woman.

Chapman introduced himself. 'Is your mother at home?'

'No, she's gone away. Is anything wrong?'

'I'm just making some inquiries,' Chapman reassured her. He asked the girl to show him a photograph of her mother, and that settled it for him. He borrowed the photograph, and visited Rene Manton's almost-blind mother, who said she had not seen her daughter in the last last three months but had received four letters from her during that time. She showed them to Chapman, who noticed a number of spelling mistakes, including 'Hampstead' without the 'p'.

Chapman took the letters and went to see Rene's husband, Bertie Manton, who was a member of the National Fire Service. Chapman found him on duty at his station in Luton.

He and his wife had quarrelled, said Manton, and she had 'slung her hook' on 25th November (six days *after* the finding of the body). He was sure of the date because it was the last day of his leave. She had

gone either to her mother's or to her brother's at Grantham. He
recognized the photograph that Chapman had borrowed from his
daughter, but not the identity photograph taken by the police. 'No,
that's nothing like my wife. I wouldn't do anything like that. . . . She's
alive.' Chapman showed him the four letters written to his wife's
mother, and he identified the handwriting as Rene's. Chapman asked
him to write a sentence which contained the word 'Hampstead'.
Manton wrote it, in what looked like the same hand as the four
letters, *and omitted the 'p'*.

Chapman thanked him for his help and, casually, asked for the
name of Rene Manton's dentist. Unguardedly Manton told him.

The dentist at once recognized the photograph of the missing
woman in life, and his record cards were in as good order as Barnett
Kopkin's in the Dobkin case. He showed Chapman a card recording
the positions of three residual roots, which he had advised the patient
to have extracted before fitting the dentures, but she had refused.
They tallied exactly with those on the dead woman's jaws. Chapman
produced the plaster casts we had made from the jaws, and these
corresponded perfectly with the dentures.

Chapman went back to Manton and charged him with murder.
Manton broke down and confessed. 'I am sorry I have told you lies
about my wife . . . I killed her but it was only because I lost my
temper. I didn't intend to.'

They had had midday dinner together at home, he said, on 18th
November. The children were all at school. Over a cup of tea by the
fireside they started quarrelling. Finally Rene jumped up and flung
her tea in his face. 'I hope it blinds you!' she shouted, and they were
her last words.

'I lost my temper, picked up a very heavy wooden stool which was
quite near my feet, under the table, and hit her about the head and
face several times. She fell backwards towards the wall and then on to
the floor. When I come to and got my senses again I see what I'd
done.'

He would have been believed if he had said he hit her only once, but
my evidence at his trial suggested much more than his story of a
sudden blow in a fit of temper.

'Did you hear Dr Keith Simpson give his evidence today?' asked
the Crown counsel, Richard O'Sullivan, K.C., cross-examining.

'Yes.'

'Did you hear him tell the jury that there were marks upon the neck of application of a hand and re-application of a hand?'

'I remember taking hold of her throat with my right hand and pushing her against the wall. I pushed her away from me and she went up against the wall.'

'And that the marks showed that the hand had been applied with very considerable force?' Counsel was relentless.

'I may have grabbed her twice, and that was in my temper.'

'You said nothing about that in your statement to the police?'

'No, sir.'

That passage killed any chance of a verdict of manslaughter.

Manton said at the trial that he thought he had struck two blows, 'one on each side of the head', but was not sure. He had thought she was dead when he undressed and tied her up because 'she did not move or answer or anything'.

He had handled her body very coolly, removing the rings and tying her up in the sacks. 'I then carried her down to the cellar and left her there. I had washed the blood up before the children came home to tea. I hid the bloodstained clothing in a corner near the copper.' He told the children their mum had gone to Grandma's, and gave them their tea. His elder daughter went out to see a friend. He gave the other three money to go to the cinema. By then it was dark. 'I brought my wife up from the cellar, got my bike out, laid her across the handlebars and wheeled her down to Osborne Road. I laid her on the edge of the river bank and she rolled into the river. I then rode home and got the children's supper ready. They never suspected anything.' No one in Luton's busy streets appeared to have paid any attention as this bicycle load was wheeled through the town.

Next morning he burned the bloodstained clothing in the copper, together with her false teeth, which he found in a glass of water. When the police searched the house they found blood at the scene of the attack, group O. They also found writing paper and envelopes similar to those used for the four letters to Rene Manton's mother. Finally, after a characteristically thorough search, Superintendent Cherrill, Scotland Yard's fingerprint 'ace', discovered a print on an empty pickle jar—now over three months old—that proved identical with the print of the dead woman's left thumb. That clinched the identification.

The heavy oak stool no longer existed. Manton had noticed that he had split it on his wife's head, and had told one of his sons to break it up for firewood. He had also, most unwisely, decided to get rid of her coat, as it might have seemed odd if she had left home without it in the middle of winter. As she had not been wearing it when her blood was flowing he saw no need to burn it, but simply cut it into pieces which he put into a dustbin. If he had left it hanging in her wardrobe he would, almost certainly, have got away with murder.

Rene Manton had dyed the coat to wear at her sister's husband's funeral. The dyer's tag nearly led to her own husband's end, for he was convicted of murder and sentenced to death. But a petition for mercy collected 30,000 signatures, and he was reprieved. He was a sick man and he died in prison three years after his wife.

CHAPTER 9

THE END OF THE WAR: GRIBBLE AND HEYS

Down West India Dock Road in Chinatown in the heart of Limehouse there are pubs galore, but none was better known to seafaring men than 'Charlie Brown's'. It had no special pretensions, for Charlie Brown himself died in the 1930s, and the pub's real name is the prosaic Railway Tavern; but you ask in Singapore or Sydney where to meet up in London next time you're in port, and it is pretty certain to be 'What about Charlie Brown's?'

So when four American destroyers anchored in the Thames in April 1944, a fair mob of US Navy men made their way on evening shore leave to drink and dance in Charlie's Continental Bar. The place was already occupied by local dockers and merchant seamen, and by 10 p.m., when 'Time, please, gentlemen' was bawled across the counter, it was difficult enough to hear. The barmaids were all over the place, the beer and spirits—always desperately short in wartime—were pretty well exhausted, and so was the 'Guv'nor', Mr Mitchell. Trouble had broken out a few minutes earlier, and an Irishman, cut by flying glass, had had to be dragged out into an ambulance by a police constable.

With great difficulty the licensee got everyone out on to the pavement at last, and was reaching up to push home the bolt on the front doors when, with a tremendous crash, the panel of one half was burst in and a long ebony-handled knife, grasped in a clenched hand, was thrust in, blind. The blade went five inches deep into the chest of a twenty-nine-year-old man named Gilbey, who was helping to shut out the mob of sailors; and as it did the licensee and his wife both saw the sleeve of an American sailor's uniform showing in the split panel. Gilbey sank to the floor and was dead, stabbed through the heart, by the time Dr Summers, the police surgeon, arrived.

Truth often turns out to be stranger than the reconstructions worked out between the police and the pathologist, especially in stabbing cases. Even a stab in the back can be inflicted in a face-to-face brawl, and there is seldom any medical evidence to show whether the victim was standing, sitting, or lying when he was stabbed. Had we not known the circumstances at Charlie Brown's, how much thought could have been wasted deciding whether the assailant had faced or knelt or sat on his victim? Who would have even suggested the stabbing might have been a blind blow through a solid door?

The mob of sailors had dispersed long before the CID appeared, and the job of finding 'an American sailor' among the 4,000 who were ashore in London that night looked hopeless. But Superintendent George Hatherill, who was to rise to the post of Deputy Assistant Commissioner, and Divisional Detective Inspector Swale, later to become Commandant of the Detective Training School in London, were determined to ferret out the man who had committed this cowardly crime, and they set about putting the comb through 'every single man on shore leave that night'. Both officers were very determined men, and they meant business however hopeless a task it looked.

Within twenty-four hours they had nailed their man! To the US Navy, who knew that hundreds of sailors from four destroyers had been ashore, and that no-one had been able to identify more than a US Navy rating's sleeve, it seemed miraculous. 'Scotland Yard get their man within hours of the crime?' It certainly looked pretty good. How was it done?

Just hard routine inquiry, and a stroke of luck: the two common ingredients of most successful crime investigations. Hatherill and Swale decided to comb all four ships' companies by a routine interview and questioning. It would have taken days, but the important point was that it was begun; for, almost as soon as they had started, an American rating said he wished to see the Yard officers. He knew a knife had been used in the stabbing, and he wasn't going to have the crime pinned on him. One of his pals had borrowed an ebony-handled knife with a six-inch-long blade from him earlier on the evening of the killing and had gone ashore with it.

'Who was it?' Hatherill and Swale were in no mood for stalling.

'Matthew Smith, a gunner,' said the rating.

It was in the bag, as easily as that. Matthew Smith, a nineteen-year-old youth, admitted he had borrowed the knife and had been drinking at Charlie Brown's that night. He said a man had rushed at him, 'swinging a club through the broken partition', and he'd 'slashed at him with a knife'. It was a nasty brawl all right, but Smith had no right to use a knife.

'If I tell the truth you will hang the murder on me,' he said, prophetically.

I found myself in a first-floor office room in Regent Street a few weeks later, giving evidence at the trial of Matthew Smith.

Why not the Old Bailey? It was very much 'open' during the war. Well, this was an American service charge, and the trial was by court martial. The approaches were screened by naval guards, in their rather sloppy-looking uniform, and the 'judge' was Lieutenant J. B. Perkins of the U.S. Navy, acting Judge Advocate, flanked by eight fellow naval officers. Accused was defended by a lawyer, a lieutenant-commander, and another officer acting as a 'friend'.

'Call Keith Simpson. Call . . .' I was idling in the cramped waiting corridor.

'Take the stand, doctor.' (This is American for 'sit down'.) 'Your testimony, doctor, is this, is it not?' (For 'testimony' read 'evidence'.)

My testimony was that Gilbey had died of a single stab wound five inches deep on the left side of the front of the chest. It had passed between the first and second ribs and penetrated the upper lobe of the lung, causing a vast internal haemorrhage. An accumulation of some 2¾ pints of blood lay in the chest cavity, and blood had also poured into the lung and reached the nostrils and mouth. Death had come quickly to the unfortunate Charles Gilbey, a twenty-nine-year-old lorry driver who had never been to Charlie Brown's before.

I had said in my post-mortem report that the weapon had a sharp point and one sharp edge, was probably less than one inch broad, and was not drawn to a fine tip. The sheath knife brought to me a few days later was an average of ⅞ inch in width and six inches in length. The blow was dealt, I thought, with an overarm thrust. At the court martial I raised the knife to demonstrate, and the defending American officer obligingly offered himself as the 'victim'.

The accused was found guilty and sentenced to the electric chair, but because of his youth he was reprieved and given a long sentence of imprisonment at Sing Sing.

It was my first taste of American court procedure. I was to see plenty of the real thing after the war, when, with my New York counterpart, Professor Milton Helpern, I visited courts in New York,

Chicago, Boston, and New Orleans. I had no difficulty in coming to
the decision to stay in England, in spite of an attractive invitation
from the Harvard University School Department of Legal Medicine
to take a post in the school similar to my own in London. I did not
then—and I cannot now—think favourably of the contests that go on
in the US courts, where the first line of attack is one's qualifications to
be standing there at all, a second one's competence in this particular
field: whether or not one has been in the top ten for twenty years and
is very well known to the attorneys in court; and a third on whether
one wasn't 'hired' to be giving that evidence; and, final indignity, how
much one's fee has been set at. Only later on come the facts and the
opinions, the evidence one has come to court to give.

Surveying the battered faces, the torn clothing, and the bloodstained
trail showing where the body had been dragged behind some bushes
for concealment, Dr Rutherford Tree, the Bedford police surgeon,
said, not surprisingly, 'This looks like murder'. Or manslaughter.
Which it was might depend partly on the order in which the injuries
had been inflicted.

The body was found in a spinney forming a ballast hole on railway
property near Kempston, in Bedfordshire, on 15th August 1944. It
was of a young man, and it was crawling with maggots. Considering
the state of decomposition, the locality, exposed conditions, and
recent weather, I estimated death had occurred ten to fourteen days
earlier.

Who was he? That might have proved a difficult question to answer
if the killer had not made it easy. When a photograph had fallen from
his victim's jacket, he later told Detective Chief Inspector Peter
Beveridge, he 'just tore it up and threw it back on the grass near the
bush where Bob was lying'. A mere twenty feet from the body, in fact.
Beveridge, who had risen to become one of Scotland Yard's wartime
'Big Five' by sheer solid determination, was not a man to overlook
such a heaven-sent clue. It was the portrait of a girl, and a woman
police officer said she had seen her at a local dance hall. They went
there to look for her, and found her, and showed her the dead man's
clothes. 'They belong to my cousin, Bob Smith.' He had been living
with her family, she said, but had not been home since the Sunday
before last, 6th August. She supposed he had gone harvesting. The
police learnt later that he was an Army deserter.

The girl said Bob had been working for a local firewood merchant named Gribble, and her father confirmed this when Beveridge went to her home. Detective Superintendent Cherrill went along, and took fingerprints from certain personal articles of Bob Smith's. They matched prints he had already taken from the dead man's fingers.

The girl said her cousin had been friendly with Gribble's son Kenneth, who was sixteen, and Beveridge had a talk with him. The youth said he had last seen Bob Smith on Sunday 6th August, at about noon. He also said, answering a question, that he had never been with Smith to the Kempston Ballast Hole. But another local lad told the police he had heard Bob Smith and Ken Gribble arranging to meet at the ballast hole that Sunday at 3 p.m. This lad also said there was some ill-feeling between the two over Bob's wages. Interviewed again, Gribble junior agreed he had made the appointment but said that after waiting at the top of the ballast hole till 2.45 p.m. he had left without seeing Smith. Then the police discovered that Smith's bicycle had been seen parked opposite the ballast hole entrance at 3.30 p.m., and it had never been taken away. Shown the bicycle, Gribble said he did not recognize it as Smith's.

Meanwhile with the coroner's permission I had taken the body back to Guy's, demonstrated it to my students, and told Beveridge a little about the murder weapon, which was still missing. It was our old friend the blunt instrument, a heavy one, and as it had not struck twice in the same place it did not need to be greatly bloodstained; but they would probably find on it some hairs from Smith's eyebrows. Beveridge thereupon ordered another search in the ballast hole, and a few days later they brought me a heavy sawn-off bough. When I examined it with a lens I found a seven-inch head hair matted to it by blood and, crushed into the wood, six eyebrow hairs that proved identical with Smith's.

Murder or manslaughter? I told the police at least four blows had been struck, and the third was a knock-out. I thought the fourth had been delivered when Smith was already lying on the ground helpless.

The first three blows had come from the front: one over the left eye region, splitting the eyebrow and smashing the eye socket inward towards the nose: a second, heavier, across the mouth, splitting both lips and knocking out eight front upper teeth; and the third a classical knock-out on the point of the jaw, heavy enough to break it. The fourth blow, very violent, had split the right eyebrow and smashed the eye socket and cheek bone; and there was a counterpressure fracture, perhaps caused by crushing on the ground, on the opposite side of the head. I could not judge the damage done to the brain as it had been eaten away by maggots. I thought it might be hard to reconcile the fourth blow with any charge less than murder, for by that time the victim must have been lying helpless on the ground.

Interviewed a third time, Ken Gribble produced an alibi, a girl friend; but under police questioning she said she had not been with him at the time. Yet the police had still found nothing to connect Gribble directly with the crime. His clothing was examined thoroughly, and not a bloodspot was found. Beveridge ordered him to be watched casually. Soon he was heard to talk freely about the killing, but without implicating himself. Beveridge waited until a month had passed; then, on 20th September, he interviewed Gribble again, this time in his father's presence. Gribble broke down. 'I did meet Bob Smith at three o'clock on August Sunday afternoon and we had a fight in the ballast hole. He threw a piece of tree at me and I hit him with it.'

Beveridge formally cautioned the youth, who raced on regardless, while Beveridge's sergeant wrote it down. 'We got to high words . . . and Bob took his jacket off and come for me. There was a fight and Bob fell over a large piece of tree wood. He picked up the bit of wood and threw it at me. I dodged the piece of tree but picked it up and as Bob came at me I struck him with it. I first struck him on the side of the face.' (That would be the blow over the left eye.) 'He hit me in the stomach, and I hit him again with the piece of tree on the head.' (Possibly the second blow I had noted, across the mouth, but more probably another inseparable from the first.) 'He was bleeding but continued to fight me, so I hit him twice more with the piece of wood on his head.' (Probably the blow on the mouth and the blow on the jaw.) 'He fell down then' (knocked out by the blow on the jaw) 'and whilst he was lying on the ground I hit him twice on the head with the same piece of wood.' (Almost certainly two blows in the same place.) 'I realized that I had knocked him unconscious. I then threw the piece of wood as hard as I could into some bushes as there was some blood on it. I then picked up Bob's feet and dragged him into some high bushes in the middle of the spinney.' Gribble said he had 'tried to bring him round' without success, staying with him 'for about ten minutes' before covering the hole where he was lying with willow-herb and a branch.

Although Gribble had dealt out far more force than was necessary for protection, and with a murderous weapon upon an unarmed opponent, the case might have ended as fights often do—without a full murder charge—but for two things. First, Gribble struck the last two blows when Smith had already been knocked out, and that always looks to a jury like a deliberate intent to kill. Second, he'd left Smith gravely hurt, unconscious, and bleeding from his head wounds, and had gone home. Without the brain, which had decomposed, I could not tell how quickly Smith had died, but he could have lived for several hours. Gribble had not called for help or made any effort to see that Smith got a chance of survival. He had said nothing.

This evidence put paid to excuses of 'it was only a fight' or 'I didn't know he was so badly hurt'. To inflict injuries that must cause any ordinary person to think, 'Oh, God, what have I done now? He's unconscious, I must get help', and then to do nothing, is to allow your victims to die. There is no question, if you find yourself standing over the body of your mother-in-law clutching a claret bottle and she's lying there bleeding at your feet, you must at least call for help, whatever happened. Whether you can't remember, decide to tell the truth, or lie about hitting the old lady, or say she must have fallen downstairs—these things matter much less than getting help, at once. It looks so much better to do this, for when you don't, you can be sure there will be some hard questioning about it. *Why didn't you?* Surely it must have been obvious to anyone that she was badly hurt, might die if nothing was done for her? You left her to die, didn't you? At the very least that becomes reduced to manslaughter; to start with the charge must be murder.

So as a result of a sudden, hot-tempered fight, the outcome of which he could not have dreamed of beforehand, this youth stood in the dock at Leicester Assizes charged with murder. Mr Justice Wrottesley explained the difference between wilful murder and the reduced offence of manslaughter, and the jury found young Gribble guilty of manslaughter. He was sent to prison for two years: his youth saved him from worse.

My scientific evidence in that case was nearly wrecked by some careless handling of the hairs, so delicately attached to the heavy bough we produced in court, and Sir Norman Kendall, then Assistant Commissioner (Crime) at Scotland Yard, sent for me one morning to say he would like to have a 'strong complaint' in letter form about this. These were early days at the new 'Yard labs', and he felt that the hard work his officers put in on such cases deserved more attentive support. It worked, and never again had I any cause for complaint in the hundreds of crime cases I examined where police laboratory help became necessary. The Metropolitan and provincial Home Office Science laboratories now have world renown for their skills and reliability.

On 9th November 1944, an urgent call for help came to Scotland Yard from the Suffolk Police. A young WAAF girl had been found dead that morning face down in a ditch near Beccles, her clothing in disarray. It was pretty obvious she had been murdered, and as there were thousands of American and Italian (POW) as well as British troops in the district, it was plainly desirable to have the Yard in at the start. Superintendent Ted Greeno, with whom I had done the 'Wigwam' case in Surrey, was put on the case, and he asked me to assist with the medical and scientific problems. In the forties the pathologist still often dealt with hairs, fibres, dust, blood, and other work now handed by the Regional Police Laboratories.

A light snow was falling when Greeno collected me from my flat, and it snowed all the way to Beccles, which we reached shortly before midnight. A tarpaulin had been placed over the body, but the ground around was covered with snow. The girl was lying prone, face down, her body and legs straight and her arms almost straight by her sides. She had been wearing full uniform, including her greatcoat, which, together with her tunic, shirt, and vest, had been drawn up over the back of her shoulders; her slacks and knickers, together with suspenders and a sanitary pad, had been torn down.

After examination at the scene the body was taken to Beccles Hospital, where I performed an autopsy with an old friend Eric Biddle, the county pathologist, at 2 a.m. Greeno went on to an Italian POW Camp, where he spent the rest of the night questioning about two hundred men.

The girl had been sexually assaulted with great violence and also penetrated from behind. The entrance to her vagina was torn, both walls were bruised about half-way up, there was a tear in her hymen—she had evidently been virgo intacta—and the private parts were heavily soiled with blood.

She also had serious abdominal injuries. Her liver had been ruptured, causing a haemorrhage into the abdomen. There was a deep bruise under her right shoulder blade and more bruising on the front surface of the spine.

On her face she had a split lower lip, a grazed nose, and abrasions on the chin. There were more abrasions on the neck and over the right breast. There was a series of numerous fine linear scratches sweeping across the high right temple, right cheek, ear, and adjacent neck; and there was grazing and bruising on the back of the right hand.

Her stockings had not been torn or bloodstained, which meant that she had neither stood nor knelt after the sexual assault. Therefore that had come last. I thought the first injuries were probably the scratches on the right side of her face and hand, which could very well have come from contact with one of the thornbushes I had seen growing on the side of the ditch. There were no signs of any preliminary struggle, nothing to suggest an exchange of blows. I thought the girl had probably stumbled and fallen on her right side and then rolled, or been turned, on to her front. Her attacker had then pinned her heavily on her face, splitting her lip against her teeth. Then he had knelt on her violently, under her right shoulder blade, torn away her clothing, and raped her.

None of these injuries had killed her. There were clear-cut asphyxial haemorrhages on the face, scalp, neck, and lungs. She had been suffocated face down in the mud.

We took scrapings from her fingernails but found nothing. We looked for foreign hairs or fibres on various parts of her body, also without success. Her murderer appeared to have left no trace. But surely he must have taken something with him. He could not possibly have emerged from that bloody struggle in the ditch without traces—of mud, of hair and clothing fibres, above all of blood. The region of the girl's private parts was so heavily bloodstained that anyone in contact with it would have been stained too.

I placed the time of death at some twenty-four to thirty-six hours before autopsy. I could not narrow it down any more, because the length of time and conditions of exposure had already reduced the temperature to that of the surroundings. No screams had been heard, nothing had been seen. All that was known for certain was that Winifred Evans, the murdered girl, had walked out of her billet bound for the signal office, where she was on night duty, at five minutes past midnight. Thereafter the only person to see her alive was the man who killed her.

She had been at a dance at an American camp, and had returned to her billet with a friend, Corporal Margaret Johns. It was very dark. 'Shall I see you to the office?' Corporal Johns had offered. 'No, thanks.' Probably the last words of her life.

Corporal Johns had then entered the women's ablution hut and switched on the light. A man was there, in RAF uniform. When Greeno questioned her she recalled the dialogue perfectly.

'What are you doing here?'

'I am lost. Is this No. 1 site?'

'No, this is the WAAF site. Get out.'

'Will you show me the way out? I am drunk and can't see.' He lurched and fell against the door.

She went out and showed him the way.

'Can I thank you?' He started moving towards her.

'No. get down the road.'

It was the road that Winifred Evans would take when she had changed into slacks, No. 1 site was less than a mile away.

Greeno concentrated his inquiries on No. 1 site. Quite soon he heard an aircraftman had been seen creeping into his bed in the dark soon after 1 a.m. At 5.30 a.m. he was up cleaning and pressing his tunic, and getting mud off his shoes, an uncommon enough exercise at that hour to have attracted attention.

He was LAC Arthur Heys, a married man of thirty-seven with a young family. He was due shortly to appear on pay parade—a perfect identification parade. Without his knowledge Corporal Johns watched the parade.

'That's him,' she said without hesitation.

When Greeno asked him Heys admitted the incident with Corporal Johns in the WAAF ablution room. He admitted nothing else, and said it was only 12.30 a.m. when he went to bed. A mile would have taken about twenty minutes for a man as drunk as he had been.

Greeno noticed some scratches on his hands that could have been made by a thornbush. His shoes were still muddy, and Greeno brought them to me. Mixed up with the mud I found brick dust, and there was brick rubble and dust in the ditch where the murder had been done.

Greeno also brought me Heys's RAF tunic and trousers. Both looked as if they had been recently sponged and brushed, and the trousers had evidently been pressed. In spite of this I found a spot of mud on both tunic sleeves, and a number of reddish and brown stains on both tunic and trousers that gave a positive reaction to specific tests for human blood. Unfortunately extracts proved too weak for blood grouping.

I also examined ten head hairs from Heys's clothing, and found four of these could not have been his own but were identical with hairs taken from the body of the victim Winifred Evans. So was a hair taken from Heys's clothes-brush.

I warned Greeno that the scientific evidence was very far from conclusive, and I warned him not to rely much on the evidence of the mud and brick dust. 'There are common features of too everyday character', evidence I would certainly agree to under cross-examination.

But Greeno thought he had a case, and the Director of Public Prosecutions agreed. Heys seemed surprised.

When Greeno arrested him he sat for four or five minutes looking at the floor. Then: 'I have been thinking,' he said. 'I can't see what evidence you have to connect me with it. Can't you tell me?'

'No,' said Greeno. 'Not at this stage.'

In the cells at Beccles, Heys was heard thinking aloud: 'I wonder what clue they have got? They must have something.' Then, to an officer guarding him: 'Chief Inspector Greeno took six hairs from my head. If any of them are found on her clothing, how am I to prove he didn't put them there? If there is any evidence against me, it is faked by the police.'

The contrary was the case. Far from planting Heys's hairs on the murdered girl's clothing, Greeno went to Heys's home in Colne, Lancashire, to collect hairs from his wife. On examination, I found these identical with those taken from the body of Winifred Evans. And, of course, in discarding the hair evidence as of no help to the case for the Crown, the Director of Public Prosecutions pursued the usual course of informing the defence of his reasons.

Before the trial Heys's CO received an anonymous letter:

Will you please give this letter to the solicitors for the airman who is so wrongfully accused of murdering Winnie Evans? I wish to state that I am responsible for the above-mentioned girl's death. I had arranged to meet her at the bottom of the road where the body was found, at midnight. When I arrived she was not there. I waited some time, and decided to walk down towards the WAAF quarters. Just before I reached this I heard a voice and stood close to the hedge. I heard footsteps. It proved to be an airman. I don't think he saw me. I then saw some one I recognized was Winnie. She said I should not have come down to meet her. A WAAF friend had offered to go along with her, as the airman ahead was drunk and had lost his way. . . .

How could the writer of the letter know Heys was drunk and had lost his way? Only two persons could know that: Corporal Margaret Johns, and LAC Arthur Heys, awaiting trial in prison.

The letter had been written in block capitals. Superintendent Cherrill found no fingerprints on it, but he said the writing was 'identical' with that on a repairs tag that had been found in Heys's belongings. The fact that Heys had been in Norwich Gaol when it was posted did not affect its value as additional evidence against him: it was admissible—and telling.

The trial at Bury St Edmunds in January 1945 was a sad day for me. The Suffolk pathologist, Eric Biddle—my old friend, who had been at Guy's—was killed in a road accident just before the trial started. His death certificate was read to the court as I waited to step into the witness box, and I found it difficult to apply myself coldly to the evidence I had to give.

The trial was doubtless even sadder for Heys. He was hanged.

About a month after our journey to Beccles a dying man was almost hurled at us from a passing car. He had been run down and dragged away under the vehicle, and it turned out that the car had been driven straight at him, as a weapon to murder him.

The victim of this crime was a retired naval captain of fifty-six, Ralph Binney. He had been walking through the City of London, minding his own business, when a young man jumped out of a car, smashed a jeweller's shop window with an axe, grabbed a tray of rings and a pearl necklace, and leaped back into the car, which immediately moved off. It was lunchtime, and the City streets were crowded. Several brave persons tried to stop the car, but jumped out of the way when the driver kept on going. Captain Binney was braver—almost stupidly so. He stepped out into the road and stretched out both arms, giving the car the choice between stopping and running him down. The driver drove straight at him. Captain Binney was knocked down and the car wheels passed over his chest, leaving him lying on the road motionless. Before anyone could reach him, the driver, seeing the road ahead was blocked, had gone into reverse. He backed rapidly for several yards, running Captain Binney over a second time; and when he drove forward again the poor man was caught up by his clothing and dragged away.

Another car gave chase, along Lombard Street and then over London Bridge. 'Help! Help!' Captain Binney was heard shouting, as he was dragged and bounced along. Down off the bridge, round the corner into Tooley Street beside the station terminus, and there Captain Binney was flung off against the kerb after a ghastly journey of more than a mile. He was brought into Guy's a few minutes later and died within a few hours. Both his lungs had been crushed and penetrated by the ends of broken ribs when the wheels of the car ran over him, and his whole body had been battered by the dragging and bumping on the road.

The car had got away and was found abandoned near the Elephant and Castle, but the City of London police soon tracked down the driver and the smasher-and-grabber, both members of a South London criminal fraternity known as the 'Elephant Boys'. The driver, Ronald Hedley, aged twenty-six, was convicted of the murder of Captain Binney and hanged. His accomplice, Thomas Jenkins, was sent to prison for eight years. He was luckier than his younger brother, Charles, who took part in a raid on a jeweller's shop in Charlotte Street, off Tottenham Court Road, two years later. He and his two accomplices were running to escape when a motor-cyclist, Alec de Antiquis, as public-spirited as Captain Binney, tried to stop them and was shot dead for his pains. The fatal shot was fired by one Christopher Geraghty, but Charles Jenkins had also carried a loaded gun and was hanged with him. A Binney Medal for bravery was struck in memory of this intrepid naval hero in the following year. Some months after this murder by motor-car I had a strange case of 'rape' by bicycle.

I was called out one evening to see the body of a woman of about fifty-five found in a country ditch near Sawbridgeworth on the boundary of Hertfordshire. She lay with her coat and frock rucked up into the small of her back, and her knickers pulled down but not off. Her vulva had been split and bruised at both sides, and she had suffered heavy crushing injuries of the face.

Rape and murder, thought the police when they found her. But it did not really add up to that. There was no tearing of the clothes, no sign of a struggle, no ordinary evidence of sexual intercourse, no strangling or other pinning marks. The genital crushing was so violent that I thought something much heavier than the male organ had been driven into the vulva. But for what other reason would her coat and frock have been pulled up and her knickers pulled down? The question only had to be asked for the answer to come to mind. She was on her way home after a session at the pub and must have been squatting in the dark road to urinate.

I estimated she had died about twenty hours earlier, which was half-past eleven the previous night. She had been drinking beer shortly prior to her death; the road was lonely and the night was dark. While she squatted—or, more probably I thought, as she was beginning to rise after urinating—a bicycle had run into her, the front wheel driven into her vulva and the handlebars or light-bracket striking her face. Bruising of the brain showed the face injury must have been very violent and would have knocked her out. A minor injury to the back of her head could have resulted from her being thrown over backward by the force of impact. Blood had poured into her throat, and she had petered out after being dragged over onto the grass verge.

CID inquiries confirmed this reconstruction. The cyclist was traced, a youth of sixteen. Tragically he had panicked and left the woman, who had not died of her head injuries—from which she could perhaps have recovered—but from asphyxia due to inhalation of blood. She might well have survived the accident if he had stopped to raise her head.

One of my last cases in the war concerned the body of an unidentified man recovered from the tidal waters of Portsmouth Dockyard. He had been dead and immersed in the water for about six to seven weeks, and had clearly been drowned. But his body was trussed up in ropes. 'It looks like murder to us,' said the CID rather heavily, as if they were only stating the obvious.

'Not to me,' I said. I could see no external injuries, no tie round the neck or strangling mark.

'But he's trussed like a chicken ready for the oven,' said the detective inspector in charge.

I traced the rope from the final loose end back to the starting point, a noose round the lower legs. Each knot had been pulled tight in an upward direction. 'I think by his own hands,' I said. I shone a torch into the dead man's mouth and saw a small strand caught in a crevice. 'And teeth.'

The police investigation confirmed that it was suicide. The man had been a strong swimmer and wanted to make sure.

CHAPTER 10

NEVILLE HEATH AND THE DIAMOND WEAVE WHIP

At the end of the war my gay young blonde secretary, Molly Lefebure, left me to get married. Her successor, 25-year-old Jean Scott-Dunn, attractively copper-haired, very warm-hearted and devoted to my interests, worked for me for the next ten years before marrying, and she did not desert me then, for I was the lucky man. (My first wife had died of multiple sclerosis the year before.) 'The first ten years are, after all, the worst,' said Jean with her nice smile, the day we married; and it was true: a marvellous twenty-year partnership followed, ending in her early death from cancer in her fifties.

Thanks to these two girls, one vital aspect of my preparing and presenting a case in court never caused me any anxiety. I knew that my 'notes at the scene', my times of arrival and departure, the list of doctors, police officers and scientific laboratory men from the Yard, the precise careful wording of the reports I made, drawings and photographs, specimens—everything I needed at my elbow when I stepped into court—would be in apple-pie order. Each of my secretaries, young girls as they were, showed an utter devotion to my survival at the hands of the lawyers. Any repute I gathered during the years they both turned out for me at such odd hours, and in such inconvenient, often dirty or frankly revolting places (Jean Scott-Dunn once sat in a men's public toilet for an hour or more whilst we worked on a murder near Gosport) was very largely due to their painstaking accuracy in note-keeping and in records and their unwavering attention to detail.

They were a tremendous help to me, too, as 'buffer' contacts. In my younger days I was typically English in my slow thawing, but they would have the stiffest visitors off the bough in a few minutes, putting them at their ease with such quiet charm that I had only to bask in the aura they had created for me. Letters that I dictated starting 'Dear Professor, your request last week for advice has come at a most difficult time' would undergo a metamorphosis in the typewriter, for I would find myself reading, 'My dear Hansen, I was so pleased to hear from you again today: it seems a long time since we last met. Your current problem in Oslo is indeed a fascinating one. . . .'

A visitor from India, offered a glass of sherry whilst waiting for me one day, asked Jean Scott-Dunn confidentially, 'What's the old man like—really?' He only found out later that this charming secretary was also the professor's wife! She could have told him more than most secretaries.

She came to me just in time for a particularly nasty case. If she could stomach that, I thought, correctly, she would put up with anything.

If ever I saw a murderer's signature on his handiwork it was the imprint on Margery Gardner's body of the riding whip with the diamond-patterned weave. The lash marks—seventeen of them, on her breasts, torso, and back—were so clearly defined that I could measure them with mathematical precision. 'If you find that whip you've found your man,' I told the police.

Three weeks and one murder later they took possession of both the man and the whip.

He rejoiced in the aristocratic-sounding name of Neville George Clevely Heath but sometimes preferred an alias like Lord Dudley or Lieutenant-Colonel Armstrong. His career, if short, was adventurous. Joining the Royal Air Force in 1937, at twenty, he soon decamped and was dismissed for absence without leave. Within three months he was caught obtaining credit by fraud, posing as 'Lord Dudley'; at his own request eight other frauds were taken into consideration. Six months after that he was sent to Borstal for housebreaking, forgery, and ten other admitted dishonesties. But he had a way with him, and when war broke out, and he joined the Royal Army Service Corps, he was considered good officer material and given a commission. Posted to the Middle East, he lasted less than a year before being cashiered for false pretences and the use of a dishonoured cheque. Shipped home via the Cape, he slipped the guard at Durban and made for Johannesburg, where he joined the South African Air Force, rose to the rank of captain, married and had a son.

At the end of the war his wife divorced him for desertion and he was court-martialled for wearing unauthorized decorations, and for other offences, and dismissed the service. He returned to England in February 1946, and within a few weeks he was caught posing as Lord Dudley or Lieutenant-Colonel Armstrong and wearing decorations to which he was not entitled. It all augured badly for his future. In fact he had less than six months to live.

On Sunday 16th June, Heath took a twin-bedded room at the Pembridge Court Hotel, Notting Hill Gate. He signed the register under his true name but falsely added the rank of Lieutenant-Colonel and an address in Romney, and said the girl with him was his wife. Actually she hoped to be, although she had only met him the evening before, at a dance in Chelsea. He proposed to her and she accepted, and agreed to consummate the marriage in advance. As she is probably still alive and perhaps happily married, it would be heartless to publish her name again. She survived that one night with Heath, peacefully enough, and had no regrets the next morning when she had to go back to her parents' home in Worthing. Heath stayed at the hotel alone.

He remained on his own until the following Thursday, when he spent an evening with Margery Gardner. She was a few years older than Heath, married, attractive, and promiscuous. They had been together, dancing and drinking at the Panama Club in Kensington, and a taxi-driver later testified that it was after midnight when they went to the hotel. Their room remained locked and deaf to the chambermaid's knocks until 2 p.m. the next day, when the assistant manageress went in. The room was in half darkness so she moved across to the window to draw the curtains. One bed was unoccupied, but a figure lay under the bedclothes on the bed nearer the door. She drew back the coverings and to her horror saw the body of a girl, bound by the ankles, arms folded behind her, naked, dead.

I was lecturing at the Detective Training College in Hendon when a message came asking me to go to Notting Hill Gate. Jean Scott-Dunn had left me her telephone number and was located under a hair dryer in Knightsbridge, so by 6.30 p.m. we were both in Room 4 of the Pembridge Court Hotel.

Even without the seventeen lash marks the girl's injuries were appalling. Both nipples and some soft breast tissues had been cruelly bitten, and a seven-inch tear ran into her vagina and beyond.

'Done with an instrument,' I told Detective Chief Inspector Barratt.

He pointed to a short poker in the fireplace. 'Something like this, doctor?'

'Something just like that.' It certainly wasn't just rough intercourse.

It was clear from the copious bleeding that this savage brutal thrust had been inflicted while her heart was still beating, and it was not the cause of death. Her blue face indicated asphyxia, and when I continued my post-mortem at Hammersmith Mortuary, I found typical asphyxial changes in the heart and lungs. As there was no sign of strangling she had evidently been suffocated.

Her body was still warm when I examined it, and her vaginal temperature was 84 degrees F. compared with 63 in the room. Allowing for the usual rise in temperature in asphyxial death, I estimated she had died about midnight or in the earliest hours of that same day. The police learnt later that the couple had entered the hotel about 12.15 a.m., and a door had been heard slamming, probably Heath leaving, at about 1.30 a.m. Nothing had been heard between those times.

Why not? How could Heath have done all that (and the whipping injuries probably came first) without her screaming the house down?

This question was partly answered later by Heath, who said he had gagged her, and a saliva-soiled scarf was found with the whip. He had also bound her hand and foot. I noted slight flushes on her wrists, and the position of her arms suggested her hands had been tied behind her. Without a struggle? Had she allowed him to tie her up?

Probably she had; it came out later that Margery Gardener was a masochist. She liked being bound and lashed. She had gone to Heath's room for pleasurable flagellation, and that may have been all he intended to give her when she offered her naked body to his whip. But she must have known the danger. Indeed, according to J. D. Casswell, K.C., who defended Heath at his trial, she was astonishingly reckless. 'It is almost certain,' Casswell wrote some years later, 'that a month before her death she had been with Heath to another hotel bedroom and had only been saved then from possible murder by the timely intervention of a hotel detective. She had been heavily thrashed, and Heath was standing over her in almost fiendish fashion.'

Heath had left his fingerprints as well as his name at the Pembridge Court Hotel before taking off for Worthing and the girl he had orthodoxly deflowered, under promise of marriage, on what was to be Margery Gardner's murder bed. She introduced her 'fiancé' to her parents, who were as charmed by the 'Lieutenant-Colonel' as she was, until his name appeared in the newspapers in connection with the crime. Heath slipped away to Bournemouth and booked in at the Tollard Royal Hotel using the romantic-sounding name of 'Group Captain Rupert Brooke'! A few days later, strolling on the promenade, he focussed his undeniable charm on a respectable young girl named Doreen Marshall, who was staying at the Norfolk Hotel. He took her for lunch at his hotel, and then dinner, and they sat talking till midnight. He wanted to see her back to the Norfolk, but she demurred and ordered a taxi. Heath persuaded her to let him cancel it, and they set off together on foot. 'I'll be back in half an hour,' he told the night porter. 'No, in a quarter of an hour,' she corrected him. They were both wrong, and the porter did not see Heath again until he looked in his room at 4 a.m. and saw him sleeping in his bed. Heath told the porter next day that he got in by climbing a ladder to his bedroom window: a little joke, he said. Then he went off and pawned Doreen's ring and watch.

Doreen Marshall was missing, and the police were informed. The manager of the Norfolk Hotel knew she had taken a taxi to the Tollard Royal Hotel on the evening she disappeared. Had she dined there? The manager of the Tallard Royal thought she might have been the girl with Group Captain Rupert Brooke. Heath laughed off the suggestion, but then phoned the Bournemouth police and said he might be able to help them in their search. They offered to send an officer with a photograph of Doreen to Heath's hotel. No, he said, he would call at the station at 5.30 p.m. He arrived on the dot.

He identified Doreen's photograph and told Detective Constable Souter that he had walked with her back to the gardens of the Norfolk Hotel. Then, he said, he had gone for a stroll along the sea front.

Souter was watching the self-styled Group Captain very closely. He thought he strongly resembled the photograph of a wanted man recently circulated by Scotland Yard.

'Isn't your name Heath?' he interrupted.

Heath denied it but found the suggestion so chilling that he said he was going back to his hotel for his jacket. The police obligingly fetched it for him, searched the pockets in front of him, and found a railway cloakroom ticket which led them straight to an attaché case containing a riding whip, leather bound, with a diamond-pattern weave. When it was brought to me I found the pattern of the weave

corresponded in fine detail with the marks made on Margery
Gardner's body.

Heath was still denying he had killed Margery Gardner when a
swarm of flies from behind some rhododendron bushes led to the
discovery of Doreen Marshall's mutilated naked body in Branksome
Chine. Her unsoiled and undamaged clothes had evidently been
removed without a struggle, but cuts on her hands suggested
defensive grasping of her attacker's knife. Probably her first major
injuries were blows of her head that would have ended her resistance.
Her wrists and ankles had been tied, her breasts bitten ferociously—
one nipple was bitten off—and slashed with a knife, her ribs buckled
and her throat cut. She was already dead from haemorrhage of the
carotid artery when her murderer split her vagina with a rough
instrument. . . .

Few men look handsome and debonair in the dock of No. 1 Court
at the Old Bailey, but this sub-human Heath managed it. Fair, fresh-
looking, good-featured, well built, he was inevitably attractive to
women. Whether he was an equally charming talker was something
we could not judge, for Casswell did not call him as a witness for his
own defence. One result of this decision was that the defence could
not fully refute the prosecution argument that Heath had never
shown any sexual abnormality before he killed Margery Gardner.
True, he had never been convicted or even charged with a sexual
offence; but even as a schoolboy he had assaulted a girl, and he had
attempted force against a young woman in South Africa; and only a
few months before the murder he had been caught beating a naked
girl, her hands bound behind her, in a Strand Hotel bedroom. His
sadistic lust had got out of control, and screams of 'Help!' and
'Murder!' probably saved her life; but to avoid publicity she declined
to charge him, and other cases may have been kept private for the
same understandable reason.

Casswell did not call Heath to give evidence because he feared he
would appear so calm, clear, and detached that the jury would never
believe him insane. Insanity was the only possible defence, and a
difficult one to establish under the McNaghten Rules. The main test,
a yardstick that any jury could understand, consisted of two
questions. Did the accused know what he was doing? And, if he did,
did he know it was wrong? It would not be enough if he was merely
unable to resist a savage urge to torture, beat, or kill.

The defence relied on the evidence of an expert witness, Dr W. H.

de Bargue Hubert, a very experienced criminal psychiatrist. He said he thought Heath had known what he was doing but not that it was wrong. In only ten minutes of devastating cross-examination the Crown counsel, Anthony Hawke, destroyed Hubert's argument and made the witness look a sorry figure. Although none of us knew it at the time Hubert was himself mentally sick, a drug addict, and within a year he had killed himself with an overdose. But no abler and fitter expert witness could have saved Heath from conviction and execution for a crime that so clearly excluded him from the protection of the McNaghten Rules.

Before Heath went to the scaffold he asked for a whisky. He was quite calm. When it was brought to him he said, 'I think I'll make it a double'.

After Heath, the Wrotham Hill murder seems almost a gentle crime, but this too was coarse and callous.

It was committed on the last day of October 1946, around breakfast time, between 7 a.m. and 9 a.m. according to the estimate I made at my autopsy the same evening. I was allowing for a rise in temperature of four to six degrees at death because of the intense asphyxial conditions I had found. The victim had been strangled with a ligature which had not been tied—there was no mark of a knot—but had been held tight for at least fifteen to twenty seconds, at an unusually high level on the neck. The ligature was evidently a folded hard cloth of some kind, and the tightly drawn impressions of the folds were set clear in four distinct lines across the front of the neck. The marks extended round the sides, especially the right, but faded at the back, showing that she had been strangled from behind on the left. In spite of the closest possible examination of the cuticle I was unable to detect any weave or pattern that would reflect the structure or form of the ligature.

There were few other injuries: a surface graze on the left cheek and a swollen left eyelid, that was all. There was no sign of sexual assault, no disabling blow to the face or elsewhere, nothing to suggest she had been felled or knelt upon or pinioned in any way. The strangling had been very forcible, fracturing the right horn of the thyroid cartilage, and she appeared to have struggled very little. One shoe was missing and her coat and stockings were torn; scratches on her legs under the torn stockings had clearly been sustained after death.

'I don't think she was killed here,' said Superintendent Frank

Smeed, Chief of the Kent CID. We were standing behind some shrubs on the margin of 'Labour-in-Vain Hill', the famous climb the A20 makes over the Downs on the London side of Maidstone.

'The tears and scratches were probably made by barbed wire,' I agreed. Evidently the dead body had been dragged, carried, or dumped, and it might have stayed hidden longer but for the missing shoe, which had been seen on the road by a passing lorry driver, who had stopped and investigated.

The Chief Constable of Kent had called in Scotland Yard, and the famous Robert Fabian was put in charge of the case. He found no clues at the scene, and no means of identification, and came to see if I could give the victim some identity after the autopsy.

'A woman of about fifty,' I told him. 'Unmarried—anyway, virgo intacta, working hands, and no marks of a wedding ring.' He added these details to the general description he was going to give to the Press. 'She was probably sitting when she was strangled,' I added. 'She was certainly seated upright for some time after she died.'

That much was clear from the post-mortem stains on her skin. When the circulation ceases the fluid blood obeys the law of gravity and settles into the lowest available vessels. The red corpuscles tend to settle first, imparting a livid colour to the affected parts. This change, which is called post-mortem hypostasis or lividity, begins within an hour or two of death and becomes marked in five or six hours. Clotting 'fixes' the stains and they then provide indisputable evidence even when a body has been moved after death. As they did in this case.

'Seated upright?' Fabian repeated. 'In a car, perhaps?'

'Probably something less upholstered,' I suggested. Livid stains cannot develop where the welling of the blood is prevented by pressure of tight clothing or by the weight of the body lying on such parts as the shoulder blades, spine, or buttocks. The staining in this case suggested the body had been on a fairly hard seat, not rough ground.

Fabian told his assistant, Detective Sergeant Rawlings, to organize a check on all lorries that had used the A20 between 5 a.m. and 8 a.m. A message went out from Scotland Yard to every police station in the country, and officers questioned many thousands of garages, haulage contractors, delivery firms, and lorry drivers, examining journey books. Nothing came of all this.

However, the dead woman was identified as Miss Dagmar Peters, aged forty-seven, who had lived alone in a small bungalow about three miles from where her body was found. Her mother, who lived near by, told the police that Dagmar used to get up at 5 a.m. once a week to visit a sister-in-law in London. Of scanty means, Dagmar would often thumb a lift, and lorry drivers usually obliged her. She was a little strange, and had, for instance, bought a man's vest in Maidstone two days earlier to wear as a scarf, for it was chilly on autumn mornings. It wasn't there when the body was found, and I thought the strangling lines were consistent with it having been used as the ligature. The motive for the murder was still a mystery. She had seemed obviously too poor to be worth robbing. But her yellow string handbag was missing, along with a purse and her door key and a brown attaché case which, her mother said, she always took to London to carry a packet of sandwiches and some little gift for her sister-in-law.

Superintendent Smeed organized a search for the missing articles, and photographs of a duplicate key and purse were published in the Press. Fabian learnt that the handbag had been crocheted by another sister-in-law, who lived at Woking. She obligingly crocheted an exact replica at top speed, and a photograph of this was published in the newspapers with a 'Have you seen this?' caption. It immediately brought results.

'Yes, I've seen it,' said fifteen-year-old Peter Nash, jumping up from tea at his father's farm in West Malling. 'It's the bag I fished up in the old lake the day before yesterday.'

His father took him to the police station, Fabian was called, and the boy took him to the spot where he had hooked his 'catch'.

'Where is it, son?' said Fabian. 'Where's the bag?'

'Crumbs! I've given it away!'

He had given it to a woman neighbour, who had passed it on to another neighbour, who had given it to yet a third, all within forty-eight hours! It had been washed, so there was scant hope of a clue on it.

But Dr Holden, the Director of the Metropolitan Police Laboratory, found three distinct types of hair in the fibres of the bag—two human, and one from the coat of a brown and black puppy. Dagmar Peters had had a puppy, with a brown and black coat.

Unfortunately this did not bring the police any nearer to the murderer. Nor did the discovery the next day of parts of the remains of the dead woman's attaché case, near the A20 road, for that was where it was expected to be found. It was also where the yellow string bag should have been thrown, thought Fabian. Why should a killer carry it across a field, over an eight-foot fence, to throw it in Clare Park Lake? Why didn't he just throw it by the roadside, like the attaché case?

Perhaps he did. Fabian asked where the lake water came from. A local Guide mistress told him that the old mill stream at East Malling ran, partly underground, to the lake. Fabian made the test, and found that an object thrown into the stream from the roadside bridge might well float all the way to the lake. He turned to the mill, which had become a cider works. It had not been mentioned as visited by any of the 1,300 lorries checked in the area on 31st October, but Fabian noticed a pile of bricks dumped at the gate. The works foreman said they belonged to a sub-contractor, who was not sure of the delivery date but said they had been brought by a haulage firm at Cambridge. Fabian and Rawlings went to Cambridge. Yes, they said, they had delivered the bricks in a four-ton Albion lorry on 31st October. Why, asked Fabian, had they not said so during the police check-up of lorries using the A20 on 31st October? 'We weren't asked,' said the manager.

It was true. The haulage firm was precisely on the boundary of Cambridge City and the County Police Forces, and each had assumed the other had checked their deliveries.

The driver of the lorry had already left the firm, but the police soon traced him. He said his name was Sydney Sinclair: Fabian was sceptical and shrewdly cornered him into admitting he was really Harold Hagger. A check with the Criminal Records Office at Scotland Yard showed he had sixteen convictions, including assault on a woman. Under further questioning he admitted he had given Dagmar Peters a lift and whilst sitting with her in the cab strangled her. 'I didn't mean to kill her, I must have pulled the scarf too tight.' He showed Fabian where he had tossed the bag away, and also where he had thrown the vest. He said he had caught his passenger trying to steal his wallet from his jacket pocket and 'got mad at her'. Fabian had woven a net that had him trapped and he was duly hanged at Wandsworth Prison.

CHAPTER 11

THOMAS LEY AND THE CHALKPIT MURDER

I was giving evidence in a civil action in the London High Court.

'It is not a matter on which doctors are generally agreed,' counsel began his questions; and I countered in similar style:

'I think there is hardly any subject on which doctors are generally agreed, but . . .'

The judge stopped me with his hand and I stood waiting for a rebuke. But the very experienced Mr Justice Cassels gave me only a wry smile.

'Doctor,' he said feelingly, 'you're telling me!' I learnt afterwards that I was the eighth doctor he had heard in the case, and opinions had covered a wide area.

Our accusatory system of justice exaggerates the conflicts for which expert witnesses are infamous, and my old friend Eric Gardner and I were once made to appear to disagree violently over a case on which we were, in fact, in almost complete agreement. The real conflict in that remarkable case was between the medical evidence and what the Lord Chief Justice called 'common sense'. I stuck to my guns but Gardner was more amenable, and, a passing coolness developed between us. Finally, after the jury had been told they did not have to know exactly how murder was done, or why it was done, or even who actually did it, a verdict was reached and the case was 'cleared up' for the police. Justice was served; but the Chalkpit Murder remains one of the mysteries of medico-legal history.

At first sight, which for me was at 9.30 on a Sunday morning, it looked like an open-and-shut case of murder. The dead man's face was plum-coloured and he had a noose round his neck. His body lay sideways in a shallow trench, six feet long and just wide enough, which could have been made for the purpose, but wasn't; it had been dug long before, probably by troops during the war; but army shovels had not filled the space behind the body with loose soil, nor had this fallen from the shelving of the trench's edge. Evidently someone had begun to bury the body.

The ground had been made a quagmire by recent heavy rains, and when we reached the trench our shoes were clogged with clay. Not so the dead man's shoes, which were clean even to the welts and soles. Washed clean by the rain, perhaps; or he might have been carried to the grave, or dragged by the feet. His jacket, waistcoat, shirt, and vest were all rucked up over his shoulders as if he had either slid or been dragged on his back to where he lay.

A dirty piece of green cloth was entwined with the noose, which was tied in a complicated tangle of knots and was so loose that it could be lifted over his head. His braces were attached only to his back trouser buttons and lay behind his body.

The trench was near the base of a chalkpit near Woldingham, in Surrey. It was a lonely, barren spot: the nearest trees were at the top of the chalkpit, thirty or forty yards away. The body had been found the previous evening, 30th November 1946. Eric Gardner, instructed as usual by the coroner, had made a preliminary examination by lamplight and estimated the man had been dead about forty-eight hours.

Called in a consultative capacity by the Surrey Police, I watched Gardner perform the autopsy at Oxted Public Mortuary. The evidence of asphyxia was exceptionally strong: a dusky skin on the head and upper neck; many small haemorrhages on the face, especially in the whites of the eyes, and under the scalp; deep cyanotic congestion of all the organs, especially the lungs; and haemorrhages in the lungs, heart, brain, stomach, and small intestine.

A line of constriction, a rope mark, encircled the neck, and the obvious inference would have been strangling with a ligature if the line had been horizontal. But it wasn't. It was lowest (and deepest) on the right side, and highest on the left, where it rose to a point under the ear, making an inverted V. A typical suspension point: it looked a textbook case of hanging.

Strangling is usually murder; hanging, almost never. Mostly hanging is suicidal; much less commonly, accidental.

In the recorded cases of murder by hanging, the victim has always been rendered physically incapable of resistance. In lynchings he was overpowered by several persons acting in concert; in the few other known cases he was either old or infirm, enfeebled by alcohol or drugs, or severely injured. The body we were examining was of a man who had been young, healthy, and neither drunk nor drugged; and apart from the hanging marks we found signs of only trivial injuries.

There were a few small abrasions on the head, and a bruise in the middle of the forehead which did not show on the surface; another bruise in front of the left hip; fractures of the tips of two ribs on the right side, with slight associated bruising, and some prodding tears on the right flank. Altogether the injuries were much too trivial to have made him unable to resist murder by hanging. They were also just the kind I had seen often in cases of suicidal hanging. The most likely cause was a broken rope and a fall to the ground.

We made the most careful search of both his body and clothing for any sign of a struggle, but found none. His hands bore no mark of injury or of dirtying.

I considered, and Gardner agreed, that the medical evidence pointed unequivocally to self-suspension.

Self-suspension is not always suicide. The dead man could also have tied himself up in a masochistic exercise and accidentally hanged himself. Such cases are not rare. He could have unbuttoned his braces in front intending sexual exposure. The green cloth might have been entwined with the noose to protect his neck from the roughness of the rope while he suspended himself for sexual pleasure.

Post-mortem hypostasis and rigor mortis showed the body had come to lie in the trench at or soon after death. Could the dead man have put it there himself? Might he have hanged himself from a tree above the chalkpit, fallen before he was quite dead, and then, partly conscious, staggered and slid downhill, finally rolling into the trench? It was a remote possibility on medical grounds alone.

Might he have been cut down from the tree and conveyed to the trench by someone else? Not necessarily from an evil motive, but with good intent? A stranger could have found the body hanging and cut it down; tried artificial respiration, perhaps; when that failed, carried and dragged him away, to seek help. Perhaps he dies then, or his would-be rescuer thinks he does; then panics about what the police might think. What to do? As if in answer, there is the six-foot trench. Dump the body on an impulse . . . then greater panic over doing it.

Bury it, then; but that takes for ever, and if he is seen doing it nobody will ever believe—panic gives way to terror, and flight from the scene.

Possible, if hardly probable. The police searched the trees for rope strands or cloth fibres, but without finding anything.

Meanwhile they had searched his pockets and found his identity card: we were still carrying those wartime relics at the end of 1946.

His name was John McMain Mudie, and he had worked as a barman at Reigate Hill Hotel, a bare twelve miles from the chalkpit where his body was found. He had last been seen leaving the hotel at about 5 p.m. the previous Thursday, his half-day: a few hours before Gardner's initial estimate of the time of death.

Aged thirty-five, Mudie had been at the hotel only a few months. They said he was quiet and inoffensive, the last sort of person to be killed or to kill himself. There was no hint of sexual perversion in the magazines and books the police found in his room. They found no clue of any kind, except perhaps a solicitor's letter threatening legal action unless Mudie returned three unsigned cheques that a property company had asked him to pass on to one of its directors. The letter was addressed to a house in Wimbledon where Mudie had lodged before getting the job at Reigate. Apparently the company director, Mrs Byron Brook, had been staying in the same house. A second letter, repeating the first, had been sent to Mudie at Reigate a few days later.

Detective Sergeant Frederick Shoobridge, making inquiries for the Coroner, went to Wimbledon and saw Mudie's former landlady, Mrs Evans. She said Mudie seemed a nice quiet man, although she had not known him well as he had rented his bed-sitter for only six weeks. Mrs Brook had lived there a mere ten days, in her daughter's flat. Mrs Evans said she had introduced Mrs Brook and Mudie in a meeting on the stairs. Afterwards she had mentioned that Mudie was a bachelor, and Mrs Brook had said, 'Well, he won't be long, with such beautiful eyes'. As far as Mrs Evans knew, that was the only time they had ever met.

When the police photographs of Mudie's neck were developed and printed one of them showed a straight line, not visible to the naked eye, forming a base to the angle of suspension under the left ear. That meant the noose had been tightened before being lifted.

The police told the press a dead body had been found in a chalkpit and appealed to the public for information. Two gardeners responded with a story of having seen a man behaving suspiciously in the chalkpit near Woldingham on the previous Wednesday, the day before Mudie disappeared. The man had been standing on the brow of the hill until he saw them and then ran very fast down the side of the pit, jumped into a parked car, revved up frantically, and reversed out in great haste. They had caught only a glimpse of his face and remembered the car better. It was a small dark saloon, eight or ten horsepower, either a Ford or an Austin; and both recalled that the figures in the registration number were 101.

The case was still a coroner's inquiry, and it was Sergeant Shoobridge who went to see the solicitors who had written to Mudie about the cheques for Mrs Brook. The solicitors told him they were instructed by the chairman of the property company, Thomas Ley, whom Shoobridge then interviewed at his house in Beaufort Gardens, in Kensington. Ley said it was all a misunderstanding. He had thought, mistakenly, that Mudie was a friend of Mrs Brook; hence the sending of the cheques. Mrs Brook had left the house in Wimbledon by the time the cheques arrived, Mudie had taken the cheques to her daughter, and there had been a delay.

Mrs Brook, who was with Ley, told Shoobridge she had known nothing about the cheques. She also said she had met Mudie only once, with Mrs Evans on the stairs.

Shoobridge went to the offices of the property company and finally reached the file copy of the letter to Mudie enclosing the cheques. A single sentence rewarded his diligence: 'Mrs Brook directed us to send the cheques to her in your care.'

The case was thereupon taken over by Detective Superintendent Roberts, chief of the Surrey CID, a quiet, most patient detective of long experience.

Discreetly investigated, Thomas Ley proved a big fish in more than one way. He was sixty-six and immensely fat, a qualified solicitor, a former Minister of Justice in New South Wales. He had returned to England in 1930, followed soon after by his housekeeper and mistress, Mrs Byron Brook. She was the same age, and she told the police that their sexual relationship ended owing to his impotence about ten years before Mudie's death. His love was undiminished, and she said his jealousy increased to the point of obsession. When she was four years short of seventy, and looked it, he accused her, quite absurdly, of intercourse with three different young men, all tenants of the same house in Wimbledon. One was her own son-in-law. Another was poor Jack Mudie.

The Chief Constable of Surrey asked for help from Scotland Yard, and Detective Chief Inspector Arthur Philpott was sent to take charge. Shrewd, tough, and uncompromising, Philpott was not awed by a former Minister of Justice; still less by a pathologist who, also uncompromising, repeated that the medical evidence would not support a charge of murder. I felt I had to take this stand before any such charge resulted in committal for trial. This was no case, I felt, for unequivocal support for the Crown, though it was for the Surrey Police that I was working; pathologists must not 'take sides'.

Eric Gardner was more helpful. Mudie might have been 'roughed up', he said, pointing to the bruises on the head and hip. The haemorrhages in the brain might not be asphyxial: he suggested these could have been concussional, caused perhaps by the injury to the forehead (although it was not even visible on the skin). The congestion of the stomach and small intestine, he added, 'could well have been from an abdominal blow—e.g., a knee in violent contact with the stomach, and indeed suggested this' (although there was no injury to the abdominal wall). Finally Gardner said he had never seen a suicide hang himself with a noose tied in a single half hitch, and he had never seen evidence of what he considered was prolonged slow asphyxia in self-hanging. I could only report that my experience was quite the contrary, and I had, of course, seen many more suicidal hangings than Gardner.

Although quite considerably my senior in age, Gardner was a 'G.P. pathologist'; that is, not a trained pathologist but one of a dying race of general practitioners still doing coroner's cases. To be fair, he did them well, but on this occasion he seemed to be trying too hard to please Scotland Yard. I stuck to our original findings, much to the annoyance of Philpott, who had other problems to solve. Mudie had been young and fit; Ley was old and fat, and could hardly have killed Mudie and carried his body to the chalkpit without help. But why should anyone help in a murder if the motive was insane jealousy?

It was not easy to hire killers in England; it would be less difficult, Philpott thought, to engage a thug if he did not know murder was meant. If Ley had hired someone to lure Mudie into a defenceless position his assistant might still not know that Mudie was dead. He would then be very frightened to learn he had been an accessory to murder. These brilliant speculations led Philpott to give the newspapers a little information of the kind they like to publish: the name and a photograph of the man whose body had been found in the chalkpit.

This appeared more than two weeks after Mudie's death and brought immediate results. Within a few hours of reading the news an ex-boxer named John William Buckingham went to Scotland Yard and told Philpott that Ley had paid him £200 for kidnapping Mudie. 'Ley told me Mudie was blackmailing a young woman and her mother who lived in Wimbledon, and that he wanted to make Mudie sign a confession and leave the country.' A woman friend of Buckingham's decoyed Mudie to Ley's house in Beaufort Gardens, where Buckingham and an accomplice named Smith were waiting for him. 'We pushed him into the front room. There was no struggle and he showed no fight. We shut the door on him and left him.' Buckingham said Ley had paid him his fee as he went out of the house.

Philpott showed me Buckingham's statement. 'Do you still say it was suicide?' he asked. I reminded him I had never said it was, but only that medically there was nothing to distinguish it from a suicide. What an exasperating man I must have appeared to Philpott!

The police soon picked up Buckingham's partner in crime, Lawrence Smith, a foreman joiner who had worked for Ley on his house. He confirmed the first part of Buckingham's story and contradicted the rest. He said when Mudie came in Buckingham was waiting with a rug in his hands while Smith himself held a clothes line. 'I put my arms round Mudie's chest, holding his arms down, standing in front of him whilst Buckingham came up behind and threw the rug over him. He then held his arms down with the rug over his head whilst I tied Mudie's ankles and then wound the rope round his body. . . . I tied the rope in the middle of his back. . . . Buckingham helped him along the passage by "jumping" him, and at the door of the room we were going to take him to, he fell forward, with Buckingham on top of him. Buckingham picked him up and helped him into the room and sat him down on a swivel chair which was beside the desk where Ley had told us to put him.' At Buckingham's request, Smith went on, he looked for a gag and found a french polisher's rag. 'Buckingham pulled the rug back from Mudie's face and tied the gag round his mouth. Smith said Buckingham then left, and he himself stayed for only ten minutes more, talking to Ley, who paid him £200 for his trouble. He said Mudie was conscious when he last saw him and he knew nothing of his death. He identified the green cloth in the noose as the french polisher's rag.

Confronted with Smith's statement, Buckingham agreed he had thrown a rug over Mudie's head while Smith tied him up, and that he had 'jumped' him along the passage, but denied that Mudie had fallen or been gagged. Philpott then told Ley of the accusations against him and invited him to go to Scotland Yard. Ley sent for his solicitor and made a statement denying the whole story.

Philpott decided he had nearly enough evidence to arrest all three men for murder but that the charge needed medical support. Gardner gave it readily, but Philpott wanted the backing of the Home Office pathologist. He came to see me at my flat in Weymouth Street, bringing Gardner, who was very pleased with Smith's account of Mudie's fall in the passage. He said the rug over the head explained why there was no surface indication of the bruise in the centre of the forehead: so Mudie could have struck his head heavily enough to cause concussion without making a mark on the skin. If Buckingham had fallen on top of him, Gardner continued, his knee could have struck Mudie in the abdomen and caused the haemorrhages in the stomach and small intestine. The 'beating up' could have been accidental.

I said I had found no reason to think Mudie had suffered any injury to the brain or stomach and intestine. I added that I did not like the idea of trying to fit medical observations to the details of a statement, and I recalled our agreed p.m. findings. Philpott said he had searched the room and found nothing to which the rope might have been attached for hanging Mudie. He asked me if someone could have stood behind Mudie and pulled the rope up. I said the rope would have had to be held up for two or three minutes. I knew of no record of anyone having been murdered in that way, and it seemed absurdly difficult: why not just strangle him? The rope had first been drawn tight on a horizontal plane and then lifted and held in a lifted position: why had it not simply been drawn tighter?

Philpott gave up. The three suspects could not be detained without a charge, and for the next week they went about in freedom. Meanwhile the police searched for more evidence. At last they found it. A few days before the murder Smith had hired a car: a Ford, dark, 8 h.p., registration number FGP 101.

Philpott arrested Ley, Buckingham, and Smith and charged them with Mudie's murder. Then he put Smith on an identity parade: one of the gardeners picked him out as the man he had seen at the chalkpit the day before Mudie's disappearance; the other gardener picked out a different man. The case was still hardly strong enough, and the prosecution decided to allow Buckingham to turn 'King's Evidence'.

At the magistrate's court Gardner said he thought Mudie had been seriously injured in a struggle before death, sustaining a head injury resulting in concussion and a blow on the stomach from a raised knee causing congestion of the intestines. He said nothing about a possible fall, and nothing about the medical possibility of a suicidal or accidental self-suspension. Of course I was not called; but my original post-mortem report was among the documents furnished to the defence, and when Ley's solicitors read it they audaciously invited me to change sides.

Usually I tended to excuse myself if asked for help by defence solicitors. I seldom seemed to have cause for any difference of opinion, and with few exceptions, emphasized the reliability of my colleagues' services: I often restricted my assistance to a perusal of photographs and the written reports of pathologists and laboratory scientists—their interpretations and so on. It was often just as helpful; indeed, I had found that if one agreed to do a second post-mortem on stale materials this was the first criticism Crown counsel would make in court. Much of the evidence had got stale by the time someone had been charged and solicitors had decided they would need help in interpreting the medical or scientific findings. The body had already been dissected at the first autopsy and preserved. Often parts of importance had been removed for further study. Knives, bloodstains, bullets, hairs, fibres, and fresh marks of injury had all gone to the labs, often to be preserved in a hardening formalin fixative, or cut up further for microscopy. There's nothing like the fresh undisturbed scene and untouched body with the knife still stuck in the chest or the strangling cord still round the neck for real evidence. Everything becomes very 'second-hand' as soon as the investigations get under way, and no one doubts that there is no substitute for attendance 'at the scene' and a first post-mortem examination on the fresh body.

In this case I had been there, and I had an additional reason for making an exception: I feared that Gardner's one-sided interpretation of the facts could, if unchallenged, lead to a miscarriage of justice. As a matter of courtesy I asked both the Director of Public

Prosecutions and the Chief Constable of Surrey if they objected to my helping the defence, and both said they had no objections whatever. It was an unusual, perhaps unique situation, but an undoubted testimonial to the impartiality of British justice.

Ley could afford to instruct two of the most famous K.C.s of the day: Sir Walter Monckton and Gerald Howard. At a pre-trial conference with them I suggested the questions to put to Gardner in cross-examination and agreed to give evidence myself if desired.

Just before the trial there was a sensational development. A man named Robert Cruikshank, who had a criminal record, went to Ley's solicitors and said he had visited Ley's house on the evening of Mudie's disappearance and found a man trussed up in a chair; in a panic, Cruikshank said, he had pulled at the rope, and now he wondered if he had perhaps accidently killed the man. I was asked if this was medically possible. My reply was the same as to Philpott's question about murder: Cruikshank could have killed Mudie if he had lifted the rope and held it up for two or three minutes: anyone could.

Two well known Treasury Counsel, Anthony Hawke and Henry Elam, prosecuted; Derek Curtis-Bennett and Malcolm Morris defended Smith. Presiding over the trial was the Lord Chief Justice himself, the much-respected and pretty terrifying Lord Goddard. Unquestionably a strong judge, whom the criminal bar addressed with care, Lord Goddard was reputed to have one weakness: having read the papers from the Magistrate's Court, he seemed sometimes to have made up his mind about a case before hearing it himself. There were early signs that this was such a case.

When Gardner entered the witness box he saw me sitting in the court, and he knew he was likely to be reminded of the opinions he had shared with me after the post-mortem examination. That prospect doubtless made him more guarded than he had been at the preliminary magistrate's court hearing. He still said the brain haemorrhages were bruises and the intestinal condition was also due to a blow, but added that both could have been caused by a fall instead of an attack. Lord Goddard, with Gardner's original deposition in front of him, clearly did not like this weakening of the case for the Crown. Didn't the signs show that considerable violence had been done to Mudie? 'I thought so,' Gardner agreed. Such as with a man after he was beaten up? 'I thought it suggested a thoroughly rough house,' Gardner, encouraged, agreed; but he repeated his opinion that Mudie could have been injured only in falling. He no longer sounded convincing, or even convinced. Finally he discarded his own theory of injury to the brain by a blow on the forehead covered by a rug. 'He could have been struck or fallen on any part of the head', and the most likely cause of the haemorrhages on the front of the brain was 'a fall or blow on the back of the head'.

I do not think the possibility of 'contre coup' had entered his head before, but it had occurred to me and I had discussed it with Sir Walter Monckton in conference. I exchanged a glance with Monckton as he rose to cross-examine Gardner.

'I don't think you told us before about the fall or blow on the back of the head,' he began smoothly. 'Objectively, you are not telling us that there *was* an indication on the back of the head of a blow?'

'No,' Gardner admitted. 'There was nothing to see there. He may have fallen on a carpet. As well as being protected by a rug,' he remembered. I began to feel sorry for my old friend: he had made his bed and Walter Monckton was going to see he lay in it.

'Is it true' (Monckton went on to the first of my prepared questions) 'that in a case of asphyxia you get some indication of haemorrhage on the surface of the brain?'

'I do not quite agree.' Gardner knew what was coming.

Monckton began reading the passages I had marked in standard books on forensic medicine. I had chosen *The Pathology of Trauma*, by Alan I. Moritz, because Gardner had often told me how much he admired it. His face lengthened as he had to listen to a lecture on his own subject from a book 'with which', Monckton said silkily, 'you are more familiar than I'. All Gardner could say was that he personally had never seen asphyxial signs that Moritz called characteristic.

Finally Monckton turned to the photographs of the rope marks on Mudie's neck. 'It is right, is it not, that there is an indication that he was pulled up at some stage?'

'There was an indication of some tension upwards.'

'When you first went into this matter, did you take the view that the rope marks indicated that the deceased was suspended by it?'

'I said there was some degree of suspension.'

'Did you say in your original report that there was no doubt the accused was suspended by the rope?'

'I cannot remember,' Gardner said wretchedly.

'I would be extremely grateful if you would look.'

'You are going a long time back, you know,' said Gardner, after consulting his notes.

'But, you see, it was a time when you felt yourself able to report about the cause of death.'

Gardner finally agreed that he had said there had been 'some form of suspension'. 'But there had been no drop,' he added.

Lord Goddard, who must have been as surprised as the jury by this evidence of hanging, came to Gardner's rescue.

'You did not think he had been hung, in the ordinary sense?'

'No, I did not.'

'You mean you could have a man lying on his back with a rope round his neck and that rope could have been pulled up?'

Knowing the rope had not been pulled or jerked, Gardner evaded the question. 'If the rope were fixed when the noose was round his neck, and if his body were sagging against the fixed rope, then that could have produced the condition I found.'

'There was no mark of jerking or pulling, merely of tightening and suspension,' I said when my turn came. I added that there was nothing to indicate whether death was due to accident, suicide, or murder.

'But this body was lying in a trench in a chalkpit,' interrupted Lord Goddard incredulously.

'Yes, my lord. I am describing the conclusions I drew from this mark. One could *imagine* a great deal, but there was nothing to show.'

Lord Goddard was not used to being taken to task by a witness for imagining too much, or for anything else; but I had noticed before that this fearsome Lord Chief Justice seemed to like opposition with a bite. He merely coloured a little, and Gerald Howard continued his examination. I explained why I thought Mudie's additional injuries were trivial, and described Gardner's theory of a beating up as 'a gross exaggeration'.

Anthony Hawke, cross-examining me, did not seriously dispute this, but questioned me about the cause of Mudie's death.

Q.   He died of asphyxia as a result of having, I would say *mainly* as a result of having, a rope tied tightly round his neck?

A.   Drawn and lifted.

Q.   You want to add 'lifted'?

A.   Yes. It was the lifting that did it.

Body of Gregston lying in the lay-by on the A6, Bedfordshire

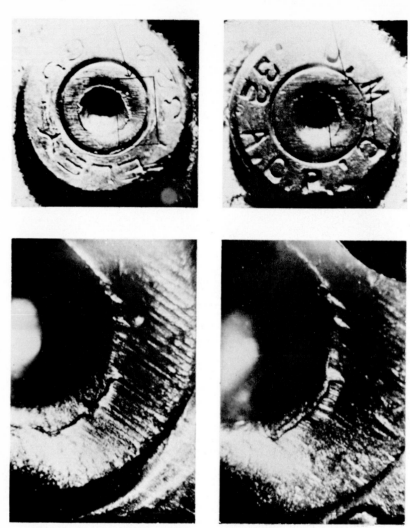

(above) R. v Boyce. Comparison of the shell-case found at the Greek King's flat with that produced by Boyce's lodger friend

(right) The author with his secretary, Miss Jean Scott-Dunn, searching the scene at Crawley in the Haigh case

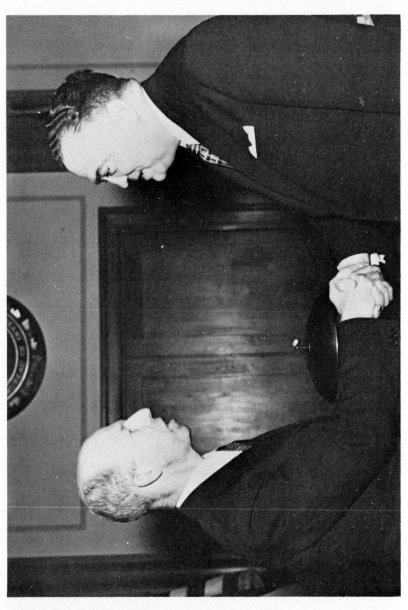

To Dr. Keith Simpson
With most cordial regards
J. Edgar Hoover

5.16.52

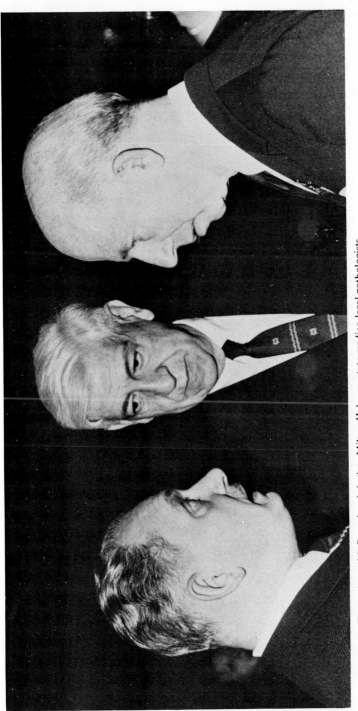

The author with Bovari and the late Milton Helpern, state medico-legal pathologists for Budapest and New York, at a European conference

The clothing as Joan Woodhouse left it in Arundel woods

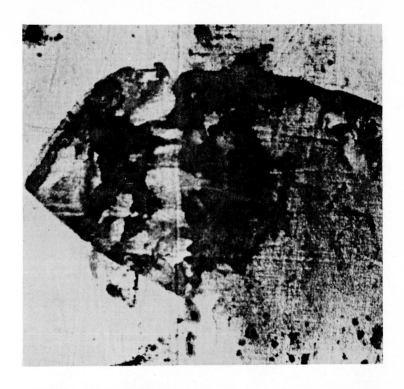

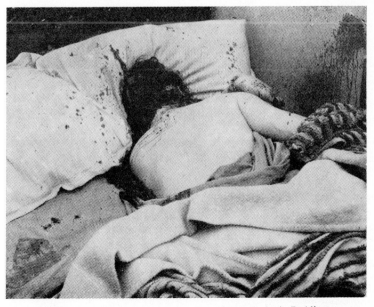

The imprint of a blood-stained axe in a prostitute murder in Paddington . . .
and the victim, as found, on the bed (see axe imprint bottom left)

The victim in the Maidenhead trunk murder concealed in a travelling trunk.
Note keys nearby

Hawke suggested death could have been caused by someone pulling up the rope and holding it up.

A. Not necessarily somebody.

Q. Not necessarily somebody?

A. I don't think we have any evidence to show . . .

Q. Not necessarily somebody?

A. No, I don't think there is any evidence.

Q. Knowing the facts, as you know them now, you do not think this man hanged himself, do you?

A. I think it is possible.

Q. What? After he had been gagged and tied up with a rope?

A. I have nothing from my examination to show he had been.

I felt I was getting a bit obstinate, but I wanted the evidence to speak for itself.

Lord Goddard interrupted. 'Doctor, you are being asked, as a man of common sense, having heard the facts in this case, do you think they point to suicide?'

'I saw nothing in the condition of the rope marks round the neck . . .'

'We are not asking you about that. We are asking you to take the whole facts of this case into account.'

'I do wish to give evidence as far as it is proper,' I told the Lord Chief Justice, 'not to give it further . . . Not to have it drawn further,' I added.

But Anthony Hawke persisted. 'Do you think that man gagged himself and tied himself up and put a rope round his neck?'

'I have no evidence . . .'

'Of course you haven't,' snapped Lord Goddard, and repeated Hawke's question. I felt he'd have loved to say: 'Don't be so obstinate Dr Simpson'.

'My lord,' I said carefully, 'I think the answer to that is that I do not know.' In fact this was precisely the state of affairs. Lord Goddard commented, 'I think so far, anyone would agree with you'.

As I was leaving the trial, feeling a little bruised, the Court Usher slipped a piece of paper into my hand. It was the triangular part of an envelope, the 'stick-down' part. On the back of it was a note from Gerald Howard, who later became a High Court judge himself: 'May I congratulate you on your stout resistance in the face of hopeless odds!' Everyone knew Lord Goddard had made up his mind beforehand, and that he was probably right. But I felt better.

Whatever the Judge felt did not prevent him from giving an impeccably fair summing up, in which he told the jury, in effect, to disregard Gardner's evidence about possible violence to Mudie before he was killed: 'I do not propose to take up time with you in discussing which of those two doctors' opinions is correct.' Lord Goddard accepted that Mudie had been suspended by the rope round his neck, and that the prosecution had not been able to prove how he had been killed: but in law, he said, the precise mode of asphyxiation did not matter if the trussing was part of a criminal assault. I felt my intervention was justified—and that Lord Goddard knew exactly what I was in fact saying—none of us knew what had happened.

The medical evidence apart, the case against Ley and Smith was very strong, and both were convicted and sentenced to death. However, a Medical Inquiry Board declared Ley insane, and he died a few months later, of a brain haemorrhage, in Broadmoor's old Criminal Lunatic Asylum. Smith's sentence was commuted to penal servitude for life. Exactly how they killed Mudie remains a mystery. With such careful planning, even to a reconnaissance of the grave, the method of murder was surely decided in advance; and probably the intention was to strangle him in the easiest possible way. One can only conjecture what happened to make the murder look so much like suicide.

No doubt Gardner felt even more bruised than I did when he escaped from Walter Monckton's cross-examination, but he had stuck his neck out unnecessarily and given one more proof of the error of trying too hard to help the police. It was his last big case (he was already dying of pulmonary tuberculosis) and I felt he wanted to leave his mark, to succeed publicly after I had said I could not help further. Happily there were never any rough words or ill feeling between us, and we remained close friends.

CHAPTER 12

HANRATTY AND THE A6 MURDER

'We've found a body in the NFS pump house on Lambeth Bridge, sir,' Chief Inspector Chapman told me on the phone. 'Seems very recent. Can you come, sir? We think he was shot.'

Well, that made a change. Shooting crimes were, until recent years, common only in the United States. They have never taken a high place in murder statistics anywhere else. In New York and half a dozen other big American cities a firearm murder takes place every day or so. London, a huge cosmopolitan metropolis, still has an average of less than a dozen gun murders a year. The United Kingdom has an enviably low position in the international murder table, and most of our modest number of killings are done by other means. This may be largely because guns are a great deal more difficult to come by than in the United States, and partly because our police normally carry nothing more lethal than a truncheon; but tradition must play a part too, for even in wartime, when firearms are legitimately carried around town, and into the home, the figures hardly vary.

Because of our national dearth of gunmen, until the 1960s there was no ballistics expert on the staff at Scotland Yard. The police relied on the help of private gunsmiths, of whom the most famous was Robert Churchill.

For the police surgeon and the pathologist the crucial question in a fatal shooting is whether the wound indicates murder, accident, or suicide: each has its distinct features. This was not a problem in the case to which Chapman summoned me on 18th October 1945, for the dead man had clearly been shot at close quarters in the back of the neck. It was equally clear that he had not been shot in the disused National Fire Service pump-house in which the body was found. It had been stuffed through an aperture in the wall of the building and was discovered by a patrolling policeman early in the morning with a raincoat covering the dead man's face. I inspected the body and the pump-house carefully with Chapman, and then said it could be taken to Southwark Mortuary. When the undertaker's van arrived it needed two men to get the body out, for it was large—almost six feet and heavily built—and the aperture was narrow. 'I imagine it would have taken two men to stuff the body in,' I said to Chapman.

The entry wound, behind the left ear, was burned, slightly blackened, split, and had bled freely after discharge. Immediately alongside the entry hole there was a 'blow-past' splitting and burning of the ear lobe. Clearly the shot had been fired from the closest possible range, with the muzzle almost touching the skin.

There was no mark on the dead man's body or clothes to suggest he had been involved in a scuffle or offered resistance or tried to protect himself. The only other injuries I found were a bruise on top of the head and a minor graze at the lower end of the right shoulder blade. It seemed certain that he had had no inkling of danger before the shot was fired.

The exit wound was about two inches above the angle of the right eye. The bullet, a .32-inch jacketed missile, had come to rest just under the skin. It lay almost horizontal, nose forward, spent. Its nose had been blunted by its passage through bone.

The weapon, then, had been pointing directly into the head, inclining slightly upward. Blood had flowed from the entry wound and from the nostrils and mouth, running down both sides of the face and over the neck to the shoulders.

'He was probably a taxi-driver,' Chapman told me.

'Then I expect he was shot from the back compartment of his cab while he was at the steering wheel. There is a sliding window access isn't there?'

I had him sat more or less upright, as he would have been in the driver's seat. Yes, it looked as if his passenger had shot him unexpectedly. Then his head would have slumped forward. . . .

When I opened the body I found some bleeding had occurred along the track of the wound and into the tissue of the right eye. I also found he had swallowed very little blood. So little, indeed, that either he had ceased to breathe or swallow within a few seconds, or he had lain after the shooting with his head lower than his trunk.

I could dismiss the idea that he had died within a few seconds. The development of the eye swelling showed that bleeding had continued for some time, perhaps as much as an hour. So he must have been lying with his head lower than his trunk. Perhaps he had toppled or been tilted on the top of the head; his shoulder blade could have been grazed at the same time. The bruise on his head had a squared pattern, the lines each being set $\frac{1}{8}$ inch apart. It was the sort of pattern you see on ridged and squared metal flooring. . . .

Chapman came and told me they had found the taxi, abandoned on a pile of rubble in North Kensington. The flooring at the back had the identical squared pattern. So he had been dumped in the rear of his own vehicle and robbed (his pockets were empty) and driven to Lambeth Bridge. Perhaps they had meant to throw him in the river and stuffed him in the pump-house instead. I estimated he had died about five or six the same morning. The shot could have been fired an hour earlier.

His name was Frank Everitt. He was fifty-six, and popularly known among taxi-drivers as 'the Duke' because he had a cottage in Gloucestershire (his 'country seat'). He was also rumoured to have had dealings with the Black Market. That was about as far as Chapman had got in his investigation when, two weeks later, a suspiciously similar murder occurred.

A man named Reuben Martirosoff, generally known as 'Russian Robert', was found dead in the back of a small saloon car parked near Notting Hill. My old friend Donald Teare, who did the post-mortem, found he had been shot at very close range, with a .32 revolver, through the back of the head. The bullet had emerged just above the right eyebrow. It was found in the front of the car, showing he had been shot while at the steering wheel. His pockets had been emptied, and his face covered with a hat.

'Russian Robert', in fact a stateless Armenian, had been a Black Market operator, and the crime was traced to two of his cronies, both Poles, Marian Grondkowski and Henry Malinowski. At Grondkowski's lodgings the police found the .32 automatic that had fired Russian Robert's bullet. It had not fired the bullet that had killed Everitt, though, and the Crown did not bring any evidence about his murder at the trial. Malinowski and Grondkowski each accused the other of killing Russian Robert, with the result that both were hanged.

In many ways they were uncommon criminals, and but for circumstances they might never have been involved in crime at all.

Grondkowski, who was thirty-three, had fought in the International Brigade in the Spanish Civil War for three years. Taken prisoner at the end, he had escaped to France, just in time for the outbreak of the Second World War. He had fought in the French Army, and when it surrendered he escaped to North Africa and joined the Foreign Legion. In 1943 he volunteered for the Free Polish Army and came to England, where he served for two years in a Special Sabotage Unit. Malinowski, only twenty-five, had fought in the defence of Warsaw in 1939, been captured by the Germans and escaped from a concentration camp, dodged his way right across Europe to North Africa, and joined the Foreign Legion, where he met Grondkowski. He too had come to England to enlist in the Free Polish Armoured Division. Both men had deserted towards the end of the war, when it was rather painfully clear that their own war aim—the liberation of Poland from both its aggressors—was not going to be achieved. But of course that did not entitle them to kill a stateless Armenian.

Malinowski accused Grondkowski of being one of Everitt's murderers, and investigations were discontinued although officially the case remained 'unsolved'.

Another shooting case happened some six months later in the village of Hollington, near Hastings. The victim was a rich cattle-dealer, John Whatman, aged seventy-three, and there was no doubt about the motive. He was found lying outside his house, which had been ransacked. A safe had been ripped open and emptied.

A thin film of snow lay over the body when I examined it at the scene of the crime at 10 p.m. on 3rd March 1946. Bloodstains suggested it had been dragged or carried to where it was found. Whatman had been shot twice, both times from behind and at very short range. One shot had entered the left shoulder two inches below the top and seven inches from the spine and had come out in front half an inch below the top and five and a half inches to the left of the midline. It did not seem the kind of shot that could have been fired with intent to kill. Nor did the other wound, in the head. Here the bullet had entered the back of the neck just above the line of the collar and an inch to the left of the midline and travelled upward and inward, like the other shot, to emerge a little left of the nose and below the corner of the left eye. The development of bruising round both wounds showed that life had persisted for some time after the shooting, perhaps as much as an hour.

There was no sign of any kind of struggle. A minor graze of the back of the left hand with slight local bruising of the knuckles could have been caused by some weak protective gesture, or by scraping past some object in being carried or dragged away.

The shoulder wound was scorched; the head wound showed neither scorching nor tattooing, and had been fired from a range of at least three feet. Presumably the shot in the shoulder had been fired first. If the gunman had tried to hit the heart he would have put the muzzle somewhere between the shoulder blades. If Whatman had started to swing round to his left the bullet could have entered farther to the left, and taken the very route it had. If Whatman had then started to run away that would explain the equally ineffective position of the second wound. But my reconstruction was not put to the test, for the case was never solved.

One fine evening in June 1946, as I was putting a week-end bag in my car at Weymouth Street, the telephone rang:

'Gerald Row Station here, sir. DDI Ball. Got a shooting at a rather important address in Chester Square. Can you come now, sir?'

I had always avoided asking the officer in charge of a case any details over the telephone, for though the operators had long ceased to handle calls personally, voices could 'cross' lines and important news could leak out quite unintentionally. To get to a job before the Press got word of it always resulted in a quieter atmosphere. Better that they should have the facts later.

The address, only a hundred yards from Gerald Row Police Station, in Belgravia, was 45 Chester Square, the wartime home of the Greek King George. There, in a ground-floor back room, slumped the dead body of the housekeeper, Elizabeth MacLindon, an attractive forty-year-old woman, shot through the back of the neck as, one glove removed, she had sat at a small table telephoning. The hand-piece dangled over the edge of the table facing her. A message pad alongside bore no information. A jagged bullet hole was dug into the wall in front of her, and a discarded .32 shell case lay on the carpet several feet behind the chair in which she sat. It proved to be a vital clue.

There was nothing to suggest a struggle, no hint that she had tried to protect herself; and it was clear from the angle of the wound that she could not have seen the pistol. No burning of the tissues, no singeing of the hairs or tattooing of the skin or clothing, meant it had been fired from a range of several feet. She had died almost immediately, and I thought she had been dead five or six days.

So far as the police could discover she had last been seen six days previously, 8th June. The King had called at the house the next afternoon and had found the milk on the back doorstep but had not investigated. A letter for Miss MacLindon, posted in Brighton the day before her body was found, asked her why she had not answered the writer's repeated phone calls. It was signed 'Arthur' but bore no address.

Miss MacLindon's sister Veronica told the police Arthur had been the dead woman's fiancé. He was Arthur Boyce, a painter-decorator working on Brighton pier. Veronica also said her sister had found an old wedding invitation in Arthur's pocket, naming Arthur as the bridegroom and a Miss Whitty of Bournemouth as the bride. He had brushed it aside: 'It was just one of my affairs and it's over now.' But the Criminal Records Office at Scotland Yard showed that Arthur had not only gone through a marriage ceremony with Miss Whitty but served eighteen months for bigamy as a result.

'Yes, that's me,' said Boyce when Inspector Ball visited him in his digs in Brighton. 'What's wrong? Is it about my fiancée? She worked at the Greek Embassy and has been missing for a week. My mother and I have been trying to find her. We were going to be married on 16th July.'

Ball searched his rooms for the gun in vain; it had probably already been thrown into the sea. A luggage label addressed to John Rowland of Caernarvon did not look a very promising clue but Ball followed it up doggedly until he traced Rowland, who was by then in the Army. He proved well worth looking for. He told Ball he had shared lodgings with Boyce in Fulham in October 1945, and when he left he discovered his .32 Browning automatic was missing from his Gladstone bag. He possessed it legally, and told the police of his loss. Also, since he thought only Boyce could have taken it, he sent him a box and label asking for its return. Boyce did not reply but unwisely kept the label.

Ball asked Rowland if by chance he had any spent bullets or empty shell cases. Yes, said Rowland, he had an empty shell case, which he had used as a spool for some spare surgical plaster.

For firearm identification the cartridge or shell case is even more helpful than a bullet. Each shell ejected from a gun bears the imprint of every minute mechanical imperfection of that weapon—firing pin, breech block, ejector bar—in considerable detail. Ball sent the two shell cases (the one Rowland had kept, and the one found behind Miss MacLindon's chair) to Robert Churchill, the gunsmith who did the police ballistics at that time. Churchill placed them together in a comparator microscope and found them identical in their firing pin depression pattern, in ejector-claw ·markings and in bolt-head/breech-face markings on the shell base. His photographs were as powerful as fingerprint evidence, and it clinched the case against Boyce, who was convicted of murder and hanged.

A famous shooting case that came on my files later was the murder of the young road research scientist Michael Gregston, in a lay-by off the A6 road in Bedfordshire in the early hours of 23rd August 1961. It was that rare thing, a murder in full view of a third person, for Gregston was accompanied that night by an attractive young laboratory assistant, Valerie Storie, who not only saw her boy-friend killed but was herself then raped and nearly killed. The case went down in criminal history as the 'A6 Murder', a prosaic name for it considering the crime took place on an isolated stretch of the A6 that already bore the more sinister name of Deadman's Hill.

According to Valerie's version, and there was no other, a man had surprised them when they were parked in a field near Windsor after dark, chatting in their car. He had tapped on the window, and when it was lowered poked a revolver in, saying, 'This is a hold-up'. He got in the back of their car and, at gunpoint, forced Gregston to drive along a route he dictated for over three hours. Finally he ordered them into the lay-by on Deadman's Hill, near Clophill. It was then about 3 a.m. 'I want to kip,' the man said. 'But first I must tie you up.' He tied Valerie's wrists with a piece of rope, and looked for something to use for tying Gregston, still in the driving seat. 'Give me that bag up,' the gunman told him. Gregston was turning to obey when the man fired two shots at his head in quick succession from very close range.

Valerie screamed. 'You shot him, you bastard! Why did you do that?'

'He frightened me. He moved too quick, I got frightened.'

She begged him to let her drive Mike to a doctor. His reply later formed a vital clue to Valerie's identifying him:

'Be quiet, will you? I'm finking.'

A few minutes later he repeated the word 'finking'. Then he ordered Valerie to get into the back of the car with him and take off her knickers. She refused until he threatened to shoot her, and then she obeyed and submitted to rape. This was quickly over. He told her to get out of the car and help him remove Gregston's dead body. He made her show him the gears and start the car for him; and then, from about five to six feet, as she sat on the ground weeping, he shot her five times in rapid succession.

Leaving her apparently dead, the man drove off. Valerie lay there, paralysed in both legs and only semi-conscious, until a farm worker discovered her at about 6.30 a.m.

I went first to the scene, as I always did, to join the police team in their initial survey, then later drove on to Bedford Mortuary. From the fall in temperature, rigor mortis, and other conditions I estimated that Gregston had died between 3 and 4 a.m. He had two .32 calibre bullet wounds of the head, shot 'through and through' from left ear to right cheek. The skin was tattooed round the entry wounds, and the range could not have been more than an inch or two; the shots had evidently been fired in rapid succession, before the head had moved.

On the following Sunday I went across from my Tring house to Bedford Hospital to examine Valerie Storie. She had similar calibre through-and-through wounds, one of the neck and four drilled-in holes in over her left shoulder and down over her arm. I thought probably all five shots, which were in a line, had been fired in quick succession and from beyond arm's range. She was lucky to be alive and would have been luckier had not one bullet transfixed her spine. 'I felt the use of my legs go,' she said to me. Sadly, this attractive girl never walked again.

When I saw her in the Bedford Hospital ward Valerie was over her initial shock and half sitting, propped by pillows, quite bright and able to chat. I did not ask what had happened, but said I had come to examine her wounds in order to help the police with their reconstruction. 'I am a Home Office pathologist,' I said, 'but I am also a doctor.' She smiled as the ward sister helped her remove her bed jacket, and made no fuss when I took several 35 mm 'flash' colour stills of her wounds. But only her face and arms moved: her legs were paralysed. I felt (as I often did) more disturbed at this tragic sight in a living creature than by a dead body.

I was impressed by her intelligence and her very clear mental state so soon after her frightful experience. Her account of the rape and of the shooting of Gregston and herself was borne out completely by my medical evidence. I was impressed too by her courage, for obviously she had to overcome great emotional stress to be able to talk about it as calmly as she did. She did not cry.

A few days afterwards Valerie was transferred—as it happened, to my own Guy's Hospital. She was still there three weeks later, when the police announced in the press and on television that they wished to interview a man named Peter Louis Alphon, who they thought might 'help them with their inquiries'—their usual euphemistic way of saying who was suspect No. 1. On 22nd September the appeal was answered by Alphon himself, and he was taken into custody. Not yet having enough evidence to charge him with the crime, the police came immediately to Guy's in the hope that Valerie was fit enough to attend an identification parade.

They could hardly have come at a worse time, for Dr Rennie was in the process of removing two bullets from her body. He sent the police away, and again refused them the next day; but on 24th September he gave way to their pressure and allowed his patient to be wheeled out on a bed to face a line of men and try to pick out the one who had killed her boy-friend Gregston and shattered her own young life. 'She was not flustered and was quite clear in her mind,' Rennie testified afterwards, 'although she was very keyed up and tense.' The conditions were far from ideal.

It was a peculiarly harrowing ordeal for Valerie: describing the crime to sympathetic doctors and policemen was nothing like so distressing as the prospect of looking again into the face of the man who had defiled and shot her. Further, as often happens at an identification parade, there was considerable police anxiety—mostly unspoken, but keenly felt—for her to pick out the man. The police believed they had the right man, they had spent a month's hard work on getting him there, her identification was vital to the evidence, and they would be disappointed if she said she could not be sure and they had to let him go.

She was still far from well and probably very vulnerable to such pressure: it probably ought not to have been imposed. But nobody can deny that that parade was conducted with scrupulous fairness. For Valerie Storie, in her somewhat emotional state, and eagerness to 'get it over', spent only five minutes on her examination of the parade before picking out a man who was not the suspect Peter Louis Alphon but a Spanish sailor, one of the similar but indisputably innocent 'controls'.

Alphon was released from custody, and Detective Superintendent

Acott said later that he now 'knew where Alphon was' on the night of the crime and for that and several other reasons he was satisfied of his innocence. It was a pity the police had pressed for an identification parade before Valerie was fit for it. It seems that if they had waited a little longer it would have become clear that they had got the wrong man: Alphon was 'somewhere else'. He led a curious life.

It was unfortunate, too, that the police did not tell Valerie before the parade that she could, if she thought it would help her, ask the men to speak. She would undoubtedly have done so, for, as she had said from the start, she had seen the murderer's face in good light only once, and then briefly, but she had heard his voice for six hours. He had, as she had already told the police, a distinct cockney accent; she remembered particularly that instead of 'things' and 'think' he had always said 'fings' and 'fink'. She would hardly have made a mistake about the Spanish sailor if she had heard him speak.

The day after the parade Valerie was transferred to Stoke Mandeville, the unit in Buckinghamshire that specialized in rehabilitating so many spinal-cord injury victims. The treatment was psychological as well as physical, and there is no doubt that from the day she entered Stoke Mandeville her emotional state improved. Meanwhile Acott had received several telephone calls from James Hanratty, for whom a search was going on: he was located in Blackpool and arrested.

Three weeks after the identification parade Valerie was asked to attend another. This time she asked if she could hear the men speak. There were thirteen on the parade, and she scrutinized them for twenty minutes. She was wheeled up and down the line several times, and asked each man to say 'Be quiet, will you? I'm thinking.' Each man had to say it twice. Finally, without hesitation, she picked out Hanratty, the man who had by then become suspected by the police much more strongly than Alphon had ever been. Hanratty was the man whose 'th's' tended to be 'f's'.

The trial of Hanratty at Bedford Assizes lasted twenty-one days, becoming the longest in English criminal history. Mr Justice Gorman was meticulously patient and fair. Naturally the defence made the most of the fact that Valerie Storie had picked out another (and certainly innocent) man at the first identification parade; and Hanratty's counsel, quick-witted Michael Sherrard, Q.C., had no difficulty in showing that the Identikit picture constructed from Valerie's information did not look much like the man in the dock. (It seldom does.) Indeed, when it was displayed for the jury to see there was a murmur of talk and even a few smiles, for the only resemblance it really bore was to the clerk of the court who was holding it up! But Valerie was an admirably cool, impressive witness, and I watched her survive a hard cross-examination unscathed. Hanratty was found guilty of murder, sentenced to death, and hanged.

Michael Gregston was dead and Hanratty was dead, but the ghost of the A6 murder has lingered on. Alphon wrote a 'confession' for a friend, Jean (John) Justice; more than a hundred Members of Parliament (including two former Home Secretaries) signed a petition for an inquiry into Hanratty's conviction; and at least three full-length books (respectively by Louis Blom-Cooper, Lord Russell of Liverpool, and Paul Foot) have questioned the jury's verdict. But no-one engaged in the case, as I was, and entirely disinterested in the innocence or guilt of the accused, as every pathologist should be—and I certainly am—could fail to be impressed by the weight of the evidence. Not only the calm Valerie Storie, but two other witnesses confidently identified Hanratty, and none of these three was shaken by cross-examination. I myself do not doubt that the Crown case has in no way been seriously dented by the books and articles written on the case.

A tragic shooting incident occurred at Londonderry, in Northern Ireland, on Sunday 30th January 1972, 'Bloody Sunday' as it came to be called. A Civil Rights Association march, held in the Bogside district in defiance of an official ban, had been followed by a riot, which was broken up by paratroopers: they were given an order to fire and thirteen civilians lay dead as the mob dispersed. Eight of them were still in their 'teens. The Government ordered a public inquiry to be held in Londonderry (Coleraine in fact), and a tribunal was set up under the Lord Chief Justice, Lord Widgery.

The father of Wray, one of the young victims, criticized the tribunal. 'In my view,' he said at the inquiry, 'the British Government have prejudged the issue.' He also complained that the Lord Chief Justice had himself been a soldier in the British Army, and for that reason was not a suitable person to hold the inquiry. Lord Widgery, as plainly fair-minded as any of the four Lords Chief Justices I have given evidence before, gravely replied, 'I respect your opinion, and you are perfectly entitled to have it. I shall do my best to conduct the inquiry properly.'

Post-mortem examinations had been performed at the time by the State Pathologist, Dr Tom Marshall, and two assistants, and the clothing had been examined in the state laboratories for fire patterns. Before the inquiry the Crown asked me to re-examine their work, for it was clear that their evidence would be cross-examined severely. I found they had not missed a point, and set out a strongly supportive report.

There had been many eye-witnesses to the shootings, but they were not all expected to agree on what they had seen, and on some points the dead men could tell better tales. One certain fact from the post-mortems was that none of the victims had been involved in ordinary fighting: apart from the fatal bullet wounds none of the bodies showed a sign of any injury (except from falling to the ground)—no fist or boot or blunt weapon or knife, no stamping or butt-ending, no explosives. Another indisputable fact was that the range of fire was beyond arm's reach. There had been no 'muzzle in contact firing' and there was no 'fire' pattern due to partly burned powder, which normally reaches about four to seven inches from the muzzle. This had been confirmed by the negative results of laboratory tests on the men's clothing, which was unwashed and unsoiled. Six of the dead men, however, had firearm powder discharge traces on their hands: they had been firing shots too, though no firearms were found on or near them as they lay dead.

There was no evidence that the firing had been indiscriminate. In only four cases was there evidence of yawing or deflection, and in these it was probably not ricochet from the ground, which disturbs a bullet's flight far more—'tearing' into the body. The angle of entry varied so much as to suggest picking off individuals who were mostly standing. It looked as if seven had been standing erect (although at the inquiry Lord Widgery—not counsel—suggested they might equally have been lying down, and I had to agree). Of the others, four had been bent forward as if ducking, and two were shot through the buttocks as if they had their backs to the fire and were heading away. In all but one of the thirteen, death had been caused by a single bullet wound. The exception, Wray, had been injured by two bullets, both through the mid-chest from right to left. This did not significantly disturb the generalization that single shots had picked off particular persons, for two separate weapons could have picked off Wray, or he could have been the 'through and through' victim of a single bullet: they were high-velocity .762 army bullets.

For the inquiry I flew to Belfast on a foggy morning and motored from there to Londonderry. It was the only time in my life that I felt I might be ambushed. At the end of the day I was asked if I would like to return to Belfast in the Lord Chief Justice's helicopter, but I felt that joining him as a travelling companion would only add to the risk. I myself was, after all, merely an expert witness, and I had never been considered in need of special protection, like many other witnesses, even at the Kray brothers' trial. Although my evidence has sometimes loaded the scales against a man on trial for his life, I have never been threatened; I was once advised not for a while to frequent Cypriot restaurants in Soho after I had given evidence in Cyprus against a man charged with murder who was nevertheless acquitted and came immediately to London, apparently to escape local revenge.

CHAPTER 13

THE VIOLENT DEATH OF
KING ANANDA OF SIAM

In June 1946 my breakfast *Times* in London carried a succinct despatch from the Associated Press in Bangkok:

9th June—The young king of Siam, Ananda Mahidol, was found dead in a bedroom at the Barompiman Palace today with a bullet wound in his head. The discovery was made by a servant shortly before noon. The Chief of Police and the Directors of the Chulalongkorn Hospital, who were called immediately to the palace, said afterwards that death was accidental. Great crowds have gathered in silent grief outside the palace. Most of them were unaware of the death of the King until news was broadcast by the Government radio at seven o'clock.

Of course, I had no idea then that I was to be caught up in all this, or that the statement that death was accidental was an official 'cover'. Whatever else the Chief of Police and the doctors put out for official consumption, they must already have been aware that it was a case of murder.

The Kings of Siam, the Chakri dynasty, who had ruled the country for seven centuries, were not ordinary mortals. The King was the 'Lord of Life', 'Divine'. None of his subjects was allowed to touch him physically, to turn his back on the royal presence, or even to cross his legs when permitted to sit in the Royal Palace. To kill him was not only regicide but deicide.

For all that, it was by no means a rare event in that country.

Of thirty-three Kings, no fewer than one-third were either murdered or murdered their rivals. State officials near the throne had killed their rulers, and there had also been other murders in the Royal Family. Being a living god was no safeguard against a violent death.

King Ananda VII, the latest to end his reign in this sad tradition, had come to the throne in 1935, at the age of ten, and survived the

Japanese occupation in the Second World War. On 8th June, a Saturday in the Year of the Dog 2489, Buddhist era (AD 1946), he was slightly indisposed, suffering from a mild intestinal upset. At 10 p.m. he retired to his private suite, dressed for bed in a light T shirt and blue Chinese silk trousers. He was protected while he slept by a guard of four men and the Inspector of the Watch. At 6 next morning he was visited by his mother, who woke him up and found him perfectly well. At 7.30 a.m. his trusted page, Butr, came on duty and began preparing a breakfast table on a balcony adjoining the King's dressing room. The night guard went off duty, and the day staff assembled.

At 8.30 a.m. Butr saw the King standing in his dressing room. The page took in the usual glass of orange juice, a few minutes later, but by then the King had gone back to bed. With a gesture he refused the juice and dismissed Butr, according to the page's own evidence.

At 8.45 the King's other trusted page, Nai Chit, appeared unexpectedly. The two pages were on alternating duty, but Nai Chit was not due to relieve Butr for another two hours. He said he had called to measure the King's medals and decorations on behalf of a jeweller who was making a case for them.

At 9 a.m. Prince Bhoomipol, Ananda's younger brother, called on the King to inquire about his health. He said afterwards that he had found the King dozing peacefully in his bed: a mosquito netting covered him over all.

Twenty minutes later a single shot rang out from the King's bedroom. Nai Chit ran in, and out, and along the corridor to the apartments of the King's mother. 'The King's shot himself!' he cried. The wording of this announcement was later to be used in evidence against him.

I was given a carefully worded description of the scene when, some time later, a Major-General of the Police of Siam came to my Department at Guy's to seek some help in interpreting what had happened. It was my first case out of England.

Ananda lay in bed within a mosquito netting, his body covered, but the arms lying outside the coverlet alongside the body. Close to his left hand was an American Army .45 Colt automatic pistol, and above the left eye was a single bullet wound.

There were no police photographs of the scene to support this account; for by the time the police appeared on the scene, everything had been irreparably 'tidied'.

One of the first to enter the bedroom was the King's mother, who threw herself, grief-stricken, on her son's body, weeping and moaning 'My dear Nand, my dear Nand!' The King's old nanny followed, and after feeling his pulse she picked up the pistol and put it on the bedside cabinet. Prince Bhoomipol, hearing the disturbance, came in, and then Butr, who put the pistol in a drawer 'for safety', thereby adding his fingerprints to Nanny's. Butr was sent to call a doctor. After he had come Prince Bhoomipal joined the Queen Mother, Nanny, and the two pages in washing the body, laying it out in clean linen, and applying blocks of ice and setting up a fan to cool it and delay decomposition, which the hot weather would otherwise have caused within a few hours.

Meanwhile various officials were arriving: the Chief of the Palace Guard, the Chief Major Domo and Protocol, the Secretary-General, and high-ranking Cabinet Ministers led by the premier, Pridi Banomyong, who had for long been an enigmatic figure in Siamese political life. As a young lawyer, together with a young artillery officer named Pibul Songram, Pridi had conspired to overthrow the monarchy in 1932. The revolution had quickly petered out, and Pridi had gone into exile. But he had returned and regained favour, along with his friend Pibul, who had risen to the rank of Field-Marshal by the time of the King's death.

Looking understandably agitated, Pridi paced up and down and said to the Secretary-General, in English, 'The King is a suicide'—a paraphrase of Nai Chit's accouncement of the King's death.

At last the police arrived; in fact, it was the Chief of Police, who had to push through the confused mob of officials to reach the body, and he was not allowed to do anything useful even then. Following protocol ('No-one may touch the Divine Body') the King's uncle stopped him from examining either the wound or the King's hands. Nobody was allowed to feel if the body was stiff or cold. All the Chief of Police could do was ask for the pistol; and when it was produced he added his own prints to those of Nanny and Butr. He noted that the weapon was not on the safety catch and that only one round was missing. No bullet had been found, but Nai Chit produced a spent cartridge case which he said he had found on the floor on the left side of the body.

Before the King's body was embalmed for official burial in a ritual tomb, the doctors of the Chulalongkorn Hospital were allowed to examine it, and they found a second wound, smaller than the first, at the back of the head. On the erroneous assumption that an exit wound is always larger and more ragged than an entry wound, they decided he had been shot through the back of the head. Rumours quickly ran round Bangkok. 'The King was assassinated'; and, more specifically, 'Pridi killed the King'. If not Pridi, one of his protégés. Two of these in particular were suspected. One was Lieutenant Vacharachai, known as Too, a former ADC to the King, who had recently been sacked. The other was Chaleo, a former personal secretary to the King.

Three days after the shooting Nai Chit showed the police a hole in the mattress behind the King's head, and a bullet was recovered.

Accident, suicide, or murder? A public Commission of Inquiry was set up to find out the truth. It was assisted by a medical sub-committee hopelessly overloaded—it consisted of fifteen doctors—general practitioners, surgeons, a psychiatrist, a toxicologist, an anatomist, and just one forensic pathologist, Dr S. G. Niyomsen, Lecturer in the subject to the University of Bangkok. The Commission began hearings on 26th June and was still in session in August, when a General Election was held. Pridi's party won; and, apparently feeling vindicated, Pridi resigned the Premiership. In October, the Commission of Inquiry reported that the King's death could not have been accidental but that neither suicide nor murder was satisfactorily proved.

In November 1947, after nearly eighteen months of rumours, intrigues, and secret struggles, tanks rumbled through Bangkok's ancient streets as the Army, under Marshal Pibul, staged a *coup d'état*. Pridi fled in a sampan. Vacharachai also disappeared. Former secretary Chaleo was arrested along with the pages Butr and Nai Chit. All three were charged with conspiracy to kill the King. A new Chief of Police, Major-General Phra Phinik Chankadi, was instructed to collect evidence for their trial. The Director-General of Public Prosecutions decided to seek an outside opinion on the medical evidence, and this was where I came in. On 13th May 1948, the Major-General came with an interpreter to see me in London.

The question was still the same: accident, suicide, or murder?

The King had been keenly interested in small firearms, and had often practised shooting with Vacharachai. He had kept an American Army .45 Colt automatic in his bedside drawer. Could it have gone off accidentally while he was examining it? Would an intelligent man who knew anything about firearms inspect a pistol with the safety catch off and the magazine fully charged while lying in bed on his back, his head on the pillow and the pistol pointing at his forehead? The idea seemed wildly far-fetched, even apart from the fact that the King's sight was so defective that he could not have examined anything without his spectacles, and at the time of his death these were lying on the bedroom table.

The position of the body made suicide almost equally unlikely. In twenty years' experience I had not seen a suicide shoot himself whilst lying flat on his back. No such case existed, so far as I knew. The suicide sits up or stands up to shoot himself.

There were other strong indications against suicide. The pistol found at the King's side was by his left hand, but he was right-handed. The wound, over the left eye, was not in one of the elective sites, nor a 'contact' discharge. The direction of fire was not inward towards the centre of the head. Furthermore the King had never hinted at suicide to anyone and had not been depressed at the time of his death.

That left only murder, for which the evidence was very strong. I thought he had almost certainly been shot while dozing, and that unconsciousness had followed instantly. The muzzle of the pistol had evidently been close to but not against the skin, giving the King no warning or any chance to try to protect himself. 'This is not a case of suicidal discharge nor of accident, but one of deliberate killing by firearm,' I concluded my report.

The trial of Chaleo, Butr, and Nai Chit began three months later, in August 1948. The court consisted of four judges presided over by the Chief Justice. The prosecution's case was supported by 124 witnesses and such voluminous documentary evidence that the defence counsel asked for an adjournment to give them time to consider it. When this was refused the counsel resigned, and there was some delay before new counsel were found. The trial then proceeded at a leisurely pace. Bail was of course refused.

The prosecution alleged that the pistol found lying *outside* the mosquito netting by the King—and it was his own property—was not the weapon that had killed him. Butr was alleged to have planted it after the shooting, presumably in a clumsy attempt to make it look like suicide.

In January 1949 I was consulted again on the case, this time by Dr Niyomsen of the University of Bangkok, the pathologist on the first team of inquiry. He came to London and stayed nine days, providing me with first-hand additional facts, which strengthened the opinion I had already given. Thus the situation of the bloodstains and the position of the bullet showed that the King's head had certainly been resting on the pillow when he was shot. In a further report I pointed out also that it would be easy to discover, with a comparison microscope, whether the bullet recovered from the bedding and cartridge case from the floor had been fired from the pistol found beside the body of the King. This had not been done.

Dr Niyomsen asked me if I would be willing to give evidence at the trial. I said I would, subject to Foreign Office approval, which was granted on the strength of an assurance by the Home Office that I did not hold any official Government appointment (I was 'consultant' to the Home Office). Dr Niyomsen said he thought I would be called to Bangkok in mid-April. However, in March, to everyone's surprise, Pridi and Vacharachai sailed up the Menam River from China and tried to seize power in Bangkok. They occupied the radio station, but Marshal Pibul's forces quickly routed the rebels, and Pridi and Vachirachai disappeared again. The trial was postponed after two of the defence counsel had been murdered, and Dr Niyomsen told me in a letter that the medical evidence was unlikely to be called until August or September. 'The trial is long and tedious,' he wrote. 'One witness may be questioned for a week and the whole case may last a year.' These were tendentious delaying tactics.

Niyomsen wrote again in September, when the accused had already been in custody nearly two years. 'The sitting takes place every alternate week, each lasting three full days.' The Director-General of the Science Department testified that the pistol found beside the King's body had not been fired for at least a week before the shooting. He also said his laboratory was not equipped with the necessary apparatus and materials for the matching test of the bullet and the spent cartridge case with the pistol which I had suggested. However, a police officer said that the bullet and the cartridge case definitely matched the pistol. Other prosecution 'experts' declared the bullet found in the bedding could not have gone through the King's head 'because it wasn't flattened as they thought it would have been by crashing through bone.' These experts continued with a lengthy consideration of the spasm of muscle that might have followed such a bullet wound if it had passed through a certain part of the brain; this had relevance as the King had been found dead as if in sleep, not contorted by spasm or gripping a weapon. And so it went on, interminably. 'I presume it will not be our turn until next year,' wrote Niyomsen: he had oriental patience.

A few weeks later two of the defence counsel were arrested and charged with treason. Of the remaining two counsel one resigned, leaving only one young but redoubtable lawyer for the defence, Fat Nasingkhla. Towards the end of the case he was joined by Chaleo's daughter, who had just graduated.

At last the medical evidence was called, beginning with the fifteen doctors who had served on the sub-committee to the Commission of Inquiry set up after the King's death. One after another gave the opinion that the King had been murdered, but not without misgivings. 'Owing to some crisis in politics in this country, it is not sure that this trial will continue,' Niyomsen wrote to me. 'If a new Government is formed, the aspect of the trial may be changed; and we doctors who confirmed regicide do not know our fate yet. We are expecting a *coup d'état* any morning on waking up; besides, Communist invasion may come any time.' I was advised to unpack my travelling case 'for the present', and it seemed to me reasonable advice.

Siam was spared both a *coup d'état* and invasion, and the medical evidence was concluded, without my personal appearance, in January 1950. More circumstantial evidence followed, and it was again summer before the defence began. All three accused gave evidence denying any complicity in the affair. Nai Chit fared worst in the witness box, partly because of his odd reason for being at the palace at the time of the shooting and partly because of his announcement 'The King has shot himself'. The trial finally ended in May 1951, two years and nine months after it had begun. In a judgment of 50,000 words the court found that *King Ananda had been assassinated*, but that Chaleo had not been proved guilty and that neither of the pages could have fired the fatal shot. However, they found Nai Chit guilty of being a party to the crime. 'The charges against Chaleo and Butr are dismissed and the two accused are hereby ordered to be released.'

Nai Chit appealed against conviction, and the prosecution appealed against the acquittal of Chaleo and Butr. After yet another fifteen months of deliberation the Appeal Court, in a judgment lasting fourteen hours, dismissed Nai Chit's appeal and, undeterred by the common doctrine of *autrefois acquit*, found Butr guilty too.

Final appeals were made to the Supreme Court, the Dakka, which considered them for ten more months and then convicted Chaleo.

Four months later, when the three men had spent nearly six years in custody, Chaleo, Nai Chit, and Butr were executed.

I was sorry not to have been able to go to Bangkok, but I have a beautiful silver cigarette box with the Royal Palace engraved on it to remind me of the case. It was presented to me in London by Major-General Phra Phinik 'on behalf of the King'. The fee for my services was paid curiously—at night, in cash, carefully counted out under a Cromwell Road lamp post near the Embassy—by arrangement! The reasons for this strange ceremony I never found out.

In due course Siam became Thailand, and Dr Niyomsen was appointed the first Professor of Forensic Medicine to the University of Bangkok at about the same time that I became the first holder of the Chair at Guy's. I never met him again; but twenty years after the trial, when I at last went to Bangkok, on a lecture visit to the Medico-Legal Institute, I found myself face to face, so to speak, with him, for on entering the main hall, there, preserved in a position of honour in the Institute in a most beautiful glass case, was—his skeleton! Macabre, yes, but a touching Oriental mark of affection for their late Chief, who had died two years earlier.

I went also to the Barompiman Palace—as an ordinary visitor— and was shown, among other things, the Royal Bedroom in which King Ananda had been shot. 'Do you know anything about the case?' asked my university graduate guide. I murmured interest only, and she set out the facts—accurately. I remained silent, merely thanking her for her courtesy: it was, after all, only history.

CHAPTER 14

TEXTBOOK CRIMES

My short students' textbook *Forensic Medicine*, which I had written mostly during the noisy nights of the war, was first published by Edward Arnold in 1947. It has been revised and reprinted many times since then, and it gained me the Swinly Prize of the RSA and made many new friends all over the world. 'I don't know you,' a letter or a visitor from a distant country would say, 'but I've enjoyed your book and I'd like to meet you'; and so another overseas contact would be made.

The book was given a generous welcome by Sir Sydney Smith, still in Edinburgh, although it challenged the circulation of his own well-known textbook. Later he was to hand over to me the Editorship of the so-called 'Bible' of forensic medicine, *Taylor's Principles and Practice of Medical Jurisprudence*, a gargantuan responsibility he had shouldered with great success for some thirty years. He was like a second father to me as I grew up in the field of forensic medicine.

A case of my own that was interesting enough to earn a place in 'Taylor' occurred in December 1947. The body of a man was discovered in a shallow stream. I sent his stomach contents to the Metropolitan Police Laboratory for routine examination, and Dr Holden found sand particles identical with a sample I had taken from the river bed. But I had already declared that the man had not been drowned, and that his body had not even been put in the water until at least one day after death.

The police were understandably worried by the lab report. The river sand could only have reached the stomach by the process of swallowing, an activity that no dead body can perform. Might I be wrong about the time of immersion?

I replied that of course I might be wrong but that in this case I didn't think I was. The water soddening of the skin was so little developed that I did not think the body could possibly have been immersed for more than eighteen to twenty-four hours before it was found. At the same time, considering local conditions and the time of the year, I thought the man must have been dead at least two or three days.

My second hypothesis was quickly confirmed. Police inquiries showed he had been dead two and a half days. But no evidence was found to support my belief that he had been dead at least a day and a half before he was put in the river.

The dead man was William Bissett, aged seventy-one. He had spent his last evening in this world drinking with a gypsy, Joe Smith, in the Cock Inn, Slough. After the pub closed, they had walked away together into the night. Bissett was reported missing the next day, and the day after that the police questioned Smith. He said at first that they had parted at a fork in the road, Bissett heading for his home in Church Street and Smith himself for a gypsy encampment on the far side of the stream. Smith was taken into custody that evening, and changed his story; he said Bissett had stumbled drunkenly and fallen on him, and he had hit Bissett and knocked him to the ground and left him there. Later still, Smith made a third statement. He said that after punching Bissett in the mouth he had robbed him of his gold watch and chain and about £30; but in this account Smith said he had watched the old man walk away, not left him lying. Smith said also that he had hidden the watch and chain on the edge of the gypsy camp, and he took the police to the spot. Next morning at daybreak they searched the camp and the surrounding area. In a shed in the camp they found a pair of ex-RAF trousers lying rolled up on the bottom of a crate, wet and bloodstained up to knee level: Smith admitted they were his and that he had worn them on the night of Bissett's disappearance. A few minutes later they found a sack containing Bissett's overcoat, jacket, and trousers roughly buried a few yards from the stream, still on the side of the gypsy camp. Finally they came on the dead body of Bissett, lying on his back half submerged in the water but with his nose and mouth well clear of it. He was dressed in his shirt and long underpants, which had been pulled down inside out over his feet. The trick of pulling down the trousers was a well-known manoeuvre by gypsy criminals to prevent the victim of a robbery from running after them and raising a hue and cry.

Bissett had not been drowned. He had gulped but not inhaled water, and there were no signs of asphyxia. He had seven injuries to the head and chest as from heavy blows from a fist, and the heaviest of these, to the left eye, had evidently thrown his head back, causing a fracture-dislocation of the neck: a 'broken neck'. There was also light bruising of the brain membrane. These injuries were severe enough to have caused death within a short period, and I could determine the approximate length of this from the fact that blood swallowed from the mouth injuries had reached the commencement of the small bowel—a vital process that might have taken fifteen to twenty minutes if the stomach was empty. Minor 'protective' bruises and grazes to the wrists and hands showed that Bissett had tried to defend himself. Hairs clutched in his hands matched Smith's. Scratches down his thighs and lower legs showed that the body had been dragged by the arms or shoulders after death.

Smith had stopped making statements, and the police still had problems. The bloodstains on the ex-RAF trousers proved to be of Group B, the same as Bissett's, Smith's own group being A; but why were they wet to the knees when the stream was little more than ankle deep? Why had Bissett's outer clothing been taken off and hidden in the gypsy camp? Smith had said he pulled Bissett's trousers down because he 'didn't want him to go to the Police Station,' but said Bissett must have taken off his own overcoat and jacket. Where had the fight taken place? And where had the body been hidden between death and immersion?

The police were still trying to answer the last question when the bombshell from the lab arrived, with its implication that immersion had preceded death. If that was right, Bissett might not have been murdered at all, only robbed with violence, after which he could have staggered drunkenly to an accidental death in the stream, gulping water before expiring. Or so a defence counsel might have argued, although it was not really possible. He could not have walked with his underpants drawn over his feet; the dislocation of the neck segments would have pinned the spinal cord and paralysed the arm and leg movements; and his legs would not have sustained dragging scratches without being dragged. And since I was insisting that he had died at least twenty-four hours before immersion, some other explanation for the sand in the stomach had to be found.

Might Smith or someone else have given Bissett water from the stream in an attempt to revive him after the fight? It was a possibility, but there was no circumstantial evidence to support it.

Could Bissett have fallen into the stream during the fight, and recovered after swallowing a mouthful? But in that case his coat, jacket, and trousers, which were all dry, would have been removed before the fight began, which wasn't likely.

Could Bissett have been accidentally dropped in the stream while being carried across it for concealment in the gypsy camp? Ah, this seemed more plausible. Gravely injured after the fight but not yet dead, Bissett might have been carried away by Smith, and perhaps one or more friends, his outer clothing being carried separately. Smith, who had also been drinking, might have stumbled while crossing the stream, so that Bissett fell and gulped water before being lifted again; and, yes, that would explain why Smith's ex-RAF trousers were wet to the knees. After a day and a half of concealment in the camp the body could have been dragged to the stream: there was thicket bramble between camp and stream, the very thing to have caused the dragging scratches on thighs and legs.

Far from destroying my original autopsy findings, the lab report about sand in the stomach had filled a gap in the reconstruction of the case. Although an alibi was raised Smith was duly found guilty of the murder.

In another case of this period that went straight into 'Taylor' the victim was also elderly, in fact eighty-eight years of age. She was Mrs Freeman Lee, the widow of a barrister, and she had lived in Maidenhead in a seventeen-room red-brick rambling mansion for forty years. Increasingly frail, senile and eccentric, she had allowed both the house and garden to fall into disrepair, coming finally to live, sleep, and eat (she had long ago forgotten the bathroom) in a ground-floor lounge.

It was rumoured that she had money, but no one really knew how much. She was seldom seen about, but occasionally tottered out to a shop or the postbox in shabby, once fashionable Victorian clothes, using a cane to steady herself.

On the morning of the first of June 1948, the local milkman saw that milk bottles he had delivered for the past two days were still standing on the doorstep. He called to a carpenter working in the neighbouring garden. 'Seen Mrs Freeman Lee about?' No, said the carpenter, and he came and peered through the lounge window and then through the letterbox on the front door: nothing. He called: no reply. The house seemed very still. He stood for a moment, then had another look. An embroidered cushion lay on the hall floor, and near by, close to an old Victorian travelling trunk, a woman's court shoe *and a bunch of keys* spreadeagled out of a leather key case.

It was enough. The old lady would never part with her keys, for she locked up everything in the mansion. The two men called the police, who picked up the old lady's solicitor on the way and forced a french window to get in. They searched the house but found no sign of her, though food, half prepared, lay dried up on a table in the disorderly lounge. P.C. Langton went to telephone his station to inform the Superintendent she could not be found. But Kenneth Thomas, the solicitor, who was also clerk to the Maidenhead Court, was idly toying with the straps that secured the old travelling trunk in the hall when something prompted him to open the lid.

Inside was the dead body of Mrs Freeman Lee, bundled up, gagged, and with her arms tied behind her back with a woollen shawl. Her head was battered and bloodstained, and the second shoe, possibly used to hit the old lady over the head, lay in the trunk beside her.

Detective Superintendent W. J. Crombie, the Berkshire CID Chief, was soon on the scene, and I arrived shortly after with my Miss Scott-Dunn. It was obvious that this must be murder, for a handkerchief gag and towel round the mouth and the way the arms were pinioned suggested she might have screamed and fought with an intruder. Her head injuries did not amount to much, and the autopsy quickly revealed that she had died of suffocation—not, as so many newspapers concluded, because she was clapped into an airtight trunk, but from the gagging. Murder had possibly not been intended, and after the handkerchief was first applied she was still doubtless able to breathe. It was this that made the case interesting to me. Any cloth gag soon becomes wet with saliva and mucus, and this moistening obstructs the 'pores' of the material. As the struggle to breathe becomes more laboured, for the gag becomes still thicker with saliva and mucus, until finally the cloth is impassable to air: it is a vicious circle.

That was what I thought had happened in the case of Mrs Freeman Lee. She had been dead at least two or three days when she was found, but the handkerchief gag was still moist. She had died not less than half an hour after her head injuries, and her body had been placed in the trunk within the first few hours after death, and had stiffened and become stained in the position in which she lay.

The house was in the most frightful chaos; everything was all over the place. No window, apart from the one used by the police, had been forced; so the old lady had probably let the intruder in by the front door.

The Chief Constable of Berkshire decided next morning to call in Scotland Yard, and Detective Superintendent William Chapman, the rubicond-faced 'Cherub', who had solved the Luton Sack Murder five years previously, arrived next day. He in turn called in the Yard's Superintendent Fred Cherrill, who had found the half thumb-print of Mrs Manton on a dusty pickle jar in the same case and was perhaps the world's No. 1 fingerprint expert.

Cherrill quickly realized the intruder was a practised burglar who had avoided leaving his prints anywhere. Door handles and jambs, window frames, furniture, and bedposts all drew a blank. Cherrill inspected a tumbler full of stout, two used plates with a fish knife and fork, another plate with a cover, the saucepan handle, fire tongs, poker, some food cans and a tea caddie—everything that might take a print. Nothing emerged but the old lady's everyday prints, everywhere. But Cherrill kept on 'dusting' around here and there in this frightful disorder, lens in hand, patiently seeking the clue that Crombie, Chapman, indeed everyone, knew was their only chance of tracing the murderer. And at last Cherrill found the vital clue. The lid of a small cardboard jewel box, no more than two by two inches, lay beneath the untidy folds of an eiderdown quilt thrown on the old lady's bed, and on the very edge of this he detected two half-impressions that looked like fingerprints; just the tips of two fingers that had held the lid to open the box.

Carefully he put it aside, and went on searching, but there was nothing else: Back to the Criminal Records Office at Scotland Yard for photographs and a search in the files.

Success! An identical print was on the CRO files. It belonged to a well-known housebreaker, George Russell, forty-five, who called himself a jobbing gardener. He was traced to an institution in St Albans and brought in for questioning. Had he ever been in that house? No. How did he account for prints being found there? He broke down and wept. 'Yes, I been there, to see the old lady about a job as a gardener'. But then he added some fatal words:

I was told she had a lot of money by another man. Did I murder this

poor aged woman for something she was supposed to have, and had not?
No. . . .

How could Russell have known old Mrs Freeman Lee 'had
not'—unless he himself had searched, indeed ransacked the house?

Russell was caught because he left his fingerprints at the scene.
They were as good as his signature because he had first made that
mistake fifteen years before, in Oxford, and his prints had gone into
the Criminal Records Office. There they lay, waiting to identify him if
he should make the same stupid mistake again. But it was not just this
that convicted him. When traced to St Albans he was found to be
wearing a scarf belonging to the old lady: he had lied about it, saying
he had 'bought it off a man in a Salvation Army Hostel'. He had lied,
too, about entering Mrs Freeman Lee's house, and he had no
explanation of the fingerprints on the jewelbox lid. Finally he had
made that silly mistake about the money Mrs Freeman Lee 'was
supposed to have, and had not'.

The judge at Berkshire Assizes, Mr Justice Hallett (a dear old boy
who had a reputation for chidings and interruptions that incensed the
lawyers in his courts, but was a fine lawyer himself on a good day)
pointed out to the jury that in those few words Russell had virtually
convicted himself.

As the jury came back into the Assize Court at Reading I noticed
two tall legal tomes that were perched on the desk in front of the
judge. The title of this two-volume work was *Russell on Crime*! The
jury announced the verdict of guilty, and Mr Justice Hallett
pronounced sentence of death. 'Russell' had this time failed 'on
Crime', and he paid the full penalty for a particularly despicable
murder.

It is strange, and in my opinion dangerous, that doctors can, and
often do, certify death without seeing the body. All that the law of
England requires is that the doctor should have been in professional
attendance during the patient's last illness and within fourteen days of
his death. Mrs Parkinson's doctor was therefore being conscientious
when he went to examine her body in the nursing home, in Worthing,
Sussex, after a nurse had phoned to say she had 'died suddenly'.

The news was not surprising. The old lady was seventy-six and
infirm, and had been going downhill for some time. But he went at
once to the nursing home, and examined the body within an hour of
the report of her death. The Matron told the doctor that the patient

had been 'troublesome' shortly before she died. 'We had to hold her hands and get her back into bed.' Small bruises confirmed this. Seeing no other mark of injury and having no cause for suspicion, the doctor issued a certificate giving the cause of death as 'chronic myocarditis, coronary arteriosclerosis, and senility', all of which she certainly had, as I was later able to testify after examining her inside as well as out; but they were not the cause of her death. If the doctor had looked more closely, and perhaps in a better light, he might have noticed an unusual blueness in her face and pinhead haemorrhages in the membranes of both eyes: from which he could perhaps have deduced that the true cause of her death was asphyxia.

Mrs Parkinson died on 25th September 1950. The next day the Registrar issued a burial order, and arrangements were made for her to be buried in the afternoon of 27th September. At about 2.30 p.m., when the funeral cortège was moving, a night nurse from the nursing home called on the doctor in a state of great agitation and, to his consternation, blurted out a story he 'could scarcely credit', he told me later. 'Such a nice matron. Couldn't believe my ears.'

His incredulity was understandable. Not many nurses' names lie in the criminal calendar. Waddingham is the only one most could bring to mind, and she committed a carefully planned morphine poisoning for gain. This was a very different kind of case. Matron was indeed a nice woman, as I was later (and most unexpectedly) to learn, and I cannot do better than forget her name.

What had happened—and the young nurse had kept it to herself for two days (and nights of sleepless worry) before she could contain herself no longer—was that old Mrs Parkinson had, on the evening she died, been very difficult over taking her sleeping pills. She'd spat them out, and abused both the young nurses who'd tried first and the matron who had come to help on hearing all the 'cufuffle'. Indeed, old Mrs Parkinson had spat in the matron's face and called her —well, the most nasty sort of names and things, and she'd struggled and shouted and the matron had had to throw herself across the old lady to keep her in bed.

'Murder! Help! Let me go, you . . .' screamed old Mrs Parkinson, by now quite beyond herself.

Matron's 'Be quiet' and 'Now stop it' had had no effect whatever, and suddenly this nice woman lost her quiet professional control.

'Matron seemed to be getting more and more worked up,' said the young nurse, who had been standing there getting pretty agitated herself. 'She grabbed the patient's hair with her left hand and pulled her head back on to the bed while she held both hands with her right. Then the patient shouted "Murder! Murder!" and', the nurse went on, 'Matron suddenly leaned over to the pillow on the right side and pulled one of the pillows over with her teeth. . . . Mrs Parkinson's face was completely covered . . . and Matron then buried her own face on the top of it, holding it down. Matron lay there for quite a long time . . . then got off the bed and said, "Take the pillow away".'

Nurse did so, and saw Mrs Parkinson's face was 'almost black and her tongue protruding and her eyes half closed'. A trickle of blood was coming from her mouth: she was still.

Nurse felt her pulse, but there was none. Nurse's watch said 10.05 p.m.

The matter might not have gone as it did but for what followed. Matron told the nurse to ring for the doctor, and added: 'You must never breathe anything of this to a living soul.' Matron rubbed the old lady's reddened wrists and removed a scarf they had wound round her legs. Worse was to follow. 'When the doctor comes, leave the talking to me.'

Nurse was told to tidy up, which she did. Like most nurses, she had a healthy respect for 'The Matron'. She said nothing when the doctor arrived, at 11.15 p.m., and Matron merely said 'Old Mrs Parkinson died suddenly this evening', as indeed she had. I felt sorry for the doctor, who was made to look as if he'd give a death certificate for any murder victim. Seen in a nice nursing home in bed, much as he'd seen her before, only dead this time, and told nothing of what had happened, how was he to be suspicious? True, the old lady's face was blue, but that could have had natural causes; and it needed a very close look in a good light to see the tiny blood spots in the eye membranes. He'd done just what most doctors would have done: gone to see the body, made sure she was dead, and, in the absence of a whisper of suspicion, given a certificate.

And then, when his former patient was on her way to the cemetery, there was the nurse in his surgery, pouring out her story of murder by the matron. The doctor immediately phoned the police, who stopped the burial, and within three hours I was performing an autopsy at the Worthing Public Mortuary, in the presence of the doctor himself and the local Chief of CID.

The blue colour had faded back from the face owing to the body lying on its back, but was well marked in the ears, nail beds and the livid stains over the back. I found pinhead haemorrhages in the scalp as well as the eye membranes, and to a lesser extent in the brain and the heart. There were similar changes to a more marked degree in both lungs.

Beyond doubt she had died of asphyxia, and since there were no marks of injury, even pressure, across the face or on the neck, it seemed reasonable to assume the nose and mouth had been suddenly obstructed by some soft object like a pillow or bedding. I knew the security of saying that the conditions were 'consistent with' rather than 'due to' when indications of detail were lacking.

The matron admitted to the police that there had been a struggle, just as the nurse had described, but said she had used the pillow only 'to leesen the sound of the noise' made by Mrs Parkinson. She did not add that she was well aware of the danger to life. She said the patient was still alive when she removed the pillow—'breathing, but not conscious'—and continued to breathe for another ten to fifteen minutes. If the pillow had suffocated her that could not be true. Nor could the matron's statement that she held the pillow over the patient for 'only a second or two'. And why not call at once for the doctor? The autopsy features were those of rapid suffocation, taking no more perhaps than twenty to thirty seconds; but not less than that, for the obstruction of breathing has to be maintained at least twenty seconds before asphyxial colour changes and pinhead haemorrhages can have time to appear. It was another case to put in Taylor.

No qualified nurse could have been ignorant of the threat to life involved, and the matron was charged with murder. The Worthing magistrates, bearing in mind the provocative circumstances, found there was no case to answer on that charge, and made the committal for manslaughter only; but the Director of Public Prosecutions restored the charge to murder, and the Crown counsel, Geoffrey Lawrence—later of Bodkin Adams fame—accused the matron of a 'deliberate, intentional, cruel act'. The judge, the tough but kindly old Travers Humphreys, plainly indicated that he was going to support a defence of provocation and instruct the jury that such a killing was manslaughter, and when she was found guilty of this he sentenced her only to three months' imprisonment; she had already served this while awaiting trial, so she walked out of court, free. Worse punishment had to follow, for her own Nursing Council had, in view of her conviction, to erase her name from the Register of Qualified Nurses. It didn't stop her working, but she could no longer call herself

SRN or take up any official post.

The sequel was as curious as any that has come my way. Nearly twenty years later my mother, who had reached ninety without suffering more than a broken wrist, became too old to live in the roomy old family house in Preston Park, Brighton, and I was fortunate enough to find a delightful nursing home for ageing folk in Hampstead, near the Heath. Matron was a charming cultured woman, who—I often said when visiting my mother—would, I hoped, still have her nice home available for me when the time came! My mother led a happy life there for several years before she died, quietly of old age.

But one summer, when I was visiting my mother, the matron said she was going away with her husband on a cruising holiday, 'and I'd like to introduce the matron who will be in charge here in my absence'.

She pressed the bell on her desk. 'Ask Mrs'—I didn't quite catch the name—'to come in, please.' And who, of all people, should walk in, but *the* matron! We had last 'met' in Lewes at the Assizes, but I could hardly use this sort of persiflage in shaking hands with her. She had gone a ghastly white on seeing me. I thought she might faint. My hostess plainly knew nothing of what had gone before, and it wasn't for me to speak of it.

Then the devil seized me, and I said, as casually as I could, 'I'm so pleased to make your acquaintance', and I added, without any malice, for I had indeed been sorry for her at Lewes: 'I do hope my old mother won't be any trouble to you.'

And, of course, she proved, as she had been before, a model matron. Nothing was ever said about the past. It was as telling a case as I could recollect of the tragic results of losing one's temper—even momentarily.

CHAPTER 15

'ACID BATH' HAIGH AND THE UNDISSOLVED GALLSTONE

'I'll come along to the police station. I might be able to help.'

It was much the same as Neville Heath had said before walking into the lions' den, never to emerge alive. John George Haigh, who showed the same bravado, with the same eventual result, was a very different kind of man. They really had nothing in common except that they were both murderers. Far from being a sex killer, Haigh was not even a lady killer; indeed, one of his mental symptoms, according to the defence psychiatrist at his trial, was his abnormal lack of interest in sex. Small, dapper, and attentive, he saved his charm for rich old ladies, like Mrs Olive Durand-Deacon and her friend Mrs Lane, whom he met in Kensington, London, at the Onslow Court Hotel. He interested her in his business of making plastic finger nails and she agreed to visit his factory. That was on Friday 18th February 1949.

'She didn't come,' he told Mrs Lane the next day. 'I waited an hour for her at the Army and Navy Stores but she didn't turn up.'

Mrs Lane was worried because her friend had disappeared. When she was still absent the next day Mrs Lane said at breakfast that she was going to the police. He offered to accompany her because he thought he 'might help'—an outsize under-statement.

A woman officer, Police Sergeant Lambourne, was put on the case, and that was bad luck for Haigh, for she distrusted him at sight. Her misgivings deepened when the hotel manager said Haigh was slow at paying his bill. Sergeant Lambourne reported her suspicions to Divisional Detective Inspector Shelley Symes, who checked with the Criminal Record Office at Scotland Yard. Haigh? Yes, he had a record, all right: fraud, theft, shady deals; convictions in Nottingham, Surrey, and London. No-one had pinned a crime of violence on him

yet. No-one had the merest suspicion that he had committed murder
at least five times in the previous five years: that a family of three
McSwanns and a Dr and Mrs Archibald Henderson had been wiped
out in London without trace . . . and all to Haigh's very considerable
financial gain.

Inspector Shelley Symes saw Haigh at the hotel and learnt that his
alleged factory was in Crawley. It turned out to be little more than a
storehouse, in Leopold Road. When the Sussex Police searched it
they found a .38 Enfield revolver and eight rounds of ammunition,
three carboys of concentrated sulphuric acid and rubber protective
clothing, and a receipt from a dry-cleaner's in Reigate for a Persian
lamb coat. The last item interested Inspector Symes most because
Mrs Durand-Deacon had been wearing a Persian lamb coat when
she was last seen leaving the hotel, and the cleaner's receipt was dated
19th February, the day after she disappeared. Then came a report that
her jewellery had been sold to a shop in Horsham for £100. Haigh,
who was still at the hotel, still eager to help the police, was invited to
return to Chelsea Station at 4.15 p.m. on 28th February.

This time the questioning was more personal, and after various lies
and contradictions Haigh realized he was not going to talk his way
out. In a break in the questioning he was left alone with Detective
Inspector Webb. 'Tell me frankly,' he said suddenly, 'what are the
chances of anyone being released from Broadmoor?'

Webb could have told him the chances were about 150 to one
against, but he very properly declined to answer.

'Well,' said Haigh, 'if I told you the truth, you wouldn't believe me.
It sounds too fantastic for belief.'

For the second time that evening he was formally cautioned.

'I understand all that,' he said impatiently. 'I will tell you all about
it. Mrs Durand-Deacon no longer exists. She has disappeared
completely, and no trace of her can ever be found again.'

Webb, playing the stolid copper, asked: 'What has happened to
her, then?'

'I have destroyed her with acid. You will find the sludge which
remains in Leopold Road. Every trace has gone.' A pause. 'How can
you prove murder if there is no body?'

Webb could have suggested that Haigh would shortly find out, but
in fact Haigh was doubly wrong. First because the Crown has to
prove a crime, not produce a dead body; James Camb was convicted
of the murder of Gay Gibson although he had pushed her body out of

a porthole on the high seas. Secondly, every trace of Mrs Durand-Deacon had not gone, as I was able to prove.

After this dramatic opening Haigh dictated a statement that took Inspector Symes two and a half hours to write down. It was a confession to the murder not only of Mrs Durand-Deacon but also of the three McSwanns and the two Hendersons, all of whose bodies he had similarly destroyed, after first drinking a glassful of their blood.

Mrs Durand-Deacon had gone with him to Crawley, Haigh said, and while she was looking at some plastic finger nails he shot her with his .38 Enfield in the back of her head. Making an incision in the side of her throat with a penknife, he had collected his statutory glass of blood and drunk it, or so he claimed. Then, removing her Persian lamb coat and jewellery, he had put her fully clothed body into a 40-gallon steel tank, and gone to the café across the road for a poached egg on toast and a cup of tea. On his return he had pumped concentrated sulphuric acid into the tank. Previous experience had taught him that after twenty to thirty minutes the tank become too hot to touch. Finally he had gone to the George Hotel for dinner and driven back to Onslow Court.

Three days later Haigh had gone to Crawley to examine his handiwork. After skimming off some fat and dumping it on the ground outside, he had pumped more acid into the tank. The next day, judging decomposition complete, he had poured off the contents of the tank outside the storeroom. His arrest and confession came seven days later.

Chief Inspector Guy Mahon took charge of the case within a few hours of Haigh's confession, and after a few more hours Jean Scott-Dunn and I were being driven in a police car to Leopold Road, Crawley. I did not have any great hope of finding much beyond residual acid sludge, but on the way down I pondered on what parts of the body might conceivably have escaped destruction.

The ground outside the storeroom was rough, with many small pebbles lying on the earth. Almost immediately, and I suppose rather impressively, I picked one up and examined it through a lens. It was about the size of a cherry and looked very much like the other stones, except that it had polished facets.

'I think that's a gallstone,' I said to Mahon.

Later, when laboratory tests had proved it to be a human gallstone (other mammals also get them), a police officer remarked to me that it was a lucky find.

'I was looking for it,' I told him. Women of Mrs Durand-Deacon's age and habits—69 and fairly plump—are prone to gallstones, which are covered with a fatty substance that would resist the dissolving action of sulphuric acid.

Almost immediately after this first find I made a second. Embedded in a thick charred greasy substance I saw several masses of eroded bone. When X-rayed, the largest of these proved to be the greater part of a left foot.

These were exciting discoveries, and I was confident that more interesting things might be found in the sludge. But not there. Covering an area of six feet by four feet, and three or four inches deep, this greasy granular mass needed patient sifting and inspection in a laboratory. I asked Mahon to have it all taken to the Metropolitan Police Laboratory, and at once he had his men lifting and packing it into wooden boxes. Altogether some 475 lb of grease and earth were transported to Scotland Yard.

Near the sludge we saw the green painted steel drum in which the body had been digested. I looked inside and saw a hairpin stuck in the grease at the bottom.

Inside the storeroom we saw three ten-gallon carboys, two of them partly filled with concentrated sulphuric acid, the third almost empty; also two stirrup pumps, a rubber apron and rubber gloves, and a gas mask. The walls were whitewashed, but I saw there was a patch of finely scattered red spots over the bench. Why should there be blood on that part of the wall? Well, Haigh said he had shot Mrs Durand-Deacon when she was looking at his artificial finger nails. If they were on the bench she would be standing in front of it and looking down; and if he had shot her in the back of the neck her blood could very well have spattered on the wall in just that place. I had the stains photographed and then carefully detached from the plaster. Later, in the laboratory, a precipitin test proved they were human blood.

I spent much of the next three days with Dr Holden and Superintendent Cuthbert in the laboratory at Scotland Yard, where we had the dirty, yellow, greasy, partly charred mass tipped out of the boxes and spread out over steel trays. From it we eventually extracted a mass of about 28 pounds of a yellow greasy substance that looked like 'melted' body fat; and when it was examined chemically it was proved to consist of animal fat. But there were other, much more interesting items in the sludge. I picked out two more human gallstones and a number of fragments of eroded bone, eighteen pieces in all. Later, after rigorous cleaning and detailed examination, using X-rays and the microscope, I was able to place eleven of them in the human anatomy. There was nothing about them to suggest they had come from more than one body. Osteoarthritis in certain joints and the fragile state of the uneroded bony tissues were evidence of late adult age. A groove in part of a pelvic (hip-girdle) bone showed it was female, and sex was confirmed by a handle of a red plastic handbag and the metal cap of a lipstick case. Superintendent Cuthbert made a plaster cast of the piece of left foot I had found, and it fitted the dead woman's left shoe. Finally, and most important, we found intact full upper and lower dentures.

So out of the sludge we had reconstructed the body of a person, an elderly woman with gallstones, a little arthritic, with false teeth, a left foot that fitted a particular shoe, carrying a red plastic handbag with a lipstick container in it; and I thought from the amount of body fat recovered that she was probably stoutly built. So much for Haigh's claim that every trace had gone.

Identity was another matter, and once again it was the teeth that did it. 'I could describe them from my notes before I saw them,' Miss Helen Mayo, Mrs Durand-Deacon's dentist, said at Haigh's trial. She had supplied the dentures about a year and a half earlier, and, luckily for us, Mrs Durand-Deacon had been a troublesome patient with inordinate gum shrinkage requiring many visits to Miss Mayo's surgery and, the dentist said, 'an exceptional amount of build-up and padding.' The dentures from the sludge were, 'beyond any doubt,' Miss Mayo said firmly, the dentures she had fitted for Mrs Durand-Deacon in September 1947.

Haigh's labours had been in vain. The remains of Mrs Durand-Deacon were identified as surely as if her body had never been given an acid bath.

Haigh, meanwhile, appeared to be going all out for Broadmoor. After the six murders to which he had already confessed he added three more, perhaps thinking, like Christie later, 'the more the merrier,' for police inquiries showed they were probably fictitious. He made much of the fact that he had drunk his victims' blood (and his own urine), and to the nine doctors who examined his mental condition before his trial he displayed, in the words of one of them, Dr Henry Yellowlees, a paranoid constitution; although the other eight, and three more who examined him after his trial, had no doubt that he was shamming insanity.

Meanwhile reports of Haigh's confessions had leaked out into Fleet Street, and the editor of the *Daily Mirror*, Silvester Bolam, decided to publish and take the consequences, although he may have miscalculated them. Describing Haigh as the 'Vampire Killer', although without giving his name, the *Mirror* entertained its readers with vivid accounts of the killing and blood-drinking and 'acid cremations' of the McSwanns and the Hendersons. The editor was charged with contempt of court, and the Lord Chief Justice and two other judges heard the case. Silvester Bolam apologized for his grave error of judgment. 'It is not an error of judgment,' said the Lord Chief Justice, Lord Goddard. 'It is a question of policy.' He ordered the proprietors of the newspaper to be brought before the court. 'Let the directors beware,' he warned. 'If they, for the purpose of increasing the circulation of their paper, should ever again venture to publish such matter as this, the directors themselves may find that the arm of this court is long enough to reach them individually.' The *Daily Mirror* was fined £10,000 and ordered to pay costs, and Silvester Bolam was sentenced to three months in Brixton Prison.

'It isn't everybody who can create more sensation than a film star,' Haigh wrote to his parents. 'Only Princess Margaret or Mr Churchill could command such interest.'

It was indeed a celebrated trial, with the Attorney General himself, Sir Hartley Shawcross, leading for the Crown, and a future Lord Chancellor, Sir David Maxwell Fyfe (later Lord Kilmuir), conducting the defence. ('I'm very glad to see that we have got old Maxy,' Haigh wrote from prison. 'He's no fool.') The judge was Sir Travers Humphreys, eighty-one years old and known for his inhospitality to any psychiatrist who ventured to appear as an expert witness in his court.

In R. *v* Haigh it was the Lewes Assize Court, and it was packed inside and besieged outside on 18th July, when the case for the prosecution began. It ended the same day, after thirty-three witnesses were called, because only four were cross-examined. Maxwell Fyfe had no questions for me, and none for Helen Mayo either. As a result there was still time for him, before we went home, to make his opening speech for the defence. He said he was going to call only one witness, Dr Yellowlees, and would ask the jury for a verdict of guilty but insane.

Three eminent London psychiatrists had examined Haigh at his solicitors' request, and the reports of two had discouraged the defence from calling them. The third was Dr Yellowlees, distinguished and widely respected, covered with degrees and honours, of the highest academic stature and authority. He spoke long and learnedly about Haigh's paranoia, but could not say he thought the accused was insane under the McNaghten Rules.

'Would it be right to say at once,' Maxwell Fyfe concluded his examination, 'that you are not prepared to express an opinion on whether he knew he was doing what was wrong?'

'That is so.'

In cross-examination the Attorney General pressed for an opinion, and finally got one.

'I will say "yes" to you if you say "punishable by law" instead of wrong,' offered Yellowlees.

'Punishable by law and, therefore, wrong by the law of this country?'

'Yes, I think he knew that.'

There was, of course, a perfectly rational explanation for all Haigh's murders, including the one for which he was tried. Murder was his business. His profit from killing the McSwanns was more than £4,000, and he had gained perhaps twice as much by wiping out the Hendersons. He had no such expectations from Mrs Durand-Deacon, but he was in debt and would get at least a breathing space with the proceeds of her jewellery (£100) and the Persian lamb coat (worth about £50).

The Crown had its own expert witnesses in court, ready to refute Yellowlees, but no refutation was needed. The jury took only eighteen minutes to make up its mind that Haigh was guilty and sane, and he was hanged in Wandsworth Prison.

The case had aroused a lot of interest in medical and scientific circles, and considerable doubt had been expressed as to the possibility of completely destroying a body with sulphuric acid. Wouldn't the stouter bones, such as the pelvis and femur, resist destruction? Dr Turfitt, Holden's deputy, performed a number of experiments to clear up the matter. He found that an amputated human foot dissolved completely in four hours, but a fresh leg-bone (of a sheep), stripped of its flesh, took four days. The important factor was the heat generated by the interaction of acid and the water present in a fully hydrated body. The bones all dissolved but the fat was resistant even to hot acid. It was lucky for us that Mrs Durand-Deacon was stout, for the preservation of our exhibits was due to the protective action of a film of fat.

But Haigh was too impatient. Another experiment showed that the acrylic resin of which the dentures were made would have disintegrated completely if they had been left immersed for three weeks. Even without longer immersion in the tank, these and other exhibits would have continued to disintegrate in the sludge, which was still strongly acid when we examined it. Superintendent Cuthbert thought that within a month most of our exhibits would have gone. It was clear from our digestive experiments that the gallstones could have lain in the yard for years, and still been proved human; but I should not have liked to present the DPP with an identification based on a couple of gallstones and a little body fat.

CHAPTER 16

WHO KILLED JOAN WOODHOUSE?

When I lectured to medical students, at Guy's or Oxford, I would often fasten their attention by saying casually, 'Now, I've had a number of prostitutes over the years'. A burst of cheering from the students, then I'd smile thinly and get into my subject.

These wretched girls know very well the risks they run in their casual pick-up relationships with men of all sorts. Though paid well enough, they are roughly treated, often gripped fiercely by the neck, half strangled, punched, and suffer fierce 'love' bites whilst giving satisfaction; and sometimes they die of the violence they receive.

Every pathologist, every crime squad up and down the country, has on the books a few sex crime murders—some of prostitutes, some of nice girls—that remain unsolved because the man responsible was a casual pick-up, not likely to be seen on the job, not a regular visitor or one of a circle of acquaintances. Fingerprints left on shoes or handbags only help when he is a 'CRO' man with his 'dabs' on the files at Scotland Yard, and even then a suspect can always plead he was not the only one there—at least not the last one to be with the victim.

In a case near Victoria Station to which I was called in 1945 a prostitute lay strangled with a stocking; some shirt fibres torn from the man she had fought with were found caught under a torn fingernail, and many prints were discovered on beer bottles and a bathroom washbasin. The tiny fibres corresponded with the texture and colour mixture in the shirt issued to men in the US Army Air Force, and a check on the service record prints of the 4,000 American Air Force men off duty that day brought *nine* of them with matching prints under the spotlight. No fewer than nine had visited the girl that night. They all admitted it. But no-one was going to admit being the 'last man in' or to strangling the girl. No charge was made, for there was uncertainty who was to blame; and it was wartime, and trained fighting men's services were vital in the European fray; more vital than the pursuit of other kinds of justice at that moment.

A more intriguing case was the murder of Joan Woodhouse, a respectable young woman who was sexually assaulted and strangled in the grounds of Arundel Castle, near Worthing, in Sussex. Her body was found almost naked; but her clothes, far from having been torn off in a sexual frenzy, were neatly folded and piled on a mackintosh, with a handbag and artificial pearl necklet on top. That was one of several mysteries in this famous unsolved case.

Joan Woodhouse, aged twenty-seven, worked as a librarian in Central London and lived at the YWCA Hostel at Blackheath. Her father, a widower, lived at Barnsley, in Yorkshire, and she arranged to stay with him over the August Bank Holiday week-end in 1948. She told her room-mate she was going to Barnsley when she set out at 8.30 a.m., on Saturday 31st July, carrying her handbag and a travelling case. But instead of going north she took a train to the south coast. At around 12 noon her travelling case was booked in at the Left Luggage Office at Worthing station: the cloakroom ticket was found in her handbag. But there was no return railway ticket. She had not been robbed. Two persons thought they had seen her alone in Arundel village, where she had probably bought the bottle of barley water that was found lying beside her. A single tablet of Luminal in an envelope was also found.

Joan's body was not buried or even covered by brushwood but lay ill-concealed by its natural surroundings of shrubs of a copse high on the side of steeply rising ground, and some distance from any road or path. Although secluded, it was a sunny spot. The body was found by Thomas Stillwell, an Arundel house painter, on 10th August. At my autopsy the next day I estimated death had taken place eight to ten days previously. I could not be more positive. A newspaper dated 31st July was found in her handbag so this estimate seemed about right.

She had been strangled, probably while lying on her back. I found typical 'fingertip type' bruises in the muscles on both sides of the voice box, and the right upper horn of the hyoid was freshly fractured. There were well-marked signs of asphyxia in the lungs and over the heart. Minor bruises under the scalp and over the spine and hip suggested she had been pressed on her back during the strangling.

The body was found lying on the back, face upward, stretched straight out across the slope of the hill, legs close together and the crutch closed. It was clothed only in pink camiknickers, brassiere, elastic suspender belt with securely attached stockings, and sandals. The camiknickers and brassiere had become twisted, as by the body sliding finally into the position in which it lay. The stockings were torn, and the skin grazed under the tears. The camiknickers had originally been fastened at the crotch by two buttons. One of these was missing, the thread being torn; how recently was not apparent. The other button was still fastened.

Joan's neatly folded clothes lay about twelve yards from the body, within view through a straight gap up the slope of the hillside, set immediately above the roots of several trees. Near the clothes I noted recent heavy chafings on the lower stems of some of the trees that I thought could have been made by the sliding pressure of footwear, perhaps in resistance to assault or during a struggle and escape downhill. A straight run down ended at the place where the body lay, and if she had been chased down this open track she might well have been thrown or forced on to the ground and strangled on her back.

The tidy removal of most of her clothing suggested she had either stripped to her undies to sunbathe or given approval to some kind of sexual attentions; but the buttoned crotch tie implied that these did not include normal intercourse. Yet there had certainly been penetration of a rough, forceful kind. I found 'fingertip type' bruises on both thighs, seven more bruises in the muscles round the entrance to the vagina, and a ball of pubic hair at the top of the vagina that could have been carried there only by the insertion of a finger or a penis. The detachment of the hair was further proof of the rough character of the sexual act. The body was too maggot-ridden for swabs for semen, and I could not tell whether or not she had been virgo intacta before the assault.

Detective Chief Inspector Fred Narborough of Scotland Yard was with me when I performed the autopsy, and he already had suspicions about the murder; but after three months of patient inquiries he had not found enough evidence to justify a charge. The case died away after a coroner's inquest: another unsolved murder.

But two elderly aunts of Joan Woodhouse were by no means satisfied. They hired a private detective to make further inquiries for them, and, as a result of what he found out, Scotland Yard decided eighteen months later to reopen the investigation. Narborough had retired, and Detective Superintendent Reginald Spooner was put on the job. I think he had little heart for it—he had already decided the scent was too old—and he did little more than conduct the whole case with meticulous care, and investigated Joan Woodhouse's life. She was a quiet girl who had had no known boy-friends, either in London or in Yorkshire, and had seldom gone out in the evenings or at weekends. She had celebrated her birthday with a quiet tea party in her room at the YWCA hostel. Spooner learnt that she had been extremely religious, and that she had been in a state of confusion about her beliefs shortly before her death.

Spooner did not consult me about my findings, which was a surprising omission for a detective of his standing considering the clear import of my post-mortem report. Even more remarkable was Spooner's own conclusion: he said he thought Joan Woodhouse was neither raped nor murdered, but lay down in the copse alone and committed suicide by taking sleeping tablets.

This was absurd. The body was too decomposed for a satisfactory analysis, but in view of the injuries no real question of her taking an overdose of drugs seemed even remotely likely. It was clear from the autopsy findings that she had been sexually assaulted and strangled. Why Spooner—a great detective, for whom I had considerable respect—should have ignored this evidence is still a mystery. Presumably he omitted to consult me because he did not want his suicide theory tested, and I can only imagine he did not want to admit defeat.

The case died again, but Joan Woodhouse's father was still not satisfied. With the help of his solicitors he applied for a private warrant against Stillwell, the man who had found the body. Five magistrates, sitting in Littlehampton, heard evidence against Stillwell for two hours, in private, and then issued a warrant committing him on a charge of murder.

It was the first such warrant for eighty-five years. The Attorney-General, Sir Hartley Shawcross, instructed the Director of Public Prosecutions to formally present the case at the Arundel Magistrates' Court, where Stillwell appeared on the murder charge almost exactly two years after the crime. The hearing lasted four days. After a retirement for consideration the magistrates said:

'We have carefully listened to the evidence placed before us, and we are of the unanimous opinion that there is not sufficient evidence to justify putting this man upon trial.'

At least two men 'confessed' to the murder of Joan Woodhouse, wasting the time of the police officers who had to make sure they were both cranks. One, living in Rhodesia, made a statement to the local police eight years after the crime. He had been living near Arundel when it occurred, and a chief inspector from Scotland Yard had to investigate: the story was palpably untrue. The other man confessed by telephone to Jack Carter, a journalist who later told the story in the magazine *True Detective*. Carter invited the man to his office, and also invited Scotland Yard to send a detective. The man made a detailed confession to Carter and admitted it was completely untrue when the police questioned him about it.

Such 'confessions' are a well-known phenomenon in well-publicized murder cases, the motive doubtless being to provide a little colour in an otherwise dull life; name in the papers, perhaps a photograph of the hooded suspect being led handcuffed to a police car. In another case of mine (in Hertfordshire, in 1956) no fewer than three notoriety-seekers had 'confessed' *before I had time to reach the police station*, only thirty miles from London; and I had set out immediately I was called.

That case was another sex crime, and it began for me with a phone call from the county CID. 'I've got a sex murder, doctor,' said Detective Superintendent Elwell, 'girl dumped in a ditch at Leverstock Green, very fresh.'

She had plainly been strangled. I could see the fold marks of a tightened scarf round the front of her neck, and her face was suffused and shot with tiny asphyxial haemorrhages. Her skirt was rucked up, and she wore no panties. 'She was dumped from a car,' Elwell told me. 'The boys who found her actually saw a man covering up the body with her coat, and driving off.' Including the boys, no fewer than eight persons had seen the man, and yet he was never caught. It seems astonishing that a man could be seen dumping his victim, seen driving away, have his car number taken by a schoolboy, be described in some detail, and yet escape into thin air. But that was, in fact, what he did.

Diane Setty was one of the girls who frequented the lay-by cafés of the Redbourne to Markyate section of the A5. She had been picked up that afternoon by a man in the Crow's Nest café and seen to get into his car at around half-past two. They were seen again twenty minutes later, apparently locked in a lovers' embrace in the back of the car, by two schoolboys cycling down Green Lane; seen by a Mrs Fitzjohn as the car drove away a few minutes later—she remembered the girl's face was 'twisted' (she was probably dead by then); the man was seen yet again on a bend in the lane by a farmworker who had to manoeuvre his car past him; and finally he was seen by three other schoolboys, farther down the lane, with the back door of the car open, soon after three o'clock. One of the boys heard leaves rustling, and they saw the man bending over something in the ditch, covering it with a coat (it was Diane's autumn overcoat) and then getting into the car and driving off at high speed.

One of the boys, who had aspirations to be a sleuth when he left school, took the car number: 'SUU 138', he wrote. Alas, when Elwell had the number traced it proved to be a three-wheel milk float! So much for amateur sleuths. The description of the man that was built up (there was no 'Identikit' in 1956) sounded splendid: 'a man of fifty to fifty-five, thickset, tanned and with an Italian look about him, horn-rimmed spectacles, greying hair' and so on . . . but it produced no-one.

I could not provide any further help from my examination, either at the scene or in the mortuary: there were no stray hairs or fibres clinging to the girl's clothing or caught in her fingernails. Two savage sexual bite-marks on the neck and breast were carefully photographed to scale, but there were no teeth to match them with. I hoped eagerly that there would be, for I was at this time developing the use of this relatively modern clue to a killer: I had had the first English case, against a man called Gorringe at Maidstone Assizes, in which a comparison of dental models and bite marks was successfully used in the Assize court.

This Hertfordshire case was exasperating for all of us: so much careful work, such painstaking labour from the police—they had taken and checked no fewer than 40,000 statements, examined 20,000 cars of the type (it seemed pretty certain it was a Rover, two-tone) for traces of the victim, held identity parades including vague 'suspects', made searches of woods and premises, rechecked months later . . . and it had all produced absolutely nothing, though it had looked so very promising at the start. The case petered out with the team engaged on it gathered rather gloomily at the old Hemel Hempstead Town Hall one afternoon to hear a coroner's jury bring in the inevitable verdict of 'Murder by some person or persons unknown'.

If the body in the ditch at Leverstock Green was, in Superintendent Elwell's words, 'very fresh', another body that came my way about the same time, found in Epping Forest, had been dead months rather than a few hours: but it had certainly been buried fresh, before the flies had had time to settle on it. There were no maggots and few beetles in that dank forest soil, and, unluckily for those who had buried it, the body was remarkably well preserved. Although it was found late in the year (on 29th October 1955) it was dressed in summer clothing, a floral frock and white shoes, which confirmed my estimate that it had been dead two or three months. As I disinterred it gently I noticed something strange about the position of the panties. They were rolled over at the waist and rucked up aslant on the hips, which suggested to me that they had been pulled on by the seat part instead of by the waist band. As it would be pointlessly awkward for a woman to pull on her panties in that unusual way I thought this service had been performed by someone else. Probably after death; after a sudden death, I suspected, the result of a criminal abortion.

I had the body, wet earth still clinging to it, removed in a heavy calibre cellophane bag to the mortuary. After cleaning up I was able to hand the police an opal ring and a wedding ring, a wrist watch, and a necklace of white beads, together with a portion of the flowered frock, and within twenty-four hours a BBC commissionaire had identified the objects as the property of his missing wife. She was a Mrs Eileen Taylor, aged thirty-one, and had disappeared on 4th August.

Meanwhile I had had the body brought to Guy's and immersed in a tank of weak carbolic, as I had done in the 'wigwam' murder. There were no maggots to drown this time, but again it proved a good way of softening off the caked earth and getting the clothing away without disintegration. On 1st November, at 3 p.m., I performed the autopsy.

In an ordinary autopsy the usual practice is to open the body with a throat-to-pubis incision and, in taking out the organs, to start at the top and work down. When a criminal abortion is suspected quite a different order is required. The commonest cause of sudden death in such cases is air embolism, and care has to be taken not to destroy the evidence of air in the womb and the veins running from it to the heart.

Air embolism can occur when a syringe is used to squirt soapy water from a bowl or jug into the womb to dislodge the sac of the pregnancy. Unless special care is taken to avoid it, the fluid level in the bowl or jug drops until the sucking valve of the syringe is uncovered and so sucks in air. The raw lining membrane of the womb is then exposed to frothed fluid, and air is forced into the veins causing air 'locks' or embolisms.

Because of my suspicions I placed containers ready to collect any fluid still lying within the vagina and womb; and, sure enough, when I opened them up, out ran fluid smelling unmistakably of soap.

I collected 25 c.c. of soapy fluid from the cavity of the womb, which still contained a partly displaced pregnancy sac. There was also air in the cavity, and I found both air and soapy fluid in the veins of the wall of the womb, from which they had reached the heart. L. C. Nickolls, at the Metropolitan Police Laboratory, later identified soap in both the wall of the womb and in a specimen of blood that I had removed from the heart. Clearly death was due to air and soap embolism.

Had the abortion been self-induced? If so, there were bound to be signs. The nozzle of the syringe would have had to be inserted into the small orifice of the neck of the womb, some four to five inches from the exterior, and it was hardly possible for a woman to do that herself without causing some injury. But I found no marks. That meant the operation was almost certainly not self-practised but had been done by someone 'with a degree of skill and knowledge of the parts'.

How long had she been pregnant? That was easy. The foetus was about fifteen centimetres long, the sex was clear, and hairs were appearing on the head: about four months.

Where had death occurred? Not in Epping Forest, for certain. She would have collapsed and died without warning not more than five to eight minutes after the inadvertent injection of air. That is the time it takes for the air to pass through the womb into the circulation, reach the heart, and get pumped to the brain and the other vital parts. The woman would have collapsed and died with alarming rapidity, taking those with her by surprise. Evidently their reaction had been to pull on her panties hastily and dump the body in Epping Forest. If they had not buried her so promptly, but given the blowflies time to lay eggs, maggots might have destroyed the evidence against them.

While I was doing the autopsy the police were interviewing Mrs Taylor's former employer, a City printing office manager named French. She had been both his secretary and his mistress. He admitted he had known of her pregnancy, but not of an attempt to terminate it; he also denied that he had ever been in Epping Forest. Unfortunately for him his wife, interviewed separately, told the police he knew Epping Forest very well. Even more significantly, a yellow pencil of Dutch manufacture had come into view as we disinterred the body, and several other yellow pencils of the same make were noted on his desk by the police officers who had called to interview French!

After some more questioning he admitted Mrs Taylor had died through an abortion that he had arranged.

'There's four of us in this,' he told the police. One of the others was a girl named Colbert, whom he had gone to see in South Street, Park Lane. After they had agreed on terms (£40) an appointment was made at an address in Bryanston Square, W.1. The abortionist was Mrs O'Regan, and her assistant was a former nurse named Williams. The first attempt was a failure. The second, forty-eight hours later, was fatal. French said he was waiting outside the bedroom with Miss Colbert when, after fifteen minutes, she was called in. A few minutes later she came out and said Mrs Taylor had fainted. French was sent for brandy, but on his return he was told 'She's gone'. He fainted. When he had recovered, and may have taken a stiff dose of the brandy, they discussed what to do.

According to French, three possibilities were on the agenda. One was to press her fingerprints on the syringe, put it in her handbag, and place her body in a busy street to be mangled by traffic in the dark of the night. A second was to throw the body in the Thames to disintegrate. The third, which they finally decided on, was to bury it in Epping Forest, 'where we used to ride together,' French said romantically. 'She loved the place.'

They 'walked' the dead woman downstairs and across the pavement into a hired car, then drove after dark to a spot in Epping Forest well away from the nearest beaten path, scraped a hole with car tools and their bare hands, and covered the body with earth and leafy debris, leaving it to rot away. After nearly three months they perhaps thought themselves safe, but someone walking in the forest caught sight of a white shoe in the brush and called the police. The womb is one of the last organs of the body to decompose, and soap, being antiseptic, effectively prevents the growth of micro-organisms; these two facts helped to preserve the body. Quick burial after death had also delayed decomposition.

The three woman named by French were traced and questioned. They were all surprised into admitting the abortion, but denied that Eileen Taylor had died on the premises. They said she had walked out into the street. The way she had died excluded this possibility. 'She couldn't have walked out,' I assured the police. 'She must have died within five to eight minutes of the injection of air into the womb.'

All four were charged with murder, but at the Old Bailey this was reduced by the Crown to manslaughter. French nevertheless pleaded not guilty, and his counsel called witnesses to prove an alibi. He said his statement had been put in his mouth by the police. The Crown had no difficulty in showing that his account of Mrs Taylor's death could not have been supplied to him by anyone, as I had not finished my autopsy or given my report when he made his statement to the police. The tell-tale yellow pencil clinched the case against him. He was convicted, with the three women, and sent to prison for three years.

One summer morning in 1971 I was awakened early by a telephone call.

'Inspector Shalter, Jersey, speaking for the Chief Constable, sir. We've got a girl on the beach. Sorry to disturb you, sir.' It was 4.30 a.m. 'Looks to us like murder. Would you . . . ?'

'Which way is the tide, inspector?'

'Coming in, sir. It's thirty or forty yards off still, but half an hour will see the spot covered. We've got good photographs.'

'Ask Dr Ralph to take temperatures internally straight away.' Dr Ralph was the local police surgeon and an old pupil of mine. 'I'll come at once.'

I took the 7 a.m. plane from Heathrow and arrived in Jersey forty minutes later. With Inspector Shalter I climbed down the steps of the sea wall to look at the scene.

'Beachcomber out early, saw the body on the sand in the half-light of dawn and ran up to the station,' Shalter said. Then he showed me the colour photographs, a magnificent series telling the whole story of the crime.

The girl's sunglasses, a handbag, and a headscarf had been found at the foot of the sea-wall steps. Blood soiled the back wall and had pooled on the sand. A couple of head hairs were stuck to the vertical wall. It looked as if the trouble had started there, and her head had plainly been bashed against the wall. From that point a long swerving trail was drawn in the sand, as if she had been dragged. Then there were three groups of kicked or rolled limb and head impressions—the latter were bloodstained, from the scalp wound—leading to where the body finally lay, sprawling, face up, legs apart. Her skirt, panties, and brassiere lay strewn on either side, leaving her almost naked. Blood lay at the vulva. Two impressions in the sand between her legs could have been made by a man's knees, and other impressions between the feet suggested toes digging in for purchase. Two sets of footprints led to (and away from) the spot, one set having presumably been made by the beachcomber. The police had made casts of both.

The girl's temperature, taken rectally by Dr Ralph, had been 97 degrees, out in the open, near naked on the beach: it must have shot up during dying, and the photographs showed why. Showers of tiny petechiae in the eyelids and conjunctivae indicated asphyxia, and finger 'blob' bruises and nail impressions on each side of the neck—more on her left, only one good one on her right—suggested a right-handed strangling from in front. The very thorough police surgeon had inspected the vulva for foreign hairs, taken vaginal swabs, and 'bagged' her hands in plastic bags, secured with Scotch tape round the wrists, for possible nail scrapings. The equally thorough and very swift-working police had searched for fly buttons, cigarette ends, pencils dropped from pockets in the sand.

In the mortuary I took the rectal temperature again and estimated the time of death as very shortly before the body was found. I also took further swabs, low and high in the vagina, and blood and urine samples for analysis. 'We'll have the levels by tomorrow morning,' I told Inspector Shalter. I had finished the post-mortem by 10.30 a.m. and had time for lunch before catching the 2.30 plane back to London.

The vaginal swabs were positive for semen, the blood and urine samples negative for alcohol and drugs. This was no drunken brawl but a plain assault and rape. The police quickly solved the case. A girl friend of the victim, whose name was Marilyn Dray, had seen her walking along the promenade at 2 a.m. with a young man of Polish-American extraction called Welch whom she knew to be working in the kitchens of a local hotel. As soon as the police started to question him he broke down and confessed. Conviction followed after a short trial in the baileywick of Jersey. It was a triumph for the Jersey police, who had acted so quickly to photograph all the 'locus' detail before it was obliterated by the rising tide. Later I sent a warm letter of commendation to the Chief Constable. The colour photographs were quite the most beautiful such records I have ever had of any scene of crime, showing in superb detail what the police surgeon had set out in his notes, and I still use them for detail in teaching. The case could really have been solved if I'd merely asked Inspector Shalter to send over the photographs—and stayed in my bed!

CHAPTER 17

COLD STEEL

A girl, sitting on a settee with her fiancé, was taunting her sister, who was cutting bread on the opposite side of a table, with her lack of success with boy-friends. The sister, exasperated, flung the bread knife hard across the table. The other girl turned her head away but the knife entered her neck behind the left ear. Her fiancé snatched it out, but she fainted and died some forty minutes later. It happened in Shoreditch.

The entry slit looked so trivial that it was hard to conceive a fatal wound. But at the autopsy I found that the blade had penetrated under the floor of the skull, through the jugular vein (causing minor air embolism), through the neck muscles between the arches of the first and second cervical vertebrae (dividing vertebral artery and vein) to reach, with the tip of the blade, the very centre of the brain stem.

It was, in fact, a typical stab wound, with little to see from the outside but with vital injuries beneath the trivial entry slit. It is the penetrating character of stab wounds that makes them so dangerous.

In another case the result of a casual 'knifing' was equally fatal. 'If the knife hadn't been on the table my husband wouldn't be dead,' sobbed Margaret Williams after the event; which was doubtless true, though no defence to the charge of murder. In this case it was an Austrian hunting knife, and it happened in Klagenfurt on 3rd July 1949. The victim of the stabbing was Squadron Sergeant Major Williams, of the Royal Corps of Signals, popularly known as Slim. He had fallen in love with Margaret at first sight, but unfortunately the feeling was not mutual. 'He was passionately fond of me but I only had a strong liking for him and did not love him,' Margaret said. 'As a matter of fact I was slightly under the influence of alcohol when he asked me to marry him,' as if lots of girls are not. But she added: 'I realized when I was sober that I had agreed to marry him, but I hadn't the heart to refuse then as I thought it would work out all right.' What a start!

They married in Scotland whilst on leave in April 1949. He was thirty-five; she was twenty-one. She stayed in the ATS and they were given a room in the YWCA Married Families Hotel at Klagenfurt, where they were both stationed. It was just one room, a bed-sitter; a fair test of marriage, and many marriages might have survived it. But, as Margaret said, their married life was not normal. 'When I agreed to marry my husband I told him that I didn't want to sleep with him until I had really fallen in love with him, and he agreed to this.' They did not quarrel much, she said: only when, after drinking, he 'wanted to make love to me'.

Their marriage, which was to end so abruptly, lasted less than three months. On Saturday 2nd July they went to the Grand Hotel, Anneheim, near Klagenfurt, for the week-end. There was a gala at the hotel, and they both drank too much but were 'quite friendly that night'. Not so the following night, when there was more drinking in the Sergeants' Mess. 'I got tight,' she said, 'and don't remember leaving there, or the journey back to Klagenfurt, but I think I remember Slim driving.' The truck was parked and they started walking to their quarters, but somehow a quarrel started. She told him to 'go to hell' and they parted company. She met four Austrians, one of whom she knew, and they went off to a Gasthof for a drink.

She was drinking and dancing when Slim came to find her. He was furious and threatened to call the Military Police; it was obvious there was going to be one big row in public if she stayed, so she walked to the door. Then 'two soldiers grabbed my arms, twisted them up my back, and marched me outside!' Slim said, 'OK: put her in the truck'. Poor Margaret was dumped without ceremony into the back of a big coal lorry. 'They kept me on the floor with my arms up my back until we got back to my quarters. They marched me upstairs still with my arms up my back . . . the front of my uniform was filthy with coal dust.' When Slim opened the door of their room they threw her in, but 'I swung round and kicked the smaller of the two soldiers. I also cursed him.' Slim then shut the door and, she said, beat her up. 'He had never hit me before.' Miserable, she got into her pyjamas and—it was probably her worst decision—decided she would sleep on the sofa . . . 'as he thought I didn't love him, and it would be a punishment to him for having dragged me all over the town.'

Things quickly grew worse. Slim asked her what she was playing at, so she told him. 'I said I was going to leave him. He told me that my mother had illegitimate children and he called me a bastard. That, of course, started another row.' She turned her back on him to get into bed on the sofa, but he caught her shoulder, swung her round, and slapped her face. 'You have jolly well asked for this,' he said.

She saw the knife on the table. 'It is my knife. I have cut bread with it, but I had been using it to make a wooden paper knife for Slim. I picked it up in my right hand, I think, and I raised it and said to Slim, "You big pig, I'll knife you if you come anywhere near me," or words something like that. He laughed and said, "You think I am scared of a little knife you cut wood with?" He came towards me and slapped my face once or twice. I hit him twice with the knife. I think the first time was on his left arm near his shoulder and the second time was farther down on his body. I saw it after, and it was down near the bottom of his ribs on his left side. He said, "That's done it", or something to that effect. He turned round and walked a few feet across the room to a chair and sat down.

'I got into bed on the sofa with the knife still in my hand and I looked across the room to where Slim was sitting and I noticed that his face had gone a grey colour. I leapt out of bed and went over to him. I noticed blood on the floor and also on his trousers, down the front on the left side. I got a handkerchief from somewhere and put it on the cut on his body and folded his arms across it to try and stop the bleeding. He didn't say anything but he was breathing and groaning. I felt his face and it was cold. I tried to warm it with my hands and told him I didn't mean it. He didn't take any notice and his eyes kept going up. I was scared and I ran downstairs and got the hall porter, who came up to the room. Then a sergeant arrived, and another sergeant, and I helped wet the bandages that they put on Slim's side. I was then taken away by one of the sergeants.' She found herself eventually in the famous No. 1 Court at the Old Bailey on trial for wilful murder.

'I did not intend to kill him, the thought was farthest from my mind. I just meant to stop him from hitting me so that we could carry on the same as before. I didn't want to kill him. I didn't mean to kill him.' If that was true it wasn't murder. But Lieutenant John MacIver, RAMC, who performed the post-mortem examination, thought Williams was already sitting in the chair when he received the second (and fatal) wound. That was much more sinister.

The Crown thought that MacIver, a young medical officer, might need support if it came to trial (as it undoubtedly would) and I was asked to put in some strengthening backing. I studied the papers and examined the exhibits, including the hunting knife, and Williams's heart, and concluded that MacIver was right.

The plan of the room and photographs taken immediately after the stabbing showed a trail of blood from the window to the chair, a distance of seven or eight feet. There was more blood on the seat of the chair and on the floor behind it.

One knife wound was above the left shoulder blade and the other had penetrated the heart. The first had bled externally; *the second had not*. Therefore all the blood across the floor had come from the shoulder wound: little had emerged from the stab over the heart for it had flowed internally into the cavity of the chest.

The question was this: could Williams have walked to the chair after he had also been stabbed in the heart?

Penetrating wounds of the heart had once been regarded as instantly fatal, but that view had long since been modified. Many cases have been recorded, in which such wounds have healed or been operated on successfully. But such cases occur only when the wound either does not enter one of the heart cavities or is so slanting that little blood escapes from it upon heart beat, owing to its slit valvular character. In this case the wound was certainly slanting, backward and downward, but the slit was gaping and must have poured blood internally and, I thought, must have caused more or less instant unconsciousness and death literally within a minute or two. The more or less instant collapse of blood pressure would also have stopped the bleeding from the shoulder. In fact, however, the stains on and behind the chair showed that the shoulder had continued to bleed for at least a minute after Williams sat down. Further, the heart wound had been delivered from in front and above, and the fact that it had not bled externally meant the victim must have been lying or sitting back: this reconstruction was fundamental to the prosecution's case.

The exhibits I examined included the chair and also the shirt and vest which Williams had, according to his wife, taken off before she stabbed him. Both were heavily bloodstained, and the shirt bore a slit corresponding to the shoulder wound. *Neither garment bore a slit corresponding to the stab to the heart.*

It seemed to me clear that Williams had been stabbed in the shoulder, walked to the chair, *removed his shirt and vest* and sat there for a minute, partly incapacitated and in pain, and was perhaps trying to staunch the alarmingly copious bleeding from his shoulder when his wife stabbed him a second time, through the heart. 'The situation and the character of the wounds as a whole,' I reported, 'is characteristic in my view of a deliberate assault of a homicidal kind, clearly likely to cause death even to a lay mind.' Mrs Williams must have dealt this mortal blow to her husband as he sat wounded and bleeding, in the chair.

But she looked a lonely, pathetic figure as she stood in the dock at the Old Bailey and pleaded 'Not guilty' to murder, and it was obvious as the case unfolded that she had had a rather raw deal with her 'Slim'. The prosecution, led by Anthony Hawke, was humane: and with three doughty counsel defending her (two K.C.s, Christmas Humphreys and Edward Clarke, and a future Attorney-General, Peter Rawlinson) everyone expected, and I think most of us hoped, that she would not be convicted of murder. I expected a severe cross-examination from Humphreys on my view that Williams could not have walked to the chair if he had already been stabbed in the heart. I had published, as he doubtless knew, cases of my own in which the victim had remained conscious and been capable of movement—in one case running to a window and jumping out—after being stabbed in the heart.

To everyone's astonishment my views went unopposed. 'No questions,' said Christmas Humphreys as I turned to face him, expecting a really tough cross-examination. Mrs Williams's heart must have sunk. What was going to be said for her?

It emerged later. It was to be left to her counsel's pleadings. 'How much time have you spent since, wondering what happened in the room that night?'

'Every night,' said Margaret weakly.

'Do you remember clearly?'

'No, I must have been drunk.'

'It is said you deliberately stabbed him as he sat in the chair.'

'No,' she said. 'I did not do that.'

Mr Justice Streatfield, a grim criminal judge, put it fairly to the jury. 'There are two alternatives,' he said, 'the first being murder; the second, which is the nature of the defence, is that the act of stabbing was in the nature of self-defence; that she was being chastised by her husband . . . and was entitled to defend herself.' The judge also offered the jury the verdict of manslaughter on the grounds that she resented chastisement and was provoked into reacting, not unreasonably, perhaps, to the hiding he was giving her.

The jury pondered for two hours and twenty-five minutes. Then they returned to their box, and the foreman, asked their verdict, said in a clear voice 'Guilty of murder'. The judge had no alternative but to sentence her to death.

It seemed to everyone a harsh verdict, and I was much relieved when the Home Secretary granted her a reprieve.

Christmas Humphreys was the Crown counsel in another stabbing case that occurred in the following year, much nearer home, in a block of flats near Waterloo Station. On 8th December 1950, a woman living on the fourth floor opened her door at 7.30 a.m. and saw a body on the landing. It was lying face down in a pool of blood outside the flat of William Donoghue, a 42-year-old bus conductor: and Donoghue himself was standing in the doorway, apparently dazed and 'in a panic', the woman said afterwards. He kept muttering, 'Is it a dummy or a body? Take it away?' And that was the start of the Waterloo Dummy Case, as I labelled this most bizarre affair.

By the time the law arrived, in the shape of P.C. 107 M, Donoghue was back inside his flat, still very shaken. 'If that is a real man, I done it,' he told the constable. 'He came home with me last night. I thought he was joking with me. He was lying on the bed making gurgling noises. I must have struck him with the bayonet and dragged him out on the landing.' All of which the constable carefully wrote down in his notebook before taking Donoghue to Southwark Police Station, where he made a longer and more coherent statement.

The evening before, Donoghue said, he had gone out drinking at six o'clock. He knocked back six or seven bottles of Guinness in the Prince Albert, leaving at about 9.45 with an unopened bottle of gin in his pocket, bound for the Brunswick Arms. There he met a friend, Thomas Meaney, aged sixty-three, who worked as a driver of a Black Maria. Meaney had so far drunk two pints of mild. Donoghue bought him another half, and laced both their drinks with gin. They left at closing time, 10.30, both very unsteady, and went to Donoghue's flat. They finished the bottle of gin, and then Meaney went to sleep on the bed while Donoghue dozed off, leaning on the table. He woke up cold and tried to get into bed. He had evidently forgotten about Meaney, for he found what he took to be a dummy figure on his bed and thought friends had put it there as a practical joke. He dragged it off to the floor, where it fell 'like a sack of coal'; then he stabbed it a number of times with a bayonet, a souvenir of the Second World War, which he normally used as a bread knife. He saw red stuff but took it to be juice from a theatrical tube arranged by his friends to mimic bleeding—part of the practical joke. Finally he dragged the dummy out on to the landing and went back to bed. He awoke at 7.20, saw blood all over the floor, opened the door and saw Meaney's body and suddenly realized what he must have done.

Detective Chief Inspector Wright found that as far as it could be checked, Donoghue's astounding story seemed to be true. When he and Meaney had left the pub they were both very drunk, but he had appeared the drunker of the two, and Meaney was giving him a helping hand. They appeared perfectly friendly and there was no hint of a quarrel. No other possible motive emerged. The police surgeon who examined Donoghue found no wounds of any kind to suggest a struggle. An empty gin bottle stood on the table, and a bloodstained bayonet. Another resident of the block had awakened at 11.55 p.m. and heard 'three distinct thuds', then silence. I also had estimated that death had occurred about midnight.

Meaney's clothing was not torn or disordered but merely rucked up round the shoulders. His coat collar was bloodstained, outside and inside, and so were Donoghue's hands; in both cases the blood was Meaney's group. A trailing smear of blood led from the landing into Donoghue's flat, where a lot more blood had been both splashed and smeared over the floor, especially near a sideboard with a broken front leg.

Meaney had been stabbed sixteen times in the left side of the head and neck. Cuts in the carotid artery and the jugular vein must have caused unconsciousness within seconds and death in a few minutes. Blood had poured into the throat and out of the nose, mouth and neck wounds. He had sliding marks on the right cheek and temple, as from being dragged across the floor. There was also bruising of the brow, eyebrows, nose, upper lip, chin, and chest that could have come from being dragged out and deposited face down on the landing floor. I found no 'protective' wounds of any kind on his hands, although both were stained heavily with blood. Thus my report confirmed all and more of the details in Donoghue's story and contradicted none.

I took samples of Meaney's blood and urine and sent them to the Scotland Yard laboratories for the measurement of alcohol. The results were astonishing. The blood figure was 347 mg per cent and the urine figure 450 mg per cent—the equivalent of about ⅘th pint of gin or whisky in the circulation. Most people, used to a drink or two, begin to feel dizzy, unsteady, confused, or nauseated and clammy at blood alcohol figures of 150 to 200 mg per cent; 250 mg is a serious level, sufficient to send a car driver to prison in Denmark or Germany whatever the circumstances; 300 mg is dangerously high, 350 mg close to menacing life, and 400 to 450 mg is fatal in itself for most people. No wonder there were no protective injuries or other signs of resistance!

Those were the figures for Meaney, apparently the more sober of the two when they left the pubs: what could Donoghue's have been?

Unfortunately it was too late to find out. In Scandinavia, where the significance of a blood alcohol reading is better understood, it would have been taken immediately as a matter of course, with or without Donoghue's consent; probably it would have been taken in the United States or Germany, too. But there is a reluctance in England, except in driving offences, partly to avoid a technical assault and partly to avoid pressure on a suspect to give evidence that might be used against him. In point of fact it would probably have been to Donoghue's advantage. If his blood alcohol reading had been measured when he was taken into custody it would have been simple to calculate with near accuracy the figure at midnight. As it could hardly have been less than Meaney's, it would have lent credence to Donoghue's extraordinary tale.

Two questions arose. First, although there was unequivocal proof of felonious homicide, could Donoghue have formed the evil malicious intent to kill? If his blood alcohol was not less than Meaney's at the time of the incident (and it was probably more) it was at a level where ordinarily a man is quite incapable of clear thinking, of forming a felonious intent, of harboring malice.

Secondly, could he have been so drunk as to be incapable of knowing he was stabbing a man? If it was a dummy, or if he honestly believed it was, could that constitute an excusable homicide, or even make the event an accident?

The case was of such medico-legal interest that John Maude, K.C., undertook to defend Donoghue. He was tried at the Old Bailey in February 1951, before Mr Justice Donovan. Donoghue was skilfully described by his counsel as 'a quiet, inoffensive, and respectable little man'. Dr Matheson, the Principal Medical Officer at Brixton Prison, who had examined him on reception, gave the helpful opinion that 'the degree of drunkenness present at the time of the alleged offence was such that he could have mistakenly believed he was, in fact, stabbing a dummy and not a human being'. The Director of Public Prosecutions concluded there was insufficient evidence to proceed on a charge of murder, and the prosecution accepted a plea of guilty to manslaughter. Donoghue was sentenced to three years' imprisonment.

A more straightforward stabbing case came my way in 1955. On 18th February, at about 8.45 p.m., a young soldier on demobilization leave entered the Blue Kettle café, near the Angel in Islington, for a cup of coffee. While he was drinking it six youths entered, several of them dressed in the current 'Teddy Boy' fashion. The soldier made it clear that he disliked their style, and a quarrel began between him and a youth called Xinaris, known locally as 'Nicky the Greek'. Threats were exchanged, and both men rose to fight, but they were restrained; then they agreed to settle the matter outside. The café was in the process of being closed, as it was after 11 p.m.

In the cobbled yard each removed his coat and jacket, and they faced up to each other. There seemed little doubt that the soldier struck the first blow with his fist. What happened next had to be reconstructed after the event. The certain fact is that when a patrolling constable heard the disturbance and went into the courtyard to investigate, it was empty except for the soldier, who was lying on his back stabbed in the throat. It was then 11.20 p.m.

The constable ought then to have called for a doctor, who would have found the soldier either dying or more probably dead and left the body undisturbed for photography to record the exact lie at death and the positions of bloodstains and of a knife lying on the ground. Unfortunately the constable summoned an ambulance, and a very different train of events began. On arrival at St Bart's Hospital the body was merely certified 'dead' at 11.30 p.m. by a young house officer who then went back to his duties. The night porter removed the soldier's clothing and stuffed it into a bin: then, without any care for possible contact traces of dirt, blood, hair, or fibres, put the naked body in a refrigerator, where it stayed for eight hours. Meanwhile the constable had picked up the knife and shown it to the café proprietor,

who added his fingerprints to the constable's. Medico-legally it was
a disastrous start to the case.

By the time the CID took charge they found nothing at the scene of
the crime except a few dried bloodstains and a flick-knife covered
with various fingerprints. The body was quite cold when it was at last
transferred to the public mortuary, the refrigeration having wrecked
any chance I had of estimating the time of death from the loss of body
heat. Not that it mattered much in this case. I found three wounds: a
stab on the left buttock, a slash across the left upper arm, and the fatal
deep stab wound, which had severed a carotid artery and opened up
the windpipe. Blood had poured out, and the soldier must have died
within a minute or two. His only other injury was a minute graze on
the back of his left hand.

Fortunately the six youths were a well-known local gang—all with
criminal records, mostly for stealing—who hung out in a near-by Fun
Fair Arcade. The CID picked up one of them, Rudolfo Farace,
known as Lou or Tony, and he was very helpful. He said Nicky had
asked him to get his knife sharpened a few days previously, and he
had handed it back, at Nicky's request, in the Blue Kettle 'just before
the trouble started'. The proprietor corroborated this, saying he had
heard Nicky whisper 'pass if over' and had suspected he was asking
for some sort of weapon. Out in the courtyard, said Farace, he had
seen Xinaris pull the knife from his trouser pocket and stab the
soldier in the left leg. 'I got frightened and went back into the café.'
They had all run off in various directions. On the way out Farace saw
the soldier on the ground 'and blood was spurting out from his neck
or his face'.

The detectives found Xinaris the same night, little more than
twenty-four hours after the crime. 'He struck me.' was the defence. A
police surgeon confirmed that Nicky had a black eye. 'I punched him
back . . . he drew a knife at me. I got hold of the knife, and then I don't
know what happened, everything went hazy. He fell to the ground so
I ran off.' But Xinaris had no wound to show he had either been
struck by the knife or grappled for it: there was no trace of a cut on
either hand. There were no bloodstains on his clothes, and the blood
smeared on the knife was of the soldier's group, not Nicky's.

He was arrested and charged with murder, and again Christmas
Humphreys prosecuted. Xinaris was defended by E. L. Mallalieu,
Q.C., M.P., who pressed Farace to admit that the knife was his and
he had given it to the soldier, not to Nicky, because Nicky had stolen

Farace's girl-friend and he wanted revenge. A neat little theory, but unsuported by any evidence. Then Mallalieu tried to persuade me to admit that the wounds could have been the result of an accident during the rough-and-tumble. I had already considered and rejected this possibility because the wounds in the buttock and the neck were stabbed clean and deep and bore no sign of the blade being turned or of the knife handle crushing the skin, as it might if the body were rolling on it. The wound in the neck was telling, for it was a deep stab into vital parts; and, of course, there was the significant fact that the accused bore no sign of having grappled for the knife. He was convicted of murder and sentenced to death. An appeal was lodged but dismissed as 'frivolous' and 'a compilation which reflected no credit on the author'. However, the Home Secretary commuted the sentence to life imprisonment: it was at a time when the sentence of execution was becoming regarded as somewhat barbarous and out of line with modern 'civilized' world practice: they were, after all, a lot of irresponsible youths.

CHAPTER 18

WITH CAMPS AND TEARE : CHRISTIE AND EVANS

In the late 1940s it became increasingly clear to Camps, Teare, and myself that we needed some common ground for the discussion of cases of unusual difficulty. Until then Spilsbury, Taylor, Temple Grey, Stephenson, and their colleagues had each pursued their work in an isolation that seemed to us both unnecessary and a little risky; it was increasingly being said that Spilsbury had no comparable opposition if there was an area for any difference of opinion, and that this was not good for justice 'being seen to be done'. It applies to us all: we need well-informed opposition, proper testing of our views and an occasional grilling in court to ensure real fair-mindedness.

We therefore invited the only man who at that time stood head and shoulders above everyone in both academic stature and experience, Professor (later Sir) Sydney Smith of Edinburgh University, to be first President of a new society, an 'Association in Forensic Medicine'. One evening, shortly after, we four met at a little Soho restaurant, appropriately named the 'Bon Accord', and founded a body that has flourished ever since, and now numbers every pathologist in the United Kingdom whose services may be called upon for crime work.

For the next ten years or so we 'Three Musketeers'—the name had stuck—took on the bulk of the medico-legal work in and around the metropolis. There was ample, for Spilsbury and Taylor had left the scene, and there was no hint of competitive envy if one or other of us was called to a 'big case'. I had the classical 'Baptist Church' case of Dobkin, the Luton 'sack murder', Heath and Haigh; Camps had Sergeant Marymont of the USAAF, Setty (Hume), and later Christie; and Teare had the 'porthole case' of Camb, the 'cleft chin' murder, Podola, and later Evans. We were all hard put to get through our day's work (so many autopsies, attendances at court, often at the quixotic convenience of the law) and the need that Spilsbury never had to build up the medical school teaching and research departments that the university had at last entrusted to us.

In spite of all this, Teare and I sensed that 'FEC' was increasingly grudging us cases that he would have liked to be called to. With increasing frequency he could be seen in court behind defence counsel in cases in which Teare or I appeared for the Crown, to try to create uncertainty, often on very flimsy grounds, in the minds of the jury. It was not in the interests of justice, and on several occasions it drew critical comment from 'Joe' (later Sir Richard) Jackson, Assistant Commissioner (Crime) at New Scotland Yard. Matters came to a head in a curious reversal of roles none of us expected when a man whose mother-in-law's body was found in a tin trunk, months after her death, was charged with her murder and committed for trial at the Chelmsford Assizes on the medical evidence Camps had given before the magistrates. He had said she had died of asphyxia. Though the body was dried up and disintegrating, Camps had told the magistrates that he had found the tiny pinhead-sized petechial haemorrhages in the lungs that gave proof of this.

Derek Curtis-Bennett, K.C., a very experienced counsel, found this difficult to accept when he took up the defence: he put the matter to each of us.

'Quite beyond the bounds of possibility,' I said, looking at the police photographs of the mummified body. The lungs were shrivelled and disintegrating—dust to dust.

'Camps has gone too far this time,' commented Teare drily.

It was just as Curtis-Bennett thought: proof of asphyxiation was lacking. 'I'll need you both in court,' he said, 'though I doubt very much if I'll need to call either of you.'

He had Teare and me sit close behind him, just to be seen by Camps as Curtis-Bennett rose to cross-examine. It worked. Camps, looking deflated, failed to repeat the evidence he had put on paper with regard to petechiae, and when he said 'I could not be certain, but I thought . . .' Curtis-Bennett realized he had gained his point. Turning round to both of us, he said, in a voice loud enough for the whole court to hear, 'Thank you, gentlemen, I think I do not need you further.'

That is what lawyers call 'not coming up to proof': failing to repeat in court what you set out in your original report. If Camps had not had firm and public opposition from Curtis-Bennett, backed by

Teare and myself, he might have got away with evidence that was not (he must have known) proper in the circumstances.

Edgar Lustgarten, himself an experienced counsel with an astute eye for detail, commented, some years later, in reviewing Robert Jackson's biography of Camps, that though setting out confidently enough, Jackson was 'first surprised, then halted, finally overwhelmed, by unfavourable evidence from sources unimpeachable' that the subject of his biography was not as sound as a Crown pathologist is expected to be.

It was disappointing. Camps had great enthusiasm for his job, and very considerable ability. But to aver, as he frequently did, that he was providing a 'new brand of forensic pathology and laboratory service' which his colleagues could not equal, was hardly calculated to maintain good working relations with his fellows: it was, moreover, untrue.

In 1960 he formed a separate 'Academy of Forensic Sciences' which he invited solicitors and barristers engaged in criminal bar work to join in an endeavour to improve standards in the presentation and handling of medical evidence in court. Again he made the mistake of belittling his fellow pathologists—this time the hundreds of hospital consultants, saying that they were not competent to perform medico-legal autopsies and court work. It was no surprise that when the Royal College of Pathologists was formed, in 1963, his colleagues failed even to nominate him for the Council, a body to which Teare and I were both elected. Camps was bitterly disappointed by this: he refused to discuss the matter with anyone, and drew further into an isolation which was in sad contrast with the amiable companionship that had existed when we all set out together on our 'careers in crime'. He died in 1973, refusing to submit himself to surgery that he quite rightly knew had been needed months earlier: an unhappy man, I felt, who had never sought, as we all have to do, the respect and goodwill of his own colleagues.

Donald Teare was a much more endearing colleague: a solid, likeable man with a good sense of humour, competent both in the field and in the witness box, very like his 'guv'nor' at St George's, Dr John Taylor—the only sound 'opposition' Spilsbury had ever encountered in court. Teare and I found our attitudes very similar, and I cannot remember a single occasion during the forty years we have worked together on which we have differed substantially in professional matters. Once only, at the Old Bailey, a 'situation' was

created by a defending counsel to whom I was giving help over an
abortion case:

'Can you,' he said to Teare in cross-examination, 'think of any
single person more experienced in this field than Dr Keith Simpson?'
He was, of course, 'building me up' for his own purposes.

Teare was equal to the occasion. He smiled disarmingly, then: 'You
embarrass me,' he said, after a pause.

He and I had, of course, equal experience in the field: it just
happened that I had written on an aspect of abortion deaths that gave
my counsel an opportunity of putting up a defence for his client.
Teare listened to a long quotation from an article I had written on
delayed deaths from air embolism in abortion, then said:

'Yes, that is of course a possibility.'

Honour was even. And we both enjoyed the situation: it had not
escaped the judge, either. He smiled.

Seldom did Camps respond with such charm. To him opposition
was a personal challenge.

Once, and only once, we three were 'on the job' together. It was a
famous case, probably the most famous for all of us.

The occasion was an exhumation, and the disinterment was
unusually well attended in spite of the unsocial hour. We met in the
Roman Catholic cemetery of the Royal Borough of Kensington at
Gunnersbury Lane on 18th May 1953, at the usual exhumation hour
of 5.30 a.m.; those who arrange these affairs, and doubtless sleep
through them, have always assumed that if timed at the crack of dawn
an exhumation will be a quiet, private affair. To make doubly sure,
and because this was a *cause célèbre*, the authorities had erected
barricades, closed the cemetery to unauthorized persons, and sent a
patrol of thirty constables to keep out the public and the Press. In
spite of these precautions hordes of newspaper reporters and
photographers with telescopic cameras lined the raised Bath Road
embankment as the coffin was lifted; and, as usual, many early risers
found time to stop and stare on their way past the cemetery railings in
the hope of a glimpse of what was, admittedly, no ordinary
exhumation. It had been asked for by the defence lawyers, not the
prosecution; the prisoner protested his guilt, not his innocence; and
another man had already been hanged for the double murder three
years before.

I represented the accused, and the Attorney-General had nominated Camps to carry out the post-mortem examination. Teare was with us because he had carried out the original autopsies in December 1949. A fourth doctor, not a pathologist but a psychiatrist, Jack Abbott Hobson, was present in the background for the defence.

We looked down into a pit nearly five feet deep, for the headstone had been lifted and most of the earth removed before we arrived. the coffin was the top of six in a common grave. The lid was cleaned and the plate exposed and photographed by the police. Then the coffin was freed at the sides and lifted out. The undertaker, the mortuary superintendent, and the gravedigger solemnly identified the plate. It said there were two bodies in the coffin: 'Beryl Evans, aged 19 years' and her daughter, mis-spelt 'Jeraldine', of 14 months. We were pleased to see that the wood, which was one-inch elm boarding and kerfed, was in good condition, with the lid only slightly warped. I consented to a slight raising of the lid to allow the escape of gases before the coffin was removed from the cemetery. Then my Jean Scott-Dunn and I escaped from all those prying eyes and cameras to breakfast at the de Vere Hotel in Kensington.

We reassembled at 8.15 in Kensington Mortuary, where we were joined by L. C. Nickolls, Director of the Metropolitan Police Laboratory, and two Chief Inspectors: George Salter, the Scotland Yard liaison officer, and George Jennings, who had identified the bodies at the original autopsies and was going to try to do the same again. Jennings was the officer who had taken down Timothy John Evans's confession and charged him with murdering his wife and daughter.

Evans was convicted only of the murder of his daughter, though most of the evidence was directed to prove that he had murdered his wife. The reason for this paradox is that English criminal law procedure does not allow a person to be tried for more than one murder at a time but may allow evidence of murders other than the one for which he is tried. When there are two or more indictments, the prosecution chooses which to take first. The case against Evans was much stronger for the murder of Beryl, and she had been killed first; but the prosecution chose to proceed with the murder of the child because it carried no danger of a provocation-and-manslaughter defence. The two crimes were considered a single transaction, and after a legal wrangle the judge allowed all the evidence concerning the murder of the wife. Everyone involved—prosecution, defence, the judge, and later the three learned judges of the Court of Criminal

Appeal—accepted that both murders had been committed by the same person, and it seemed indisputable at the time; but another judge, Brabin, reviewing the evidence sixteen years later, was to conclude this assumption was probably false. There is a common belief that the Brabin Inquiry found that Evans did not kill his wife. As a matter of fact it found that he probably did.

Evans had been convicted of the murder of his daughter Geraldine on 13th January 1950, after a trial at which he refuted his confession to the murder of both Beryl and Geraldine and accused the chief witness against him, John Reginald Halliday Christie, of having committed both murders himself. Christie had had opportunities as he lived in the same house, but as he had no apparent motive the Crown counsel dismissed the accusation as 'bosh'. The jury concurred and Evans was executed.

Three years later the remains of six more female bodies were found in the same house. Two had died several years before Beryl and Geraldine, the other four afterwards. When Christie was caught, wandering on the Thames Embankment near Putney Bridge, he admitted he had killed them all. Later he confessed also to the murder of Beryl Evans, and that was where I came in.

There was no mystery about Christie's motive for murder, which had been thought non-existent at the trial of Evans. Camps and Nickolls discovered this before his arrest. Two of the bodies were only skeletons that had been buried in the garden about ten years before; but the other four had been dead only a few months and, by chance, had been stored in cool dry surroundings (Christie's kitchen alcove) with some air movement, almost perfect conditions for preservation. All were more or less clothed, but none wore knickers. In the most recently dead (about twenty days) Camps found whitish material exuding from the vulva and inside the vagina. He took vaginal swabs from all four bodies, and under the microscope three of these showed the presence of spermatozoa. The exception was Christie's wife.

The exhumation of Beryl and Geraldine Evans had as yet nothing to do with the Evans case, which was officially filed as solved. Christie's lawyers had decided his only possible defence was insanity, and they thought seven murders might seem slightly madder than six. Christie was sane enough to appreciate this opinion, which he paraphrased for the prison chaplain: 'the more the merrier' was the way he put it to that shocked clergyman.

It seemed hardly likely that a relatively small addition to Christie's score could make any difference to the verdict at his forthcoming trial, but the reason for the extraordinary public interest in the exhumation had little to do with Christie. If he had killed Beryl, Evans had not, and therefore might well not have killed Geraldine either. (Christie had not confessed to the murder of the child, but reticence would be understandable: there could be no extra merriment in the destruction of a girl so far from nubility.) So we knew, when the lid came off that coffin, that we were looking for evidence that might prove an innocent man had been hanged.

Christie was, in the psychiatrist Hobson's words, a 'pathological liar'. He also affected to be a strict moralist, and each of his confessions included a spurious justification for the crime. He pretended the murder of his wife was a mercy killing; in two other cases he said his victim had started a fight; finally he said Beryl Evans had asked him to help her to commit suicide.

Christie's four most recent victims had all been killed by strangling with a ligature, and he said he had used the same method on the two that time had reduced to skeletons. In three of the four bodies Camps had examined (Mrs Christie was the exception) he had observed clear signs of carbon monoxide poisoning which had been confirmed by examination of the blood with a spectroscope. Vaginal swabs from the same three bodies proved that sexual intercourse had taken place at about—one can never be sure whether it was before, during, or after—the time of death.

Christie's first confession to the murder of Beryl Evans—made to his solicitor, Roy Arthur of Clifton's, in Brixton Prison—followed the same pattern: gassing to unconsciousness, followed by strangling with a ligature and sexual intercourse. When he repeated his confession to Dr Hobson, Christie said he was not sure which of the latter occurred first. Clifton's had supplied me with a copy of Teare's original autopsy reports and asked me if I thought there was anything in the medical evidence that supported his confession.

The strongest item was that Beryl (and Geraldine too) had been strangled with a ligature, Christie's invariable technique. Most stranglers use their bare hands. On the other hand Teare's report showed that Beryl had been beaten up before death: a black eye and a bruised upper lip suggested punches on the face, and there were more bruises on her thigh and leg. These injuries were alien to Christie's style of murder. Teare had also noted two marks on the posterior wall of the vagina—one an old scar, and beside it a small bruise which, Teare said at the magistrate's court, 'could have been caused by an attempt at forced intercourse or in a struggle'. Later he thought it had more probably been a self-inflicted injury caused by a syringe that Beryl seemed to have been using to try to abort herself (she was four months pregnant). Her body was found fully clothed except that she wore no knickers, but Teare did not take a vaginal swab for laboratory examination. 'Had he done so, he would almost certainly have found traces of Christie's spermatozoa,' Ludovic Kennedy wrote in his best-selling *Ten Rillington Place*; and I doubt if a more reckless over-statement can be found in all the millions of words written about the Evans-Christie case.

Teare's report was most revealing in something it did not say. If Christie had gassed Beryl, her skin and tissues would have been cherry-pink. This characteristic sign of carbon-monoxide poisoning could not possibly have been overlooked by a pathologist of Teare's care and experience in a case of obvious murder. Camps had observed it very clearly on three other bodies, two of which had then been dead about two months. Beryl's body, almost equally preserved, had been dead less than a month at Teare's autopsy. Moreover, with characteristic thoroughness Teare had made a routine laboratory test for carbon monoxide and found none.

I would not in any case have expected to be able to find a residue of carbon monoxide in a body that had been buried more than three years, but there was another reason for the exhumation. When the police searched that notorious house where Evans and Christie had lived they found a two-ounce tobacco tin containing four separate tufts of human pubic hair. They had been teased out, forming ringlets, each of which occupied a corner of the tin. They were all interlocking so that they were held in what Mr Justice Brabin described as an 'artistic display'. Clifton's gave me to understand that Christie acknowledged ownership of these trophies and had said he had taken one from the body of Beryl Evans.

Kensington Mortuary, built in 1883, was typical of the kind of premises we had all three been campaigning to have scrapped. The post-mortem room was walled with glazed white tiles and had two operating tables, each lighted by a 500-watt bulb overhead. The lighting was adequate: a detail of some importance, as it was in this room, with exactly the same lighting, that Teare had performed the original Evans autopsies and that Camps had examined the bodies of Christie's last four victims.

A whitish mould hung down in stalactites from the inside of the coffin lid. The shroud was overgrown with the same mould, but the bodies were clearly outlined underneath. The child lay on top of the mother, who was on a bed of brown damp sawdust. We waited for Chief Inspector Jennings to see if he could identify the bodies for the second time in the same mortuary. This proved unexpectedly easy, for, to everyone's surprise, both bodies had been marvellously well preserved for identification purposes, by the formation of adipocere.

Adipocere is seldom well developed in bodies buried in coffins, which seem to decompose more rapidly than those without, but it had been favoured by some unusual conditions: the cold weather at the time of death, the position of the bodies in the outside washhouse, and the effect of the rather wet common grave and the well-drained sandy soil.

At the first autopsy the child's body had been described as almost black with post-mortem changes: now it was whitish-yellow. Camps lifted out the little body and stripped off a second thin shroud, and we saw that the mother's body was equally well preserved, and of the same whitish-yellow colour, except for an area on both thighs, which was pink.

Cherry-pink!

'I want specimens of the thigh tissue for carbon-monoxide analysis,' I told Camps.

'Yes, of course I'd like you to do that,' Teare said to me immediately.

He was cool and unflurried, and clearly confident that my tests would prove negative. It was a tense moment, but the only person flustered was Camps.

'I'm in charge here,' he said tersely. 'I'm going to do this my way.' It was pure bluster, and I could only think he was irritated by our agreeing on the matter before he could say a word. He would have preferred us to argue and ask him for a ruling. 'I'll deliver all the specimens to Nickolls, and you can examine them at Scotland Yard,' he added in a truculent tone.

I had of course, a right to examine anything I wished for the defence, but I said nothing, and the moment of tension passed. As

Camps continued the autopsy I noticed that the cherry-pink colour
was beginning to fade. It had evidently been preserved by the contact
with the body of the child and was disappearing on exposure to the
air. I thought Teare probably had good reason not to worry: it looked
like nothing more sinister than 'post-mortem pink'. The tests would
show.

The hair on Beryl's abdomen and pubis was in a normal condition,
and appeared complete except for a small portion that had adhered to
the shroud. I could not see any sign of a tuft having been cut out—but
there was no trace either of the removal of a sample by Teare at the
first autopsy. I asked him how much he had taken. 'Just a pinch': he
held a few hairs between his thumb and forefinger to demonstrate. I
showed Camps the area of abdominal wall I wanted for further
examination, and asked also for a sample of the debris containing
hairs that had sloughed out of the skin.

Camps reopened the body by cutting Teare's sutures. The organs
were remarkably well preserved. The lungs, although dehydrated,
were easily recognizable.

They were pink, cherry-pink, just like the area over the thighs.

Again the colour disappeared on exposure to air.

The heart and other organs gave clear evidence that Beryl had died,
as Teare had said, of asphyxia. Then, most remarkable of all, came
the uterus, vagina, and vulva all in one piece, complete with pubic
hair, just as Teare had removed it for examination three years before.
We could measure the uterus and see that it had been in a pregnant
state. I inspected the vagina and cervical canal and saw the two small
marks on the posterior vaginal wall which Teare identified as the scar
and the bruise he had noted at the original autopsy. The pubic hair
gave no evidence that a tuft had been cut away.

Four teeth in the garden had not been proved to belong to either
skeleton, and so we had arranged for Beryl's jaws and teeth to be sent
with them to Bernard Sims, the lecturer in Dental Pathology at the
London Hospital. I looked at Beryl's teeth and saw the crowns were
cherry-pink. We had all seen 'pink teeth' in cases where no question of
carbon monoxide had arisen, but of course this too called for
analysis.

The material that we had earmarked for laboratory examination
was placed in sixteen jars, each sealed by Salter, carefully labelled, I
approved the re-burial of the body on behalf of the defence, and it was
put back in the coffin with Geraldine and interred the same evening.

Nickolls and I made a joint examination of the materials at the Metropolitan Police Laboratory, with the Lab liaison officer, Chief Inspector Salter, looking on. As Nickolls was sure to be called by the prosecution at Christie's trial, and I had been engaged by the defence, I was careful not to give anything away; and under the surface of our common professional interest this good friend of mine was equally withdrawn from me.

L. C. Nickolls—'Elsie' to those who penetrated his veneer of sharp wit and caustic barbed comment—had succeeded Holden as Director of the laboratory in 1951. I had already worked with him on several cases before he mentioned to me casually, on a train back to London from a West Country poisoning trial, 'I don't suppose you know, but I got my first job in the Civil Service as a result of a testimonial by our family doctor, a G.P. called Dr Simpson of Brighton.' There was a twinkle in his eye, for he knew Dr G. H. Simpson was my father.

Nickolls had already proved his worth as a Director of a Midlands Home Office laboratory, and at the Scotland Yard labs he was a winner: a good organizer and a natural 'chief', quick to perceive the right types for an efficient lab staff and tireless in trying to improve the standard of equipment. It was certainly not his fault that we had to examine Beryl Evans's pubic hair and Christie's trophies with a comparator microscope that compared unfavourably with the instrument in my own lab at Guy's.

We had first gone over the material from the autopsy again with a hand lens to see if the pubic hair had been defaced in any way. I concluded that while Teare could well have plucked a few hairs, in the way he had shown me, without it being evident even at the time, a specimen the size of Christie's trophies could not have been removed without leaving a visible mark. The cut ends of hair would still be showing if it had been cut, and if it had been plucked (to be trimmed afterwards) the area would show on the skin.

Taking a representative sample of Beryl's pubic hair, we compared it with each of the four tufts in Christie's tobacco tin. Three of these were entirely different. The fourth, however, was identical in colour, thickness, and general microscopic structure. The hair was mid-brown and of a very common type, and equally identical specimens could have been found on about 15 to 20 per cent of the population—literally millions.

We examined each of the identical specimens in greater detail, to see if there was perhaps an unsuspected difference; and we found that most of the hairs in Christie's trophy had been cut at both ends. In each case one cut was recent, and had presumably been made by Christie when he took the hairs from the body; the cut at the other end had rounded off and was about six months old. The hairs in the sample from Beryl's body were uncut.

There were a few exceptions, but the ends of these were rounded, while old cut ends of those from the tobacco tin were quite heavily frayed.

The conclusion was inescapable: the hairs in the tobacco tin could not have been taken from Beryl's body at the time of her death.

Next we examined the parts of Beryl's body on which we had seen the distinct pink coloration. There was no blood left, so we ground up some of the muscle tissues with a little water, and filtered it in a Buchner funnel. If carboxyhaemoglobin was present the filtrate would be strongly pink. It was practically colourless and had no traces of carbon monoxide.

The dental experts who examined the 'pink teeth' reached a similar conclusion.

Nickolls of course gave me what Camps had refused: material from the exhumation to examine in my own laboratories at Guy's. I repeated the tests we had made together, with the same results: the tests were only repeated in order that the defence should feel satisfied that they were 'independent'.

'I am obliged to say that not only has exhumation proved unrewarding,' I concluded my report to Clifton's, 'but to some extent (in the failure to match hair samples) providing evidence which goes to dissociate any sample of hair found in the possession of Christie from the hair of Mrs Evans. I hope Counsel will appreciate that, under the circumstances, I can offer no useful assistance to the defence . . . with reference to the deaths of Beryl or Geraldine Evans.' I also expressed the opinion there was nothing in Teare's original autopsy that appeared to have been overlooked.

Clifton's wrote asking me if there could have been carbon monoxide in Beryl's body when she died. I replied that if there had been it was very probable it would no longer have been detectable at the exhumation, three and a half years later, but that it would have been evident a month after death, when Teare performed his autopsy. 'No one could reasonably suggest that a pathologist of Dr Teare's ability and experience could possibly have overlooked coal-gas poisoning in a case of such a nature,' I added. 'One is always on the watch for more than presents itself as the main issue in crime investigation.'

This at least was one matter on which Camps and I were agreed; Teare could not have missed carbon monoxide if it had been there.

Three days after I posted this additional report to Clifton's, they asked the police to take a statement from their client in Brixton Prison. They could, of course, have done this any time since his arrest, more than two months earlier, but presumably they wanted him to know the results of the exhumation before he committed himself on his alleged murder of Beryl Evans. I think his statement shows he had tried hard to avoid saying anything that might be discredited by my report or by Teare's original autopsy report which I had endorsed:

She begged of me to help her go through with it, meaning to help her to commit suicide. She said she would do anything if I would help her. I think she was referring to letting me be intimate with her. . . . I got on my knees but found I was not physically capable of having intercourse with her owing to the fact that I had fibrositis in my back and enteritis. We were both fully dressed. I turned the gas tap on and as near as I can make out, I held it close to her face. When she became unconscious I turned the tap off. I was going to try again to have intercourse with her but it was impossible. I couldn't bend over. I think that's when I strangled her. I think it was with a stocking I found in the room. The gas wasn't on very long, not much over a minute, I think. Perhaps one or two minutes.

It was rather different from his 'confession' to his solicitor and his psychiatrist. The time of the gassing had been reduced to minimize the post-mortem evidence; for the same reason sexual intercourse had been reduced to an attempt, the intention being left intact; and not a word about 'scalping' Beryl's pubic hairs. On the contrary. Christie added a postscript to his statement:

The pubic hair found in the tin at 10 Rillington Place came from the three women in the alcove and from my wife. I feel certain of this, but I can't remember when or how I took it.

Christie, who purported to be hopelessly confused, especially about times and dates, could also be remarkably precise and alert. Three days later he wrote: 'There is the possibility that as the gas tap was only used for a very short time (1 to 1½ minutes), after a month (app.) there may not have been signs in the body.' What he did not know was that a minute or two was hardly long enough to make Beryl unconscious, and that a dose large enough to cause loss of consciousness would also cause a visible saturation in the blood.

Christie was tried for the murder of his wife only, and the prosecution did not lead any evidence about his other ghastly crimes. The defence made up for this, and in the witness box Christie repeated his confession to killing Beryl Evans. I was in court, at his solicitor's request, but I was not called to give evidence. If I had gone into the box I could only have supported Nickolls's opinion that none of the tufts in the tobacco tin could have been taken from Beryl Evans's body at the time of her death. Yet the opinion was rebutted, to everyone's surprise, by Dr Hobson, the psychiatrist who had watched the exhumation and the subsequent autopsies.

Hobson, who was Consultant Physician in Psychological Medicine at the Middlesex Hospital, had been called to give evidence about Christie's state of mind in support of the insanity plea, and this took up some considerable time. Right at the end of his evidence Derek Curtis-Bennett asked him about the tuft from the tobacco tin that resembled Beryl's pubic hairs. 'Can you tell us how, if they are Mrs Evans's, both ends became cut?'

'Yes,' said Hobson. 'Very many women trim the hairs actually on the sex parts, on the vulva . . . it is particularly common in pregnancy, particularly in pregnancies which are unwanted, and with wives of unsympathetic husbands.' (This was not at all my experience in a wide variety of autopsy cases.) 'I think again,' Hobson went on, 'an abnormal person, the sort of person who would collect gruesome trophies like this, would be much more likely to collect hairs from the sex organ itself than from the abdomen.' Nickolls and I had found correspondence of one coil of hairs in the tobacco tin with Beryl's pubic hairs; therefore, Hobson said finally, 'it is still not impossible that those in the tin were the hairs of Mrs Evans.'

Hobson had not been present at the laboratory examinations or he would not have assumed that we had failed to inspect the ends of the vulval as well as pubic hairs. But his remarks apparently took the prosecution by surprise: the Attorney-General scarcely cross-examined him on them, except to suggest they were 'pure speculation', which Hobson denied. In his closing speech the Attorney-General conceded that the hair in the tin could have been Beryl's. He could afford to do so. Whether Christie had killed Beryl was of such little importance in this trial that Hobson himself had not even mentioned the possibility when giving evidence about Christie's mental state. Pinning a seventh murder on Christie would not affect the answer to the only question at issue, which was whether or not he had been insane according to the M'Naghten Rules. In spite of Hobson's pleas the jury decided Christie had not been insane, and he was found guilty of murder and sentenced to death.

But had he killed Beryl Evans? The question that mattered so little at Christie's trial assumed immense importance outside the court. Suddenly British justice itself was put on trial. Members of Parliament, the public, and the Press demanded an official investigation. The Home Secretary appointed a senior Q.C., John Scott Henderson, to carry out an inquiry in private.

Scott Henderson asked Nickolls about Hobson's vulval-hair theory, and Nickolls gave two reasons against it. He said the hairs in the tobacco tin were long and coarse and therefore pubic, rather than short and fine; and the only cut hairs we had found on Beryl—which Nicholls said were vulval—were rounded at the ends and not frayed like those in the tobacco tin. Had I been asked to give evidence (I merely had to attest to my report to Clifton's) I would have supported Nickolls entirely on the second point. We had found no hairs on Beryl with frayed ends like those in Christie's trophy. I would also have said I did not think pubic and vulval hairs could be distinguished all that easily.

Hobson said the fact that some of Beryl's vulval hairs had been cut supported his theory, and he also told Scott Henderson he thought Teare could have missed the signs of carbon monoxide at Beryl's original autopsy. The fact that it had been detected in the three bodies from Christie's kitchen alcove was, Hobson thought, 'due to Camps's brilliance'. This seemed a remarkable judgment by a psychiatrist, especially as Camps, by no means modest about his abilities, had said Teare could not have missed it. Hobson added the suggestion that if Beryl had inhaled gas for only a minute or two, as Christie had said, 'the struggle which followed would have resulted in deep breathing, which itself would have washed out all traces of carbon monoxide from her body'. As a matter of fact the effect of a struggle would have been the opposite: she (and also Christie) would have inhaled more gas.

Scott Henderson preferred the opinion of three pathologists to that of a psychiatrist on both the pubic hair and the carbon monoxide.

After interviewing Christie himself in prison he concluded that his confession to the murder of Beryl was false and that there could be no doubt that Evans had killed both his wife and his child. He published his report on the day set for Christie's execution, on which date Christie was duly hanged.

That was still not the end of the affair. Fifteen years later, after continued pressure, the case was reheard in public, at the Royal Courts of Justice, by Mr Justice Brabin, a quiet scholarly man of great patience. The main hearings took place on a total of thirty-two days, spread over several months. The Evans family were represented by counsel (Sebag Shaw, Q.C.); so were Teare, Camps, Hobson, and the Metropolitan Police. I was not. We all repeated our evidence, and again the three pathologists concerned were in complete agreement. Mr Justice Brabin accepted our opinions, rejected Hobson's theories, and dismissed Christie's' confession' to the murder of Beryl as false. His final conclusion was, however, quite unexpected. '*More probably than not*,' he said, '*Evans had killed Beryl but Christie had killed Geraldine.*'

If so, Evans had been executed for the wrong murder. He was thereupon given a posthumous free pardon and his body was exhumed, not for a second autopsy but for reburial outside Pentonville Prison.

A Member of Parliament who objected to the free pardon pointed out that Mr Justice Brabin had confirmed Evans's guilt in the murder of his wife. The Home Secretary replied that Evans had been pardoned because it was for the murder of the child that he had been tried and hanged. If the prosecution had chosen to proceed with the charge of killing his wife, as Evans' defenders thought it should have done, and if he had then been convicted and executed, as was likely, presumably no pardon would have been forthcoming, and his remains would still lie under a prison yard.

'One wonders about the possibilities of there being two stranglers living in the same tiny premises,' Derek Curtis-Bennett said in his defence of Christie; and disbelief in this coincidence was the whole basis of the widespread public belief that Evans might be innocent. Nobody questioned his conviction until the bodies of Christie's victims were found. But the Brabin report upheld the coincidence, and it never seemed to me very far-fetched. Coincidences are far more common in life than in fiction.

In her Introduction to *The Trials of Evans and Christie*, F. Tennyson Jesse pointed out that Christie's last three victims, each of whom he met only in London, had all been treated for venereal disease in the same hospital at Southampton. Another coincidence, although he did not call it that, was revealed by Ludovic Kennedy in his book *Ten Rillington Place*. He was the first to publish a bizarre extract from the brief to Evans's counsel, referring to the pre-trial hearing at the magistrate's court:

The evidence given by Dr Teare appears to be open to the comment that his expert opinion travelled beyond justifiable inference from his examination of the corpse, in so far as he purports to suggest that there might have been an attempt at sexual penetration after death. The case is sufficiently horrible without disgusting surmises of this nature being introduced into the minds of the jury.

The defence counsel, Malcolm Morris, Q.C., agreed. 'If Evans was guilty, it made things worse,' he explained afterwards. 'It could not, on such facts as I then knew, possibly assist the defence.' Morris, of course, had no idea at that time that the man Evans accused of the murders was a homicidal necrophile.

'Here was the vital, the missing link between Evans's claim that Christie had done it, and the reason why he had done it,' Ludovic Kennedy commented. 'Here, so to speak, were Christie's fingerprints . . . in the light of what we know now, it pins the crime fairly and squarely on Christie.'

It does nothing of the kind, as Mr Justice Brabin made clear, because Teare never said what was attributed to him. In the magistrates' court he repeated what he had written in his autopsy report on Beryl: 'There is an old scar in the posterior wall of the vagina and beside this is a little *ante-mortem* bruising.' The Latin phrase *ante-mortem* is rarely used outside the medical profession, but *post-mortem* is part of the English language. When we do not hear a sentence completely we automatically fill in the blank from what we assume to be the sense, and familiar words are more likely to suggest themselves than the esoteric. Baillie Saunders, the solicitor's clerk who drafted the brief to counsel, was over eighty when he listened to Teare's evidence before the magistrate, an age when it is not unusual to be a little hard of hearing. So the misunderstanding is easily explained: the coincidence was eerie.

Christie never boasted of his murders but seems to have been reluctant to remember them. In his statement to the police on arrest he admitted the four they told him they had discovered but said nothing about the two skeletons in the garden. Only when he was asked later did he admit responsibility for these too. He had been in custody almost a month before he first 'confessed' to the murder of Beryl Evans.

'Do you remember whether or not you killed anybody else other than those seven people?' his counsel asked him at his trial.

'I do not remember. If somebody said I did, well, I must have done.'

When he was in custody he was asked, among other things, if he might have killed Christine Butcher, the seven-year-old girl, strangled with a ligature near Windsor Castle, whose body I had examined. He thought he had not, but only because he had not been to Windsor. Scott Henderson also asked him if he might have killed other people, and again he was non-committal.

One piece of evidence suggests he had at least one other victim, perhaps four.

In the postscript to his last statement to the police Christie said the pubic hair in the tobacco tin had come from the four bodies found in his house. Nickolls checked this and found that one of the trophies could have come from Mrs Christie, whose hair was of the same common colour and type, but none could have belonged to any of the three women found in the kitchen alcove.

Two of the other three trophies were also of common types, and Nickolls thought they might have belonged, respectively, to the skeletons in the garden, according to the descriptions of the women and some head hair that had been found. One of these two trophies was the tuft with the frayed ends that we had found otherwise identical with Beryl Evans's pubic hair.

It seems odd that Christie should have said hair came from the bodies in the alcove if in fact it had come from those now reduced to skeletons; not very likely that in his last four murders the only trophy he took was from the one woman with whom he did not have peri-mortal sexual intercourse; and even more odd that one of his trophies had definitely not come from any of the unfortunate women known to have been involved.

CHAPTER 19

THE INNOCENCE OF DR BODKIN ADAMS

Doctors are in a particularly good position to commit murder and escape detection. Their patients, sometimes their own fading wives, more often mere ageing nuisances, are in their sole hands. 'Dangerous drugs' and powerful poisons lie in their professional bags or in the surgery. No one is watching or questioning them, and a change in symptoms, a sudden 'grave turn for the worse' or even death is for them alone to interpret. They can authorize the disposal of a dead body by passing the necessary death certificate to the Registrar of Deaths, who has no power to interfere unless there is some statutory shortcoming in the way the certificate is filled out, or death appears due to accident or violence of some kind, or the wording is so vague or unintelligible that the Registrar has to seek the help of the Coroner.

Are there many doctor murderers? Have whispers or frank allegations ever resulted in exhumations and the discovery of crime? Or are doctors above suspicion?

No one can know, but if doctors do take the law into their own hands, the facts are only likely to emerge by chance, through whisperings of suspicion or, rarely, through carelessness in disposal of the dead body, as when Dr Buck Ruxton threw the remains of his wife and her maid Mary Rogerson in an open ravine at Moffat in Dumfriesshire.

Dr Crippen lied stupidly about his wife's 'disappearance', paraded Ethel le Neve in her jewellery, and then tried to escape the clutching hand of the law by his historic dash by liner to America, with his girl-friend dressed as a boy. Sheer stupidity.

Dr Neill Cream had the impudence to publish scurrilous letters, print misleading circulars, and eventually complain to Sergeant McIntyre of Scotland Yard about the investigation into the deaths of his prostitute victims by strychnine: he could have remained silent.

Dr Lawson walked into a private school to poison his crippled brother-in-law with aconite in a piece of cake and was caught when the chemist supplying the poison read the account of the murder. Dr Clements, Palmer the Staffordshire horse-racing doctor, Dr Pritchard, Dr Smethurst, Dr Waite, Dr Webster—all but the last used poison and might well have escaped but for faulty planning or behaviour, or some mere chance.

But there are 70,000 doctors in England and Wales alone, so a mere handful of professional murders in fifty years speaks generally very highly of their moral fibre, or the ease with which they can conceal crime.

There is another area where doctors are at risk of suspicion over the deaths of their patients. When patients are suffering intolerable discomfort from inevitably fatal cancer or have lapsed into permanent coma from brain injury or tumour, it is lawful for a doctor to use pain-killing narcotic drugs to ease the process of dying. It is not euthanasia, but a humane and understanding professional service.

Now of course this can be misinterpreted in a more sinister way. Pain-killing and hypnotic drugs can not only put people to sleep: they can kill if they are overdone; and the area between painless sleep and death is a no-man's land without very sharp definitions. Some patients welcome gentle nursing out of their intolerable existence; others may have no choice in the matter.

Dr John Bodkin Adams, a portly bespectacled Irishman of sixty, had practised medicine for years in Eastbourne, and had many elderly patients on his list. Some were on sleeping pills or capsules, some needed more powerful narcotic drugs like morphia or heroin, and some were eking out a month-to-month existence in Eastbourne's comfortable nursing homes. Dr Adams did not hold himself out as a particularly distinguished diagnostician, he was just an ordinary doctor seeing to his patients' minor ailments and guaranteeing them a comfortable existence and a good night's sleep. Did it ever cross his mind to kill any of his old ladies? Would any benefit have come from it? Was there a legacy persuasive enough to tempt a successful doctor to crime? Would an elderly Rolls-Royce or a canteen of cutlery in an antique chest be likely to turn the head of a professional man in a good way of living?

You would not think so, but in 1956 a mere whisper on the seafront deck chairs of Eastbourne grew into a *bruit* and then exploded into a scandal that achieved arresting treatment, first in France, in *Paris Match*, and finally on the front pages of the English national newspapers. What had been happening to Dr Bodkin Adams's wealthy old ladies? Was it safe to go into a nursing home in Eastbourne? What were the police doing about it? Hints of crime grew into virtual allegations of murder.

'Something must be done about it,' they said, and eventually gossip and rumour, fanned by the newspapers, forced the Sussex Police to investigate, and then to call for help from Scotland Yard. Detective Superintendent Herbert Hannam, a very unusual sort of policeman, was sent to make inquiries. Well dressed, possibly slightly conceited, confident, certainly well aware of his powers and not without experience (though hardly of this kind of scandal) Hannam set out to get to the bottom of the affair.

The next event, in July, was a call to the pathologist Francis Camps to perform an autopsy on the body of Mrs Gertrude Hullett, a rich widow who had died in her mansion at the top of Beachy Head. Camps, who normally prided himself on his speed, spent a long time in the mortuary, but without finding any evidence helpful to the police. Hannam, still suspicious of Dr Bodkin Adams, asked for the exhumation of two of his other patients; whereupon Dr Adams, a subscribing member of the Medical Defence Union, got in touch with the secretary and asked for help. The MDU undertook to handle the affair on his behalf and, if it became necessary, to employ a skilled lawyer in his defence. Harsh rumours of 'wicked old doctor', 'satanic streak' and 'calumny' revolving round his head could from now on be left to his legal advisers. He might not sleep well, but at least he was not alone.

The first step taken by the MDU was to ask me to 'watch' the exhumations, which, in the event, did no more harm to Dr Bodkin Adams than the autopsy on Mrs Hullett. Only one of the two bodies was in good enough condition to enable Camps and me to agree on the cause of death, which was cerebral thrombosis, *precisely what the doctor had certified*. No analysis for the drugs he had prescribed was fruitful, owing to the lapse of several years between death and exhumation.

Hannam persevered, and in December he arrested Dr Bodkin Adams and charged him with the murder of yet another patient, also a rich widow, Mrs Edith Alice Morell.

On the face of it the case looked hard to prove. There was no body (an obvious handicap in a case of alleged poisoning) as Mrs Morell had been cremated, at her own request. She had died six years before. She was eighty-one, and half paralysed by a stroke, after which she had been given from six to twelve months to live, only to survive another two and a half years under the care of the doctor now charged with her murder. She had left an estate of £157,000, out of which the doctor received an elderly Rolls-Royce and a chest containing silver valued at £275 . . . hardly a rich legacy.

However, the Crown was able to convince the magistrates that there was a prima facie case against him. Records of his prescriptions of morphia and heroin were produced: nurses testified that the drugs prescribed had been administered, even when the patient was in a continuous coma, and that she had shown signs of opiate poisoning; and a very distinguished physician said the drugs could only have been given with the intention of killing her.

The expert was Dr Arthur Douthwaite, a Senior Physician at my own hospital, Guy's, where he also taught therapeutics. The MDU naturally wanted to find out all they could about him, and I had to tell them he was a much respected expert in his field, Editor of the famous *Hale-White's Materia Medica*, and a fine doctor of outstanding merits and principles. I had known him first as a teacher, when I was a student, and later as a fellow-member of the staff and a personal friend. But in this affair we were on opposite sides, and the MDU were determined to find out anything that might undermine the value of his evidence against Dr Bodkin Adams. I was able to tell them that, far from being opposed to the administration of heroin, he had, in fact, led a deputation to the Home Office asking that no ban should be placed on its manufacture or use in England. I suggested also that we should inspect the order book for hard drugs in a private London clinic used by Dr Douthwaite, and this showed that he had had considerable recourse to both morphia and heroin for his own patients. I prepared charts to demonstate this fact: happily we never had to confront him with them.

The case was heard at the Old Bailey, and to defend Dr Bodkin Adams the MDU chose one of the most skilful and persuasive lawyers the English Bar ever had: Geoffrey Lawrence, Q.C., later Mr Justice Lawrence. Opposing him, following an established tradition in cases where murder by poison is alleged, was the Attorney-General himself, Sir Reginald Manningham-Buller: they were then of entirely different qualities, though each, of course, of outstanding repute. The first important witnesses were the four nurses who had attended Mrs Morell . . . four very ordinary nurses for whom this must have been a terrifying ordeal.

Nurse Helen Stronach, the first of these, said that during her tours of duty the evening routine was unchanged: at 9 p.m. she gave Mrs Morell ¼ grain of morphia, and at 11 p.m., when she was still dopey and half asleep, the doctor came and gave the patient another injection, but what it was the nurse did not know.

Lawrence asked her if she had written all this down in the nurses' report book. 'Yes, every time we gave an injection we wrote it down—what it was, and the time, and signed our names.'

'Everything that happened of significance in the patient's illness would have to go down in the book; everything that was of any importance?' Lawrence suggested in his lightest voice.

Nurse Stronach was unsuspicious. 'We reported everything,' she said stolidly.

'So that if only we had those reports now we could see the truth of exactly what happened night by night and day by day when you were there?'

'Yes. But you have our word for it.'

Lawrence's face relaxed. It was just the answer he wanted; for he had more than her word: he had the books.

He produced them suddenly, like a conjurer pulling a rabbit out of a top hat, and asked Nurse Stronach to identify them. She just stared at them unbelievingly. Normally such books were destroyed after the patient's death. The Attorney-General was equally astonished, and dismayed, as Lawrence began to read out quietly the entries that Nurse Stronach had to admit she had made. 'We have now been through the whole of your records for that time,' he concluded, 'and we have not found a single instance where you gave that injection of one-quarter grain of morphia by itself you were talking about. And you recorded only one or two visits by the doctor, and then we find you know exactly what injection was given.'

Nurse Stronach had nothing to say: Lawrence had effectively destroyed her credibility.

The second nurse, Sister Mason-Ellis, was in a happier position than Nurse Stronach. The report books were now out in the open, and the Attorney-General was careful not to lead any evidence that contradicted them. In cross-examination Geoffrey Lawrence read out her report of the afternoon before Mrs Morell's death. '"Awake but quiet. Half a glass of milk and brandy 3 drachms taken." It is quite obvious from that report that she was not in a coma?'

'Well,' said Sister Mason-Ellis, unwisely hedging, 'not according to my report'.

Counsel raised his eyebrows to simulate surprise. Had she not agreed that the reports were where the truth was to be found? 'You do not want to go back on that now, do you?'

'Not at all.'

'So when you wrote "awake", she must have been awake?'

'She must have been.'

'Therefore she could not possibly be in a coma.' Another 'kill'.

Nurse Randall, who came next, was to have been one of the Crown's star witnesses, for she had been with Mrs Morell during the last hours of her life. In his opening speech the Attorney-General had promised that Nurse Randall would describe this period in detail. 'The night nurse will tell you Mrs Morell was very weak, except for occasional spasms. She was in a coma. At 10 p.m. the doctor came and himself filled a 5 c.c. syringe with a preparation.' The Attorney-General held up a 5 c.c. syringe to show how big it was. 'The doctor gave this syringe to the night nurse and told her to inject the contents into the unconscious woman. She did so. The doctor took the empty syringe and refilled it with a similar quantity—far too large a quantity on each occasion to be morphine or heroin—and told the nurse to give the second injection to the patient if she did not become quieter. The nurse did not like giving another large injection from this unusually large syringe, whatever it was, and later in the evening she telephoned the doctor. She received her instructions and it was her duty to obey them. She gave the second injection. Mrs Morell gradually became quiet, and at 2 a.m. she died. Why were those large injections given to an unconscious woman on the doctor's orders? The prosecution cannot tell you what they were . . .' Manningham-Buller sounded confident enough.

Lawrence was again well primed. The night nurse's written report was there before she came into the witness box. The Attorney-General did not ask her to repeat the evidence she had given at the lower court, for her written report told a very different story. 'Patient very weak and restless. 9.30 p.m., *paraldehyde 5 c.c.* given intravenously by the doctor. 11.30 p.m., very restless, no sleep. 12.30 a.m., restless and talkative and very shaky. 12.45 a.m., seems a little quieter; appears asleep. Respiration 50. 2 a.m., passed away quietly.'

No spasms, no injections given by the nurse, no phone calls, one injection by the doctor, when the patient was not unconscious but restless; not with a sinister 'preparation' kept secret from the nurse, not with a lethal dose of powerful morphia or heroin, but a reasonable dose of safe, old-fashioned paraldehyde, which any nurse could recognize a mile off by its revolting smell.

Nurse Randall, the night nurse, still said in her evidence that she had telephoned the doctor and given a second injection, but Geoffrey Lawrence made short work of that. Why wasn't it in her report? Why give the injection when the patient was not restless but quieter and seemed asleep? 'Your memory isn't very trustworthy?' 'It appears not to be.'

Unwisely, in view of the cross-examination to come, the Attorney-General had led Nurse Randall to describe Mrs Morell's jerky spasms, a common sign of withdrawal from opiate poisoning, in her last hours. 'They were so bad I could not leave her, and they almost jerked her out of bed . . . I had never seen jerks as bad.' But they were not bad enough, Geoffrey Lawrence noted smoothly, to be recorded in her report. 'I wrote that she was very shaky.' Shaky? Was that her word for spasms that almost jerked the patient out of bed? 'I just don't know. I suppose I wrote it down quickly.'

Answering a question from the judge, Nurse Randall made an effort to help her side. 'I think 4 c.c. or 5 c.c. of paraldehyde is a very large dose,' she said. Lawrence was on his feet in a flash. 'Do you know,' he asked her, 'that the British Pharmacopoeia full dose is 120 minims or 8 c.c.?'

The fourth nurse to give evidence, Sister Bartlett, had shared the last night duty with Nurse Randall. She too bravely repeated some of the evidence she had given at the magistrates' court: the patient had 'twitching spasms, and was semi-comatose.' Geoffrey Lawrence gravely read out her written reports. 'Awake, restless, talkative.' Hardly semi-comatose? And not a spasm or twitch or even a shake.

The Crown had expected the nurses' evidence to be short and not seriously disputed, but with the report books Lawrence had been able to challenge it point by point and largely destroy it, and the process had taken a week. The next important witness was Dr Douthwaite, who had also given evidence at the magistrates' court and had come to the Old Bailey expecting to be asked merely to repeat it. 'The prosecution will call a medical authority', the Attorney-General had promised in his opening speech, 'who will tell you that in their view Mrs Morell could not possibly have survived the administration of the drugs prescribed in her last five days.' But that evidence was no longer good enough, for the nurses' report books showed that Mrs Morell had been given only a small proportion of the drugs prescribed for her at the end. Douthwaite had said he thought Bodkin Adams must have meant murder if he gave his patient 41 grains of morphia and 39 grains of heroin in her last five days, but this was plainly not so. According to the calculations of the Crown's chemist, the discrepancy between prescription and administration in that period was 30 grains of morphia and 22 grains of heroin. With these drastically revised figures, and with the nurses' recollections replaced by the evidence of their reports, would Dr Douthwaite still say he thought Dr Bodkin Adams was trying to kill his patient? If he wouldn't, the Crown might as well give up.

It is easy to imagine the subtle pressure put on Dr Douthwaite by the prosecution lawyers, their respectful and perhaps unduly persuasive blandishments to induce him to give the evidence they needed to keep the case going. It is difficult, though, to understand why he yielded. The amounts of morphia and heroin actually administered to Mrs Morell, including maximum estimates for 'special injections' given by Dr Bodkin Adams himself, were considerably less than the amounts commonly given by Douthwaite himself in his private clinic, in particular for elderly patients of precisely the kind treated by Bodkin Adams; and this could be proved from my charts.

But Douthwaite showed no sign of any misgivings when he entered the witness box, a striking figure, well over six feet tall, handsome, greying, frank and honest. In style at least he was a model witness, clear and incisive.

'Is there, in your opinion,' the Attorney-General asked him, 'any justification for injecting morphia and heroin immediately after a stroke?'

'No justification whatsoever.'

'Is it right or wrong to do so?'

'Wrong. In all circumstances wrong.'

Bespectacled old Bodkin Adams was purple in the face, almost bouncing in his chair in the dock. You could see he'd thought of at least six objections to such a hard rule. Douthwaite did admit that pain might introduce the need—later on, but not otherwise. He really did lay in to old Bodkin Adams. 'Morphia would give rise to addiction . . . to dependance on the doctor . . . people over seventy should not have heroin unless they are suffering from some incurable disease'.

'What conclusion do you draw from the dosage administered in the last days?' the Attorney-General asked finally. 'What conclusions do you draw as to the intentions with which that dosage must have been prescribed?'

This was the crux of the case. Had this elderly seaside doctor merely been handing out rather too heavy sedative doses to his more troublesome senile patients, or . . . ?

The court was dead silent as Dr Douthwaite slowly pronounced the words:

'*The only conclusion I can come to is that the intention on 8th November was to terminate her life.*' (She had died on 13th November.)

Geoffrey Lawrence knew better than to comment on the enormity of such a sentence—and on a fellow doctor! 'Quel acharnement quand même contre un confrère dans le malheur!', wrote a French journalist in court (they were there from all over Europe).

Instead Lawrence nibbled round the edges. Dr Douthwaite had been wrong in assuming, when he gave evidence at the magistrates' court, that 'for the last three or four days of her life this lady had been in a continuous coma'. It was not so. And had the doctor 'made any inquiries' about the symptoms of her stroke and the treatment she had for it in Cheshire, where her illness had started?

Dr Douthwaite was in trouble. He had not done so. He had said in conference 'it would be interesting to know' but he 'did not regard it as my duty to find out facts of that sort'. He had been told that 'the information was not available'.

Geoffrey Lawrence started the pressure.

'It would be most *important* to know before condemning the doctor's treatment from the start, as you did yesterday, what happened in Cheshire?'

Douthwaite agreed that 'it would be *interesting* to know'.

Slowly counsel produced from under his desk a document. It was another rabbit from the conjurer's top hat: the clinical record from the Cheshire Hospital! What a body blow for the prosecution! The Medical Defence Union had indeed done its job well.

Lawrence read from the document, which covered the ten days Mrs

Morell had spent in the hospital. For every night there was a record of
morphia injection. 'Does the field of condemnation that you are
spreading from this witness box include Dr Turner of Cheshire for
having given the patient morphia after a stroke?'

Dr Douthwaite could hardly change horses. 'If that was the
treatment for the stroke, yes.'

'It does?' Lawrence threw up his hands in a despairing gesture.
'Good gracious me!'

The Crown's case was already crumbling. Altogether four doctors
had seen the patient, and all had prescribed morphia. Was everybody
wrong except Dr Douthwaite, who never saw her?

I could only feel sympathy with this distinguished physician. He
had overstated his case, and this was the pay-off. But it was only the
beginning of a long ordeal. Hour after hour, as Arthur Douthwaite
stood in the witness box, focus of attention, alive to the need to
choose every word of reply with the utmost care, Geoffrey Lawrence
eroded the main substance of his medical argument. His former
absolute certainty became more qualified. 'I don't know what was in
the doctor's mind.'

'Did you not before?' rapped out Lawrence. 'When you saw
murderous intent?'

No answer.

Tiring during the afternoon, Douthwaite (who later told me it was
the most exhausting test of his mind and body he had ever endured)
yielded that 'heroin *is* useful'. He could 'remember a woman of
seventy-three who had it prescribed'.

'So it is sometimes prescribed?'

No answer.

My charts were ready for production, to remind Douthwaite how
much morphia and heroin he had prescribed himself, but it was
unnecessary to press him on this. The judge plainly felt that
Douthwaite had overstated his case. Looking straight at him, he
asked:

'If the doctor (Bodkin Adams) were to go into the witness box and
say, "I disagree entirely with his view", he would be guilty of
perjury—he would be saying he held a view which he cannot honestly
hold?'

It was an impossible position for any consultant to maintain. As
the judge pointed out, he was saying, in fact, that the treatment
Bodkin Adams used was not just wrong and dangerous and caused

death, but could not have been due to error, ignorance, or incompetence, and must have been due to an attempt to kill.

Although the trial lasted another six days, to become the longest for murder in English criminal history (the trial of Hanratty for the A6 murder, which lasted even longer, came five years later) the case for the Crown was already lost when Dr Douthwaite was at last released. It has often been said that, but for his ill-judged stand on this very important medical issue, Arthur Douthwaite would have been in the lobby, possibly even elected President of the Royal College of Physicians in the following year. I was sure he had been over-persuaded by the Crown's legal advisers, and when as old friends we talked about it afterwards he told me how chagrined he felt at having been 'hoisted on a petard' of his own making. His experience at the hands of Geoffrey Lawrence was a warning to all doctors who go into the witness box that the real strength of any evidence is its reasonableness: it has to be both sound and defensible, and to look so to the jury.

To learn from the experience of others is never quite so telling, but one would have expected the discomfiture of Douthwaite to exercise at least a temporary restraint on any doctor who happened to witness it. Yet the expert witness called by the defence, Dr John Harman, Consulting Physician at St Thomas's Hospital—who had advised Lawrence on his cross-examination of Douthwaite, with such deadly effect—also stuck his neck out in much the same way, and with similarly painful results. Describing a morphia convulsion, he gave a most impressive and detailed display, twitching and jerking, eyes bulging and palms thrust out, doubling himself over backwards in the witness box—a dramatic performance that was highly publicized in the evening newspapers; only to admit under cross-examination next day that he had never seen a morphia convulsion in his life!

Dr Bodkin Adams was of course acquitted of the charge of murder. He was tried later under the Drugs Act on a minor charge of 'loose' prescribing of hard drugs, which was a purely technical offence. As a result of his conviction he was somewhat surprisingly struck off the Medical Register, but his name was later restored and he was free to continue to treat rich elderly widows with such quantities of morphia and heroin as he considered appropriate.

One mystery remained. The defence had proved that the amount of morphine and heroin prescribed (and supplied by the chemist) greatly exceeded the amount administered to Mrs Morell: what had happened to the rest?

'There must be some channel existing by which the drugs prescribed were improperly disappearing,' the judge said to the jury in his summing up. 'One knows that dangerous drugs are things in which there is an illicit traffic, and you might think that someone was dealing dishonestly with them, and that someone must either have been the doctor himself or one of the nurses. If you were ever to get so far as to begin to wonder which of those people was most likely, you would in fairness to the doctor have to bear in mind that two of the nurses have told lies about this matter in the witness box. One of them lied about whether the drugs were kept locked or not—that was Nurse Stronach—and one of the others, either Nurse Mason-Ellis or Nurse Randall, lied about their conversation in the train' (which was on whether the drugs had been kept in a locked cupboard or in an unlocked drawer).

The judge added that he was not accusing any of the nurses of stealing or illegally dealing in the drugs, but only warning the jury against drawing an inference prejudicial to the accused. In the event no-one was ever charged. No doubt there was what in the wine, or milk, trade is called 'spillage', but the truth of the matter was never made public.

CHAPTER 20

THE POISONERS: RADFORD AND ARMSTRONG

The moment anyone says, 'Well, one thing's certain, you won't see any more Maybricks, Armstrongs, or Seddons', famous arsenic poisoners, you hear that two doctors in Warwickshire have decided to withdraw a certificate they had just issued to certify that a woman patient whose last illness had puzzled them had died of gastro-enteritis. A month later William Waite, the chauffeur to Lord Leigh of Stoneleigh Abbey, is charged with the murder of his wife by giving her repeated doses of arsenic. Waite's interest in his wife had waned. He had taken to a girl-friend, and, said the Crown counsel at his trial, 'it was only a few hours after a clandestine love-making with her in a car that he was giving his wife the final doses of poison', concealed in a drug capsule provided for proper treatment.

Why was it not all spotted by the doctors? The victim had lost weight to a very serious degree without explanation: her skin was dry, her hair falling out; she kept having attacks of vomiting 'for no reason' and she had 'polyneuritis'—the lot, you would say. Yet the doctors seemed blind to the possibility; no tests for arsenic had ever been made.

The truth was they never thought of it. Murder by poison in their quiet Warwickshire practice? And in a nice home with a distinguished peer's faithful servant coolly committing the crime under their very noses? Unthinkable! So it is not thought of. And it is when it never crosses anybody's mind that the cunning murderer fools everyone. Do many escape detection? No one knows, but so few murders come to light when puzzled doctors refuse to issue death certificates and a post-mortem is made for the coroner that it does not seem to be a big problem. But how many puzzled doctors just take a chance with the death certificate? Quite a lot: there is no doubt whatever about this, and, crime apart, it is dangerous; it can result in bad statistics at the very best and failure to award compensation for compensatable illness at the worst. Isn't crime even worse? Personally I doubt whether one overlooked murder is as serious a fault as one mother deprived of industrial or accident compensation for her dead husband's children, for life. It seems a moot point.

One of the coolest murders by arsenic that ever came to lie in my crime files took place in, of all places, a sanatorium. Frederick Gordon Radford killed his ailing wife under the very noses of the doctors and staff, and he very nearly got away with it.

Margery Radford had been ailing for about two years before she died of 'pulmonary tuberculosis' in the Milford Sanatorium at Godalming, in Surrey. She had become thin and pale, coughing, seedy, suffering from this wretched lung disease for nearly seven years in all. Maybe she had never been fit enough to make an attractive wife for Radford, a virile and good-looking man who worked as a laboratory technician at St Thomas's Hospital, a mile from the sanatorium. He had grown bored with his wife lying so long in hospital and had found a girl-friend. Margery Radford had a shrewd suspicion about this.

Six days before she died, wasted away by her long illness, she confided to Mrs Formby, a friend who visited her regularly, that she had for some time been suspicious also of the tasty extra titbits of food and occasional bottles of mineral drink her husband had been bringing or sending her: she thought they might contain poison. She had felt ill, even vomited, after eating a jelly, some plums, and 'only yesterday', she said, 'part of a fruit pie' that her husband had given to her own father to bring in for her.

'Please do something,' she pleaded. 'Send this pie to Scotland Yard and have it analysed, for I am sure it has been poisoned.'

Instead, after consulting her husband, Mrs Formby sent the pie, wrapped in brown paper, to the Superintendent of the sanatorium. She also wrote a covering letter, which she posted separately. When they arrived the letter went into his secretary's in-tray and the parcel was put on his desk. It was a Saturday afternoon, and when the Superintendent dropped in around teatime there was no-one in the office to tell him who had sent the nice-looking fruit pie. Assuming it must have been a friend, he took it home and began to eat it. He swallowed about one-sixth of the pie before he was seized with pain

The author in 1976

Examining the remains of Baby Armstrong in the seconal case at Portsmouth, with Chief Superintendent Salter, Yard Liaison Officer

The heating apparatus in the motel bathroom in the Trist case in Portugal
Butane generator and inadequate ventilator

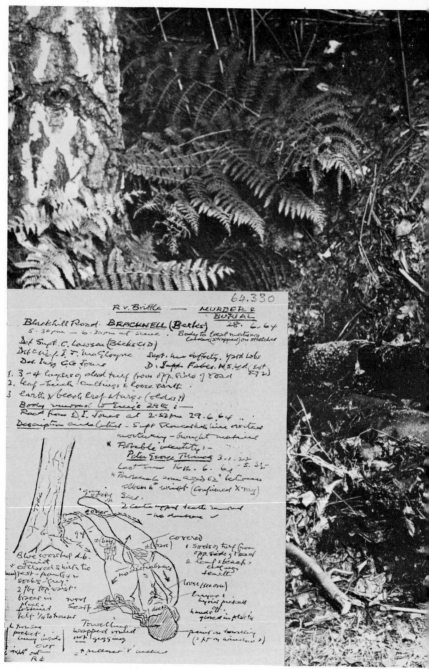

Body of Peter Thomas as found in the Lydney murder; and a page from the author's n

scene

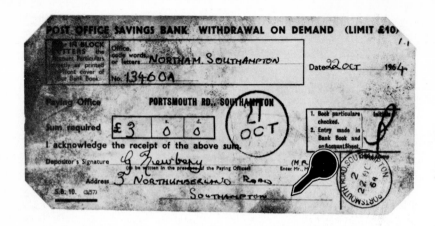

The post office withdrawal slip in the Southampton taxi murder . . .
and enlargements of the fingerprints

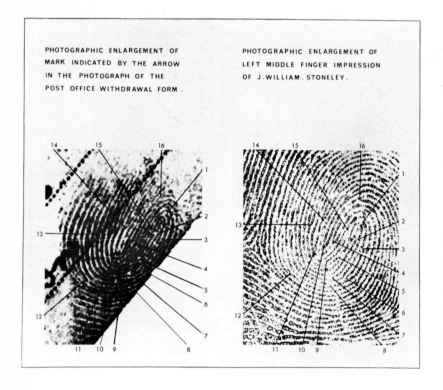

PHOTOGRAPHIC ENLARGEMENT OF
MARK INDICATED BY THE ARROW
IN THE PHOTOGRAPH OF THE
POST OFFICE WITHDRAWAL FORM.

PHOTOGRAPHIC ENLARGEMENT OF
LEFT MIDDLE FINGER IMPRESSION
OF J. WILLIAM. STONELEY.

The author working at the exhumation of a murder victim in Antigua, West Indies

Still on the job – 8 a.m. Battersea Park

and felt sick. He retched but could bring nothing up. He went upstairs to his bed and vomited so violently that little blood vessels in his eyes burst with the agony. He nearly died.

He could not make it all out. Something in the pie? He was uncertain what to do, and lay in bed meanwhile, sick and quite unable to eat. He was still off colour and weak, with mild stomach ache, when he went to his office on Monday morning and read Mrs Formby's letter explaining why she had sent the pie. He took the remains of it to Mrs Radford, who identified it. Her case record showed she had vomited three or four times on the day her father had brought it. The Superintendent called the Surrey police.

The next day, Tuesday 12th April 1949, the remains of the pie were sent to Dr G. E. Turfitt, then analyst at Scotland Yard laboratories. He found it contained *3 ¼ grains of potassium arsenite*, one of the most dangerous of all the arsenic powders! He telephoned his finding immediately to the Surrey police. On the same day Margery Radford died.

The Surrey CID Chief, Superintendent Roberts, took charge of the inquiry, and next day I went down for the autopsy. Turfitt came too, to make immediate tests for arsenic.

There was not much doubt that Margery Radford had been ill with her lung disease for a long time. The tuberculosis was so advanced no-one would have given her much of a chance. But analysis showed arsenic in the stomach and bowel, the liver (2¾ grains here alone), kidneys, the skin and nails, the hair. It was everywhere, and for a thin little creature like Mrs Radford (she weighed only 4 stone 13 pounds) it was more than enough. Six-and-a-half grains or so in all; more than three times the minimal lethal dose. Her hair contained arsenic both in the roots and for a distance of 5 centimetres from the base of the hair. Since hair grows at about 0.44 millimetres every twenty-four hours, it was fair to assume that the first administration of arsenic had occurred some 100 to 120 days before death. She had been systematically poisoned over a period of three months; and the doctors and nurses who attended her daily had never suspected that her more rapid deterioration, pallor, loss of flesh and appetite, and vomiting were due to anything but natural causes. Had there been even the slightest suspicion, a sample of the stool or hair or nail clippings would have confirmed it in a day.

Nobody thought of it. Even if the husband was not very attentive—known to be having an affair with another woman—

why should he kill a dying wife? Why should anyone murder a woman who obviously did not have much longer to live?

Radford used those arguments when the CID told him what analysis revealed, although at first he appeared shattered. He could hardly deny he had bought the pies and drink and asked his father-in-law to deliver them to the hospital, and when he was told arsenic had been found on both the food and in his wife's body he held his face in his hands.

'I don't know anything about it,' he said at last. 'That means murder. I know it looks black against me.' There was a long pause. 'I .admit I bought the pies and gave them to Mr Kite to take to my wife. Why should I want to kill my wife? I knew she was going to die anyway.' Then he looked straight at Superintendent Roberts and said slowly: 'I would not be such a fool as to use arsenic with my experience, as I know the police could find it easily enough. If you think I did it, charge me, and let a judge and jury decide.'

Remember, he was an intelligent technical laboratory assistant. There was just a possibility he was not double-crossing the police. Superintendent Roberts decided to hold his hand. After Radford had agreed to go to the police station the following afternoon for the opening of the inquest he was driven home. As he got out of the car he invited the police officers to come in for a cup of tea, but they understandably declined. That was the last they saw of him. Next morning he was found dead in bed, and already cold. He had poisoned himself, not with arsenic but with the much faster-acting prussic acid.

There is little doubt that if Mrs Radford had not asked Mrs Formby to have the pie analysed, or if Mrs Formby had not acted on this request, the patient's death would have been certified as due only to pulmonary tuberculosis, and her murderer would have got away with it.

Dr Bernard Johnson, a Portsmouth G.P., had no reason to be suspicious when he was called urgently, in July 1953, to see Terence Armstrong, aged six months, and found him dead. The child had been seen by Johnson's partner, Dr Ian Buchanan, earlier that morning. When the emergency call came, at 1.20 p.m., Buchanan had gone off duty to play golf. The child's father, John Armstrong, had made the call sound so urgent that Johnson left his lunch to hurry to the house. He arrived at 1.30 p.m., and Terence had just died. His father, a naval sick-berth attendant, had been home for lunch, but was already back on duty at his station at Haslar. His wife, Janet, said Terence had been a poor colour and difficult to rouse. Dr Johnson had no idea why the little boy had died so suddenly, and said so, adding that he could not give a death certificate.

'Will there have to be an inquest?' asked Janet Armstrong.

Dr Johnson said later he 'thought it odd' that the bereaved mother should ask this question, but she was naturally very upset and he dismissed it from his mind.

Johnson reported the death to the coroner, who instructed Dr Harold Miller, a Portsmouth hospital pathologist, to carry out a post-mortem examination, which he did at 5 p.m. the same day (July 22). Miller found nothing to account for the sudden death, but from the child's throat he recovered what looked like a red skin of some kind, disintegrating: and there were several more in the stomach. Could the child have eaten poisonous berries?

Meanwhile the coroner had also sent a police officer, Sergeant Bulley, to make the usual inquiries at the Armstrongs' home. Bulley was most surprised to find the bereaved parents watching television, and they did not strike him as at all grief-stricken when he asked them the day's events. They told him Terence had been unwell the previous evening, over-sleepy and wheezy. John Armstrong had applied artificial respiration until he was breathing normally, and then had phoned Dr Buchanan. The doctor had called at 8.40 a.m. and 'couldn't make much of it', according to Janet Armstrong. Her husband had come home for lunch at 12.15 p.m., as usual, and found Terence seriously ill.

'His breathing was shallow, otherwise his colour was normal. I touched his hand and he turned blue in the face. I pulled away his pillows and applied artificial respiration again. He turned white and then turned his normal colour, but he was still sleeping. I returned to Hasler on duty, where I rang Dr Buchanan again about 1.20 p.m. and left a message for the doctor to attend my son.'

Sergeant Bulley was astonished. A sick-berth attendant should surely know that an infant needing artificial respiration was in mortal danger, a case for an immediate emergency telephone call. Yet Armstrong had got on his bicycle and pedalled off to Haslar Naval Station, more than four miles away, before calling to his doctor for help.

Sergeant Bulley took the child's last feed-bottle and a vomit-stained pillow to Dr Miller, who told him Terence might have eaten poisonous red berries. Back at the Armstrongs' house Bulley learnt there actually was a *daphne mezereum* bush in the garden, full of the scarlet summer berries notoriously attractive to little children. But how could a baby of six months have reached them? That was easy: he had a sister, Pamela, aged three.

Bulley reported the news to Dr Miller, who sent the dead child's stomach contents to the County Analyst with a note 'suspected daphne berries'. By then the red 'skins' Miller had seen had disappeared but the gastric fluid was pink. 'No daphne or other berries,' the analyst reported, and added, obviously without realizing the significance of it, 'but some uncooked maize starch and the synthetic dye eosin'. Eosin, a pink dye, is used in colouring the capsule of some drugs—notably of the sleeping powder 'Seconal'.

The coroner authorized burial, but the investigation was taken up by the Hampshire CID. It was still almost three weeks after the child's death that, in reply to a phone call from Detective Inspector Gates, Dr Miller first suggested that both the maize and eosin might have come from the encapsuled sleeping drug Seconal, a powerful barbiturate and obviously highly unlikely to be prescribed for a child of six months.

Gates reported to his chief, Superintendent Walter Jones, who immediately had the remains of the stomach contents transferred from the County Analyst to the Scotland Yard laboratories. From this material Lewis Nickolls recovered the equivalent of $\frac{1}{3}$ grain of Seconal. He extracted a further $\frac{1}{50}$ grain from the vomit stain on Terence's pillow.

Gates went back to the Armstrongs and asked if there had ever been Seconal in the house. Both denied it. Police searched the house and also John Armstrong's locker at Haslar but found nothing. Gates went on to question the naval authorities about their medical stores, and learnt that fifty $1\frac{1}{2}$ grain bright pink eosin-tinted Seconal capsules had been stolen from a poison cupboard at the Royal Naval Hospital in February 1955, five months before Terence died. Armstrong had been working in the hospital at the time.

An exhumation order was issued by the Home Office and at the usual hour of dawn we started digging in the Portsmouth cemetery. Another $\frac{1}{20}$ grain of Seconal was recovered from the disintegrating organs. Taking into account the wastage of material at the first autopsy, Nickolls estimated that Terence had swallowed from three to five 1½-grain pink capsules. The drug is fast-acting, and I told Superintendent Jones that I thought such a dose would kill a child of six months well within an hour.

Terence had died just before 1.30 p.m. His father had been in the house from 12.15 to 1 p.m. So had his mother. Either parent could have given him the fatal dose.

What about the child's sickness the previous evening? Janet said both Terence and his sister Pamela had vomited at 4.30 p.m., shortly after tea of Farley rusks and milk. Terence was asleep when her husband came in at 7 p.m. and deeply asleep, 'breathing heavily', at eleven. After giving artificial respiration Armstrong had pushed his fingers down the infant's throat to try to make him vomit, but without success. Armstrong left for work at 7.30 a.m., an hour before the arrival of Dr Buchanan, who found Terence awake, crying, and apparently well, with no fever and no sign of ill health. The Armstrongs both said that at 12.15 p.m. Terence was again deeply asleep and difficult to rouse.

I told the police that a sub-lethal dose given before 4.30 p.m. would have left the child merely drowsy at 11 p.m., not unrousable, and the effects would have entirely worn off by 8.30 next morning. Seconal is not cumulative. There could have been two separate attempts to kill the child: if so, the first, unsuccessful attempt had been made when only Janet was in the house. Whether the stain on the pillow containing Seconal was made by the vomiting at 4.30 p.m. or shortly before death the following day could not be established.

Although the Armstrongs were young—he twenty-four, she merely nineteen—Terence had been their third child. The first, Philip, had died when less than three months old in March 1954. Dr Stone, who had attended him at the time, certified that death was due to broncho-pneumonia, although he told me he had found no stethoscopic signs and there had been no rise in temperature. Dr Stone had been eighty-two at the time, and I did not think he had much clinical acumen. The police asked for an exhumation order, and again we went digging at dawn. 'There won't be much of the body left after all this time,' John Armstrong suggested to Inspector Gates as they stood in the cemetery. He was right. I collected what material I could from the rotting skeleton, but, as we anticipated, Nickolls's analysis proved negative. Superintendent Jones had no proof that Philip Armstrong had not died from natural causes, though he suspected it.

Jones invited Armstrong to go to the station to 'assist the police in their inquiries'. Armstrong knew his rights and declined. 'I'll come if I'm arrested, but I want to know the charge.' He asked his wife to telephone for his solicitor.

'I have seen a document,' Jones said slowly, 'that reports evidence of poison in your son Terence's body.'

'Yes, berries,' replied Armstrong.

'No, it was Seconal. You know what Seconal is?'

'Yes, but neither of us ever had it in the house.'

Jones and Gates had reached the limit of their inquiries. It was left to the Director of Public Prosecutions, Sir Theobald Mathew, to decide whether they had found enough evidence to justify a charge of murder against John or Janet Armstrong or both. The decision was that a jury would probably not be convinced. So they remained free, and John Armstrong wrote his version of the case for a Sunday newspaper. It looked as if Superintendent Walter Jones had failed to nail his man.

A year passed, during which the Armstrongs quarrelled and drifted apart. On 24th July 1956, two days after the first anniversary of Terence's death, Janet applied for a separation order and maintenance, but the Gosport magistrates refused. She walked out of court in tears of frustration and rage.

'Is there anything you'd like to tell the police, Mrs Armstrong?' It was Detective Inspector Gates at her side. 'Anything at all?'

She hesitated only a moment. 'Yes, there is.' And she made and signed a statement that was eventually to reunite her with her husband, in the dock at Winchester, where they were tried jointly for the murder of their son.

Her statement was not a confession or even an accusation, but she made the damning admission that there had been Seconal in the house. She said her husband told her he had been taking some himself, but after the police called he told her to get rid of it, saying he might be blamed for Terence's death or at least for having stolen the capsules from Haslar. 'I took the capsules out of the bottle,' she told Gates. 'I should say there were six or seven pink ones, and I threw them on the rubbish heap at the bottom of the garden.'

A wife is entitled to cherish and obey her husband, whatever he does, and therefore is immune from a charge of being accessory after the act. But Janet had been in the house and with the child, on and off, about the time of the fatal poisoning. Nobody knew who had given the capsules, and there was evidence that she might have administered a sub-lethal dose the day before. Therefore the charge against them both was murder.

I knew the trial would be a testing one for me when I heard the defence were being assisted by Francis Camps. I could be sure he would spare no effort to loosen, if not pull apart, medical evidence he could criticize, particularly the precise timing of the absorption of Seconal.

Nickolls and I had been led to believe the Seconal that had been administered was in the normal gelatine capsules, and it was on this assumption that we gave our evidence at the preliminary hearing. I said I thought the fatal dose 'must have been swallowed well inside one hour, almost certainly within half an hour before death'. Then it was learnt that the Seconal stolen from Haslar had been in a new type of capsule made of methyl cellulose. This did not dissolve nearly as quickly as gelatine, but allowed the drug to leak out, so that it must have been more slowly absorbed. I carried out a series of experiments before the trial started and found that capsules made of methyl cellulose did not leak substantially until some twenty or thirty minutes after swallowing, and then needed another twenty minutes for the dose to become fully effective. This new timing still gave John Armstrong the opportunity of poisoning his son, although it was a near thing.

I could now anticipate the questions Camps would suggest when coaching the defence counsel; neither of whom was likely to miss a point. John was defended by Malcolm Wright, Q.C., and Janet by Norman Skelhorn, Q.C., as skilled and pertinacious as any defending counsel before he became Sir Norman Skelhorn, Director of Public Prosecutions. I survived a very testing cross-examination, worn down a little, but by no means battered.

As usual in a poisoning case, the Attorney General, at that time Sir Reginald Manningham-Buller, led the prosecution. John Armstrong admitted having 'surreptitiously recovered', in his own euphemism, drugs from Haslar, and having them in the house at the time of Terence's death. 'But as soon as I asked Janet to dispose of the remains of the drugs she said she had already done so.' Janet denied this and said she had been wrong in stating that Terence was already in a poor state when John had come home for lunch: it was not until 12.45, she said, that Terence's condition became worse. She added that in the meantime she had been in the kitchen cooking her husband's lunch and had not gone in to the baby. It was what the lawyers call a 'cut-throat defence,' each accusing the other of the crime.

In his summing up Mr Justice Pilcher reminded the jury that they did not have to find *both* of the accused either guilty or not guilty, and it took them only forty-three minutes to find John Armstrong guilty and to acquit Janet.

I was pleased that I had not been bested by Camps, in spite of his efforts for the defence. Three years later the boot was on the other foot, for I was asked by solicitors at Windsor defending Sergeant Marcus Marymont of the USAF to help prepare an 'apellate brief' in the hope of reversing a conviction for murder. Marymont had been found guilty of poisoning his wife with arsenic. This time Camps and Nickolls had put the medical case for the Court Martial prosecution. Could I prise their case apart? Alas for the prospects of a reverse contest. I read their evidence with care but I could find no fault with it. Putting up a fight for a cause already lost only damages one's repute with the lawyers, and the law: distasteful 'contests' between experts such as those between Spilsbury and Bronte are happily things of the past: they more often arose from professional 'needle' or frank jealousy than from a desire to see that justice was done.

CHAPTER 21

THE TRIST CASE IN PORTUGAL

When I entered the field in the mid thirties an international conference of forensic pathologists was quite a rare event, but since air travel has cut time to ribbons we have met literally all over the world. In the last two decades I have addressed such meetings in most European capitals from Stockholm to Budapest, in the Far East, in Sydney and Melbourne, New Zealand, in Toronto, New York, New Orleans, Los Angeles, and the Caribbean, in Rhodesia and South Africa . . . the world was an oyster which seemed easily prised open if one had world colleagues and experience in this kind of pathology.

More, so many countries lacked real experts in the field that I have had calls from foreign Governments to murders in Cyprus, Bermuda, Barbados, St Lucia, and other Caribbean islands; and I have been asked for advice on cases in Canada, Australia, France, Kuwait, Gibraltar and the Virgin Islands. Invitations have been so sedulous and hospitality so generous that I have no right to grumble because once, just once, I was told to keep out and refused permission to go and see the bodies at my own expense.

This happened in Portugal, the country to which a Brighton dentist, Arthur Trist, set out by car with his wife and two little children in February 1959. They were on a holiday that ended abruptly and tragically in the Vale dos Gatos, near Lisbon, where they stopped at the Muxito Motel. After putting the children to bed Trist and his wife tucked in to a meal of Lagos Obidos clams and veal escalope, retiring to their detached chalet at 11 p.m. Next day the maid knocked on their door at 10 a.m., again at noon, and yet again at 4 p.m., without getting a reply. She called the motel manager, who forced an entry to the chalet. The children, hungry, tired, and puzzled, told him Mummy and Daddy 'won't wake up', and he soon realized they would never wake up again.

Arthur Trist was lying spreadeagled on his bed dressed only in a pyjama top. His wife, Patricia, more fully dressed, was kneeling against the edge of the other bed in the room. There was no sign of forcible entry or of ransacking, and nothing that the police could find to suggest murder or suicide.

The procurator of Almada District instructed medical officers (corresponding to our police surgeons, not pathologists) to examine the bodies. They found no injuries or other clues to the cause of death except vomit stains on the face and clothes in both cases. The British Consul in Lisbon, Leslie Blackwell, telephoned Trist's parents and the children were flown home. Harry Weaver, a journalist on the *Daily Mail*, scenting a story, flew to Lisbon, where he was told death was due to food poisoning: specifically to those Lagos Obidos clams.

Weaver asked the obvious question: how many other people had been affected? He was told, to his surprise, that clams from the same batch had been eaten by other guests at the motel, and that the restaurant staff had finished them off, and nobody had so much as a tummy ache. Jose dos Reis, a waiter, told Weaver he had eaten the five clams the Trists had left, and said they were excellent, and so was his health. Puzzled, Weaver got permission from the motel manager to look round the Trists' chalet, and tried to discover what they had been doing between eating dinner and being struck down dead. The manager showed him exactly where the bodies had been found. A bathroom adjoined the bedroom, and one of the couple, apparently Arthur Trist, had had a bath: there was a water-level mark on the bath tub, although the water had been let out, and four spent matches lay near the water heater. Mrs Trist had evidently rinsed stockings in the washbasin beside the bath. That was all they seemed to have done. Their beds had not been slept in. It looked as if they had been taken ill suddenly and violently, and simultaneously—or one of them would have been able to call for help.

Back in England, Weaver made contact with a doctor named Cyril Pragnell, who had been a fellow student and a close friend of Arthur Trist at Guy's. Dr Pragnell, who had attended my lectures in forensic medicine, suggested to Weaver that they should ask my advice. Pragnell was greatly concerned about the children's future, which was likely to be affected substantially by the cause of their parents' death. For before setting out on holiday, Arthur Trist had taken out an accident insurance for £10,000.

No doubt he had in mind some car accident or a bathing tragedy whilst abroad, but the cover was not limited to these and the policy defined an accidental death in the usual terms: 'If the insured should sustain bodily injury resulting wholly and exclusively from violent accidental external and visible means, which injury, solely and independently of any other cause, caused his/her death.' That would not include food poisoning, which insurance companies treat as an illness; but it covered risks like fire, crumbling masonry, and other misadventures that might befall a policy-holder in a hotel. But surely there would be some evidence of such an accident? Food poisoning might not seem likely in the circumstances, with the waiter and everyone unscathed, but there was the vomiting, and what else could have caused their death?

Food poisoning is not the only cause of vomiting, which is also a common event in the last phases of carbon monoxide poisoning—a very sudden and silent killer. I asked Weaver about the water heater in the bathroom, which was evidently run off butane gas. Was the supply cylinder inside or outside the bathroom? Outside. Was there any smell of gas? No. Did the water heater have a flue? No. (Ah, getting warm.) What was the ventilation like in the bathroom? Minimal. (Much warmer.) If the Trists had been almost overpowered by carbon monoxide in the bathroom, but had just managed to stagger out, might they have collapsed where their bodies were found? Yes, the positions seemed just right for that.

Carbon monoxide poisoning due to a faulty or inadequately ventilated gas installation in a hotel would surely fit into the insurance company's definition of an accident.

Had the Portuguese medical officers perhaps jumped to a false conclusion and failed to look for the evidence? No Government official likes to admit a mistake, least of all to foreigners, so we proceeded with caution and tact. I did not tell the Portugese authorities, as I regularly pointed out to my students, that we shall all die after our last meal (but it doesn't necessarily follow that it killed us); nor did I remind them—for surely they would have known—that it was out of season for the plankton that makes clams dangerous. To begin with we merely asked for copies of the post-mortem reports. In reply we were told the bodies had been removed to the Institute of Legal Medicine in Lisbon for analysis, and that certain 'toxins' were suspected. After some 'reminders' we were told that the analyses had confirmed that death was due to food poisoning, but the Institute declined to produce any toxic material, cultures, bacteria or other scientific evidence. Under gentle pressure they later admitted 'there were slight traces of carbon monoxide' in Mrs Trist's body 'but not enough to cause death'.

'Why not in both bodies?' I asked. 'They were together.'

It was clear from the post-mortem reports that the Portuguese experts had taken only organs for analysis but not the vital blood and muscle samples for testing for carbon monoxide. Evidently they had tacitly adopted the assumptions made by the medical officers at the scene, and the question of carbon monoxide fumes had been completely overlooked. I could hardly believe that the inquiries had been as casual until I found that the post-mortem report on Mrs Trist recorded the condition of *both* lungs although she had had one removed by Lord Brock, the famous surgeon, several years previously, as a check with his records confirmed.

I told Pragnell I was willing to go and examine the bodies and the chalet immediately the Portuguese gave permission, and then he and Harry Weaver flew to Lisbon. At the motel the friendly manager opened the Trists' chalet for them and they surveyed and photographed the bathroom. It was quite small: eight feet by four feet six inches, and ten feet high. They examined and tested the water heater, and were satisfied it did not leak. But, as Weaver had said, it had no flue and the bathroom ventilation was most inadequate, consisting of half a small circular window which was closed and only finely louvred. It was clear from their replies to questions that since the tragedy no tests had been made on the electrical or gas supplies in the chalet or on the ventilation.

Pragnell succeeded in getting an interview with the Director of the Institute of Legal Medicine, but all his other requests were refused. He was not allowed to examine the bodies, to take samples or blood or muscle, or to question the Portuguese experts. Finally Pragnell passed on my suggestion that the cause of death might be carbon monoxide poisoning and asked if I could examine the bodies and the scene. This brought an official riposte from the Public prosecutor in Lisbon, saying that his Government experts had already 'solved the problem' and that it would be contrary to Portuguese law to allow any foreigner to check either the police reports on the chalet or the post-mortem findings. My suggestion that gas fumes in the bathroom might have caused collapse with vomiting and death was scornfully dismissed on the grounds that it was made without my having 'seen the bodies or taken cognisanse of the elaborate analyses that were taking place in Lisbon'.

Elaborate? Elaborately misdirected, rather—to clam toxins and histamines and the like. Testing for the presence of carbon monoxide takes two or three minutes, and the averagely intelligent 'lab boy' can do it.

However, the decision of the Portuguese authorities was final, and I was not allowed to go to Lisbon to examine the bodies. I played what proved to be a trump card: The family of the deceased asked, through the usual formal channels (not our medico-legal or press channels), if the Portuguese Government would allow the bodies of the Trists to be buried in their native land. Of course the request could not be refused.

Sixteen days after death, the bodies were flown in sealed coffins to Heathrow and immediately taken, not to an undertaker's chapel, but to my mortuary at Guy's. They were accompanied by an official document from the Public Prosecutor giving his final decision that 'the cause of death was *ill defined*'. It took me only a few minutes to define it—and beyond dispute.

The bodies were mere hulks, bereft of all their organs, but that didn't matter. Within ten minutes samples from the legs showed carbon monoxide in muscle fluid of 52 per cent in one and 50 per cent the other, the equivalent of at least 60 per cent in the blood—lethal saturations of gas fumes. But even before the tests I was sure my theory was right. I was sure the moment the coffins were opened, and I saw the characteristic cherry-pink colour of the skin. How all the Portuguese 'experts' missed that remained the only unsolved mystery. It was no more than a case of simple thinking and deduction of Holmesian type: looking at what there was to see, and seeing its significance.

I got my colleague Donald Teare to make an independent examination of the bodies and he agreed with my opinion. My figures for the carbon monoxide saturation were further confirmed by L. C. Nickolls, then Director of the Metropolitan Police laboratory, and by Squadron Leader Fryer at the RAF Medical Research Laboratories. Meanwhile the Chief Chemist to the Calor Gas Research Division made a mock-up of the chalet bathroom and installed a water heater of the same model. His experiments showed that an accumulation of 0.28 per cent of carbon monoxide could develop in one hour. 'This concentration,' he reported, 'could be fatal in half an hour'.

We informed the Portuguese of our findings and invited their experts to come at any time and examine the bodies, the materials, and the laboratory tests we had made. They refused the invitation, denied the possibility of gas poisoning, and elaborated their food-poison theory.

That did not worry me or Pragnell or the Trist family. Dr Ian Milne, the coroner into whose London district the bodies had come, was told of the circumstances and held a public inquest at Southwark, as he was entitled to do with unsatisfactory matters coming into his area of jurisdiction. Our evidence satisfied not only this shrewd London coroner, but also a solicitor who was in court with a watching brief for the London and Lancashire Insurance Company, which had accepted the Trist policy. Having heard my findings, he told the court 'any proper claim' would be met, and, without further litigation or cost, the £10,000 was paid to the children within a week. It was all paid over to them intact, as none of the experts involved in the case claimed a penny for their services.

'A triumph for English obstinacy,' the coroner called it. Harry Weaver paid me a nice compliment in the last chapter of his story for the *Daily Mail*: 'The mystery had been solved by a pathologist sitting in his office a thousand miles away.'

One does not expect a medal for helping two orphaned children to get justice, but I hardly thought I deserved to be put on the carpet. It was on a very elegant if slightly threadbare carpet, in a lofty room in Whitehall from which perhaps Lord Palmerston had dispatched gunboats to teach foreigners a lesson. Times had changed; the elegant (but also slightly threadbare) Foreign Office dignitary who lectured me so severely wanted to send 'our oldest ally' nothing more menacing than a billet-doux. Disturbed relations had arisen, he said, eyeing me coldly, as if I ought to have thought of the political consequences before questioning the toxicity of the clams, over this 'sad case'. Would I care to write a letter myself to the authorities at Almada or in Lisbon, to help repair the damage, or would I like the Foreign Office to draft one for me to sign?

The only part of his homily that I agreed with was that the case was indeed sad, for an innocent couple had been killed, and their children orphaned, by a Portuguese contraption that exceeded the British standard Code of Practice safety level by eight times. As it did not appear that this was the kind of comment the Foreign Office wanted me to make in my letter, I told the official I would have no part in such humbug, took up my hat and walked out.

I was disturbed by the incident, because there is no place for deception or dishonesty in a calling that is dedicated to the discovery of truth. Diplomatic and political considerations should never be allowed to impede or divert medico-legal experts from their duty to try to find out what really happened, no matter whose feelings or prestige may be hurt.

Once, in a speech of my own a year or two later, I said this at a meeting of the European Académie de Médecine Légale, which happened to be held on that occasion in Budapest. Early next morning a large black Russian car arrived at my hotel, and I was requested to accompany the driver and an ominously forbidding-looking 'comrade' to the City Hall. After nearly two hours' indoctrination in French by the Chairman of the City Council on the efficiency of the Hungarian Government service in legal medicine, I was released at a back door, to walk away on the pavement like an unwelcome visitor at the Hall. My wife was agreeably surprised to see me walk into our hotel again: people have been 'held' for questioning for indefinitely long periods in European gaols for saying less.

CHAPTER 22

THE MURDER OF BRENDA NASH

Perhaps the most despicable of all crimes—certainly the one that rouses the public to such a fury that women will throng the approaches to a court, brandish fists, and shout abuse at the prisoner when he is brought to trial—is the sex violation and murder of little girls. The victims are nearly always 5 or 6 to 12 years old and usually bright little things. Some wretched mother has nearly always been 'driven out of her mind' by grief and anxiety in the interval before her child is found cruelly raped and strangled, sometimes battered out of existence by a man she can only think of as a monster. To the public he is, and the women would lynch him if he were not always given police protection on the way into court for trial. To the psychiatrist he is just a pervert.

The criminal records are unfortunately full of such cases, and my own files contain some particularly gruesome examples. Let me recount two.

On Sunday 8th July 1951, a girl of 7½ called Christine Butcher left her home in Windsor carrying her black china doll. Her mother had seen her standing near the training headquarters of the famous boxer 'Sugar' Ray Robinson during the afternoon, and when she failed to return home the police were alerted; in the Windsor area, the Home Counties, and the Metropolitan area.

Parks, the local woods, riverside walks up and down the Thames, Runnymede, Windsor Great Park itself were all searched in vain during the next two days. Then, at dusk on 10th July two visitors to Windsor were walking through Steven's Meadow under the shadow of Windsor Castle when they came upon her body. Christine lay hidden by the long grass, clutching the big black doll she had last been seen hugging. Her blue raincoat spread over her, covering her blotched face.

Police were called to the scene, then Superintendent Walter Crombie, the County Chief of CID. He telephoned me in London and I went down at once with my secretary, Jean Scott-Dunn. Superintendent George Salter of the Scotland Yard laboratories was there when I arrived.

The 1 a.m. scene in that beautiful meadow, scene of the Royal Shows, was eerie. It was dark but the black outlines of the historic castle stood out against a sky lit by the orange glow of city lights. We all crouched or knelt round the body in the glare of car headlights and set about collecting every item, every scrap of evidence there was. Jobs done at 1 a.m. in open ground have to be as good as any at noon in the comfort of a Park Lane hotel when it comes to facing counsel at trial. We had to find everything.

Christine had been strangled with the belt of her blue raincoat, tied tightly round her neck and secured by a double knot. Strands of the long grass in which she lay were caught up in the knot, showing that she had been murdered in the exact spot where her body lay. She had been cruelly violated both before and after death.

An hour later I performed the autopsy at the mortuary of the King Edward VII Hospital, Windsor, without finding a useful clue. Her nails were cut short, and scrapings revealed no foreign material. The police tested her doll for fingerprints and found only her own. Dr Holden of the Metropolitan Police Laboratory filed details of clothing, hair and blood samples, also soil and grass, in the hope of comparing them with a suspect's clothing or footwear; but no suspect came within striking distance, although a famous Yard detective, Superintendent Colin McDougal, was put in charge of the case. It was no use. Christine's killer escaped, as so many child murderers do: they lure the little girls off the street or into the woods for 'some large blackberries' or with a promise of 'sweets' and few are seen alive again.

Little children are easily lured away by strangers and, as the great Canadian pathologist Boyd once wrote, 'life's little candle is easily snuffed': they are no match for their assailants, who all too often escape the proper consequences. These cases are as difficult as any the police have to solve, but they are also among the most important, for the assailant may have, like Straffen, an irresistible impulse to repeat the crime; as in the following two cases.

A Girl Guide of twelve, living at Twickenham and referred to simply as Barbara (for obvious reasons her full name was withheld), was abducted by a man in a car and driven into open country, abused for three hours and finally raped, but fortunately not killed. On the contrary, he drove her back to within a mile of her home. She kept her wits about her and described him, correctly, as a thickset, dark-haired man of about forty, with a 'starfish' scar puckering his right cheek; and, also correctly, she said the car was a black Vauxhall Wyvern.

The case occurred on 9th September 1960, and police inquiries were proceeding in a routine way when, on 28th October, another Girl Guide disappeared. She lived at Heston, about three miles from Barbara's home. Her age was eleven, and her name was Brenda Nash. The police asked if anyone had seen a black Vauxhall Wyvern in the area on the evening of her disappearance, and found two men who had seen one parked and driven off at just about the right time and place. One of the witnesses, a man named Wakefield, thought he might recognize the driver.

Detective Superintendent Hixson of Scotland Yard took charge of the case, and organized a search of the country around. He also detailed subordinate officers to question all owners of black Vauxhall Wyverns who lived in the district. On 24th November, when Brenda had been missing nearly four weeks, Sergeant Nicholson visited a man named Arthur Albert Jones, who lived at Hounslow, a bare mile from Brenda's home. He was forty-four, and lived with his wife and their sixteen-year-old son. He was dark, thick-set, and had a scar on his right cheek. Where had he been on 28th October, the night that Brenda Nash disappeared?

'At my sister-in-law's, in Beckenham,' he said. 'My wife and I went over to see about a vacuum cleaner.'

Sergeant Nicholson saw Jones's sister-in-law, Mrs Eldridge, the next day, and she confirmed the alibi. It looked as if this promising line had petered out. Then a little more than two weeks later, on Sunday 11th December, three small boys playing Cowboys and Indians on Yately Common, near Camberley, saw a girl's shoe sticking out from some loose bracken at the bottom of a ditch. Looking more closely, they saw that it was attached to a foot. When the police came and pulled away the dead grass and broken-off bush branches, they found the decomposed body of a girl dressed in Girl Guide uniform with shoulder tabs of the 5th Heston Company. 'BRENDA FOUND' was the headline in the next morning's newspapers.

That Sunday afternoon I was reading in my country home at Tring when the telephone rang.

'Superintendent Jones here, sir. We've got a case in Camberley. Can you come down? Yately Common, sir. We could meet on the bridge at Camberley.'

It was bitterly cold. It was drizzling. It was getting dark. But there was no alternative. Taking a pair of Wellingtons, I drove to the bridge at Camberley to meet Detective Chief Superintendent Walter Jones, one of the most remarkable and successful detectives I ever met. He had been Chief of the Hampshire CID for eight years, and solved every murder case he had investigated. Yately Common was just inside Jones's county, so when the body was found he took over the case from Hixson of the Yard.

Characteristically, Jones had called a fire engine to the scene, so that I could examine the body under the light from arc lamps. Next day I performed the autopsy at Cambridge Hospital, Aldershot, in the presence of Jones.

She had been lying there dead about six weeks, I thought; and we knew she had been missing forty-four days. She had been strangled and the grip on her neck was no momentary act, for asphyxial changes showed it must have lasted at least a quarter to half a minute. She had also been hit on the head, but not a disabling blow. She had struggled. She had not been raped, but the disarrangement of her knickers and vest suggested an attempted sexual assault. There were some foreign green fibres on her outer clothing, and a piece of chain was found under her head. Her body had been found about twenty yards from the main Camberley-Reading road, and some twenty-five miles from her home in Heston.

Walter Jones ordered a complete re-checking of all statements taken from persons questioned about Brenda's disappearance; and that led to a fresh check on the alibi of his namesake, the man with the scar, Arthur Albert Jones. He was invited to the station to help the police with their inquiries. 'BRENDA: MAN HELD 20 HOURS' was the newspaper headline on 29 December. The story the paper could not tell was that Jones had been put on an identity parade *and picked out by the Girl Guide named Barbara* as the man who had raped her on 9th September.

Jones was charged with that crime and remanded in custody. Chief Superintendent Jones went to see Mrs Eldridge, who broke down and admitted the vacuum-cleaner alibi was false! Neither Jones nor his wife had visited her on the evening of 28th October, when Brenda Nash had disappeared.

Two days later Jones's solicitor handed the police a statement which he said was his client's final truthful statement of his movements on the night of 28th October. According to this statement, Jones had driven to the West End of London and gone with a prostitute, and had not arrived home until 2 a.m. because of engine trouble in his car. His wife, he said, was angry and wanted to know where he had been. He told her about the engine trouble, but she was not satisfied, and refused to speak to him the next morning at breakfast. Then the papers published the news of Brenda's disappearance and police inquiries about a black Vauxhall Wyvern car. Mrs Jones asked her husband if he knew anything about it. 'You don't think I know anything about that?' he replied. Then he admitted he had gone with a prostitute; and to avoid shame and embarrassment Jones persuaded his wife and her sister to say he had been to Beckenham that evening about a vacuum cleaner.

The piece of chain found under Brenda's head matched other pieces found at Jones's house, and the green fibres on her clothing were similar to fibres from a green rug in his car. That was the total scientific evidence, and there was at that time nothing much else to connect him with the murder. But Barbara's identification and the breakdown of Jones's alibi made the rape charge much stronger, and on 15th March he was tried at the Old Bailey for this offence. The Senior Treasury Counsel, Mervyn Griffith-Jones, prosecuted. Chief Superintendent Walter Jones was not concerned in this case but he was keenly interested in the evidence, especially that given for the defence, for it could bear on his enquiries.

Jones, on trial, said he had an alibi for the evening of 9th September, the date of Barbara's rape. He had driven to the West End and gone with a prostitute, and had not arrived home until 2 a.m. because of engine trouble in his car. His wife, he said, was angry and wanted to know where he had been. He told her about the engine trouble, but she was not satisfied, and refused to speak to him the next morning at breakfast. The papers carried headlines of Barbara's rape and police inquiries about a black Vauxhall Wyvern car, and Mrs Jones asked her husband if he knew anything about it. 'You don't think I know anything about that?' he replied. Then he admitted he had gone with a prostitute.

Walter Jones compared this evidence with the written statement made by Jones to his solicitor on 4th January. The two alibis were almost word for word identical, except that the earlier one was for 28th October, the date of Brenda Nash's disappearance!

Arthur Albert Jones was convicted of the rape of Barbara and sentenced to imprisonment for fourteen years. This earned him a place on the picture pages of the next day's newspapers. And the man named Wakefield, who had earlier told the police he had seen a black Vauxhall Wyvern parked and driven off at Heston in the evening of 28th October, walked into Hounslow Police Station with a newspaper in his hand and pointed to Jones's photograph and *said that man was the driver!*

Other witnesses came forward to testify that Jones had been in Heston that evening, and a fellow prisoner named Roberts said Jones had confessed to him that he had killed Brenda. 'I done it,' he had said, according to Roberts. Prisoners dislike men on such charges: ordinary murderers are 'kings', but child ravishers are 'dirt'. Roberts reported the conversation to the prison Governor, who passed it on to the police.

Finally, a woman named Miss Carruthers, who worked at a hairdresser's, recalled that at the time of Brenda Nash's disappearance another employee had told her that her uncle had a black Vauxhall Wyvern and seemed anxious. . . . The girl who told her this was Christine Eldridge, the daughter of Mrs Eldridge of Beckenham. Christine had been within earshot when Jones and his wife had persuaded her mother to support his false alibi.

Wakefield and another man who said he had seen Jones in Heston both picked him out on an identity parade, and on 10th May Chief Superintendent Walter Jones walked into Wandsworth Prison and formally charged him with the murder of Brenda Nash.

The trial was held on 17th June, again at the Old Bailey and again with Mervyn Griffith-Jones the leading Counsel for the Crown. After only three months he still had a very clear recollection of the alibi Jones had given in the witness box at his trial for the rape of Barbara on 9th September of the previous year; and before him, in the papers delivered to the Director of Public Prosecutions, was the alibi Jones had given in writing, through his solicitor, for 28th October, the date of Brenda Nash's disappearance and probably of her murder. Almost word for word the same! But could the jury be allowed to know that the accused had told this tale before?

It was a delicate point of law. Normally the accused cannot be

asked questions that 'tend to show' he has been convicted or even
charged with any offence other than that for which he is being tried,
and Griffith-Jones trod very delicately when he asked the accused
about a similar explanation he had given to his wife on 'another
occasion'; and he brought out the duplication, word for word, of the
two stories without once using the word 'alibi'.

It took the jury only seven minutes to find Arthur Albert Jones
guilty of murder. Mr Justice Sachs sentenced him to 'life'
imprisonment, to commence when he had finished his fourteen years'
sentence for rape. Appeals were lodged against both conviction and
sentence, and the former went to the House of Lords before it was
finally dismissed.

A child who survives assault can at least speak and even identify her
assailant, as Barbara did: but a baby who is battered has to lie helpless
while the guilty parent or guardian glibly explains away the injuries to
a credulous doctor or nurse, social worker or even police officer. 'Fell
out of the pram, off the table, or down the stairs', to account for
crushing skull injuries and so on, can be a cover-up for ferocious
punching, kicking, beating, or hurling against a wall.

The Battered Baby Syndrome is a relatively modern phenomenon.
Ordinary ill-treatment of infants—lack of proper care and attention,
starvation and neglect—is an age-old tragedy; so, of course, is
infanticide, the killing of the new-born by distraught mothers. But
the brutal bashing, beating, and sometimes killing of infants by
parents or guardians who lose their tempers is a comparatively new
crime; and when the results of it were first noticed by an American
radiologist, Dr Caffey, about 1944, he thought the increase in the
numbers of infants with fractures sent to him for X-ray must be due to
a new bone disease, a kind of fragility of bone in which fractures
developed in ordinary play or even spontaneously. The so-called
Caffey Syndrome was not properly recognized for another ten years.
Then Dr Silverman, also American, established that the injured
infants had perfectly normal skeletal structures, that their injuries
were traumatic, and that they could not have been caused by the
explanations given by those in charge of them. Two years later, in
1955, two more American doctors, Woolley and Evans, bluntly
proposed that parents or guardians were to blame.

Nobody wanted to believe it, and seriously injured infants would
frequently be treated in hospital and discharged back to the care of

those who had injured them, only to suffer again. Health visitors and child welfare officers continued to be all too easily fobbed off by highly implausible excuses. It soon became clear to those interested in the problem that England was having its share of such cases, and that they were often going unrecognized. 'What is really needed is a *cause célèbre* with front-page treatment in the press,' Dr Eric Turner wrote in the *British Medical Journal* in 1964. A month or two later I happened to have such a case.

It had begun in December 1963, when Laurence Michael Dean, aged eighteen, called a doctor to look at his daughter, Susan Moon, aged four months, whom he had found dead in her cot. He said only that she had been 'off colour' for a few days. The doctor noticed and commented on some surface bruising; Dean said she had hit her head on the cot a few days before. The doctor had not been visiting the family or the child, so he reported the case to the Coroner, who ordered an autopsy. Dr Francis Camps found a fractured skull, several fractured ribs, a ruptured liver, and numerous recent bruises, notably in the inner abdomen, under the jaw, and over the scalp. The father explained all these by saying that when he found her not breathing he tried artificial respiration, giving her the 'kiss of life' and thereby fracturing her ribs and, in order to hold her head up, gripping her throat and so making the stranglingly tight marks on her neck; while pressing his hand into the pit of her stomach might have caused the injuries to her abdomen, and perhaps in rocking her he fractured her liver. The astonishing fact is that these explanations were accepted, and at the inquest an 'open verdict' was returned.

Dean walked out a free man, moved to Wadhurst, in Sussex, and married Susan Moon's mother before she bore him another child. Named Michael after his father, he lived for only five weeks, and he died in a doctor's arms. Dean said he had been perfectly well until, shortly after a feed from a bottle, he started to whimper. 'I picked him up and he stopped crying.' Back in his cot, 'his breathing sounded heavy'; and Dean picked him up and carried him downstairs. A neighbour took them both to a near-by doctor, who rocked Michael in his arms in an attempt to revive him. The baby died, and the doctor did not need to look very closely to suspect the father's account was very far from being the whole truth. The little body was brought to me at Guy's for autopsy.

I found nineteen separate fresh bruises in six different parts of the body, including the head, deep bruising of the upper abdomen, and a ruptured liver. Dean then gave an explanation for some of the injuries. As he was nursing Michael on his knee, he said, the baby started to roll off, and in trying to save him 'my knee came up and hit him in the abdomen'. I said I could not accept Dean's story.

The two deaths were reported to the Director of Public Prosecutions and considered together in the trial of Dean for murder, of which he was convicted at the Old Bailey on 19th January 1965. It was the first English conviction for murder in such a case; but the 'on dit' was growing, and the Dean case was no sooner over than I walked downstairs from No.1 court into court No.5 at the Old Bailey to give evidence in another battered baby case and to tell a horrified court that I had found seventy-three separately countable injuries on the surface of the child. Five days later I was giving evidence at Reading in yet another case of a baby whose death had been caused by parental cruelty. The mother had been in the habit of tying her child's hands behind his body and shutting him in his bedroom, believing he could not get out; but he had reached the bathroom, where he had tripped and struck his head; lying unconscious at a freezing temperature,he was found dead next morning. My autopsy showed that he had been struck many times and kicked at least once.

The Reading case was before magistrates, and the maximum sentence they could impose was only six months' imprisonment or a fine of £25. Plainly this was hopelessly inadequate in this and other similar cases.

In the north country a child of six months was slapped across the face by his father so fiercely that he was blinded for life. Medical evidence was given that 60 per cent of his face was covered with bruises. One leg was badly bruised, the X-ray showed a thigh had been broken, and there was a brain haemorrhage. Again the sentence was six months.

In another case, at Mansfield, the father of a child of four months was given the same sentence for having burned his baby's face, broken one of his legs and one of his arms, and cut his tongue to stop his crying. 'It never took to *me*, that child; always upsetting *me*, making my turns come on; I didn't do it on purpose; I still love the baby. It would keep on crying,' the man told a Detective Chief Inspector.

While punishment of such parents was inadequate, what was really important was the safe care of the child. Towards the end of my time (in the mid-seventies) the incidence of battered babies fell away

markedly, largely as a result of a higher threshold of awareness—
among doctors, nurses, children's care centres and the like—of this
disturbing crime; and possibly also of treatment by social workers,
less by psychiatrists, of the parents under stress who might 'take it out'
of their children. For my part I did all I could, by public lectures and
writing in journals, to get the condition properly recognized for what it
really was: a serious current stream of crime that had to be controlled
if it could not be stemmed altogether.

The problem remains. Babies are still battered, sometimes fatally.
In a survey published in 1977 the NSPCC estimated that in the
previous year about 8,000 infants suffered such ill-treatment, and
about one hundred of them died of their injuries.

CHAPTER 23

THE LYDNEY MURDER — A RIDDLE OF MAGGOTS

The police record for clearing up murders in England and Wales could hardly be better. Of the 150 or so real murders—not technical homicides—they hear about each year, only a handful have to be written off as unsolved. But how many more are unknown to the police? How many murdered persons are buried or, worse, cremated, as ordinary natural or accidental deaths? How many are hidden so successfully that their bodies are never found and recognized as human remains?

It's anybody's guess, of course. But it seems certain that some murders escape detection, for some come to light by pure chance. The body of Peter Thomas, for instance, could have remained for ever half buried in a Berkshire wood but for its unlikely discovery by two thirteen-year-old boys looking for bait for a Sunday fishing expedition.

The bait they were after was maggots, the larvae of flies that lay their eggs on the carcases of dead animals. So off they went one Sunday, young Tony King and Paul Fay, to Bracknell Woods, in the hope of finding a dead pigeon or rabbit, as they had several times before. On this occasion, 28th June 1964, they found the maggots before the carcase—a seething mass of fat white maggots, on a mound of rough sods of turf loosely covered with beech cuttings lying a few feet off a forest path. The boys at once started to pull the turf away, and were so pleased that they hardly noticed the stench as they dragged the sods aside to get at the maggots—until they caught sight of a decomposing forearm with the remains of a hand at the end.

The fishing expedition ended before it had begun. Being sensible boys, they left everything, including the precious white maggots, and ran to the nearest police station.

'There's a dead body buried in the woods,' they told the duty sergeant in their commendably matter-of-fact style.

Shortly after I was rung up out of my Sunday afternoon snooze in the garden at my cottage at Tring, and by 5 p.m. I had joined Detective Superintendent Arthur Lawson, chief of the Berkshire CID, at the scene, where I set about a more scientific disinterment of the lightly buried body. I stopped to allow photographs to be taken at every stage as I removed the turf cuttings and sprays of beech wood; looking around, I noticed there were no beeches in the vicinity. From Lawson I learnt there were none in Bracknell Woods. Had the body been brought there dead, then? The police searched very thoroughly but found no appropriate tyre tracks or footprints.

It was the body of a man, lying on his back, fully clothed, with his head wrapped in towelling. How long had he been there; or, rather, how long had he been dead? It was much too late to try measure the loss of body temperature, and rigor mortis would certainly have come and passed off again long before. The body was disintegrating, and the police assumed it must have been dead for six or eight weeks.

'At least nine or ten days, but probably not more than twelve,' I told Lawson, who stared at me in disbelief. 'It's astonishing how quickly maggots will eat up the flesh,' I reminded him. 'I've seen a body reduced to this state in *as little as ten days*.'

I thought it safe to assume the maggots were larvae of the bluebottle *Calliphora erythocephalus*, but I preserved samples because the maggots of other flies of the calliphorine type, with slightly different hatching times, are not dissimilar to the naked eye. The ordinary life history of the bluebottle is quite simple. The eggs are laid in daylight, usually sunlight, and in warm weather they hatch on the first day. The tiny 'first instar' maggot sheds its skin after eight to fourteen hours, and the second instar after a further two to three days. The third instar, the fisherman's maggot, feeds voraciously for five or six days before going into a pupa case. The larvae I was looking at were mature, indeed elderly, fat, indolent, third-stage maggots, but they were not in pupa cases. Therefore I estimated that the eggs had been laid nine or ten days earlier. Adding a little more time to allow for the bluebottles getting to the dead body, I reckoned death had occurred on 16th June or 17th June.

Lawson telephoned the Scotland Yard missing persons bureau and learnt that a Peter Thomas had disappeared from his home at Lydney, in Gloucestershire, on 16th June, and that Detective

Superintendent Horace Faber of the Yard had been down there helping the local police in their investigation. Faber was so interested in the report of the body in Bracknell Woods, though it lay more than a hundred miles from Lydney, that he joined us at the scene the same afternoon.

Because of the extensive decomposition and maggot infestation I had decided to examine the exposed parts—head and neck and hands—as they lay. This was a fortunate decision, for as the neck came into view I saw a pool of liquid blood over the left side of the voice box—and not at any other site. (I found later it was the only pool anywhere in the body.) The small bones of the larynx were crushed on this side, and I picked them out loose.

'He received a blow across the throat,' I said. 'Not a violent constriction but a blow.'

'What sort of a blow, doctor?' asked Superintendent Faber.

'A punch, a kick, a bottle—'

'What about a karate chop with the side of the hand?' Faber had been on Commando training in the war.

'That would do very well.'

When I continued my examination in the mortuary I found blood in the main windpipe and bronchial passages and a few asphyxial haemorrhages on the surface of the heart. I saw no sign of any skull or other fracture, but the disintegrated liquid state of the brain made it impossible to discover whether unconsciousness might have been caused by some other blow. In the absence of any other positive finding I attributed death to bleeding into the windpipe from the blunt injury to the throat. This would have disabled the victim so that he would have been likely to inhale the blood and die in a few minutes.

But was he the missing Peter Thomas? I put his age between forty and fifty: Thomas was forty-two. When stretched out, the body measured 5 feet 3 inches: Thomas was said to have been 5 feet 3 inches or 5 feet 4 inches. He had neglected attentions to his teeth so the dental data were no use. But it was said he had broken his left arm in youth, and X-rays showed an old fracture of the left forearm. He had a criminal record, so his fingerprints were on the files: the experts succeeded in getting some impressions of the skin peeling off his finger-pads which were identical with both the records and prints found in his home at Lydney. A tailor's tab in the jacket of the dead man's suit also led to Thomas. Beyond doubt Superintendent Faber had been right in his hunch—it could hardly have been more—that the man who had disappeared from Lydney had ended up dead in Bracknell Woods. How?

Peter Thomas had been living very simply in a tumbledown wooden bungalow outside this little Welsh border town, alone except for his dog. He pretended poverty and drew unemployment pay although he had inherited about £5,000 from his father three years before. Letters found in his home revealed that he had recently lent £2,000 to William Brittle, a heating engineer salesman of Hook, Hampshire, and the loan was due for repayment in the month Thomas had disappeared. It was a strictly business loan. Brittle had advertised in a Cardiff newspaper offering a 'quick return' on a loan for an 'agricultural prospect'. Thomas, against the advice of both his solicitor and his bank manager, had lent him the money at 12½ per cent interest (a moneylender's rate in those days) for six months.

Questioned by Faber, Brittle said he had motored to Lydney and repaid the debt on 16th June, the very day Thomas had disappeared. But there seemed to be no proof that the money had been received. Faber pressed Brittle to say how he got this large sum? Not from agriculture, he admitted. 'I got an accumulator on a roll-up system at the races,' he said. Faber asked him for the names of the winning horses but he 'could not remember them', nor could any of the bookmakers or betting shops in the district recognize his photograph. As evidence that he had been to Lydney on 16th June Brittle mentioned that he had given a hitch-hiker a lift on the way back home.

Brittle's car was 'taken apart' at the Regional Forensic Science Laboratory without yielding anything more suspicious than a single beech leaf under the driver's mat. No beeches grew anywhere near Brittle's Hampshire home. A few scattered bloodstains were found on the sleeve of Brittle' coat: group O, the same as Peter Thomas's: but as it happened the same, too, as Brittle's. The police found out that while in the army Brittle had attended a course in unarmed combat which would have included the use of 'the chop'. Although the blow required training rather than great strength, Brittle did not look like a man who could commit murder with one bare hand. 'What, killed by *this* man?' his counsel, the redoubtable Quintin Hogg, asked scornfully at his trial. 'Felled like an ox at one blow?'

Meanwhile Brittle's hitch-hiker had been found from his description. A golf caddy, he confirmed the truth of Brittle's story that he had

gone to Lydney that day. To repay Thomas or to kill him? If Faber's
suspicions were correct, Brittle had stopped to pick up the hitch-hiker
on his way back when he had Thomas's body in the boot of his car.
That would have been very cool; and, as Quintin Hogg was to point
out, the most thorough and expert search of the vehicle had failed to
produce a trace of the body. Wrapped in cloth or a sack or bag, of
course, this might well be.

Faber had been working doggedly on the case for four months
when a man named Dennis Roberts, a nylon spinner, came forward
to say he had seen Peter Thomas at Gloucester bus station, studying
the timetable, on *20th June*. Roberts said they had exchanged
greetings (they had once worked together in a sawmill) and he was
sure of the date because it was the only day in his life when he had
been on strike.

If Thomas had been alive on 20th June, the whole case against
Brittle collapsed. His day of opportunity to kill Thomas was 16th
June, and if Thomas was alive on 20th June, he had been dead only
eight days at the most when I saw his body (and the tell-tale maggots)
in Bracknell Woods.

'Is that possible, doctor?' asked the anxious Faber, who had
brought Roberts's statement to my laboratory at Guy's.

'No, it isn't.' I answered immediately. 'And I am ready to stand up
to severe cross-examination on the point if it comes to trial.'

Faber looked as if I had taken a great load off his mind. If I had
answered that one could never be absolutely sure about such a
matter, the case would have crumbled and Scotland Yard would have
lost confidence in me—with good reason. Why, if I had not been
really sure, had I pinpointed the time of death with confidence at the
start?

Faber asked me for a written statement that he could attach to his
report for the Director of Public Persecutions, and I dictated one on
the spot to my secretary Jean Scott-Dunn. It was as unequivocal as the
estimate that I had given in my original autopsy report:

Guy's Hospital, 21st October 1964.
I have today been shown by Detective Superintendent Faber a copy of a
statement made by Dennis John Roberts to the effect that on Saturday,
20th June he saw a man whom he recognized as Peter Thomas at a bus
station. The condition of the body when examined in the wood suggested
in the first instance, while still at the scene—'some nine or ten days,
possibly more'—was a minimum period. Nothing in the post-mortem

state of the body suggested any special conditions likely to have accelerated the ordinary process of maggot infestation and disintegration of the body.

And to put a final 'nail in the coffin' I added:

I have had considerable experience in the timing of death and would regard Dennis Roberts's statement as being wholly inconsistent with my findings.

To prosecute or not to prosecute? The question was for the Director of Public Prosecutions in London, and he considered it for several weeks. He took the opinion of Senior Counsel, and finally decided the case was not strong enough. He could not ignore Roberts's statement, and it might well deter a jury.

All Faber could do then was to refer the case to the Coroner at Bracknell and let his jury hear the evidence; which they did, in an inquest lasting seven days. Nobody expected a Coroner's jury to commit Brittle for murder after the DPP had declined to do so, but to everyone's astonishment the jury found Thomas had been murdered on or about 17th June and they named Brittle as the person responsible. The Coroner committed him into custody, and he was tried at Gloucester at the spring assize of 1965.

His counsel, Quintin Hogg, Q.C.—later Lord Hailsham, the Lord Chancellor—was making a trial return to the bar after a distinguished career in the upper echelons of politics. Long before that he had been a very promising young barrister, and I expected a really testing cross-examination, especially when I heard he had taken the trouble to consult another Home Office pathologist, Dr David Bowen, and an entomologist, Professor McKenny-Hughes. It was a good thing I had decided to bottle a few maggots on that Sunday afternoon in the woods, for McKenny-Hughes wanted to see them and check if they really were the larvae of *C. erythrocephalus*, as I had said.

When I was examined by the Crown counsel, Ralph Cusack, I set out as clearly and briefly as I could the nature of the fat, third instar maggot, not yet pupated, yet plainly having passed the growing-up stages from the day the eggs hatched. I further set out the several periods of time that (it was accepted, I said) eggs took to hatch, and the three stages of maggot instar to develop before pupation. I added up the times and then said, as deliberately and purposefully as I knew how:

'So I had no doubt in my mind at the time'—I emphasized that I had made up my mind at the outset—'that this man had been dead some ten days.' Nine or ten was a minimum.

Cusack brought his examination to a quick finish. It was late in the afternoon, and he did not want to give the defence counsel the chance to discuss my evidence with his advisers before cross-examining me. But Quintin Hogg was an equally shrewd tactician.

'Doctor,' he began, 'may I assume'—counsel likes to use this phrase instead of 'I am sure'—'that you made notes during the successive stages of uncovering that body in the woods?'

'Yes, I have them here in court.' They were before me.

'My lord,' he said, 'I am going to ask that they be duplicated by photostat and handed to the members of the jury in the morning.'

The judge agreed, and Quintin Hogg was able after all to consult his advisers before cross-examining me, and I expected them to supply him with an armful of questions, skilfully worded to probe any weaknesses in my evidence. Next morning I braced myself when he got to his feet and pulled at his gown.

'Doctor,' he began, 'I have only to say, of your notes, that the sketch which accompanies them is of more help to me in understanding the lie of the body than the police photographs!'

I was off the hook. He was not going to challenge me on my evidence.

But he still had Professor McKenny-Hughes, who was certainly more of an expert than I on the habits of the bluebottle and maggots. If anyone could pick holes in my evidence he was the man.

'Professor, you have heard the evidence given so far in this case,' he began. 'Will you kindly tell the court in what respects your views as to the times of egg-laying and hatching of the larvae differ from those of Professor Keith Simpson?'

The distinguished entomologist ran his fingers through his wispy hair and favoured me with a jovial beam. Was he going to enjoy himself cutting me up into little pieces?

'Well,' he said, still smiling, 'I'm not sure there's anything I really . . .'

'Professor,' interrupted Quintin Hogg rather desperately, 'can we agree about one thing?' His witness nodded and waited. 'Let us suppose that the bluebottle lays its eggs on the dead body at midnight on the . . .'

'Oh, dear me, no!' exclaimed the entomologist. 'No self-respecting bluebottle lays eggs at midnight. At midday, perhaps, but not at midnight.'

There were stifled giggles in the public gallery, lawyers and reporters hid their smiles with their hands, and even the judge's face twitched. Poor Quintin Hogg tried again.

'At what period, then, Professor, would you expect the eggs to hatch?'

'Well, it all depends.' The professor seemed oblivious of the effect he was creating. 'You see, in warm weather—'

'Yes, Professor, we know it was June and quite warm,' Counsel came in hastily. 'How many hours would have elapsed before the first maggots were hatched?'

'Well, I agree with Dr Simpson,' said McKenny-Hughes, looking as if he expected everyone to be pleased about that. 'Say eight to fourteen hours for the first instar, and . . .'

'And these maggots would settle down on the dead tissues at once?'

'Well, maggots are curious little devils,' the entomologist said engagingly. 'Suppose this is a dead body.' He had taken out a matchbox and placed in on the edge of the witness box. 'And suppose you have a hundred maggots here.' He indicated them with an expansive spread of his hands. 'Ninety-nine will make their way towards the body, but the hundredth little devil'—the professor was back in the lecture hall, completely unmindful of his real surroundings—'he'll turn the other way.'

Mr Justice Phillimore's face twitched again, the Crown lawyers hardly dared to exchange glances, the jury looked relaxed and almost happy, and Quintin Hogg's frown deepened into a furrow as he told the professor very frostily that he had no more questions for him.

But the defence had three more witnesses who were not at all as acceptable to the prosecution.

First, Dennis John Roberts told how he had seen and spoken to Peter Thomas at Gloucester bus station on 20th June. 'Hello, Dennis,' Thomas had greeted him, he said; and Ralph Cusack, Q.C., who led for the Crown, could not shake him in cross-examination.

Next Mrs Jane Charles, of Lydney, said she had seen Thomas walking along the road towards Blakeney village on 21st June. She knew the date because it was the longest day of the year. She had been a passenger in a car and could only have glimpsed him briefly, but she was sure it was Thomas whom she knew. Finally Mrs Gwendoline Padwick, of Blakeney Stores, also said she had seen Thomas on 21st June, in her shop, buying matches. He was a regular customer, and she knew the date because she had just made out a cheque for her mother, who was staying with her for the first time.

Cusack pressed both women hard in cross-examination. It was, as he pointed out, a long time ago—nearly nine months—and their memories could have played them false. He asked them what else they could remember of that day, and of the previous day. What else had happened? What had Thomas been wearing? And so on. All three witnesses seemed perfectly honest persons—they had been 'found' by the defence but there was not a breath of suspicion about this—and the question was simply whether they had each made an honest mistake.

Quintin Hogg decided not to call Brittle, doubtless because he did not want his client exposed to cross-examination by the very skilful and penetrative Ralph Cusack. 'He has already made three long statements,' Hogg said, as if these rather contradictory accounts put his client in the clear. He went on to speak confidently of the three witnesses who said they had seen the dead man after 16th June; and since just one of them had been enough to raise sufficient doubt to stop the DPP from prosecuting, it seemed quite likely the jury would acquit Brittle. But, in the event, they decided my maggots were more reliable in their hatching habits than Quintin Hogg's three alibis, and found Brittle guilty of murder. He was given a life sentence.

The case was particularly satisfying to me. My insistence on the timing of death had become pretty well known, to the police, the Director of Public Prosecutions, the lawyers—and the Press, who would have scented a public disgrace for me if I'd been wrong.

CHAPTER 24

GANGSTERS IN LONDON: THE BROTHERS KRAY

One evening in October 1964 a tramp walked up a farm track seven miles outside Southampton, looking for a place to sleep. He found a cosy billet under an arch of low trees but someone had got there before him, or rather been put there, for the man he saw lying on the ground had his head bashed in. The tramp moved off to seek other lodgings.

The body was found soon after daylight. Its temperature at 9.30 a.m., taken by the police surgeon, was 110 degrees F., and rigor mortis was still present when I performed the autopsy at 5.30 p.m. I estimated that death had occurred in the early hours of the morning. The development of the bruising from his injuries showed plainly that he had not died at the time he was assaulted, probably not for several hours. He had, however, been so brutally beaten up that he would have been immediately knocked out. His scalp was split, his left ear almost severed from his head, and the back of his head bore much evidence of a final bashing after he'd slumped forward from the first blows. An injury to his left hand suggested he might have raised his arm to defend himself at the outset. From the stains due to the flow of blood from the first two wounds I thought he had been seated when attacked, and dumped, still alive, quite shortly afterwards.

He was soon identified as a Southampton taxi-driver named George Newbery, and he had last been seen in the town by other drivers at 10 p.m. When the murder hunt began the tramp came forward and told the police he had seen the body at about 11.15 p.m. Almost certainly Newbery was then still alive, although dying and indeed beyond human aid. Meanwhile his taxi had been found on some waste ground near Six Dials—a pretty tough area of Southampton not far from Newbery's own home. Blood was splashed all over the roof lining of the car, over the driver's seat, and on to the adjacent pillar. I thought he had clearly been attacked, whilst seated, by a passenger from behind.

Newbery, who was sixty, had been given this terrible battering with some blunt weapon: an iron bar or pipe, a tyre lever, a jack handle, or something of that kind. The police searched the bushes near the dumped body, and found a rusty gas pipe which I was shown next day at Scotland Yard. It was bloodstained at the nutted end and could very well have done the job.

The man in charge of the case was Chief Superintendent Walter Jones, who had caught the killer of Brenda Nash. This was his fortieth murder in his twelve years of Chief of the Hampshire CID, and *not once* so far had he failed to arrest his man and obtain a conviction in court. The Chief Constable felt no need to call in Scotland Yard, and Jones soon put together a regional crime team for an investigation that he expected to be long and was indeed difficult, but ultimately once again successful.

It was the kind of case that can give the police immense trouble, for anyone can pick up a taxi-driver, clobber him, relieve him of his cash, and dump the body miles away without leaving a clue. Jones found nothing in the car, no fingerprints except Newbery's, no foreign fibres or hairs, nothing on or around the body, nothing on the gas pipe. He therefore started house-to-house checks in an area one mile around the Six Dials, and set another team screening the docks before ships sailed. The *Queen Mary* had unfortunately sailed that morning, but two huge liners, the *Reina del Mar* and *Andes*, were only about to leave. Some sixty police officers went through the crews of these and other ships in harbour, questioning seamen and searching their belongings and especially their clothes. A signal was sent to the captain of the *Queen Mary* to search for bloodstained clothing, and officers questioned the crew on the ship's arrival at New York. Nothing emerged.

Meanwhile Jones had learnt from Newbery's widow that the dead man had had a Post Office Savings Account and that his account book was not in the house. Jones warned the General Post Office that the account might be 'raided' and, sure enough, a £3 withdrawal form on the account came shortly after through the official accounting machinery. It had been cashed between 1 and 2 p.m. on the day the body was found. That let out the crew of the *Queen Mary*, which had sailed before one.

Jones had the withdrawal slip tested for fingerprints, without much hope: it had been handled by dozens of clerks in different departments of the Post Office. *But prints–sweaty, greasy finger-prints–were found on the form*! A clue at last.

Both the Hampshire files and the CRO at Scotland Yard were searched for a similar print, disappointingly without result. The owner of it did not have a criminal record: from which Walter Jones deduced, correctly, that he was probably young.

The crews of all the ships that had been in harbour except the *Queen Mary* were fingerprinted, and the handwriting on the withdrawal form was compared with the writing on all kinds of official documents: seamen's cards, Labour Exchange and work application forms, driving licence forms (it wasn't Newbery who had driven his taxi to Six Dials), anything the police could legitimately lay their hands on. A mountainous pile of statements, alibis, house-to-house, dock-to-dock, warehouse and ships' crew details, some from the Mediterranean and South Africa, piled up—a mass of more than 100,000 documents—and still no clue. The police offered a reward of £500 for information: no response. After more than two months it looked as if Jones's fine record for solving crime was about to end.

But Jones was not deterred. If the man he was looking for was too young to have a criminal record, time could put that right. He had asked for all new offenders' prints to be compared with the prints on the withdrawal form, and that was precisely how the case was finally solved. John William Stoneley, a cable maker of twenty-one, was caught trying to break into a Southampton garage, and his prints were found to be identical with those on the withdrawal form. He had been granted bail because he was going to be married. He was charged with murder at Eastleigh magistrates' court on the day that had been fixed for the wedding. With him was his partner in crime, George Ernest (but of course known as Bill) Sykes, a dairyman of twenty-three. The evidence included a confession in Stoneley's handwriting that he had given to Superintendent Walter Jones whilst 'assisting the police in their inquiries'.

Stoneley said he had not meant to kill Newbery, and had struck him only once; but my evidence was that he had unquestionably been struck seven blows, the last five of which were set parallel, close together, over the back of his head, and had been delivered, in my opinion, in quick succession when he was slumped forward, disabled and probably unconscious as a result of the first two blows: this was no odd single blow but a savage beating up: plain murder.

Stoneley concluded his confession with a sentence that was enough to lose him any jury's sympathy:

'His death was caused by him not getting help.' It wasn't, really. Not even immediate skilled treatment could have saved his life. But the idea that it was somehow Newbery's own fault, when the only persons capable of getting help were his attackers, was grotesque.

Both men were convicted of murder. Stoneley was sentenced to death, later commuted to life imprisonment; Sykes to 'life'.

Five months later a nineteen-year-old girl, Pat Mundell, married Stoneley in the Church of St Michael's and All Angels at Princetown, on Dartmoor. She was given away by the prison welfare officer and the best man was another prison officer: no hymns, no music, just thirteen minutes together back at Dartmoor, then more 'life' for Stoneley.

Superintendent Walter Jones had solved his fortieth consecutive murder case. In the following year the Crime Writers' Association awarded him their first 'Sherlock Holmes Pipe'. Shortly afterwards he retired, to keep a Hampshire 'pub' near Winchester. I call in when I am that way.

Violence of a more blatant kind shattered the calm of a Whitechapel pub called 'The Blind Beggar' early in the evening of 8th March 1966. The public house was almost deserted except for a group of five men sitting at the bar and drinking light ales. The only one whose name matters was George Cornell.

Shortly before 8.30 p.m. two of the group made their excuses and left. The other three stayed on drinking and talking. Soon afterwards a car drew up outside and two men walked in. Cornell raised his head and had just time to say 'Well, look who's here' before one of the men pointed a pistol at him and shot him between the eyes. As Cornell dropped off his stool a second shot was fired into the ceiling. Without a word the two men walked out, and the car drove off.

The barmaid, who had ducked behind the bar, went to the wounded man, and someone called an ambulance and the police. The man's two drinking friends disappeared. The murderer and his companion had not worn masks or even hats, but nobody in the pub could say what they looked like. The barmaid agreed, with a marked lack of enthusiasm, that she might be able to identify them.

Cornell was taken to the London Hospital, and was dying when he

arrived. Had he been dead he would have been p.m.'d by Camps; but
he was transferred to the West End Hospital for Brain Surgery, so
when he died, hours later, I got the job—at the Westminster
Mortuary. Camps was livid.

Cornell must, I thought, have been taken entirely by surprise.
Neither hand had been raised in a protective gesture, and the entry
was set squarely between the eyes. The absence of powder marks
showed the shot had been fired from some feet away, out of arm's
reach. I extracted the bullet from Cornell's head. Detectives had
picked up two empty shell cases from the floor of the pub, and it
would have been a simple matter to identify the murder weapon if it
was ever found. The police believed the shooting was the work of a
gang operating a protection racket in the East End. Public anxiety
was growing.

Superintendent Butler came from Scotland Yard to take charge of
the case, and it was not long before informers told him where to look.
Three days after the crime he called at a flat in Lea Bridge Road,
Walthamstow, and invited two men to Commercial Street Police
Station for questioning. They were brothers, already well known to
the Yard and their name was Kray. They both assured Butler they had
not been near the Blind Beggar that evening and said they knew
nothing of the killing. The flat was searched but no pistol was found.
Butler asked Ronald Kray to go on an identification parade. (He
might as well have asked Reginald Kray, for they were identical
twins.) The suspect was a good deal less nervous than the barmaid of
the Blind Beggar, who hardly glanced at the men paraded in front of
her before telling Butler she could not recognize anyone as the
murderer of Cornell. At the inquest she protested she had not seen the
actual shooting, and the coroner gave the only possible verdict:
murder by some person or persons unknown.

A perfect murder, then. Committed openly, unhurriedly, before
eye-witnesses in a public place in the heart of London. The killers
walked in, picked off their victim, and drove away without anyone
raising a finger. Cornell's four companions had vanished without
trace. Like others who knew the murderer's identity, they were
evidently too frightened to talk to the police. For London, a relatively
law-abiding capital city, it was a new and alarming state of affairs. If
it could be done with such impunity once, it would surely be done
again, and again. This was gang warfare.

It is unlikely that George Cornell was widely mourned. Indeed, the metropolis was a healthier place without him. He had a record of violence and had indulged in torture, and had recently entered the West End pornography business. Indirectly it was this that led to his death. In a chance meeting late at night at the Astor Club, in Berkeley Square, another gangster demanded rather than asked to be taken as a partner in Cornell's 'blue film' trade.

'Bugger off, you big poove,' was Cornell's reply, for which he was nearly shot on the spot: but the other man was restrained by his friends, who thought it was the wrong time and place. Early evening in the Blind Beggar was deemed a more suitable occasion to punish Cornell's insolence with a bullet between his eyes.

It was the cocksure casualness of the murder that most appalled the police. If they could get away with that, what more might they do? Who else might be killed?

The answer, although the police did not learn of it until some months later, was Jack McVitie, known as 'Jack the Hat' owing to his disinclination to reveal his bald pate. He was another hardened villain with a record of violence: once he pushed a girl friend out of a car he was driving and broke her back. He was game for any kind of crime, from protection rackets to drug-dealing—even murder, for a price. He made an unsuccessful attempt to kill a potentially dangerous witness for a reward of £500. Among other troubles Jack the Hat drank too much, and might then get quarrelsome. He was seen in the Regency Club, 'North London's Smartest Rendezvous', with his hat at a rakish angle, a sawn-off shotgun in his hands, threatening to kill his employers. A few days later, he unwisely accepted an invitation to a private party in a basement flat in Stoke Newington. It was an evening in October 1967, eighteen months after the technically unsolved murder of George Cornell.

'Where's all the birds, all the booze?' Jack the Hat shouted when he entered the flat.

There were no birds, no booze. Five men were in the room and four more had come with McVitie. Somebody put a pistol to his head and pressed the trigger, but the gun jammed. Then the others jumped on him.

Jack the Hat made for the window and got head and shoulders through, but they yanked him in again by his legs. One man held him from behind while another stabbed him with a knife—once under the eye, then in the stomach and chest, and finally through the throat, impaling him on the floor: or so an eye-witness said later. There was no autopsy, for McVitie's body was never found. Not one of the witnesses of his murder who later turned Queen's Evidence could say what happened to it, except that it was wrapped in an eiderdown and driven away in a car. At the last moment someone went into the garden and retrieved the telltale hat that had fallen from McVitie's bald head in his attempt to escape. The knife and the jammed pistol were thrown into the Grand Union Canal by Queensbright Road. The knife was never found, either, but when the police dragged the canal nearly a year later they brought up a jammed .32 automatic.

No word of this cold murder leaked out, and it was some time before the world or the police knew that Jack the Hat was dead. He was reported missing, by the woman he had been living with, the morning after he was murdered; but he was the sort of man to leave home suddenly at any time. His murder could easily have remained unknown for ever but for the fact that the police had not given up the case of the murder in the Blind Beggar. Instead, a team of police, under two fine detectives, Chief Superintendent Jack du Rose and Chief Inspector 'Nipper' Read, had been formed expressly with orders to clear up the Cornell murder and other recent East End gang crimes which it was suspected the Kray gang had organized.

After months of work the detectives at last broke through the 'wall of silence' and began to collect evidence. Most witnesses were still reluctant to speak freely while the men they feared remained at large, and the police therefore had to take them into custody with the case still far from complete. On 9th May 1968, they arrested the Kray twins, their older brother Charles, and fourteen other men.

Almost as soon as the prison gates clanged shut on them, information started to pour in. Detective Superintendent Mooney at last convinced the barmaid at the Blind Beggar that she was safe from reprisals, and she at once identified Ronald Kray as the man who had shot Cornell. Later she recognized John Barrie as his companion. Her evidence was supported by John Dickson, who said he had driven Ronnie Kray and Barrie to the pub. Dickson was invited to turn Queen's Evidence, and so was the twins' cousin, Ronnie Hart, who reported the murder of Jack McVitie in all its horrifying details. Considerable subterfuge was necessary to get this information, for Hart had been remanded in custody, with the others, in Brixton Prison. When visiting him Chief Inspector Read posed as a Home Office inspector or a prison visitor, even as a clergyman, for fear of 'springing the gate' or stirring up reprisals; and prisoners wanted for

questioning were called away 'for a medical examination'. The
evidence collected in this way was worth all the trouble. Hart said it
was Reggie Kray who first tried to shoot Jack the Hat and then killed
him with a knife while Ronnie Kray held him from behind.

The trial began at the Old Bailey before Mr Justice Melford
Stevenson, a tough judge, eight months after the arrests, with ten men
in a cage-like dock, an imposing array of lawyers, and a swarm of
police officers, uniformed and CID. Heavily guarded, the accused
were brought to court each day in a high-speed convoy, and vital
witnesses like the barmaid from the Blind Beggar were secluded and
protected as if they were public figures in danger of assassination.
Ronnie Kray was charged with the murder of Cornell and McVitie,
Reggie with killing McVitie; the others with being accessories to
these crimes.

There was a scene at the start of the trial. Some of the prisoners
tore off the numbered labels they wore to indicate who was who, and
Ronald Kray shouted at the judge, Mr Justice Melford Stevenson:
'This isn't a cattle market!' They won their point, the labels being
pinned to the dock in front of them, but it was their only victory.

The barmaid at the Blind Beggar was plainly under a considerable
strain, and looked pale and drawn. She was the mother of two
children for whose safety she had feared for months, when she had
been too afraid to speak. As I watched her give evidence I thought she
would 'pass out' at any time.

'The first man shot Cornell in the head,' she said. 'I saw Cornell
start to fall from the stool. Then I just turned and ran down into the
cellar.'

'Did you see the man who shot Cornell?' asked Kenneth Jones,
Q.C., prosecuting.

It was an electric moment. Did she dare? There was a few seconds
hesitation, then she raised an arm and pointed: 'It was No. 1 over
there. Ronald Kray. I have seen him before a few times. I have seen
him in the public bar, and also in the East End of London.'

'Have you any doubt.'

'No—oh, no. That was him.'

Of course John Platts-Mills, Q.C., defending, got at her over her
silence at the time. She had lied to the Coroner in 1966, when her
memory must have been fresher, pretending that she had not seen the
shooting. 'Why?' he asked.

'I was terrified I would get shot,' she said, quite simply. She was still frightened, had nightmares, could not sleep.

The other vital Crown witness, Ronald Hart, was one of no fewer than twenty-eight self-confessed criminals who were spared punishment on a promise of giving evidence for the Crown. Hart described to a shocked jury how Reggie Kray had skewered McVitie with a carving knife while brother Ronald held him from behind. He denied he was giving evidence just to save his own skin. 'It was to save my life and the lives of one or two other people as well,' he said; adding, rather against character, 'Some of us have got consciences.'

Ronald Kray caused a surprise in court when he announced from the dock that he was going to give evidence. His theme was that the whole thing was a cooked-up job: the police had been after him since he had slipped out of their hands in 1965. 'It's all lies,' he snapped. 'Everything these prosecution witnesses have said about the murder is all lies.'

He was arrogantly defiant towards Kenneth Jones, who cross-examined with an ill-chosen sarcastic, 'so you are really rather hard done by' attitude. 'They do it because they don't like us, 'retorted Kray.

'To run,' Jones suggested, 'is almost a confession of guilt?'

'It just shows what justice is to you if you think that to go from one pub to another makes you guilty of murder,' replied Kray coldly.

But later he got angry with the rather portly Crown counsel, screaming 'you're just a fat slob!' When he was called to order from the bench he rounded on the judge himself: 'And you're biased too!' he shouted, pointing an accusing finger at Mr Justice Melford Stevenson. 'I've had enough of your comments.'

Reginald Kray exercised his right to stay out of the witness box. The trial lasted thirty-nine days, and was surely one of the costliest as well as the longest in English criminal history. Twenty-three counsel, among whom were nine Q.C.s (five of them Recorders), two M.P.s, a former M.P., an Attorney-General of the County Palatine of Durham, and an Old Bailey Commissioner—£500 a brief, and £60 to £80 'refreshers' each day—the legal costs alone must have been about £75,000. The state paid, for all the accused, including the Krays, got legal aid. But it was money well spent: the foul air this gang had created had cleared.

Nine of the ten were found guilty of the charges against them. Each of the Kray twins, convicted of murder, was sentenced automatically to life imprisonment 'which I would recommend should not be less than thirty years,' said this firm judge—a sharp contrast to the more usual ten or twelve. If his recommendation is followed they will be sixty-five when they come out. John Barrie, Ronald's partner in the Blind Beggar, also got 'life', with a recommendation for not less than twenty years. The others were awarded imprisonment for ten to fifteen years. Charles Kray got ten years.

Murder was not intended by the three tough young men who ransacked a luxurious flat in Falmouth House, Bayswater, but two dead bodies were left for the porter to find the following day, when he began wondering why the occupants did not answer the telephone or doorbell and showed no signs of life. Using his master key, he entered the flat in the evening of 13th March 1968, and found it in great disorder, with drawers pulled out and clothing, papers, and other articles scattered about. The tenant, a stockbroker of 58, Michael St John O'Carroll, lay dead on a bed in one room; his girl friend, Janet Williams, 23, who had lived with him for six months and was expecting a baby, lay dead in the same position in the next room. A 999 call brought a police patrol, and soon afterwards the CID were on the scene. I arrived only twenty minutes later, and between us we started to unravel the affair.

Both victims were fully dressed, and from measurements of temperature and rigor mortis I estimated death had occurred in each case in the late evening of the previous day, a point that was to prove unexpectedly important. They had both been bound and gagged and stabbed behind the left ear with a carving knife, which lay in the passage. But the cause of death in each case was asphyxia, 'due to (mechanical) obstruction to breathing', I said in my report; for it was not possible to determine the proportionate contributions made by gagging, suffocation, and, in the case of Janet, constriction of the neck. Both lay face down, with the head covered by pillows, and Janet had a ligature, a white scarf, tightly round her neck, not knotted but twisted at the back. The knife wound, in each case about an inch deep, had been made in a very tender part of the body, probably in an attempt to persuade them to reveal where they kept their money and valuables.

It was plainly robbery that had brought the murderers there. Jewellery, cash, a cheque book, and bank cards were all missing. The flat had not been forced, so it looked as if at least one of the intruders had been known to either O'Carroll or Janet. Drink bottles, glasses, and cigarettes left around in the lounge added to this belief.

Two days later O'Carroll's car, a fast Lancia coupé, which he had left parked in the City, was found abandoned at Abbotsinch Airport, Glasgow. Two men had tried to sell it in Glasgow the day before. Meanwhile all newspapers carried big headlines of the double murder, and this started the crack that eventually opened the case. One of the men who had helped to ransack the flat had left it before his companions, and he was appalled to read that O'Carroll and Janet had been 'tied, tortured, and strangled', as the *Evening Standard* put it, when he thought he had been involved in nothing more serious than robbery with violence. He wasn't going to take the rap for two murders he hadn't committed, and decided to go back to London and give himself up to the police.

He was Raymond Cohen, 23, a trainee football manager. His partners in crime were Michael Ellis, 22, who taught swimming, and David Bolton, 30, a dancing instructor and apparently the brains of the affair. Bolton had known Janet when she was herself a dance hostess; and she and O'Carroll had been taking lessons together regularly at the school of dancing where he taught. A month before the murders Bolton lost his job, and he was on the way to losing his home when his landlord got a court order against him for £50 arrears of rent. Exactly ten days before the murders he was invited to a party at O'Carroll's flat. He found himself briefly in a world of luxury where an odd fifty pounds meant very little, and when he looked again at the twenty-eight-day court order he decided where to get the money. He asked his old friend Ellis to help, and Ellis introduced Cohen as the third man. Bolton said he thought the jewellery alone would be worth £15,000 to £20,000.

Bolton went up alone to the fifth-floor flat, and Ellis and Cohen followed a few minutes later. As Janet opened the door, Bolton, who was standing behind her, threw an arm round her face and pulled her back into the flat, where she was gagged, trussed, and left on the bed. Bolton told Cohen to go out and sell the jewellery they took from her, and he went off to 'Harry's' in Earls Court. Their haul did not quite come up to expectations. For the jewellery and a cheque book and two bank cards 'Harry' paid only £220. This was shared out when Cohen returned to the flat, and then they all waited for O'Carroll.

The broker returned early in the afternoon. He was immediately jumped on and bound. A wrist watch and five pounds were taken

from him, and he was carried, trussed, to the phone to tell his
secretary he wouldn't be back again that day. He need not have added
those last two words.

Asked for money by Bolton, O'Carroll said half-laughingly that he
was on a £3,000 overdraft. Bolton then said they would have to sell his
cars. Ellis left the flat at 3.30 p.m. to try to sell Janet's Mini, but he
had no luck and returned at 4.30 p.m. Cohen was then sent to the City
to collect O'Carroll's Lancia from a car park, and was told to take it to
Bolton's flat at 10 p.m. When he left the flat, he said in his statement,
O'Carroll and Janet were both still bound but alive and unharmed,
and he never saw them again. He collected the Lancia from a car park
at London Wall, went to watch Chelsea play Sheffield Wednesday at
Stamford Bridge, and drove to Bolton's flat at ten. Then Ellis and
Cohen drove the car to Glasgow and tried to sell it. When they failed
Ellis proposed to take it to Ireland. At Stranraer, on the way to the
ferry, Ellis handed a newspaper to Cohen, who then read the shaking
news that he was on the run for murder.

'Ellis told me they had had to kill them because O'Carroll tried to
press the service bell,' Cohen said later to the police. 'Ellis said that
Bolton just put his arm round O'Carroll's throat and he died. Ellis said
that he himself had killed Janet. He said they were both strangled.'

After Ellis had told Cohen this they went on to the car ferry, but
when they noticed they were 'getting strange looks' from the ferry
staff they turned and drove out of the town. Cohen asked Ellis to
drive him to the airport. 'I was surprised he did not mind doing this,
knowing fully well that I was intending to return to London.' It took
Cohen all next day—wandering around Fulham, going to a cinema, a
club called 'Blazes' and a casino, where he won £50 playing blackjack,
only to lose £110 at another gaming club—to make up his mind to tell
the whole story to the police.

Cohen eventually went with his father to the 'back yard' at New
Scotland Yard, and on saying they had come to make a statement in
connection with the murders they were told by a constable that they
had 'come to the wrong station', and were redirected to Paddington
Green! With an alert that was country wide!

Bolton and Ellis were caught soon afterwards, and the case against
them was strengthened by the finding of a clear fingerprint on an
ashtray. At their trial at the Old Bailey Ellis's counsel confirmed
Cohen's report of the murders. 'O'Carroll made a dash for the service
bell, and Bolton came up behind him and put his arm round his neck.

O'Carroll just collapsed. The girl had seen everything, so Ellis strangled her.'

The shrewd Mr Justice Sebag Shaw, an old hand at defending crooks in his barrister days, sat on the Bench, presiding at his first criminal trial upon appointment as a High Court judge. He sentenced Bolton and Ellis each to fifteen years' imprisonment for robbery to run concurrently with life imprisonment for murder.

Was O'Carroll really killed 'mugging' with an arm? I said in evidence that he could have been. In a recent case I had examined from Broadmoor one prisoner had murdered another in exactly that way, and no mark was left on his victim's neck. However, O'Carroll had also been gagged with a pair of tights and might have had his breathing further obstructed by being trussed on his face. Similarly Janet could have been strangled by the towel twisted round her neck, but she also must have found it difficult to breathe owing to a black stocking gag tied tightly through her mouth and secured behind the neck, and she too lay face down. There were three causes of asphyxiation in each victim, and it seemed to me that their proportionate contributions were equivocal.

I was not cross-examined on this, and felt reinforced in my feelings that it is always better to set out exactly (for the Crown and the defence) areas where any very positive views would lack support when tested. The Chalkpit case had been perhaps the most outstanding example of this. I didn't know exactly what had happened in Ley's house in Kensington, and I said so. I have always done this at the outset, even though it might look less decisive. In this respect I had no wish to emulate the inflexibility of Sir Bernard Spilsbury, whose positive evidence had saved the old lag Loughans from conviction of the murder to which he later confessed, and had doubtless led to convictions at other trials that might otherwise have ended with sufficient doubt in the jury's minds for acquittal.

On one point in the Bayswater murders, however, I was able to give positive evidence that greatly influenced the course of justice.

'I had nothing at all to do with the murders, and I was only aware of them when Ellis told me about then,' Cohen had concluded his statement to the police. Nevertheless he was charged with murder. But if he had left the flat at 4.30 p.m., as he said, and as the police came to believe, he was, by my timing, certainly innocent. My firm opinion on this point induced the prosecution to drop the murder charges against him and he was tried only for complicity in the robbery. Mr Justice Sebag Shaw sent him to prison for two years.

Timing the crime was equally important but not quite so simple in
an earlier brutal double murder in which I became involved. The
victims were a jeweller and his wife, Frederick and Cissie Lucas, and
their seventeen-year-old daughter had the horrific experience of
finding their battered and bloody bodies when she returned from
work to her home at Leigh-on-Sea in the evening of 6th June 1945.
When I examined the bodies at 12.30 p.m. next day Lucas's
temperature had dropped down to that of the surroundings, and I
was satisfied that he had been dead at least twenty-four hours. But his
wife's body was still relatively warm (the internal temperature was 77)
and I did not think she could have been dead more than twenty hours.
I estimated that she had died between 4.30 and 6.30 p.m., when her
daughter had found her body, and her husband some time between
6.30 and 12.30 in the morning. The latter estimate was supported by
his wristwatch, which had been smashed when he tried to defend
himself—there were protective type grazes and bruises on the backs
of his hands—at exactly nine o'clock. His brain was severely
lacerated, and the limited amount of intracranial bleeding indicated
that death had followed quickly on the assault. It seemed there was a
period of at least seven and a half hours between his death and his
wife's.

This proved perfectly reasonable, for her injuries were less severe,
her brain being only contused, and the accumulation of blood
suggested that circulation had continued for some time after the
assault, probably several hours. Both attacks, therefore, could have
occurred at 9 a.m.

A more intriguing puzzle in this case concerned the weapons. Each
victim had been struck a number of times—he six, she three—with a
blunt instrument while standing or kneeling, and each had received a
very heavy and probably final blow from a different weapon—a flat
instrument, like a board—while lying on the ground. The same flat
weapon could have been used on both victims; but it looked from the
wounds as if the blunt instrument used on Lucas had been a piece of
ornamental furniture, while the first three blows on his wife's head
had not been made by any such fashioned article.

More than one assailant, perhaps; or why should a lone attacker
have changed weapons so many times?

A possible reason for one such change occured to me when I

examined the wounds. The first six blows sustained by Lucas were clearly violent enough to have broken the weapon used to inflict them. This theory was confirmed by the discovery of a broken and bloodstained leg of a stool. The police also found a bloodstained board that could have been used to inflict the flat injuries on both Lucas and his wife. No other weapon was found to account for Mrs Lucas's blunt injuries, but it occurred to me that they could very well have been made with the edge of the board.

Only one change of weapons in both assaults, then: and only one assailant. His name was Young, and he was convicted at Chelmsford at the Winter Assizes.

CHAPTER 25

GORRINGE AND HAY: THE MARK OF THE BEAST

With a little more luck I might have been able to identify Neville Heath as the murderer of Margery Gardner by something more personal than his diamond-patterned riding whip. He had bitten both her nipples and soft breast tissues most ferociously, leaving what must initially have been very clear bite marks on her skin. Unfortunately, from my point of view, and perhaps from her own, she had not died immediately but had lived long enough for the bruising caused by the bites to begin to spread into the tissues, so masking the outline, spacing, character, and shape of the biter's teeth.

A little more than a year later I found a bite mark on the breast of another dead woman I was called in to examine, and this looked more hopeful as she had evidently died before much bruising could develop.

The case occurred at Tunbridge Wells in the first hours of New Year's Day, 1948. The young woman, Mrs Gorringe, had gone to a New Year's Eve dance with her young husband, and they were seen leaving the dance hall shortly before midnight. A few hours later, still in her dance frock, her body was found behind a lorry in a yard near the hall. Detective Superintendent Frank Smeed, then Chief of the Kent County CID, woke me on the phone, and I went straight down.

Her head had been battered in and she had been strangled; and there was a bite mark on her exposed right breast. A clear mark, evidently made by the two upper front teeth and four lower teeth; and I thought they showed such unusual irregularities of spacing and lie that I told Smeed it might be possible to identify the murderer by his teeth. Her husband was already suspected (they had been heard quarrelling when they left the dance hall, and Smeed was not at all satisfied with his account of his subsequent movements) and I suggested a wax impression should be taken of his upper and lower teeth. This proved more difficult than we had expected. Smeed found it impossible to rouse any dentist in that part of Kent so early in the morning of New Year's Day, and in the end he persuaded me to do the job myself. Casts were prepared from my very primitive and rather ham-fisted Stent wax impressions, and printer's ink bite patterns were taken from the casts. Fortunately the suspect's teeth were so badly spaced and angled and curiously shaped that there were a number of direct comparisons to make, and on every point these irregular features proved identical. My evidence survived cross-examination at Gorringe's trial, and he was convicted and sentenced to death, although later reprieved.

It was one of the very earliest cases in which such evidence was given, for though bites are by no means rare in sex killings, this case bore sufficient detail to enable me to satisfy the Assize Court of the identification of the murderer by his teeth-marks: the first of its kind in Britain.

Dentists, both in the academic world and in practice, were nevertheless slow to become interested in forensic odontology, in spite of other examples I had like the cases of Harry Dobkin, the Luton Sack Murder, and 'Acid-Bath' Haigh, as well as the notorious Neville Heath. The dental profession's lack of interest was well illustrated by the fact that I, a pathologist without any training in dentistry, was invited to lecture on the subject early in the 1950s in the United States and in Scandinavia, where Gösta Gustafson with his wife Anna Greta had done much of the pioneer work, especially in assessing age by microscopy of the teeth. It was perhaps an even greater honour for me, a mere Sassenach, to receive a call for help from the land of my ancestors. The Scots have a historic tradition in forensic medicine, with great figures like Christison, Littlejohn, the Glaisters, and Sydney Smith and great cases like Madelaine Smith, Burke and Hare, Ruxton and the like, and they just never had come south of the Border for advice and help. But in 1967, Dr Warren Harvey, their own expert on forensic dentistry, expressed a view that they needed to consult 'a forensic scientist with considerable personal knowledge of the dental aspects of proving identity from bite marks'. From a list of names of 'men known personally from four nations' the choice fell on me—and I was delighted, for it was a case bristling with interest.

The case had begun on 7th August 1957, when the battered and strangled body of fifteen-year-old Linda Peacock was found in, of all places, a cemetery, in the little country town of Biggar, between Edinburgh and Glasgow. She had been reported missing the night before, and at 6.40 a.m. two patrolling constables found her lying between tombstones under a yew tree.

No attempt had been made to rape her, and her knickers were in place and undisturbed; but her anorak, blouse, cardigan, and brassiere had all been pulled up, exposing her breasts. It was the police photographer, Detective Sergeant John Paton, who noticed the oval area of bruising on her right breast and thought it might be the mark of a bite. So did the police surgeon and the pathologist who was to perform the autopsy, but it was Sergeant Paton alone who grasped its possible importance. He took no fewer than fifteen photographs of it, at the cemetery and in the mortuary, and sent an immediate urgent message about it to Detective Inspector Osborne Butler, of the Identification Bureau of Glasgow Police.

Butler was about to have morning coffee when the message came, and he left his cup untouched. Butler knew nothing about teeth and bite marks—yet—but he was an expert at matching the jemmy with the door. He had fifteen years' experience of examining and photographing marks made by tools, firearms, other weapons, and a variety of objects that could be identified from marks made by their irregularities or other peculiar characteristics. He reached the mortuary before the autopsy had begun, and immediately suggested calling in Dr Warren Harvey, an expert in forensic odontology and lecturer to the Scottish Detective Training School.

Meanwhile the police investigation was handled, tirelessly and most astutely, by Chief Superintendent William Muncie, Head of the Lanarkshire CID. In the first week he and his subordinates interviewed no fewer than 3,000 persons, eliminating all who could have any connection with the crime except a short list of twenty-nine men from a local detention centre—a sort of boy's borstal. At Warren Harvey's request dental impressions were taken from all of them, after they had given written permission ('I have been told that this is in relation to the investigation into the death of Linda Peacock. . . . It has been made clear to me that I can refuse. . . . It has also been made clear to me that should my dental impressions be linked with other evidence in the case they may be produced as evidence'). The impressions were taken at Glasgow Dental Hospital, and models were cast. Each model was identified only by a number, and great care was taken to prevent Harvey and Butler from receiving any hint of the identity of the man on whom Muncie's suspicion was beginning to focus.

From the reaction round the bite mark it was clear that the girl had died within a few minutes of being bitten, and the teeth marks were quite distinct. There were, however, only five marks, of which two were merely small dark rings with pale centres. The largest mark, a very dark oval about 13 mm by 7 mm, looked the most interesting. Harvey thought it was too big to have been caused by a single intact tooth: he suspected it had been made either by a sharp or jagged tooth or by two adjacent teeth. Comparing each model in turn with transparencies of the breast, Harvey and Butler were able to exclude several as having no teeth capable of causing this large abrasion. Others could be ruled out because they were either too regular or too irregular to fit the pattern of the bite mark in any orientation, and eventually the short list was reduced to five. Of these the most likely appeared to be number 14. It looked as if a sharp-edged lower right canine could have caused the largest mark, and the four other marks on the transparency appeared to fit the model reasonably well if the assailant's head had approached the girl's breast from below, which seemed the most likely orientation.

It was at this stage, after about two weeks' work on the problem, that Harvey and Butler, carrying their photographs and transparencies and twenty-nine models, came on the overnight train to London to see me at Guy's. I was much impressed by their work and also picked out number 14 but shared their own doubt whether the identification was yet strong enough to justify an arrest, let alone to put before a jury. We discussed how it could be tested further, and when they went home they set to work to check the occlusal movements of each of the five suspects. For this they took fresh dental impressions, and made new models in tough acrylic resin instead of plaster, mounted them on a modified articulator or hinge, and, as soon as a suitable female body appeared in the mortuary, made trial bites on the breast. The result was not only definite but devastating. It seemed to throw the most solid doubts on number 14 having caused this bite on Linda's breast—if not to eliminate it.

Harvey and Butler started from the beginning again, re-examining all twenty-nine models and this time focussing their attention on the two curiously shaped abrasions: the small dark ring marks with pale centres. Harvey had found no description resembling these marks in the literature of bite marks, which was admittedly rather scanty and mostly in foreign languages like Swedish and Japanese. What kind of teeth could have made such unusual marks? Examining the whole range of models with this single question in mind, they found the answer in the upper and lower right canines of suspect number 11. The tip of each of these teeth was marred by a small but definite pit. As an experiment Harvey pressed each in turn into the nail bed of a thumb: and for the first time—it was a thrilling experience—they saw marks exactly like the rings on the dead girl's breast.

The next step was to determine the orientation and to find how well number 11's teeth fitted the other marks on the breast. Even before comparing the breast transparencies with the model Harvey could foresee the startling result.

The ring marks were on the left side (from the observer's viewpoint) of the area of the bite. If they had been caused by right canines, the orientation of the assailant could only have been from above the girl's shoulder; when he bit her breast his head was, so to speak, upside down, if her head was considered right side up.

That would have been the only possible orientation even if the ring marks, which lay roughly one on top of the other, had been of the same shape and size. In point of fact the upper mark was a circle one millimetre in diameter while the lower mark was more oval-shaped and measured one mm by two mm. The pits in number 11's canines measured exactly the same, but here the upper was one mm by two mm, and the lower was one mm in diameter. By this conjunction the unexpected orientation was confirmed.

'Since, to put it mildly, this orientation seemed strange,' Warren Harvey wrote afterwards, in a paper on the case, 'a further attempt was made to orientate the other four short-listed models. But apart from the already discredited number 14, none of the others fitted at all.'

Number 11 fitted perfectly. The large abrasion corresponded exactly with the upper left incisor, which was broken and sharp, and the adjacent upper left lateral, which had a hooklike cavity from which a filling was missing. Harvey's final opinion of the orientation was that the assailant had come over the girl's right shoulder from behind while she was sitting.

The medical evidence showed that this was not so far-fetched as it might seem. The mark of the ligature round her neck was most pronounced in the front and least at the back, showing she had been strangled from behind. Blood in front of her left ear, from one of her head wounds, had clotted while she was vertical. Her left wrist had been tied with a piece of string (burned off after death, leaving a scorchmark and a blister), and her arm had probably been held behind her. And, although Harvey and Butler did not yet know it, mud had been observed on the knees of number 11's jeans that night, suggesting he had been kneeling on the ground.

At this point, five weeks after the murder, Harvey and Butler told Chief Superintendent Muncie that they were considering only number 11, and he replied that number 11 was his suspect too.

Number 11 was Gordon Hay, and he was seventeen. At the time of the murder he was a pupil at an approved school a few minutes' walk (and less than two minutes' fairly fast run, the police found on testing) from the yew tree in the cemetery. On 6th August one of the masters saw Hay in the school dining-room just before 10 p.m.; another master, putting out the lights, saw him in bed, wearing pyjamas, at 10.30 p.m. But just before 10.30 one of his room-mates had seen him come in, his hair blown about, his face dirty and sweating, and with mud on the knees of his jeans. Screams had been heard coming from the cemetery at 10.20 p.m., and Linda Peacock had probably died, according to the autopsy report, between 10 and 11 p.m. Gordon Hay possessed a boat hook which could have been used to inflict Linda's head injuries; in his pockets police found string exactly similar to a piece found in the branches of the yew tree, and a cigarette lighter that could have been used to burn it. The youth had met Linda at a fair the day before her death, spoken to her for less than a minute, and afterwards told a friend he would not mind having sex with her.

All this circumstantial evidence was clearly insufficient, and the dental evidence was crucial. Harvey and Butler came again to London, and showed me the latest results of their work. I encouraged them to make a more detailed study of Hay's teeth and to prepare scaled 'overlay' transparencies. They fitted the scaled bite-mark print perfectly: that was beyond doubt. But there were few points of identification. Gösta Gustavson, in his book *Forensic Odontology*—then the only textbook on the subject in the world—had suggested a minimum of four or five adjacent teeth corresponding with bite marks for a positive identification: here there were only three, and not adjacent. But I thought quality might make up for lack of quantity if the pits in Hay's canines were as uncommon as Harvey suspected.

Back they went, to take a third impression of Hay's teeth, this time with a sheriff's warrant. Copper ring as well as composition impressions were taken of his canine teeth, and the pits were photographed both in black and white and in colour. Hay could not have been more co-operative, and even gladly agreed to having his tattoo mark photographed. Harvey, keen as nuts, called in other experts and investigated Hay's whole dental and medical history, even checking with the public analyst on the fluorine content of the water he had drunk as a child. He established that the sharp-edged, clear-cut pits, which were like small craters on the pinnacles of the tips of the canines, were not due to caries or to wear but to hypocalcination. Finally *he examined 1,000 canines in 342 boys aged sixteen and seventeen* and found only two with pits, only one with a pit and hypocalcination, and none with two pits in the same mouth. Meanwhile Butler, with consummate skill, prepared final trans-parancies of the models of Hay's teeth for superimposition on the photographs of the breast.

All this took another month; and when they brought their exhibits to me on a third visit to London, I could only say I had never seen such fine bite-mark photography and dentition matching. 'A jury should have no difficulty in understanding this evidence, and appreciating its simple strength,' I said in a written report. 'It is akin to tool-marking evidence or fingerprints.'

A few weeks later Hay was arrested and charged with murder. The trial took place at the High Court of Justiciary in Edinburgh and lasted nine days. The typescript of the evidence ran to nearly 1,100 pages of foolscap, of which about 400 were taken up with medical and dental evidence.

'Forensic odontology, as it is called, is a relatively new science,' said the judge, Lord Grant, in his summing-up, 'but there must, of course, always be a first time for everything.' It was certainly the first time in Scotland that a man charged with murder was identified by a bite mark.

The prosecution star witness was undoubtedly Dr Warren Harvey, and he spent a whole day in the witness box. Impressively clear, although suffering a throat affliction, he took care not to overreach himself in giving his evidence. Asked about the enlargement of the transparencies in relation to the measurement on curved surfaces, he said 'I would hate to be taken too far out into deep water because I am not an expert.'

'Perhaps you will paddle with me so far?' asked the defence counsel, W. I. Stewart, Q.C.

'Not too far, please.' He remained cool and efficient.

Harvey admitted candidly that much of his investigation was experimental.

'You came to the view that the orientation of the bite meant that the attacker came down from behind over the girl's right shoulder. Did this surprise you?' defence counsel asked.

'I had had so many surprises by then that I was not quite so shocked as I might have been.'

'In this particular case were you learning as you went along?'

'Yes,' Harvey admitted readily, 'but it is accepted that few people in the world have worked on more than a handful of cases; in contrast Professor Keith Simpson has had at least seven cases which, I think, qualifies him for the Guinness Book of Records!'

When I was in the witness box the defence counsel, as I had expected, quoted from the Swedish expert Gustafson's book, to which I had written a foreword published in an English translation. 'Do you agree with the view expressed in that book that at least four or five teeth, and they say they are adjacent teeth, should correspond exactly before a positive identification can be made?'

'I think it is a sound view,' I answered, 'but I think probably a better attitude is a general one, that is to say that the more points of comparison that can be pointed to, the more certain the proof, and the fewer the less certain. I would not fix any given number of 3, 4, 5 or 6 but I would say the more you can point to, the more certain you can be of real matching.'

'Would you agree that the leading experts in forensic odontology seem to live outside Britain?'

'I think they have made strides in this field which have preceded those which have been made here and, therefore, they have become leaders.'

The Solicitor-General, Ewan Stewart, Q.C., was quick to re-examine me on Gustafson's book in order to make the point that the references at the back included ten of my articles or books, the largest number quoted from any single author.

A jury of fifteen considered their verdict for two and a half hours. Although in Scotland there is the extra option of a 'not proven' verdict, they found, by a majority, that Hay was guilty of murder. As he had been under eighteen at the time of the crime the Lord Justice

Clerk was obliged to sentence him to be detained during Her Majesty's pleasure. The sentence mattered nothing to Warren Harvey and myself: what we were concerned to see was that such remarkable dental evidence convinced the court. The Lord Justice Clerk had left little doubt about his acceptance of our evidence.

CHAPTER 26

THE TRIALS OF STEVEN TRUSCOTT IN CANADA

In 1967 Gollancz the publishers sent me a copy of a new book, *The Trial of Steven Truscott*, written by Isabel Lebourdais, and asked for my comment. They also sent a copy to Francis Camps, who apparently approved of the book and told Gollancz he 'did not think the medical evidence could possibly stand up to scrutiny', adding that he 'would have no objection' to his views being published; which, of course, they were. Rather than be caught up in a public argument with Camps, I restricted my remarks to a review of the book for the *Medico-Legal Journal*, in which I said Miss Lebourdais seemed to me to be indulging herself in unfounded, biased and emotional criticisms of the Canadian Police, their pathologist, and the Canadian Courts. It was hardly surprising that Gollancz did not quote any of my comment in their sales advertisements or on the jacket of the book.

However, the book sold well, and disquiet grew all over Canada. One former student of mine at Guy's, then doctoring in Canada, wrote to me to ask if I could not interfere 'for the sake of justice'. I did: but it was at the invitation of the Canadian Government, and it was to support those who had been lashed so publicly by Isabel Leboudais's vitriolic pen that they had been forced to concede to public demand for a retrial. I went to Canada soon after for what was to prove an historic retrial of a young man who had already spent eight years in prison for murder.

Steven Truscott was only fourteen in 1959, when the murder occurred. His father was a warrant officer in the Royal Canadian Air Force, and the family lived in the married quarters of the RCAF Station near Goderich, Ontario. Lynne Harper, the twelve-year-old daughter of a Flying Officer, also lived at the station. The two children were in the same grade at the school and knew each other well.

On Tuesday 9th June 1959, Lynne sat down with her parents to a meal of turkey, cranberry sauce, peas, potatoes, and 'upside-down' pineapple cake. It was about 5.30 p.m. A quarter of an hour later she was washing the dishes, and then she walked over to a meeting of the Brownies on the green near the schoolhouse.

About 7 p.m. Steven Truscott, wearing red trousers and riding his green racing bicycle, arrived on the green. Lynne walked over to him, and they were seen chatting amiably for a few minutes. Then, at about 7.05 p.m., two women saw them walking across the grass with the bicycle to the paved County Road. There Lynne sat on the crossbar and Steven pedalled northward.

About a mile from the school the road crossed the Bayfield River, and there was a swimming hole by the bridge. It was a popular resort that evening, which was very warm, and it happened that two boys came out of the water and started off back to the Air Station soon after 7 p.m. One, Richard Gellatly, aged twelve, was riding a bicycle; the other, eleven-year-old Philip Burns, was on foot.

So there they were, Steven and Lynne riding north, Richard and Philip heading south, on the County Road; bound to meet. And, sure enough, at about 7.25 p.m. Richard met Steven and Lynne, who were still going north, alongside a small wood known as 'Lawson's Bush'. But Philip, walking behind, did not meet them. He was quite certain he did not see them on the road, although he was only just behind Richard and reached home at 7.30 p.m. Philip's evidence was strengthened by that of two playmates who were out looking for Steven, and who asked Philip if he had seen Steven, and he said he had not. The obvious inference was that Steven and Lynne had left the road very shortly after passing Richard, and that would be while they were still alongside Lawson's Bush.

About 8 p.m. Steven was seen again in the school area, alone. 'What did you do with Harper, throw her to the fishes?' one boy asked him. Outwardly calm, he said he had taken her up to No. 8 highway, which intersects the County Road about a quarter of a mile north of the swimming hole. He walked for a few minutes with his brother and some friends and then went home.

When Lynne had not come home by 9.15 p.m. her mother went looking for her. Her father, Flying Officer Harper, joined the search and finally reported her missing to the Air Force Police. Ontario

Provincial Police were notified at 11.30 p.m. At 11.40 a missing person message was broadcast not only on the police radio network but on commercial stations in the area. Both Air Force and civilian police were out early in the morning, searching barns and empty houses. At 7.45 a.m. Flying Officer Harper, having heard Lynne had been last seen with Steven, called on the Truscotts. Steven said he had taken Lynne to No 8 highway and she had hitch-hiked a ride. This sounded so improbable to Harper that he asked the boy point-blank 'Are you sure?' Steven said he was.

Later in the morning the police questioned Steven, who amplified the same story: 'she got a lift in a grey 1959 Chevrolet with lots of chrome and bearing yellow licence plates'. Yellow plates indicated a Michigan car. This information was broadcast across the police radio network without result. By nightfall the girl was still missing, and not a clue found.

Next day, Thursday, the police and the Air Force organized a shoulder-to-shoulder search through Lawson's Bush. At 2 p.m. Lynne's body was found, covered by a few branches, lying on her back in a copse less than a hundred yards from the County Road. She was naked except for her blouse and vest. The blouse had been torn and was tied tightly round her neck. Her clothes were scattered around.

Dr John Penistan, Oxford trained, the consulting medico-legal pathologist to the Province, arrived on the scene at 4.45 p.m. He noted that the girl's legs lay forked apart, and two mounds of earth between her feet could have been pushed up by a man's shoes in the course of rape. A crepe-sole pattern was clearly marked on the earth.

The temperatures in the last two days had been not far from tropical, hastening decomposition. The girl's vagina was already riddled with maggots, and any brushing or tearing of the delicate entrance folds had been disintegrated. Penistan found some bruising and swelling of the vulva, but it was too putrified to justify any detail. He found no fluid, seminal or bloody, in the crotch region.

After Penistan had finished examining the body it was turned on its left side for the police to photograph the ground beneath. (This was an important step, as it turned out.) At the same time Penistan searched for seminal fluid or blood on the leaves and soil but without finding a trace. The body was then removed to the mortuary, where he performed an autopsy at 7.15 p.m. the same day. Vaginal swabs were found to be positive for seminal fluid. Lynne's body bore twig

and undergrowth impressions suggesting she had not merely lain but
been pressed on her back. The cause of death was asphyxia due to
strangling with a ligature.

When had she died? The most helpful of all guides—the fall in body
temperature—was no longer available, since the body loses all its
natural heat in eighteen to twenty-four hours. Rigor mortis, one of
the least certain of all factors, though its chemistry is better
understood than it was, had 'almost passed off'. But the police could
tell Penistan exactly what *and when* Lynne had last eaten, and he
could measure the amount of food left in her stomach. Penistan knew
the emptying time of the stomach was not a mathematical problem
but depends on emotional factors as well as the amount and type of
food in the meal. Fear slows, but anger hastens gastric emptying, so
that might operate either way. Severe injury can paralyse all
movement, but the girl had not received any injury until she died. After
weighing up all the factors Penistan wrote: 'I find it difficult to believe
that this food could have been in the stomach for as long as two
hours, unless some complicating factor was present, of which I have
no information. If the last meal was finished at 5.45 p.m., I would
therefore conclude that death occurred prior to 7.45 p.m.' Penistan
made this telling estimate without reference to anything outside his
post-mortem, and indeed before Steven Truscott was even suspected
of the crime. Penistan took the stomach contents to the Attorney
General's laboratory, where tests identified the stomach contents as
similar in detail to the meal she had eaten on the Tuesday evening: it
had definitely been her last meal.

Steven Truscott had not been suspected at the beginning because
his story sounded reasonable and, as Detective Inspector Graham
said afterwards, it was not the type of crime he would attribute to a
boy of fourteen. But there was an obvious discrepancy between
Steven's evidence and that of Philip Burns, and his account of
Lynne's hitch-hiking looked much less plausible after her body had
been found in Lawson's Bush. Murderers don't move the bodies of
their victims nearer home; and, besides, Dr Penistan had already
shown that it was almost certain that she had been sexually assaulted
and killed where her body lay. So Truscott's story of his parting with
Lynne, which had originally been accepted without question by
everyone except her father, came under closer scrutiny. Where had he
been when he saw her picked up on No 8 highway? He said he was
standing on the bridge by the swimming hole, a quarter of a mile

away. Was it likely he could have seen the car so clearly from that distance, even to the colour of the licence plates? Graham decided to question the youth again.

It was 7 p.m. on Friday 12th June, just twenty-four hours after the autopsy, that Steven Truscott was taken to Goderich Police Station. Nearly three hours later the police took him to the Air Station for a medical examination. This was made, with the consent of Steven's father, by the Truscott family doctor, Dr Addison, who found marks on the youth's penis. On each side of it, he said, there was 'a brush burn of two or three days' duration the size of a 25-cent piece'. It was then exactly three days since Lynne's disappearance. An RCAF medical officer, Dr Brooks, examined Steven at the same time and agreed. Both doctors thought the brush marks were the result of a rape. They also found a wound on the back of his leg, two or three days old, that could have been caused by barbs in the wire fence that surrounded the area where Lynne's body had been found.

While Steven was being medically examined, police officers were executing a search warrant at his home. They found his red trousers, freshly laundered, on a clothes-line in the cellar, hanging alone. Grass stains were detected on the knees, and there was a tear in the back of the trousers that corresponded with the injury on Steven's leg. Steven was known to have had a pair of crepe-soled shoes, and said to have been wearing them the night Lynne disappeared, but the police could not find them, and in fact they were never found: had he destroyed them?

The youth kept to his story, but that evening the Crown Attorney decided to charge him with murder. The Juvenile and Family Court Judge gave permission for him to be lodged in the County Jail, and he was admitted at 3 a.m. on Saturday 13th June.

At his trial three boys gave evidence for the defence, one saying he had seen Steven and Lynne on the bridge by the swimming hole and pedalling north, and the other two saying they had seen Steven in the same area; but none of them had said anything of this during police inquiries or even when they heard of Truscott's arrest. Their stories had only surfaced on 16th June, when Steven's father was trying to collect evidence for his son's defence.

Steven Truscott was found guilty of murder and disappeared into prison, and the case was forgotten until Gollancz's publication of Isabel Lebourdais's book eight years later. This blew into a storm of criticism over the conviction, and the Canadian Director of Public

Prosecutions asked me to put a comb through the book and comment on the author's complaints.

As I had said in my review of the book, it seemed to me too disturbed by emotional involvement to be a sound criticism of the case. It was highly tendentious, irrational, and medically ill-informed. The author relied upon textbooks long since out of date: a 1929 edition of Glaister's *Medical Jurisprudence*, and a *Recent Advances in Forensic Medicine* of about the same date. I was very surprised to learn that Francis Camps had not only endorsed Gollancz's book but had gone so far as to write a private letter to the Attorney General of England expressing his concern over the conviction—a letter that he was to regret bitterly before the case was dead and buried for the second time.

I had reviewed the book before I saw the papers in the case, which the Canadian DPP sent to me. When I read Penistan's long and detailed post-mortem report I realized, with growing admiration, that he had given the most patient, thorough, and skilled attention to what was, on the face of it, just another murder. I had seen many such reports on behalf of both Crown and defence solicitors, and I did not remember, in thirty years, having seen a more thorough or painstaking report, or any more impartial deductions. I wondered where he had studied, and learnt he had qualified at Oxford. 'You examined me in my finals' were almost his first words to me when we eventually met. Sadly this fine pathologist died shortly after the re-trial at Ottawa—still a man in his prime: it had, I thought at the time, been a great strain for him.

Some of Miss Lebourdais's criticisms were based on pure ignorance. Referring to the vaginal swabs, she asked why the semen had not been grouped: Steven Truscott's blood group was known, and if he was a secretor, as 75 per cent of the population are, the semen would be similarly grouped. The answer to this was that it had been grouped, and that it was the same group as his blood. But it so happened that Lynne Harper had the same blood group and was a secretor, and the semen was, of course, mixed with her vaginal mucus, so that this item of potential evidence had to be discarded.

On other points Miss Lebourdais puffed out her case with manufactured observations. For example: 'After she was dead the killer proceeded to complete the knot, for no possible reason except the strange wish to leave everything tidy.' There was no evidence for either the alleged action or for the motive imputed.

Of the theory that Lynne had been strangled with her own blouse Miss Lebourdais said simply that it could not be done. She would have been wiser to say she did not see *how* it could be done, for when we reconstructed the strangling, using an identical stock blouse on a policewoman, we were able to demonstrate that it was perfectly possible.

Miss Lebourdais also said, correctly, that part of Lynne's blouse was missing when it was exhibited at Truscott's trial, and she argued, unreasonably, that this was fatal to the case for the Crown. There was no mystery about the missing piece of blouse, and after we had reconstructed the strangling Penistan demonstrated exactly how it had become detached. 'Cut it there,' he said, indicating on the ligature. I cut the blouse we were using, and the very piece that had been mislaid from the original blouse fell away. Penistan had cut the ligature in the undertaker's mortuary at Stratford, an ill-lit building that was then crowded with doctors, police officers, photographers and their stands. When the ligature was removed all interest was on the body, and the missing piece of cloth was doubtless overlooked or forgotten and later swept up by mortuary staff and discarded.

Penistan's report and the excellent police photographs taken at the scene proved beyond any real doubt that Lynne had been assaulted and murdered exactly where she lay. This disposed of the contention made by Miss Lebourdais, supporting Steven's story of seeing the girl accept a lift in a car on No 8 highway, that she had been hi-jacked and murdered out of the district. Miss Lebourdais wrote much of perplexing tears in the skin and bleeding, when in fact the marks were quite simple, common to many similar sex killings: a long scratch on her left leg, a laceration—Miss Lebourdais called it a 'gash'—on the back of the left shoulder, and various other small cuts and abrasions on the backs of her hands and legs and torso, all clearly shown in the photographs, seemed to me to be just the kinds of mark I would expect to see if a struggling body had been pressed against or held down in that type of undergrowth.

When I first considered Miss Lebourdais's criticisms of the laboratory work in the case I asked, rather hesitantly, if any pathological material or specimens had been preserved or filed. The answer was overwhelming. When I went to Toronto for a conference in July 1966 I found that every single laboratory specimen except for the food matter, every smear, every microscope slide (and there were many) still lay in the files in the Ontario State Crime Laboratory. A practising pathologist could but admire the thoroughness with which every detail of forensic medical and scientific evidence had been recorded and retained, eight years later. I wondered how many of us could emulate that. I wondered also if Miss Lebourdais, before embarking on her criticisms, had asked for experts to examine the scientific exhibits or medical findings, of which she could have had little personal knowledge. She had not, I found. She relied instead upon very outdated textbooks of 1928 and 1929, which she quoted at length.

She quoted extensively, from the same aged books, against the evidence of the stomach contents as a guide to the time of death. Here again Penistan had been marvellously thorough. He had noted the condition and volume of the stomach contents, recorded that a very little was passing for a short distance into the small bowel, had it all examined in the laboratory. I was able to examine every simple laboratory exhibit again eight years later in Toronto, before submitting my report for the re-trial in October 1966.

The exact time of death was as vital a piece of evidence in this case as in any I had known in thirty years' practice. So much depended on it that the Canadian Director of Public Prosecutions himself, and his Senior Counsel, Don Scott, came to London to talk to Professor Hunt of Guy's Hospital Medical School, a world authority on stomach emptying. I happened to be at a meeting of pathologists in Copenhagen with Dr Milton Helpern, the Chief Medical Examiner of New York, when the Canadian Attorney General's office rang from Toronto to propose a conference. I asked Helpern to come with me back to London as I wanted his opinion too. Imagine a DPP, Senior Counsel, an English and an American medico-legal expert converging on a London teaching hospital to meet an expert in stomach emptying! But so much public anxiety as to the justice of Steven Truscott's conviction had been aroused by Miss Lebourdais, Gollancz, Camps and the Canadian Press that I was determined to see that no stone could be left unturned in establishing the real truth.

Professor Hunt expressed the view that 'the conclusions drawn by Dr Penistan tally with those which I have reached after a close study of the literature and more than fifteen years' personal research in this particular field' . . . and ended, 'I am satisfied that Dr Penistan was entirely correct to conclude as he did under the circumstances'.

Stephen Truscott's virtual retrial took place at the Ottawa Supreme

Court before a 'jury' of eleven experienced judges, and concerned itself mainly with the medical evidence. Most of the original witnesses repeated their evidence. Detective Inspector Graham, who was shortly to become Commissioner of Police of Ontario, and Dr Penistan were both unshaken in cross-examination by Mr Martin, Truscott's very able lawyer. A charming police girl played the role of 'victim' in a demonstration of how the ligature was tied and cut, which proved unexpectedly dramatic. When the blouse was cut the loose piece not only fell away but fluttered out of sight under a bench—perfect evidence of how easily it could have 'got lost' in the ill-lit, crowded mortuary at Stratford. I could hardly conceal my delight at this quite unrehearsed happening before the judges.

Dr Petty, a well-known American pathologist from Baltimore, Maryland, was called by the defence to support Truscott's story of seeing Lynne driven away in a car on No 8 highway. Petty somewhat rashly said that areas of pallor on the dead girl's cheek and left shoulder front showed that she had lain, at some time after death, in a different position from that in which she was found. He encouraged defence counsel to infer that this could have been through being carried dumped in the boot of a car. But Dr Petty seemed to have overlooked the significance of one of the photographs. The pressure marks on the face and shoulder had clearly been made when the body was turned on its left side so that photographs could be taken of the ground beneath. Dr Petty also tried to show the court that when twigs lie on the ground they are like—and he produced—numerous ball-pointed pens scattered on a table. The demonstration fell as flat as the pens, for most of the judges had doubtless walked over rough untended brushwood themselves. The suggestion that Lynne had been killed outside the district was given its death-blow by Milton Helpern. 'What?' he exclaimed in his rich American voice. 'Murdered and then brought back near to her home and put there with her shoes and things scattered around? It just don't make sense!' It was as plain an 'Oh now' remark as I have heard in court, and the defence counsel did not pursue the matter further.

Dr Petty, again, was asked to support the view that death could have taken place later than 7.45 p.m. He suggested arching of the small of the back seen in a photograph indicated a more pronounced degree of rigor mortis than Dr Penistan had noted, as if arching of the back were not normal in those who keep their shape. I said I was 'very surprised to hear any pathologist make such a suggestion'. I was almost as surprised to hear Dr Petty suggest the 'goose-skin' change in the skin indicated a greater degree of rigor than Penistan had measured.

Professor Hunt was not called by the defence, for it was left to me to quote his opinion on the stomach emptying in support of my own original report. All I needed to add was that, in the absence of any evidence to the contrary, it must be assumed Lynne Harper was an average subject whose stomach emptied at the normal rate. In cross-examination Martin referred to my little textbook on forensic medicine and asked if there was (knowing well there wasn't) any mention of the reliability of stomach contents in determining time of death. In agreeing that there wasn't, I said the book was written for medical students and was not intended to be comprehensive. Doubtless to the pleasure of my students, if they saw it, the *Whig-Standard* of Kingston (Ontario), reporting my evidence, rendered the last word as 'comprehensible'.!

One pathologist called by the defence argued that Lynne 'could have died within one hour—or up to nine or ten', because reliance on gastric emptying 'could be dangerously misleading to the investigating officers'. But Francis Camps, after some earlier criticisms, said to his own counsel that 'Dr Penistan's conclusions were very fair'. Camps had failed to 'come up to proof'.

It was a disastrous trial for Camps. When Don Scott rose to cross-examine him he produced a letter. 'Just look at this letter, and tell the court if that is your signature to it.'

Camps took the letter, his colour rising perceptibly. 'Yes, it is. It was a private letter, and . . .'

'Never mind about that. I am going to read it to the court.'

It was Camp's letter to the Attorney General of England, and it proved to be an unsolicited offer to give evidence for the convicted youth in Canada if a rehearing took place.

Camps was livid at the exposure. He had plainly touted for work in addressing himself to the Attorney General in this way, and Scott belaboured him with his unethical offer of services, then tore his objections to pieces, one by one. Camps glared at me as the instigator. When Scott had finished, Camps, red in the face and plainly very angry, stormed out of court, forgetting his briefcase! Scott looked at me with a smile of triumph on his face. He never told me how the letter had come into his hands and I didn't ask.

Steven Truscott, by then twenty-one, finally gave evidence in his own defence. (He had not gone into the witness box at the original trial.) He denied having seen any of the witnesses who said they had seen him on the County Road. He explained the sores on his penis by saying he had had them for six weeks before his arrest. (If he had, he had not consulted anyone about them. Moreover, he had not said they had been there six weeks when they were found after his arrest.) After much argument about these unusual lesions, including a description by a dermatologist of allergic rashes on Truscott during his detention, the Crown accepted that there could have seen some pre-existing condition but held that it had at least been aggravated by a sexual assault.

Truscott, like Camps, had to hear a damaging letter he had written read out to the court. While serving his sentence he had written to the Parole Board asking for 'a chance to prove that one dreadful mistake' would ensure that he 'won't make another'. Asked why he wrote this if he was innocent, he said he thought if he 'continued to argue his innocence' he would 'stand less chance of getting out'. The Press, who had been staunchly behind him until that day, were plainly worried by this letter.

Feelings had run high in Canada during the hearing, and Miss Lebourdais appeared on television each evening during the trial to recount the day's events in court—an astonishing feature of Canadian public relationships; but the jury of eleven experienced criminal bar judges were unlikely to be influenced by this. In the event the Crown, and Dr Penistan, triumphed. The judges rejected Steven Truscott's story and opposing medical evidence and decided there had been no miscarriage of justice. Truscott went back to prison. There was some general sympathy for him and he was released in the summer of 1969.

'Was it possible, as a matter of common sense, that the boy could have raped the girl and strangled her in such a short time and returned home so calm and collected?'

I was asked this question in a discussion after I had read a paper on the case to the Medico-Legal Society. In reply I told of a case I had concerning a girl on Waterloo Station who was in an advanced stage of pregnancy. To go to the toilet, she excused herself from her boy friend, who was positive afterwards that she was away only seven minutes because they had a train to catch and he had been watching the station clock. She emerged carrying a rather heavier suitcase, and no longer pregnant. They boarded the train. Most people would have said it was utterly impossible for the girl to go to the toilet, give birth to a child, clean herself up and board the train in such a short space of time, but it was a fact.

Truscott, similarly, had had enough time. Curiously this point was not raised by the defence, nor by the court. His calmness was not surprising to anyone who knows how people behave after committing terrible crimes: look at Haigh, Heath, Hanratty or ... so many others.

CHAPTER 27

CARIBBEAN CRIME:
THE BLACK POWER OF MICHAEL X

During the period 1970–75 I had a succession of cases in the West Indies. None of these islands is large enough to have its own crime laboratory service, and when a major crime occurs they sometimes seek outside help. So it was that I had, successively, a drunken head-bashing in the Virgin Isles, a rape and strangling on the foreshore in Hamilton, Bermuda, and double murder and arson in the hills behind Castries, the harbour where so many tourists put in for a day or two in the lush tropical island of St Lucia. Not long after this, I was called to Trinidad to examine the body of Gale Benson, dug up out of a grave Abdul Malik, better known as 'Michael X', had had dug for her after 'execution' in his garden; and on the way back to England after the Assize Court hearing of this case in Port of Spain, I dropped in at Antigua to help Scotland Yard police officers who had been called out there to investigate the murder by shooting of a rich Englishwoman found in an acacia grove.

In most of the smaller 'paradise, palm-beach, and pineapple' islets the standards of pathology are low when serious crime occurs, and some of my cases had been poorly handled at the start. In one, the District Medical Officer, acting as pathologist, had 'completed a post-mortem examination' and written a three-page report on his findings, when, I found at my re-examination, he had not even looked inside the body at all. He was unabashed when, as my re-examination of the body went on in a hot undertaker's parlour, it became clear that he hadn't done his job, and I felt I had to say to the police officers standing around us that we had better refer to his 'post-mortem' as a 'preliminary examination'.

Early one morning on 10th June 1971, an estate house on the

mountain side of Castries, the old port of St Lucia, burst into flames. Neighbours raised the alarm, but by the time the old fire engine had got into its arthritic bumbling run up the tortuous road out of town the house was a shambles, pretty well burned out.

The firemen found two charred bodies among the mosquito netting and timber debris of a ground-floor bedroom and assumed they were the remains of James and Marjorie Etherington, who had lived there, a couple in the Fyffe banana business.

No one felt any suspicion. A local police surgeon examined the charred bodies at 5.30 a.m. The police looked around the house. The Caribbean Government pathologist flew in to see the bodies the next day and reported that they had died as a result of the fire. The charred hulks were put into plastic bags, sealed together in a zinc-lined coffin and buried in St John's Churchyard on the neighbouring isle of Barbados.

It was an insurance man who smelt crime. Nosing around a day or so later in the ruins of the house, he found earthy footprints on the floor of a rear scullery, beneath a broken louvred window—broken inwards, and in a part of the bungalow neither involved in the fire nor used by the fire brigade in putting it out. Nearby a piece of green plastic hose ran out over a window sill: it had been assumed by everyone it was there to water the garden.

Insurance men in most parts of the world are pretty suspicious of fire-raising, and this agent put the end of the hose to his nose. It smelled strongly of petrol! He traced it round the back of the house to the garage, where a car stood with its petrol tank open, the filler cap on the ground. It was arson, and murder!

Nigel Fuller, a young Cambridge science graduate on the staff at Scotland Yard, flew out next day and raised the charred floorboards, to find under them some four or five centres of fire with hydrocarbon residues from petrol. I went the next day to look at the bodies and, in effect, to perform the first proper post-mortem examinations. I was met by two Yard detectives, Superintendent Morrison and Sergeant Osborne, who had already 'got a line' from inquiries in St Lucia that several men had been seen hanging about near the bungalow during the evening before the fire. The local Commissioner of Police, Samuel Brooks, had three well-known criminals brought in for questioning.

'That was pretty quick work, Mr Brooks,' I said.

He smiled—an 'all over' smile. 'It's simple,' he said. 'If I get any real trouble on the island I bring these three in: Florius, the ringleader, Faucher and Anthony Charles, who just does what he's told. If they haven't done it, they always know who has!'

He was bang on. Florius had burn marks on his neck and arm, and fingernail scratches on his chest and cheek. Anthony Charles was scratched on his shoulder and arm. None of the three had an alibi, and all had come into money on the day of the fire. But they wouldn't admit any violence—just to robbery. They had left the couple tied up. No killing. No fire. That was just an unfortunate coincidence, and we had to prove otherwise, said Florius, the ringleader.

At 6 a.m. next day we assembled in St John's Church graveyard near Georgetown, Barbados, and started to dig. For lack of privacy the scene surpassed even the exhumations of Beryl and Geraldine Evans in Kensington. Hundreds of gaily dressed men and women jostled outside the graveyard walls, and there were ice-cream stalls and hordes of children with great white eyes eager for an entertainment that had never come their way before. Policemen digging up dead bodies! Murder! English scientists! Scotland Yard!

Three hours later I was distraught with frustration. Only one elderly gravedigger had turned out, and he had an old spade and two enamel bowls, each rusted through and leaking much of their contents every time they were lifted to the edge of the grave. This was eight feet long, six feet across, made for two to lie side by side, and they were five or six feet down. The old man tired quickly but wouldn't have anyone else work with him: he was the official gravedigger, so it was his job. He'd walk out if anyone got down into the grave with him. Occasionally he cried. Every ten minutes or so he took a rest. Occasionally he had a 'Coke'. Then he set off again, slower than ever. It was three hours, and the sun was scorching all of us, before we saw the coffin lid, and *then the grave pit sides caved in*! An hour later the heavy double coffin was at last tilted enough for the canvas straps to be passed under it.

The smell was awful when the lid came off in Queen Elizabeth Hospital, and my audience in the post-mortem room rapidly dwindled as I examined the charred bodies. In spite of the fire damage I could see that the man's skull had been shattered above the left ear by some blunt instrument. Beneath it a blood clot indicated surface bruising of the brain. I thought the blow had probably been powerful enough to have caused unconsciousness, but it had not killed him: I found soot particles in the deepest part of his lungs, and colour changes in the blood and muscles suggested he had also inhaled carbon monoxide. The cause of death was asphyxia due to inhalation of fire fumes. The woman's body was more destructively burned, charred, and disintegrated. Of the skull only the base was left, with a little brain attached; but the remains of a plastic-covered clothes line, running between her charred teeth, showed she had been gagged and left to burn. The red colour of her muscles suggested she too had inhaled fire fumes (through her nose).

When I left Barbados for London I had some difficulty in retaining possession of my large black gladstone bag, for an officious young air cargo officer said it was too big even for the first-class cabin. I said I had travelled much with it and was not going to part with it: I dared not say it had the remains of two dead bodies in it, on their way back to my laboratories at Guy's. Passengers don't like to have corpses in their cabins; and air staff don't like a dead body on board anyway, not even in the hold. In the end I got a security officer to persuade the cargo duty man that there was some 'pretty highly confidential Home Office matter' in the bag and I just could not let it out of my sight: it had the Police Commissioner's sanction. Grudgingly the young man gave in.

Laboratory tests on samples of blood and muscle confirmed the presence of carbon monoxide in both bodies, and there was little doubt that the couple had been callously left to die in the fire.

Three months later Florius, Faucher, and Charles stood their trial in the stiflingly hot courthouse at Castries. Nigel Fuller and I sat dripping perspiration, he to give evidence of arson, I of murder. We had little opposition from defence counsel, bewigged and all London trained. Faucher, speaking from the dock, said Florius had told him they had to burn the victims, 'as in England they have a new method to make the dead talk'. It seems Florius actually believed electronic records could be taken from the dead on to tape. 'If we burn them, ashes don't talk'. The Attorney-General, John Renwick, picked this up in his closing speech, pointing out that the ashes had talked very eloquently through the evidence of Nigel Fuller and myself. All three men were found guilty and hanged.

It isn't every week that a cultured voice on the phone says 'Foreign Office here, professor. I'm ringing to see if you could go to Trinidad tomorrow morning. It's the case of Michael X, Black Power man. Local police have found the body of an English girl buried in his garden and say it's murder. Would like your help.'

'Why—er, yes, of course.' But I was uncertain where I was supposed to be tomorrow, like the absent-minded Hilaire Belloc who, due to give a public lecture, rang his secretary in London to say 'I'm at Crewe, my dear, where should I be?' Then I remembered it was Friday night. It couldn't have been better, for I was at my country home at Tring, easing off for a quiet week-end.

'Yes, of course,' I repeated. 'I can leave in the morning.'

'Splendid,' said the very English voice at the other end. 'We'll have your tickets left at the BOAC desk at Heathrow. 8.30 for 9.15 Flight BA 697. We'll let Trinidad know. Can we send a car for you?'

What a quiet week-end! By Saturday evening I had flown 4,000 miles to Piarco airport, been driven fifteen miles out of Port of Spain to the garden at Arima, met the Commissioner of Police, Eustace Bernard, looked over a burned-out house and the graves where two bodies had been found, and had slept fitfully at the Hilton. By Sunday at 9 a.m. we were all in the airless post-mortem room at the General Hospital, examining and photographing sodden, smelly victims' clothing, stab wounds, weapons. At 2, after a discussion over lunch, we set out for the West Coast bay where another victim, Steve Yates, had been 'accidentally drowned' shortly before. By 5.30 I was in a bath. By 7 at a Chinese restaurant downtown in Port of Spain, being entertained by about twenty local doctors, including old pupils of mine, and lawyers. By 10, after a hair-raising dash to the airport while excuses were made to BOAC about my being detained, climbing aboard the BA 697 (now 698), and the stewardess was saying, 'Haven't I seen you before, sir?' It was the same crew going home after a day's rest in the sun. Back at Heathrow 8 a.m. Monday.

'Give you two guesses where I've spent the week-end,' I said to my Guy's secretary, Hilary White, at 9.30 a.m.

'I've seen it in the newspapers,' she replied. 'Enjoy your trip?'

Well, I had always got a lot of enjoyment from the occasional calls on crime jobs abroad. They gave me a 'lift' out of the run of ordinary work in England.

'Yes, Miss White,' I could truthfully say. 'A jolly good week-end' . . . stifling a yawn. A full Monday's routine work lay ahead. It's always next day you begin to feel tired.

This was indeed a job that had suddenly stirred the world press. Michael X, or Abdul Malik, was trouble anywhere, and newspapermen were alive to any development, though they hardly expected the murder of an English girl to be the next news.

Born in Trinidad, the son of a Portuguese planter called de Freitas and a Port of Spain black girl, he had come to London, married a black girl in Notting Hill, and manoeuvred his way into the world of prostitution. He became a ponce, drank, gambled, and drifted into the 'real estate' of Rachman, the racketeer property man, who terrorized the coloured district of Paddington by employing thugs like Malcolm de Freitas to persuade his tenants to relinquish their legal 'security of tenure' and so send the value of his property soaring.

Malik, as he called himself, was fascinated by reports of the Black Power movement in the United States, which was headed by a militant who called himself Malcolm X. The young man from Trinidad adopted the name of Michael X, founded a 'Racial Adjustment Action Society', and became self-appointed Messiah to London's black community. 'When you think of me you can think of Hitler . . . he had power,' he told his followers. He taught integration with *power*, a policy that led to his imprisonment for twelve months in 1967 under the Race Relations Act, for advocating shooting any white man seen with a black girl. He jumped bail in the summer of 1969 when on further charges of robbery and demanding money with menaces, and was next heard of in Trinidad in 1970. The British authorities did not seek to extradite him, preferring to leave him wherever he was rather than to allow him to stir up racial conflict from a platform in London. He had wealthy friends—Sammy Davies junior, John Lennon, writer Alexander Trocchi, Nigel Samuel, the millionaire's son—and not a few followers who quite honestly believed him to be a black man's Messiah, incapable of the crime that eventually proved his downfall.

Among those who fell for him was an attractive English girl in her twenties. Gale Benson, daughter of a man of character and integrity—a *Who's Who* figure, Captain Leonard Plugge, author, traveller, naval inventor, and former MP for Chatham. Her relationship with Malik was not physical, certainly not sexual; she lived with a Muslim disciple of his, Hakim Jamal. But Malik had a Svengali-like hold on her. He never for a moment contemplated abandoning his wife, Désirée, but exercised a ruthless control of the will of this girl Gale. They met at a party, and Malik described her as 'the prettiest woman I had ever seen—long straight black hair and her skin like a dark olive'. He said he had 'done all manner of evil things to her and she never complained; but I didn't love her for this, I hated her. Once I tied her spreadeagled on a bed and beat her until I was tired.' She didn't care. She was utterly slave-like in her devotion to him, and she was only one of a number of equally fascinated white girls.

Gale and her lover, Hakim Jamal, followed Malik to Trinidad when he fled from London in 1969, and at first things went well for them all. Malik returned to protection rackets and prostitution and graduated to politics. Meetings spawned marches, then Black Power demonstrations, ending in an Army mutiny that caused the evacuation of Police Headquarters in 1970. Malik was in this to the neck, and when it was suppressed his popularity waned. He ran short of money, and towards the end of 1971 was very pressed to complete purchase of a £20,000 bungalow he had rented in Arima, some twenty miles from Port of Spain. He started an arms racket, organized armed robberies, and (his fatal mistake) put a well-known criminal called Joseph Skerritt on a raid on a country police post. Skerritt wouldn't obey, and Malik quite simply ordered his execution. A trench was dug by a gang of which Skerritt himself was a member—he was told it was to facilitate drainage—and when it was ready Malik decapitated the recalcitrant with a cutlass and buried him. When the trench was filled in Malik ordered his gardener to 'plant something' in it. Some lettuce went in next day, and did well! The code name for doing a job of this kind was 'to plant a tree', and Malik's gang knew that any of them might fall a victim at any time.

Skerritt was killed on 8th February 1972. Only a few days later the body of another member of the gang, Steve Yates, was 'lost' in a bathing excursion to Sans Souci Bay, a quiet inlet I bathed in myself safely enough. Everyone was on edge and tempers flared. Gale had not been seen for more than a month, and no one seemed inclined to ask about her. Outsiders kept well clear of the gang.

Then suddenly the whole dirty business came to light—literally. Malik left for Guyana on a 'lecture tour' with his wife, and that night his bungalow was set alight by one of his gun-runners. As soon as Malik settled into a small hotel in Georgetown he got news of the fire, and he reacted curiously. He wired his lawyer in Port of Spain to get an injunction to bar anyone from visiting the premises. But he was too late. The Fire Brigade had been followed in by the police, and an inspector thought a patch of lettuces in the garden were growing far 'too tall and yellow'. His men dug them up, and found Skerritt's grave. Two days later they found a second grave. Nearly five feet under the surface they unearthed the body of a woman wearing a print frock and rose-coloured panties: a white woman.

I took samples of soil when I looked at the grave two days later, soon after my arrival in Trinidad. Police Commissioner Bernard drove me back to the Hilton, and conversation died when we entered the bar. They all knew why I was there: the evening *Argus* had my photograph on the front page, and it was no good pretending I was just another travelling salesman.

The press from all over the world were already flying into Piarco airport, and I spotted not a few of them sipping rum-and-Coke at the Hilton bar, conveniently close, at dinner, walking on the terraces or round the pool. One never knew—I might possibly let drop that I needed a taxi at 6 a.m., or had ordered a 'conference room' that night. In fact, all I was interested in was bed. Plans had already been made for a morning call 'to go to church', but on the way we turned into the hospital, where Gale's body lay, and were too late for the church service.

The body was provisionally identified by Police Superintendent McPhillip: later her London dentist, Roland Knight, examined her teeth and recognized twenty-five of her thirty-five fillings as his own work. Bearing in mind the conditions and depth of the burial, I estimated she had been dead about two months, and had thus been killed and buried more than a month before Skerritt.

There was no sign of a disabling blow and no hint of sexual assault. Her face was uninjured, and she had evidently resisted the attack. I found a bitten-off finger nail, not her own, in her throat behind the tongue. There were ten slashed cuts in the front of her chest, all confined to the skin. A single one-inch stab cut on the back, below the tip of the shoulder blade, was similarly superficial. A through-and-through wound of her left arm at elbow level, with a four-inch entry slit and two-inch exit, looked typically 'defensive'. Finally there was the single stab wound that had killed her, entering through a three-inch vertical slit at the root of the neck and penetrating six and a half inches down into the left chest. It had cut through the tip of the breast bone and sunk deep into the left lung, causing the escape of both blood and air into the chest. I told the police they could look for a long knife, sharp-pointed and with at least one cutting edge capable of penetrating over six inches. Impeded as it was by bone, the thrust must have been made with considerable force. This injury would in itself have been fatal, but it was not the only cause of death. In the back of her throat and in her windpipe and air passages I found dirt or earth, similar to the sample I had taken from her grave: more lay clinging to the lining of her stomach. The fact that she had inhaled and swallowed soil particles showed that she had been buried alive, and the consequent obstruction to breathing must have accelerated her death. The fact that the fingernail in her throat had been neither coughed up nor swallowed suggested it had entered just before she was buried, and that she had died very soon afterwards.

The dead girl's lover, Hakim Jamal, was found by a newspaper reporter in Massachusetts, looking, he said, for Gale. 'I've been searching since she disappeared in Trinidad three weeks ago.' Nobody else on the island had seen her for nearly two months, according to the Trinidad police, who had meanwhile asked the police in Guyana to arrest Malik. They found his wife still in Georgetown, but Michael X had disappeared after making his agent shave off his beard. 'I said I was not a barber, but he forced me at scissor point,' the agent said later in court. 'I was emasculated,' he added.

The clean-shaven Malik had donned a rough new suit, put on dark glasses, and set off for the Brazilian border some 300 miles away. He got only 60 miles when a surveyors' party saw him stumbling, wet and exhausted, in the jungle, armed only with a knife and a fishing hook and line. It was dusk and they directed him to a woodman's hut. One of the party recognized him and rang the police. When Malik awoke next morning at dawn it was to face three Guyanan policemen with pistols levelled. 'Please don't shoot,' was all he said.

In August Malik was tried for the murder of Skerritt, convicted and sentenced to death. The Trinidad Government still had him indicted on the further charge of murdering Gale Benson, perhaps for fear that he might, on appeal, escape the first conviction. Two other men, Stanley Abbott and Edward Cheddi, were also charged with the murder of Gale, and in October I went back to Trinidad to give evidence at the magistrates' court. While I was in Port of Spain I accepted an invitation to give what seemed a timely 'pep' talk to the Trinidad and Tobago Medical Association about the doctor's job in a suspected crime.

The magistrates committed both Abbott and Cheddi for trial, but this was not held until eight months later, in July 1973. Meanwhile Malik was still in gaol, using all possible appeal machinery and still widely feared outside. In May 1973 Hakim Jamal was killed by five gunmen in Boston, in front of his family: it was commonly believed that Michael X had ordered the 'execution' from his own condemned cell. This may have accounted for the way I was looked after when I returned for the trial of Abbott and Cheddi. Plainclothes security men sat in the corridor outside my bedroom day and night (as if I were a co-respondent) and another couple managed to follow me if I went out for a dip in the pool. There were fears that Malik might be about to stage another coup, like the one three years before when he had the entire Police Force besieged in the Central Police Station!

The Assize Court No. 1 at Port of Spain was impressive, a long and broad courtroom with large windows thrown open down one side, a high ornate ceiling. Mr Justice Garvin Scott, in full red robe and wig, received the usual respectful bows of the Attorney-General, the Solicitor-General, and defending counsel, and, after a few perfunctory objections, the jury was sworn in. One of the accused objected to my being in court to hear the Attorney-General open the case, in which he would indicate what I and other witnesses were to say, so I left the courtroom to wait in either a black hole of Calcutta where some thirty other witnesses were perspiring or the sun-baked balcony outside. Each was intolerably hot.

I slipped into the air-cooled Court No. 2 to pass the time. It was a retrial in another stabbing murder. The Crown's only witness of the affair, who had given a detailed account of it at the first trial, was again in the tall old mahogany witness stand.

'And now, Mrs Charles,' said counsel. 'will you tell the court what you saw on May 8 last?'

There was a long pause. Counsel waited confidently enough, for at the first trial she had told her story well.

'Well, Mrs Charles?'

'Ah done remembah nutt'n',' she suddenly blurted. 'Coconut done fall on mah head since, an' ah done know nutt'n'.'

It put paid to the case. What a delightfully simple way of having the memory wiped out—at least in the Caribbean!

I was just getting warmed up to counsel's dilemma—he asked Mrs Charles to stand down for the time being, in the hope that her memory would return—when I heard my name called in the corridors. My turn next door in Court No. 1. And no chance of pleading 'de coconut fall'!

In the event my evidence was not disputed, and it was largely confirmed by another Crown witness, Adolphus Parmesser, who had taken part in the murder. He said Gale had been lured to the scene of the crime by Steve Yates, the man who was later 'accidentally drowned'. He had shown her the pit that had been dug, and she had asked what it was for. 'To put fresh matter to be decomposed,' he answered, and then pushed her in. After a furious struggle it was Yates (they said) who forced his cutlass down her neck.

Abbott and Cheddi were both convicted and sentenced to death. Michael X's last appeal was rejected by the Privy Council in London in November, and he was finally hanged, almost two years after the murders of Gale Benson and Skerritt.

CHAPTER 28

THE LORD LUCAN CASE AND OTHER UNFINISHED BUSINESS

Of the unsolved mysteries in my files perhaps the most tantalizing was the case of a married couple with the name—not very appropriate, apparently—of Love.

On 5th December 1960 a giant grab hopper called 'Gallion's Reach' was dredging in thirty feet of water in the Royal Victoria Dock. At about three in the afternoon one of the grabs picked up the chassis and engine of a car. An hour later the hopper retrieved more parts of the vehicle, and then a shout from alongside reported a body in the water, which had evidently tumbled out of the car when it was being raised. The master of the hopper, Alfred Holland, hauled in the body with a boathook and handed it over to the CID. It was a headless female torso, disintegrating, the fat swollen by adipocere, and I thought it must have been immersed for very many months since most of the limbs had come away. Only the right leg was still attached: it was intact, and covered by a stocking and a fur-topped bootee. I calculated that the woman's height was about 5 feet 4 inches, her age between 50 and 60. An appendix scar was still discernible.

More dredging the next morning brought up other parts of the car, a woman's metal bracelet, and a man's wristwatch. Then came several loose bones and bits of bones, and a man's shoe, a brogue size 8½, with a foot in it. Finally came a man's shirt with a decipherable laundry mark.

So I had the remains of at least two persons, and when I had put the pieces together as far as possible I was satisfied that I did not have any part of a third person too. From the man's bones I calculated his height as about 5 feet 10 inches and estimated his age at 30 to 40. The condition of these relics suggested immersion for years rather than months.

The car was a Wolseley. The number plate had rusted, but the last two figures, 30, could still be read. Within hours the police had traced the vehicle to a garage owner named Jack Love, who had disappeared with his wife Mary from their home in Tottenham, north London, four years before. Mrs Love's daughter Joy identified her mother's bracelet and bootee and her stepfather's watch and shoe. She had been living with them when they disappeared. They had both been at home when she returned from work at midday, and the car was outside the house. Her mother, in fur coat and bootees, had gone out at about 12.45 p.m. saying she had an appointment at the Ministry of Pensions and would be back about half-past four. Joy's stepfather went out shortly after without saying where he was going. When Joy herself went back to work, at about 1.45 p.m., the car was no longer outside. She never saw either of them again.

Jack Love was thirty-four and Mary was fifty-seven, and they had been married only a year; but he had been her lodger for seven years before that. Mary had inherited a substantial amount of money and had been supporting her rather idle husband, financing his unsuccessful business ventures—garage owner and car-hire dealer— but still keeping a firm hold of the purse strings. He had a history of depression and psychiatric treatment, and had been discharged from the RAF as mentally unstable. He had been drinking heavily in the last three months before their disappearance.

I agreed that both bodies could have been immersed for as long as four years. The difference in the degree of preservation was doubtless due to the fact that hers had been inside and his outside the car.

Was it an accident? It seemed unlikely, for the Loves had had no reason to be in the dock. It would have been an unusually discreet accident, too, in such a well-patrolled area, for nobody had reported seeing or hearing the car go over the side.

Suicide? He was depressed, but she wasn't. Her daughters scoffed at the idea of a suicide pact.

Crime, then? Could he have killed her, put the body in the boot of the car, and driven it over the quay with the intention of jumping out but not making it? I could not answer the whole question, but I was able to tell the police that her body had not been lying in the boot of the car. Her right leg was bent at the hip and knees as in a sitting position, and part of a coiled seat spring was deeply embedded in the middle of her disintegrating back.

Murder and suicide? Did he drive the car over in order to kill himself and his wife? It was possible, but there was no evidence.

The heads of the Loves were never found. They had rotted off, not been cut or sawn. I X-rayed all the bones but discovered no evidence of any type of injury. As no organs were present the cause of death was unascertainable: it seemed likely both had drowned.

Inevitably the coroner recorded an open verdict. He added an advice to the relatives against cremation, in case fresh evidence should come to light. It never did.

In 1945 I had three cases in as many months of what looked at first like sexual murders but evidently were not.

Constance Williams, whose body was found by the side of a military road near Plymouth, was a normally developed girl of fourteen. A post-mortem examination was performed by a senior west country pathologist, who gave the cause of death as asphyxia but found little to account for it. He reported that there was 'very little external evidence of any degree of violence'. He noted a 'minute bruise' over the front of the neck, but otherwise 'there were no bruises of any kind round the neck'. The local pathologist had evidently not turned the body over, or he could not have failed to see bruises of the back of the neck which were still very clear when I performed a second post-mortem a day later. I found also that there were in fact two separate bruises of the front of the neck, one on each side of the midline, and there was more extensive and deeper bruising in the muscles underneath. The left wing of the voice box was bruised but not fractured, probably because of the great resilience of the part owing to the girl's youth. It was clear to me that she had been strangled by a hand applied with very considerable force in front and maintained as asphyxia developed. She had been lying on her back and pinned to the ground, counterpressure being the cause of the bruises in the back of the neck which the local pathologist had overlooked. He had also failed to notice that the girl was seven months pregnant.

She had been strangled where she was found, probably late in the evening before. There were showers of petechial haemorrhages on her face and further intense asphyxial changes in the lungs, showing that her strangler must have maintained his grip for at least twenty to thirty seconds. Since she would have lost consciousness within only a few seconds there was little doubt about the intention to kill.

Plenty of evidence of violence, then; but, surprisingly, almost no signs of a struggle, although she had been a healthy girl, clearly strong enough to defend herself vigorously. A single small bruise on one knuckle might have been sustained in delivering some defensive blow; it could equally have resulted from her hand striking the ground. Her nails, although long enough to scratch, were untorn; scraping proved negative, and the cuticle of the fingers was undamaged.

The girl's pregnancy was undisturbed, and there was no evidence of sexual assault or of violent intercourse. The condition of the vulva and hymen showed she had been used to intercourse, and I recalled the case of another girl in a Kent field who had been raped by *two* US servicemen, one pinning her by the throat while the other had intercourse, and who had died of strangulation during the proceedings. The sexual assault had been accomplished with ease, giving the impression of consent owing to the absence of violence or injury. But in the case of Constance Williams there was no evidence even of consenting intercourse. If it had occurred it must have been either with sheath protection (unlikely, when she was seven months pregnant) or without emission, for vaginal swabs were negative.

The police had a suspect, but for lack of more evidence no arrest was ever made.

A month after this case I was called to the Isle of Ely, where the body of a young woman in WAAF uniform had been found lying face downward on the bank of the river Nene. Her skirt was rucked up round her waist, showing that she wore no knickers. Otherwise she was fully dressed except for one missing stocking and both shoes. P.C. Jack Cox, who was called to the scene, turned the body over and noted dark marks on her face which he thought might be bruises. He saw a dark fluid seeping from her vagina, and promptly called in the CID. Before the day was over the case was in the hands of Detective Chief Inspector Thorp of Scotland Yard, and shortly after midnight I was examining the body in Thorney Public Mortuary. It had by then been identified as that of a WAAF girl of twenty-eight named Florence Childs.

I estimated she had been lying dead on the river bed for about two weeks, and the body appeared to have been more or less completely submerged since death. Decomposition was too far advanced for the usual signs of asphyxia to be visible, but silted matter lay in the body orifices (including the vagina) and extended into the deepest parts of the bronchial tubes of both lungs; and this gave the strongest presumptive evidence that she had inhaled water while alive, and died from asphyxia by drowning.

The marks on the face that P.C. Cox had thought might be bruises were normal discolorations due to decomposition. I found only three surface injuries on the whole body. One of these, a half-inch-long split in the scalp, showed no vital bruising, but the skin split would have allowed blood to flow into the water rather than spread under the skin. The other two—one on the back and one on the shoulder blade—were even more trivial skin grazes but had plainly been sustained in life. There was no sign of any major injury or disease that might have caused her to collapse or fall into the water, or affected her natural ability to save herself from an involuntary immersion. She was a married woman, and no evidence of sexual interference, violent or otherwise, was present: the vaginal swab was negative.

I had to report that I had found no real cause for suspicion of foul play on medical grounds. The river Nene at that place is very fast flowing and tidal, and a distinct undertow coupled with cross-currents make it dangerous for bathing. The spot where the body was found would have been submerged at high water, and the body had evidently been left by a receding tide. The police found no footprints or other suspicious marks in the soft mud, and nothing in the dead woman's personal history to throw any light on the cause of death. She had not been drinking. It looked as if she had fallen into the water by accident; it was strange that her knickers were missing, but some women do not wear them.

Another unsolved murder in my files occurred in Epping Forest one November evening in 1952. Kenneth Dolden, an RAF man on release leave, had parked his car in a glade and was sitting in the back seat with his fiancée, Jacynth Bland, when the door was wrenched open by a man wearing a grey cloth cap pulled down over his eyes and with a muffler or handkerchief masking the lower half of his face. 'Get out,' ordered Dolden. The man leaned forward and fired three shots into Dolden's body. Miss Bland said later that the shots seemed muffled and she thought the gun might have had a silencer. Dolden managed to stagger out of the car, but immediately fell. Miss Bland ran to the road to call for help. Seeing another car parked, she gasped out her story to the driver and his woman passenger, and they all drove to the nearest police telephone box.

The police told Miss Bland to wait for them at the box, and the other woman stayed with her. The driver of the car said he would go back to the glade to try to help the shot man, but he was not there when the police arrived and he was never seen again. His passenger told the police he had picked her up that evening and had said his name was Bill. There was no reason to suspect him of being involved in the crime, and presumably he did not want someone else, such as his wife, to know that he had picked up a girl and taken her to the forest.

Dolden had died of the wounds in his chest and abdomen. The chest injury was plainly a contact wound, and the other two shots had been fired from the closest possible quarters short of actual contact. Beyond doubt his murderer had shot to kill.

Dolden was still breathing when he reached hospital, and in brief spells of consciousness he gasped out a dying statement to the detectives at his bedside:

'Hit on head . . . three shots fired at close range. . . . Man had mask on. . . . I have no idea who he was. He had cap on. . . . I tried to kick him . . . wearing overcoat. No idea how old. I had been there about half an hour. . . . Handkerchief round nose. . . . I think whoever it was was after car. There was no other car anywhere near when I drove into trees.'

Theft of the car seemed an unlikely reason for the murder, but the police never found a better one. Nothing in the lives of Dolden or of his fiancée suggested a more personal motive, and no clue to the murderer's identity was found. From his point of view it was, in fact, a perfect, if senseless, crime.

The fourth of this little group of cases occurred in East Anglia, and it bore some uncanny resemblances to the first. Again the girl was only fourteen, normally but not precociously developed; again there was no sign of sexual attack; and again murder was clearly deliberate.

Daphne Bacon's body was found in a rye field at Aldringham, and she had been beaten to death with a rough stick, bough, or some similar blunt weapon. Unlike Constance Williams she had been able to put up some resistance. She had sustained at least five very violent blows on the head, which she had tried to ward off with her hands, and then two further similar blows of greater weight while she lay on the ground. Finally she had been dragged by the feet to the spot where her body was found.

That fine detective Edward Greeno took over the case, and, hearing that the girl had murmured 'a soldier came . . . and hit me' before she died, had 30,000 troops 'combed'. A bloodstained ear of corn was found by Sergeant Long in the pocket of one, and Greeno had him 'in'. He lied about where he'd been at the time of the murder—and was sentenced to death and reprieved.

The Earl of Lucan, whose name is still in the 'Red Alert' category of Interpol files, was nicknamed 'Lucky'; but whatever luck he had in his favourite occupation, gambling, ran out in the end, which came in the evening of 7th November 1974.

It was about 9.45 p.m. when a woman staggered into the bar of the Plumber's Arms, in the West End of London, bleeding from her head and screaming, 'Help me! Help me! I've just escaped from a murderer. My children, my children!' she added, between sobs. 'He's still in the house.'

As the landlord, Jack French, said later, in a masterpiece of understatement, 'That kind of thing doesn't usually happen around here.'

She was the Countess of Lucan, and her house was at 46 Lower Belgrave Street, only thirty yards from the pub. When the police broke in a few minutes later they found no man but only the three children, all unharmed. The Earl's son and heir, aged seven, and his younger sister were asleep in their beds. The eldest child, ten-year-old Lady Frances, was merely bewildered and anxious to know when her mother was coming back. But Lady Lucan was in an ambulance bound for St George's Hospital, where she was to stay a week. She had seven scalp wounds and was in a state of shock. 'It was my husband who attacked me,' she told the police at her bedside. She later repeated this at the inquest on her children's nanny, Sandra Rivett, whose dead body was discovered bundled up in a canvas mail bag in the basement of the house.

The police found Sandra's body when they were searching for Lady Lucan's attacker, and it was still warm to the touch. The divisional police surgeon certified death, and I performed a post-mortem examination at ten the next morning. Death was due to a number of severe blunt head injuries, three on the face and at least six on the scalp. The skull was not fractured but the brain was bruised and considerable bleeding had occurred. There was also heavy bruising on both shoulders as from 'near misses', and some 'protective' type bruising on the back of the right hand. A series of four in-line bruises on the front of the right upper arm was consistent with a forceful grip by a hand. Death had taken place before the body was doubled up and put into the bag.

The police showed me a bloodstained piece of lead piping weighing some $2\frac{1}{4}$ pounds which they had found in a room on the ground floor. Surgical plaster strip had been wrapped round it. It could have caused Sandra's scalp, shoulder, and head injuries, and could also have been used to inflict Lady Lucan's injuries. When the police asked her what she thought had hit her she said, 'I know it sounds silly, but it felt bandaged'.

Lady Lucan said in her statement that she and her daughter Frances had been watching television in her bedroom when Sandra looked in and asked if she would like a cup of tea. That was just about five minutes before the nine-o'clock news. Sandra went down to the kitchen in the basement, and Lady Lucan never saw or heard her again. At about 9.15 she went downstairs to find out what had happened to the tea. On the ground floor she looked down the stairs to the basement and saw there was no light on. She called Sandra's name, and heard a noise from the ground-floor cloakroom. 'I walked towards the sound and somebody rushed out and hit me on the head. There were about four blows. I screamed. The person said, "Shut up". I recognized the voice. It was my husband. He thrust three gloved fingers down my throat. We started to fight. He attempted to strangle me from in front, gouge out my eye. . . . I grabbed him by his private parts. He then moved back.' Apparently that was the end of the struggle. 'I asked him for a drink of water. We went into the downstairs cloakroom and I had a drink. It was dark. Following this we both went upstairs to my bedroom. My daughter Frances was still there. I sent her upstairs. I said I felt ill. We looked at my injuries together. After that he laid a towel on the pillow and I lay on it. I understood my husband was going to get a cloth to clean up my face. He went into the bathroom. I heard the taps running and I jumped to my feet and ran out of my room down the stairs. I ran to the Plumber's Arms. . . .'

Ten-year-old Lady Frances Lucan confirmed much of this, although she thought it had happened earlier. 'After a while Mummy said she wondered why Sandra was so long. I don't know what time this was, but it was before the news came on the television at 9 p.m. I said I would go downstairs to see what was keeping Sandra, but Mummy said no, she would go. I said I would go with her, but she said no, it was OK, she would go. . . . Just after Mummy left the room

I heard a scream. I thought maybe the cat had scratched Mummy and she had screamed. I wasn't frightened by the scream and I just stayed in the room watching television. I went to the door of the room and called out 'Mummy' but there was no answer so I just left it. At about 9.05 p.m., when the news was on the television, Daddy and Mummy both walked into the room. Mummy had blood over her face and she was crying. Mummy told me to go upstairs. . . . I got into bed and read my book. I didn't hear anything from downstairs. After a while I heard Daddy calling for Mummy. He was calling out, "Veronica, where are you?" I got up and went to the banisters and looked down, and I saw Daddy coming out of the nursery. He then went into the bathroom, came straight out, and then went downstairs. That was the last I saw of him.'

Police forced the front door a few minutes after 10 p.m. By 10.20 Sandra's body had been found and Sergeant Graham Forsyth of the CID had arrived. At 10.45 Dr Smith, the police surgeon, certified that she was dead. A quarter of an hour later Lord Lucan's mother arrived. 'I am sorry to have to tell you that your daughter-in-law has been attacked and is in hospital, and the nanny to your grandchildren is dead,' said Sergeant Forsyth. 'I knew something was wrong,' she replied, 'because my son telephoned me a short while ago and told me to come here.'

Lord Lucan had telephoned his mother at about 10.45 to tell her that 'a terrible catastrophe' had occurred. 'He said he was passing the house and he saw a fight going on in the basement between a man and Veronica,' the dowager countess told Forsyth. 'He said he went in and interrupted the fight. He said "Veronica is shouting and screaming". He sounded very shocked. He also mentioned the nanny and said she was hurt. I asked "Badly?" he said, "I think so." He told me to get the children out as soon as possible. I said to him, "Where are you going?" He said, "I don't know." He then rang off.'

Less than two hours later the Earl of Lucan surfaced at Uckfield, in Sussex, forty miles away, and called at the house of his friend Ian Maxwell-Scott. Maxwell-Scott was not at home, but his wife Susan admitted Lord Lucan, observing a damp patch on his trousers. He repeated the story he had told his mother with additional details. 'He said his wife was very hysterical and cried out that someone had killed the nanny and almost in the same breath accused him of having hired the man to kill her. . . . I think he used the words "It was an unbelievable nightmarish experience", so extraordinary that no one would believe him. He said he felt that his wife would try to implicate him. He said he reckoned no one would believe him.'

At 12.15 a.m. the Earl of Lucan again phoned his mother, who was by then back in her flat at St John's Wood. Susan Maxwell-Scott heard his side of the conversation. A police officer who was with the dowager countess heard hers. Lord Lucan asked first about the children, and she told him they were with her. Then he asked about Veronica, and was told she was in hospital. His mother asked him if he would like to talk to the police. He hesitated, and then said he would phone again in the morning and talk to them then.

Mrs Maxwell-Scott watched Lord Lucan write two letters. Then, refusing to stay the night, he left at 1.15 a.m., saying he 'must get back to sort things out'.

Detective Chief Superintendent Ranson, who took charge of the case, said later that he expected to see the Earl walk into the police station that morning accompanied by his solicitor. At the same time Ranson took the precaution of sending a message round the world through Interpol: 'Richard Bingham, Earl of Lucan, wanted for murder and attempted murder. Please arrest. Extradition will follow.'

The Earl was never seen again. Two days after his disappearance a car was found, in the Channel port of Newhaven, which had been lent to him by a friend two weeks before. The front seats were heavily stained with blood of group A (Lady Lucan's group) and of the much less common group B (Sandra Rivett's group). In the boot of the car the police found a piece of lead piping bound with surgical plaster in the same way as the similar piece of piping found stained with blood at the scene of the crime.

The Earl of Lucan had left his wife nearly two years before these events, but had called regularly to take the children on outings. Sandra Rivett had been their nanny for only two months. Her murderer had evidently entered the house with a key, and killed her when she went down to make the tea. I found that considerable bleeding had taken place from her skull injuries into the throat, the glottis and main air passages, and because she had been 'knocked-out' this would have precipitated death within a minute or two. An unconscious person cannot clear the air-ways by coughing.

There were no signs of robbery in the house: plenty of valuables lay around. There appeared to be no reason for anyone to have murdered the nanny. Almost certainly she must have been killed in mistake for Lady Lucan.

Both women were 5 feet 2 inches in height, but otherwise they were not alike. However, anyone who knew their habits would have expected Lady Lucan to be making the tea. She would come downstairs at about that time of the evening, on a Thursday, for Thursday was Sandra's usual evening off. By chance she had changed to Wednesday that week. As Lady Lucan said, 'it would be unusual to find Mrs Rivett in the kitchen on a Thursday evening but it would be a usual thing for me to be there.' The murderer had evidently planned to kill Lady Lucan and to take her body away in a sack.

The police found that a passer-by could not have seen a fight in the basement through the venetian blinds, and a warrant was issued for the Earl's arrest. The inquest on Sandra was adjourned for seven months. Then, with the Earl still missing, the whole story was brought out. The verdict of the coroner's jury was 'Murder by Lord Lucan', and the coroner formally committed the Earl to be tried at the Central Criminal Court. 'I don't want my children to see me standing in the dock,' he told Susan Maxwell-Scott before he vanished; and they haven't.

CHAPTER 29

STILL ON CALL

In 1960, in a magistrates' court in Cyprus, the defence counsel asked me how long I had been engaged in medico-legal work, how many autopsies I had performed, and how many of them were criminal stranglings. He was hoping, of course, to show what a small part of one's experience is in actual crime. I was able to answer that in some thirty years I had personally performed autopsies on fifty-seven murders by strangling; and I added, without being asked, that not one of these had been committed by a woman. That was the last thing in the world that counsel wanted to hear, for his case was that the strangling of the girl victim was the work not of his client, a man, but of his client's wife.

Every doctor in the witness box must expect to have his qualifications as an expert tested, and he will naturally disconcert counsel in this sort of way if he has the chance. But giving evidence is not a game, and I never went out of my way to try to score off counsel.

Stepping down from the box one afternoon in 1970 I was very flattered to receive from the usher a pencilled note that had been handed to him by the Senior Clerk to the Old Bailey, Leslie Boyd, who must have seen more doctors and pathologists giving their evidence in Court No. 1, scene of England's most famous trials, than any other living person. 'If I may respectfully say so,' the note ran, 'I *still* think you give evidence better than anyone else I know or can remember—and that includes Spilsbury!'

I carefully filed the note with another shorter one, also pencilled and indeed written on a torn-off corner of an envelope, which was similarly delivered to me in 1968: 'If I may say so, you were magnificent in the box. Thank you.' It was signed 'Gerald Howard'—Mr Justice Howard, who had presided at the trial.

Such testimonials are precious. Another came unexpectedly in a letter from Colonel T. E. St Johnston, C.B.E., at that time Chief Constable of Lancashire, granting me formal permission to reproduce some police photographs in one of my books: 'I am very glad to have this opportunity to write to you again because, although you will not remember it, you conducted the first post-mortem that I ever saw when I was a young P.C. at Walham Green in 1938.' I remembered him very well, on a wet and foggy November day, knocking at the door of Fulham Mortuary, helmet dripping with rain, asking if he might watch a post-mortem. Of course I invited him in, although I suspected it was shelter and perhaps a cup of tea he was after. He seemed a very intelligent young officer, and I said afterwards, 'He's the sort who might go far'. He did! Later, as Sir Eric St Johnston, he became Chief Inspector of Constabulary, the premier post any young P.C. could ever aspire to . . . the 'Field Marshal's baton in the knapsack' that Napoleon carried in his youth.

Every doctor, for all his professional detachment, still has his feelings. My own have not changed greatly after many thousands of post-mortem examinations.

Even as a young man I felt no emotional disturbance when I performed post-mortems on elderly or infirm subjects, or those released by death (or during operation) from the sufferings of incurable illness. Many old people die in their sleep, or so suddenly that they 'never had a day's illness' to complain of; and then death seems to me indeed almost a happy event, or at any rate the least sorrowful. But when I have seen children—the joy of life to most of us, with their eager faces and carefree smiles—crushed under lorries, electrocuted through fiddling with inquisitive fingers, or incinerated in house fires that must have terrified them, I have always felt sad: there but for chance fate were my own children, or grandchildren.

I have felt saddened, too, by the deaths of young mothers leaving families to mourn a hopeless love. I myself lost two wives from incurable illness during my working life, and am still saddened by the memories of empty, lonely days and nights. But when I have seen strangled girls who had deliberately taken the occupational risks of prostitution, drunken sots who toppled downstairs to their death, or the adolescent victims of the lure of drug addiction, I have often said without the slightest emotional disturbance, 'Better out of this world—really. Never a chance of being a happy and useful citizen.'

Brutal murder cannot fail to cause any doctor—indeed any ordinary mortal—the revulsion and bitter resentment that judges must try to suppress. But I think I can fairly claim that such feelings have never—literally never, even with battered babies—crept into my evidence at court.

I once did a post-mortem by telephone, and the story is worth telling, for step by step the case unfolded itself before me as I lay in bed in England early one morning, just asking for more information. It happened in 1971, and began with a harsh ringing of the telephone bell at 3.15 a.m.

'Sorry to wake you so early, sir, but we've got a nasty-looking case here and wonder if you'd help.'

'Where's here?' I asked, hoping it wouldn't be more than ten minutes away.

'Guernsey, sir. Detective Sergeant Brown speaking. I wondered if you could fly over this morning.'

'Tell me something about it, sergeant.' I wanted to know how urgent it seemed before taking a plane to the Channel Isles.

'It's a lad of fourteen, in a living room in his parents' home, dead, with blood all over the place, things in disorder, handle pulled off the door. His parents went out around eight last night, got home just after midnight, they say, and—they say—found him dead, like that.'

'What does the police surgeon say?' I asked.

'That's the trouble,' said Sergeant Brown. 'He was called at 1.30 a.m. and says the whole body had gone into rigor mortis and that the boy must have been dead seven or eight hours. That puts it at around six o'clock last evening, when his parents admit they were still in the house. We don't know what his wounds are,' Brown added. 'He's covered with blood, and it looks nasty.' He meant it looked like murder.

I wondered if the police surgeon was right about the rigor. 'Did he take the temperature of the body?' I asked. Sergeant Brown said he did not. 'Then I suggest you call him out again and get him to take it, at once. And ask him to take it again, in an hour's time, so that if it's still falling we can work out how fast. Ring me later.' I went back to sleep.

At half-past five the phone rang again. Sergeant Brown reported that the lad's temperature was 93 at 4 a.m. and 92 at 5 a.m.

'Then he can't have been dead since six o'clock last night,' I said. 'It must have been nearer eleven or twelve—just before his parents came home. It looks as if they're in the clear.'

'The rigor mortis . . .'

'It wasn't rigor. It must have been cadaveric spasm, the stiffening that comes on sometimes at the moment death takes place. It means the boy must have been very frightened or very taut at the time he died. Now I suggest you take the body to the mortuary and clean it up a bit, and see where he's bleeding from. Give me another ring.'

At half-past seven the bell rang again. 'He's got a deep four-inch cut on the sole of one foot, sir. that's his only wound.'

'I've never seen a murder, not even a fight, with just a cut on one foot,' I said. 'Barefoot or socks, I suppose?'

'Socks, sir. And now you mention it, there was a broken glass tumbler or something, on the floor near the door.'

'He must have been staggering about in the dark or drunk or . . .' I was wondering about drugs.

'I forgot to mention,' said Detective Sergeant Brown, 'that there was a strong smell of whisky about the place, and a half-empty bottle of Scotch on the sideboard. I thought it was probably intruders.'

'Did the boy smell of it when you cleaned him up?'

'Come to think of it,' said Sergeant Brown, 'he did.'

'Well, I don't know,' I said, settling back in my bed on my elbow, 'but it looks very much as if he may have been having a go at the booze in his parents' absence; in the dark, perhaps, so as not to be caught. If he got drunk and staggered about, dropping the glass or knocking it on the floor, he could have stumbled on it, cut his foot and got into a panic—the frightened state we needed for cadaveric spasm—as he bled and died. *Could be.* What about the door handle coming off?'

'Oh, I've asked about that, sir. It's always coming off, so there's nothing in that.'

It was nearly 8 a.m. 'I think all we need is a sample of his blood on the morning plane,' I said. 'We'll see if it's got a high alcohol. If it's over 150 or so, I think we've solved the problem on the phone.'

It was 173 mg per cent! Very drunk for a boy of fourteen. The case was finished by midday.

That case was exceptional, for usually I welcomed every opportunity to fly to new places. In 1973, the year I was due to relinquish my university appointment at Guy's, I had:

1   Circuited the world, lecturing in India, Bangkok, Hong Kong,

Australia and New Zealand, returning via Fiji and Mexico.

2   Visited Monte Carlo to lecture for the American 'University of Young Presidents', a mob rich as Croesus who liked to study their marginal problems—like population pressures, crime control, drug addiction, and social trends—in the greatest luxury. Prince Rainier and Princess Grace attended my talk.

3   Given a Memorial Lecture at Bergen University to a large assembly of students who greeted me with a parade of their university brass band (in top hats and flowing top coats), awarding me the 'Order of the Leading Cow', a minute silver bell on a blue riband, not awarded to women!

4   Paid three successive visits to the Caribbean for the murder-exhumation of the Etheringtons and trial of the three men who had butchered them in their home overlooking Castries in St Lucia, one of Nelson's hide-outs in 1797.

5   Dealt (unfortunately without a visit to the island) with the mystery of a skeleton found in a cave on the north coast of Cyprus, a wartime relic.

6   Solved for the Canadian Police the problem of a drunken North American woman found after arrest hanging in a police cell in Edmonton and alleged by the Press to be a police 'hounding' of the poor suicide.

7   Visited Bermuda to give evidence for the Crown against a man who had waylaid, punched, strangled, raped, and drowned a local English girl, leaving her in a creek under the local Dinghy Club.

8   Visited Trinidad to exhume the body of Gale Benson.

9   Accepted an invitation to tour India, Nepal, and Ceylon on behalf of the British Council, lecturing and advising on medico-legal services.

. . . And, of course, continued, when 'at home', to do my routine job 'on the beat' in London, Birmingham, High Wycombe, Portsmouth, and wherever else some wretched victim had been found dead.

In the autumn of 1973 I was succeeded as Professor of Forensic Medicine at Guy's by Keith Mant, who had been my valued first assistant since he came to me from the War Crimes Commission soon after the war. No-one has had a more loyal colleague of such utter reliability. He was soon in 'at the deep end' with the murder of 'old Gossy' in his shop at Clay Corner, Chertsey, and as the 'Yard pathologist' in the famous Tow-path murders at Teddington, and emerged from both with credit. He continued his services to the police and the Home Office with the kind of repute for reliability and integrity that I hoped I had as I eased myself out.

In 1976 the BBC filmed a 'profile' of my professional life for the *Horizon* television series. My colleagues were charmingly complimentary about it, and I have not yet had a summons from the General Medical Council suggesting it was 'serious professional misconduct'—blatant advertising! Doctors have always been restrained from indulging in the 5 A's: adultery, advertising, alcohol, abuse of privileges, and associating with unqualified persons. I seem, as I see retirement on the horizon, to have escaped all five.

When I retired from the Chair of Forensic Medicine at Guy's I did not give up my job as Home Office Pathologist, and at the time of writing I am still in Court most days and doing a large variety of postmortems. What other profession could offer all the excitement, travel and interest that I have had? So different from catching the 8.15 to the office in the City every day; or from looking down throats and examining smelly feet, handling people and trying to sort out their psychosomatic problems. My patients never complain. If their illness is perplexing, I can always put them back in the refrigerator, talk over the problem with my colleagues, and come back to it later. Of course the first twenty years had to be something of a grind: of course I had to turn out at all hours, go anywhere, stand around with dead bodies in ditches and fields, backyard sheds and filthy rooms, suffer the disinterest in my convenience that judges and lawyers seem to enjoy meting out to the young doctor. But what rewards! And even the judges begin to look younger and behave more reasonably as time goes on: we had all been young colleagues or amiable opponents years before.

My hard-working Scots father often used to say to me as a schoolboy: 'Nothing that is worth having is easy to get. You've got to work for it.' It was both wise and true, at least of a career in medicine. No doctor achieves repute without much study and a fair leavening of that quality the Scots have so often seemed to possess—industry. I know of no finer and more rewarding career than medicine . . . and, particularly for the few who have the good fortune to practise it, forensic medicine. Retire? I can't (at present) think why!

I suppose, eventually, my mind will fritter a little at the margins. I said once, at lunch, in my own hospital, with a group of my fellow-doctors round me, that it is very difficult for someone who is getting older to realize that his own mind is beginning to fray at the edges. And I added, rather incautiously, that my wife had instructions when this happened to me to come into my Tring garden and have 'a little accident' with a shotgun. A voice down the table instantly—too instantly, for my liking—said: 'She's left it a bit late, hasn't she?' I had asked for it.

INDEX